W9-ACX-519

Dragon Knights

Written and Illustrated by
Mineko Ohkami

Volume 6

RECEIVED

DEC 23 2011

By_____

HAYNER PUBLIC LIBRARY DISTRICT
ALTON, ILLINOIS

OVERDUES 10 PER DAY, MAXIMUM FINE
COST OF ITEM
ADDITIONAL $5.00 SERVICE CHARGE
APPLIED TO
LOST OR DAMAGED ITEMS

HAYNER PLD/ALTON SQUARE

TOKYOPOP®

Los Angeles • Tokyo

Translator - Agnes Yoshida
English Adaption - Stephanie Sheh
Retouch & Lettering - Songgu Kwon
Cover Layout - Anna Kerbaum

Senior Editor - Luis Reyes
Production Manager - Jennifer Miller
Art Director - Matthew Alford
VP of Production & Manufacturing - Ron Klamert
President & C.O.O. - John Parker
Publisher - Stuart Levy

Email: editor@TOKYOPOP.com
Come visit us online at www.TOKYOPOP.com

A ☒ TOKYOPOP® Manga
TOKYOPOP® is an imprint of Mixx Entertainment, Inc.
5900 Wilshire Blvd., Suite 2000, Los Angeles, CA 90036

© 1991 Mineko Ohkami. All rights reserved.
First published in Japan in 1991 by Shinshokan Publishing Co.,
Ltd., Tokyo, Japan. English Publication rights arranged through
Shinshokan Publishing Co., Ltd.

English text © 2003 by Mixx Entertainment, Inc.
TOKYOPOP is a registered trademark of Mixx Entertainment, Inc.

All rights reserved. No portion of this book may be reproduced or
transmitted in any form or by any means without written permission
from the copyright holders. This manga is a work of fiction.
Any resemblance to actual events or locales or persons,
living or dead, is entirely coincidental.

ISBN: 1-59182-102-9

First TOKYOPOP® printing: February 2003

10 9 8 7 6 5 4 3 2 1

Printed in the USA

From the Chronicles of Dusis, the West Continent...

The Beginnings: Nadil and Lord Lykouleon

When the Yokai Nadil kidnapped the Dragon Queen Raselene, The Dragon Lord Lycouleon ventured to the Demon Realm to rescue her. He defeated Nadil by cutting off his head, thereby saving Raselene, but not before the demon leader rendered her barren, unable to give Lykouleon a child... and the Dragon Kingdom an heir. Now, the demon and Yokai forces, under the command of Shydeman and Shyrendora, plot to attack Draqueen, the Dragon Kingdom, and retrieve their leader's head in the hopes of reviving him. The Alchemist Kharl and the rogue Yokai Bierrez have also entered the contest for power of all Dusis.

The Dragon Knights: A Motley Trio

Rath is the Dragon Knight of Fire and has accompanied the fortune teller Cesia to Mt. Mfartha, though his reluctance to be entirely forthcoming about his motives may be a point of concern. Thatz, a human thief, is the Dragon Knight of Earth and is currently engaged in a search for the mysterious three treasures. Rune, in a battle with the Demon Fish Varawoo, healed the Water Dragon, thereby unlocking its seal and becoming the Dragon Knight of Water, but not without sacrificing the Elfin Princess Tintlet who remains in a sleep spell, keeping the Demon Fish Varawoo safely sealed away.

The Future: Missions Abroad

Rune's quest to solve the mystery behind the disappearance of the Faeries has brought him to the Faerie Forests, but thus far he has discovered nothing about what may have happened. Meanwhile, Lord Lykouleon travels with Alfeegi to foreign lands to solicit help in the war against the demons. But they find most people unwilling to join the Dragon Clan's ranks. Less settling, however, is the appearance of a poisonous black smoke that has enveloped the land and caused great sickness.

CONTENTS

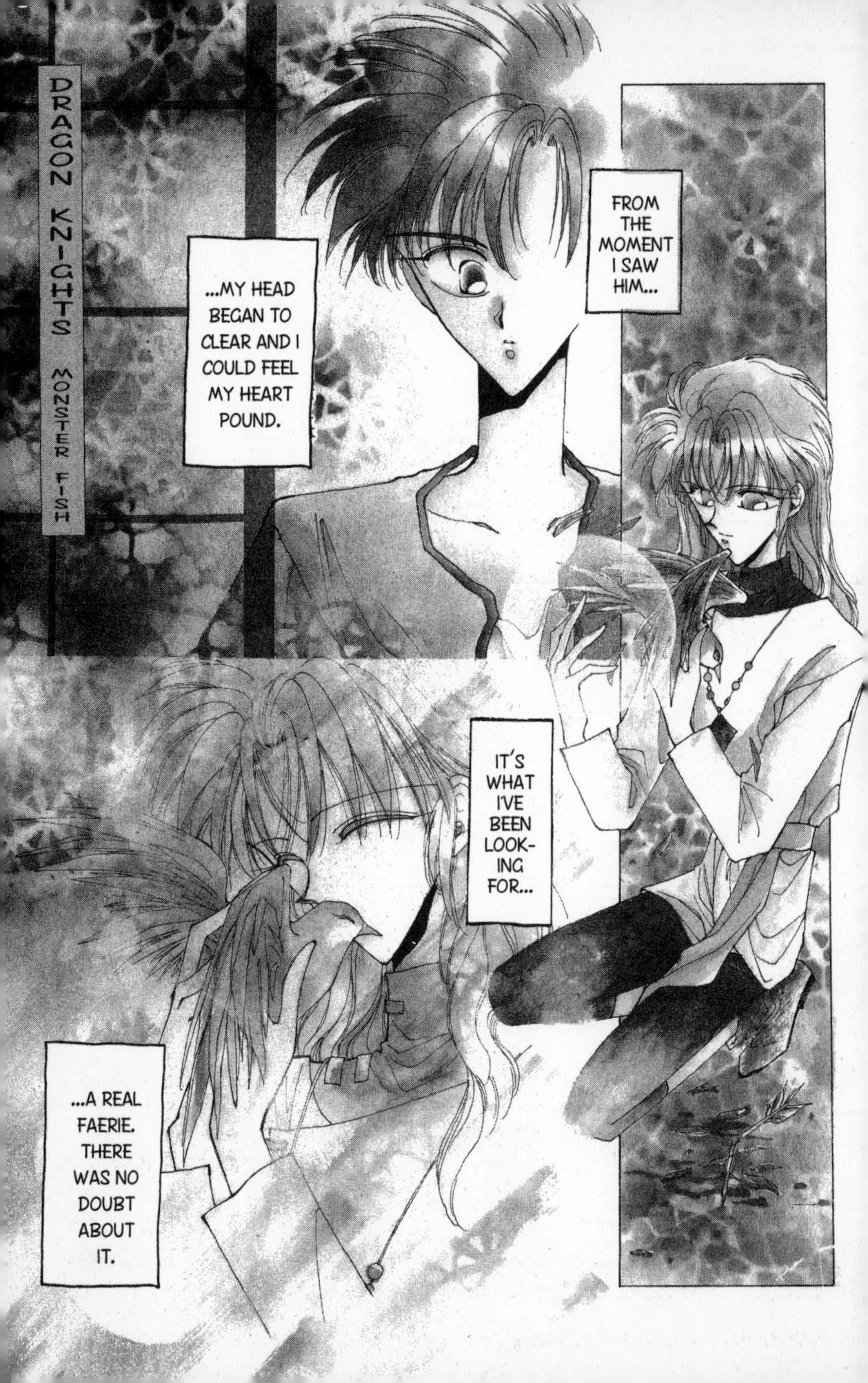
FROM THE MOMENT I SAW HIM...
...MY HEAD BEGAN TO CLEAR AND I COULD FEEL MY HEART POUND.
DRAGON KNIGHTS
MONSTER FISH
IT'S WHAT I'VE BEEN LOOK-ING FOR...
...A REAL FAERIE. THERE WAS NO DOUBT ABOUT IT.

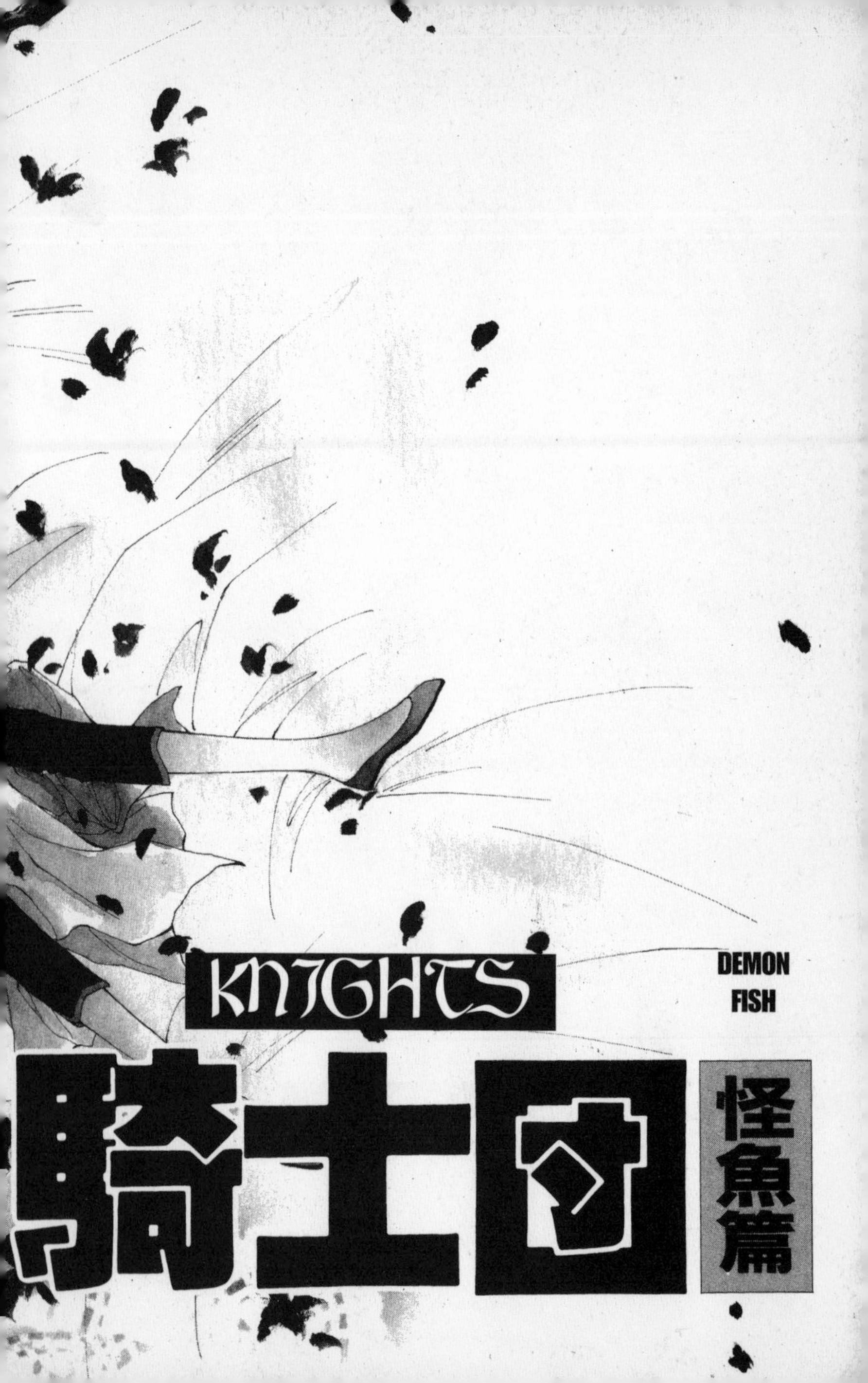
KNIGHTS
騎士団
DEMON
FISH
怪魚篇

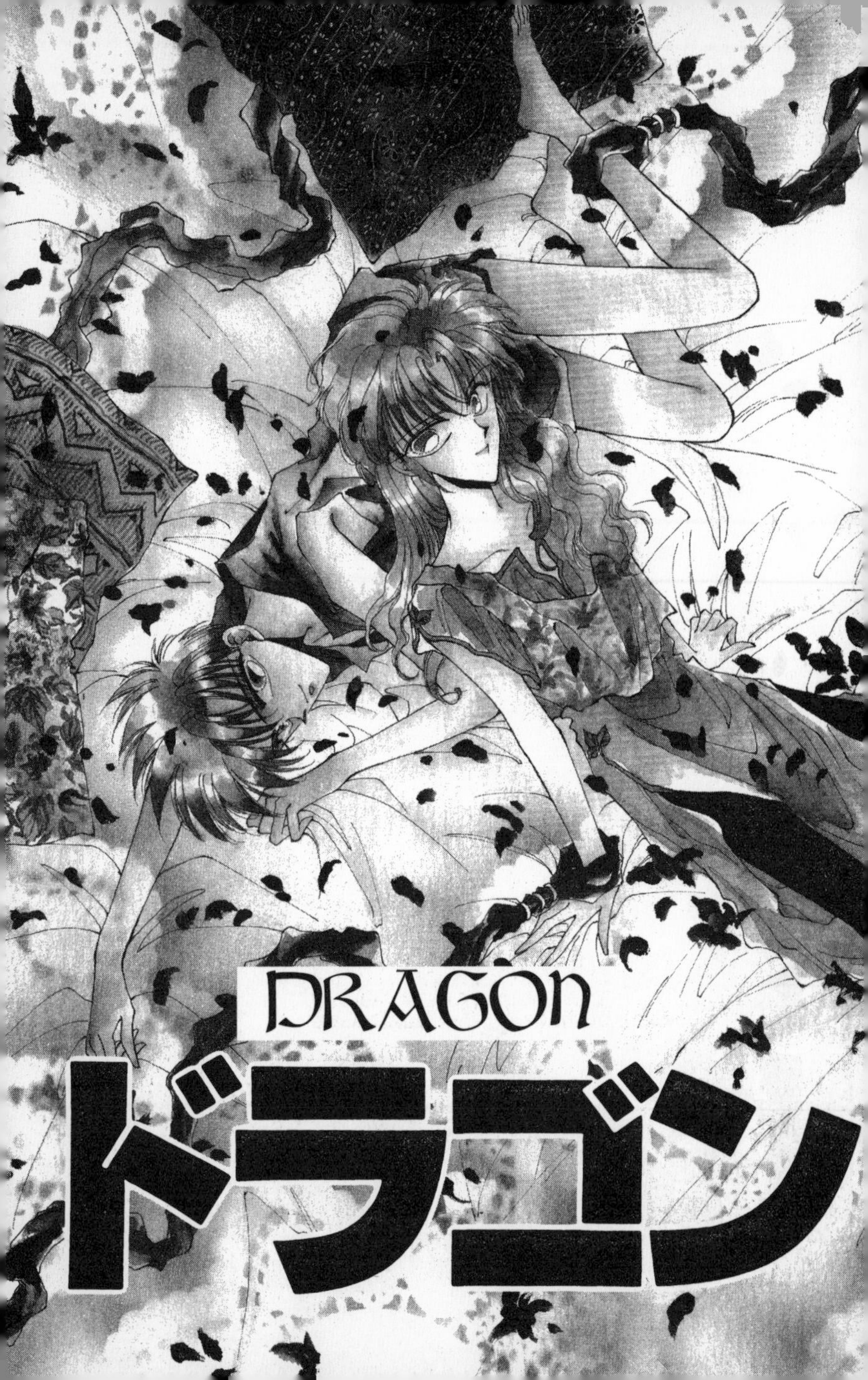
DRAGON
ドラゴン

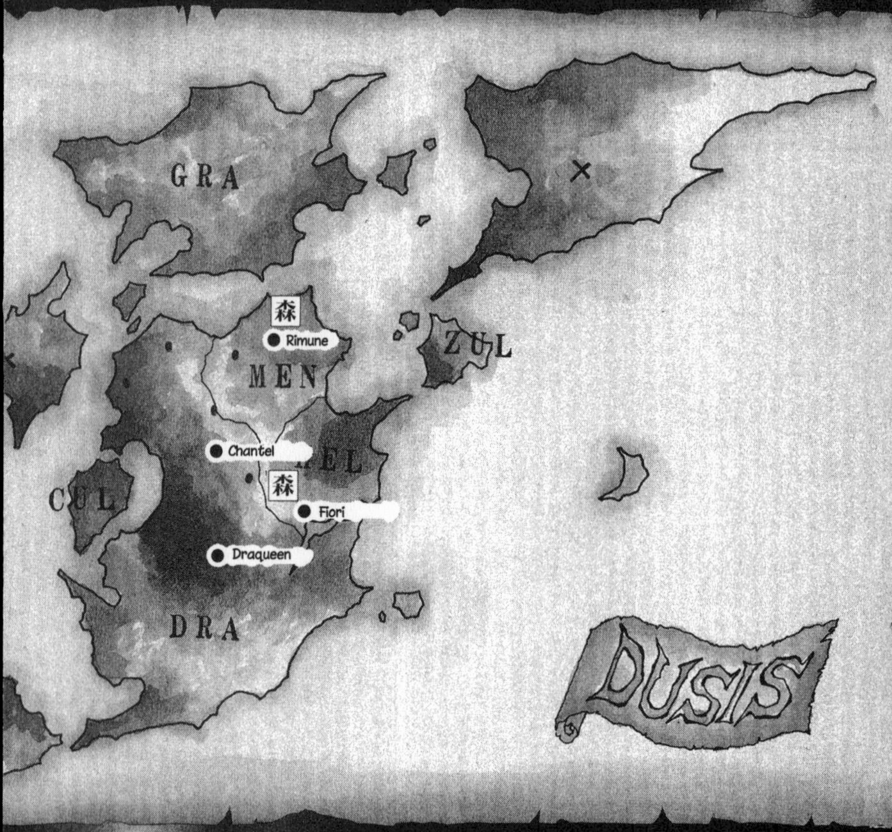
GRA
森
Rimune
ZUL
MEN
Chantel
CUL
森
Fiori
Draqueen
DRA
DUSIS

森 = forest

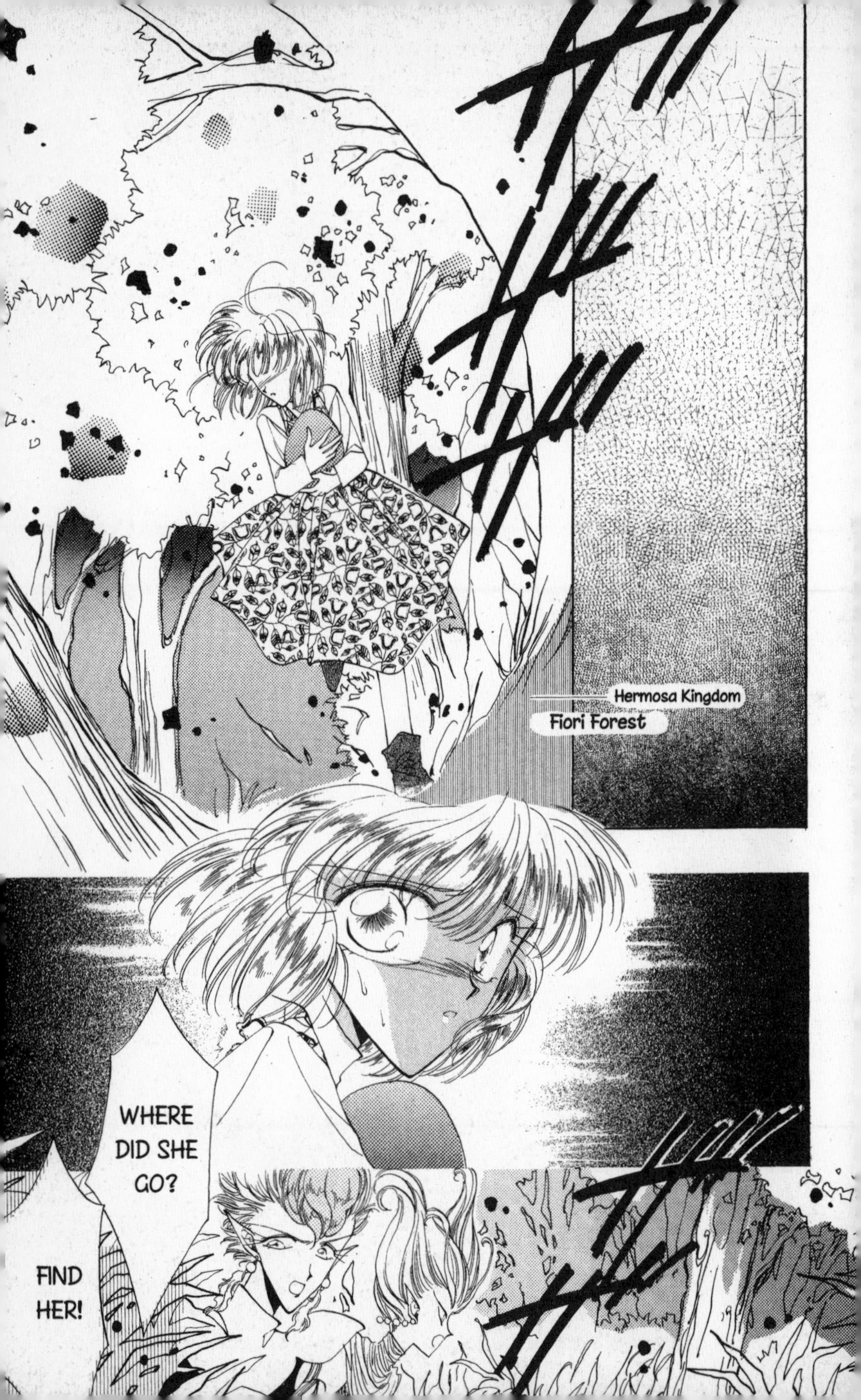
Hermosa Kingdom
Fiori Forest
WHERE DID SHE GO?
FIND HER!

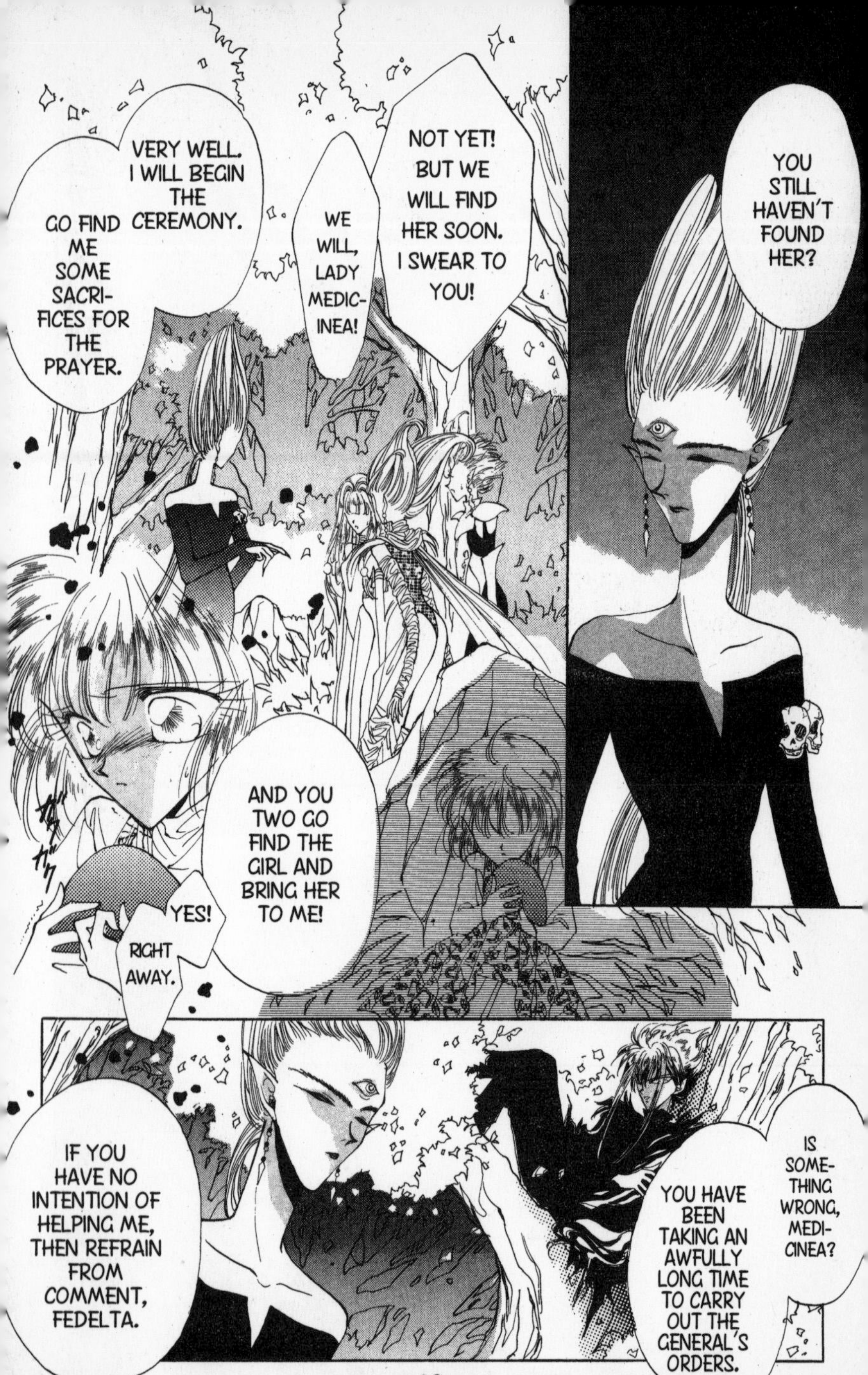
YOU STILL HAVEN'T FOUND HER?
NOT YET! BUT WE WILL FIND HER SOON. I SWEAR TO YOU!
WE WILL, LADY MEDIC-INEA!
VERY WELL. I WILL BEGIN THE CEREMONY.
GO FIND ME SOME SACRI-FICES FOR THE PRAYER.
AND YOU TWO GO FIND THE GIRL AND BRING HER TO ME!
YES!
RIGHT AWAY.
IS SOME-THING WRONG, MEDI-CINEA?
YOU HAVE BEEN TAKING AN AWFULLY LONG TIME TO CARRY OUT THE GENERAL'S ORDERS.
IF YOU HAVE NO INTENTION OF HELPING ME, THEN REFRAIN FROM COMMENT, FEDELTA.

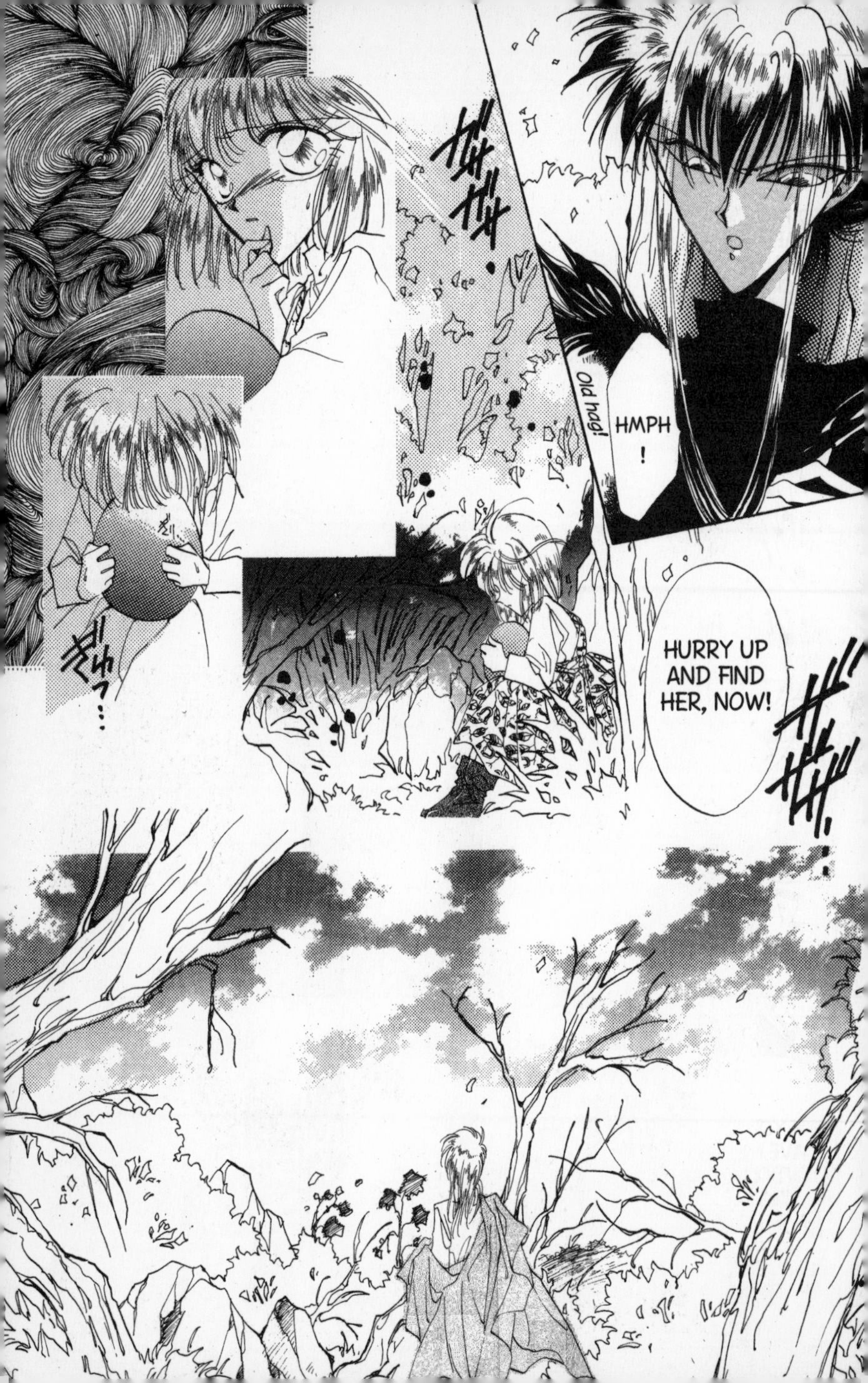
HMPH!
Old hag!
HURRY UP AND FIND HER, NOW!

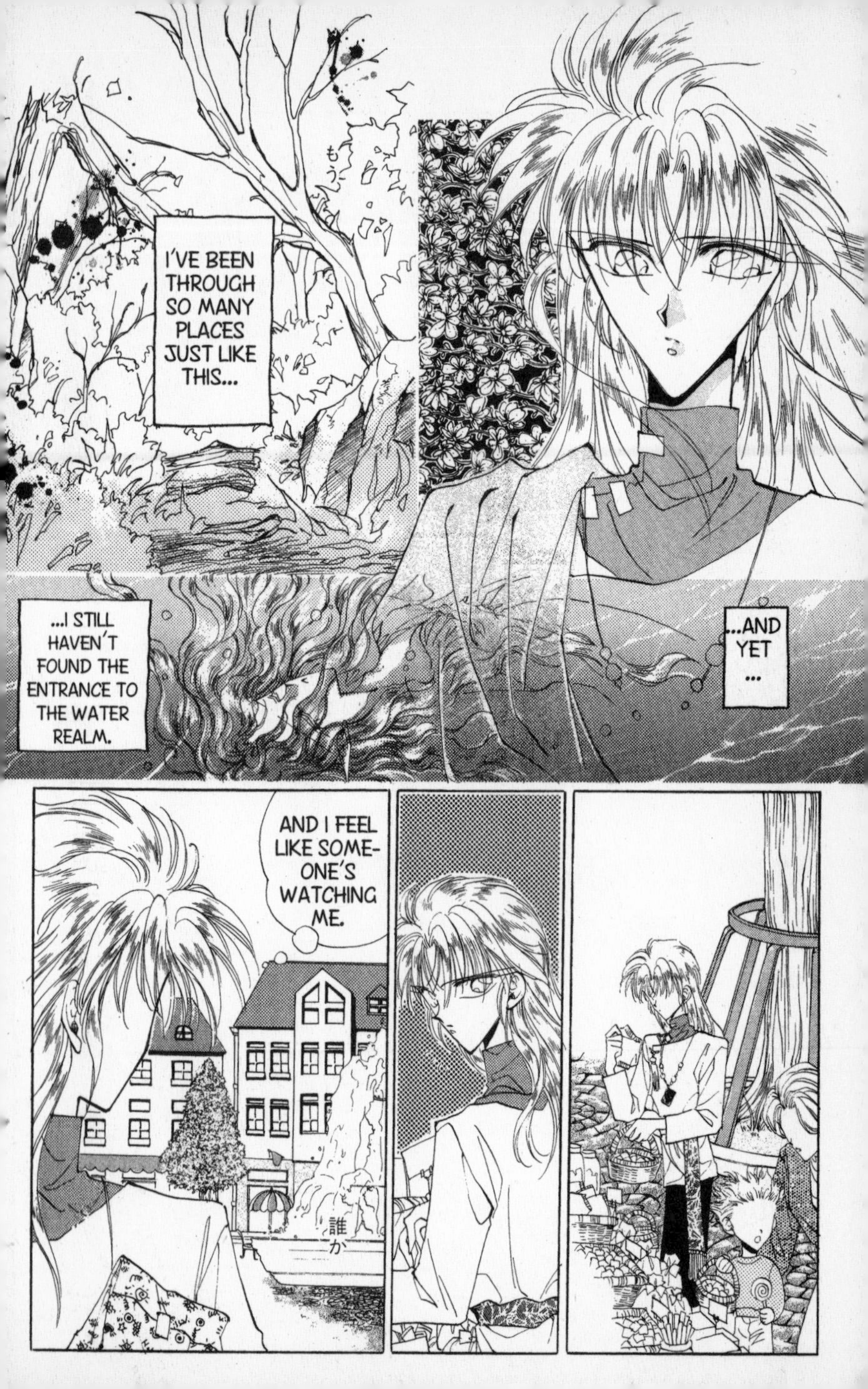
もう
I'VE BEEN THROUGH SO MANY PLACES JUST LIKE THIS...
...AND YET ...
...I STILL HAVEN'T FOUND THE ENTRANCE TO THE WATER REALM.
AND I FEEL LIKE SOME-ONE'S WATCHING ME.
誰か

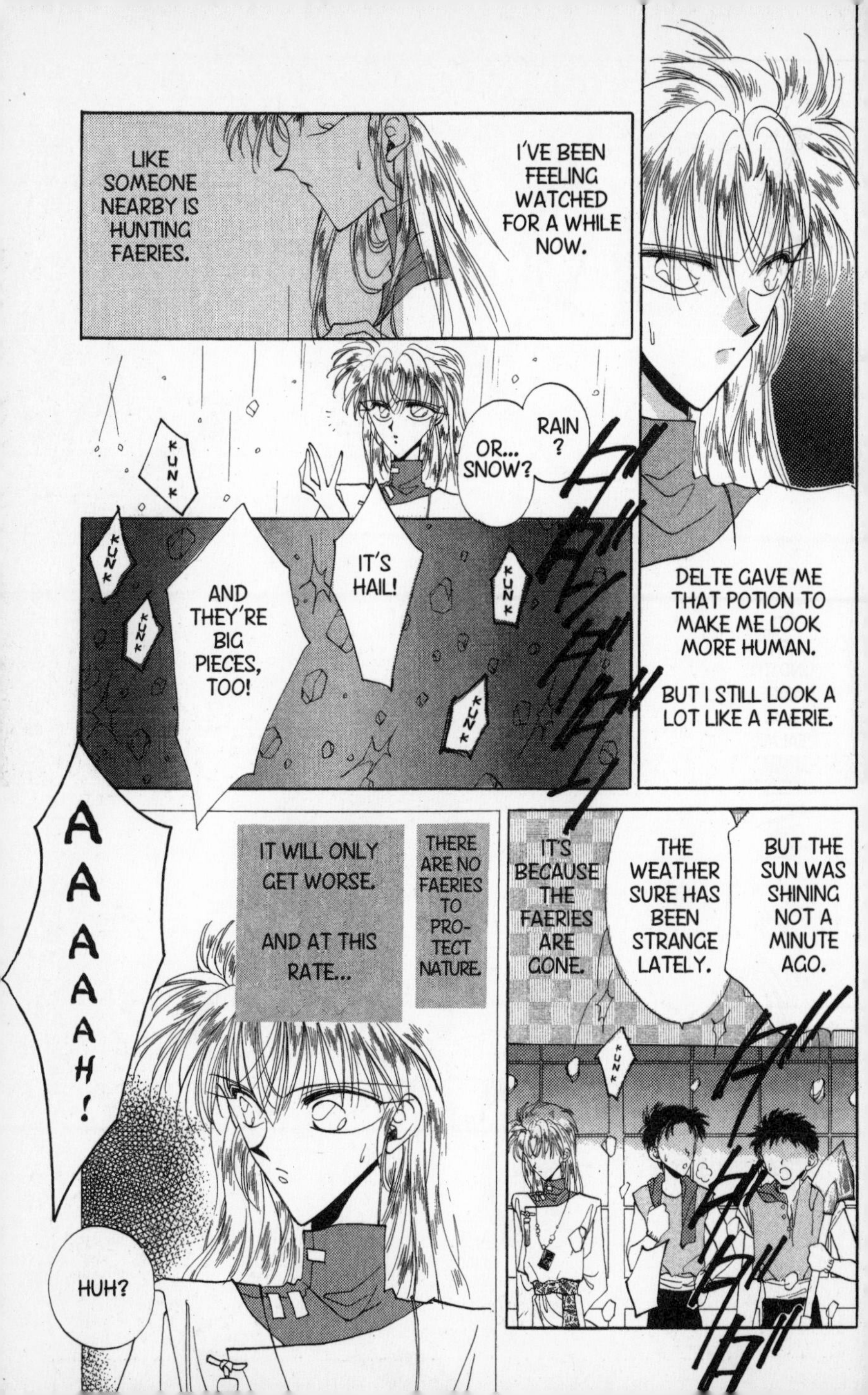
DELTE GAVE ME THAT POTION TO MAKE ME LOOK MORE HUMAN.
BUT I STILL LOOK A LOT LIKE A FAERIE.
I'VE BEEN FEELING WATCHED FOR A WHILE NOW.
LIKE SOMEONE NEARBY IS HUNTING FAERIES.
RAIN? OR... SNOW?
KUNK
KUNK
IT'S HAIL!
AND THEY'RE BIG PIECES, TOO!
KUNK
KUNK
KUNK
BUT THE SUN WAS SHINING NOT A MINUTE AGO.
THE WEATHER SURE HAS BEEN STRANGE LATELY.
IT'S BECAUSE THE FAERIES ARE GONE.
KUNK
THERE ARE NO FAERIES TO PROTECT NATURE.
IT WILL ONLY GET WORSE.
AND AT THIS RATE...
AAAAAH!
HUH?

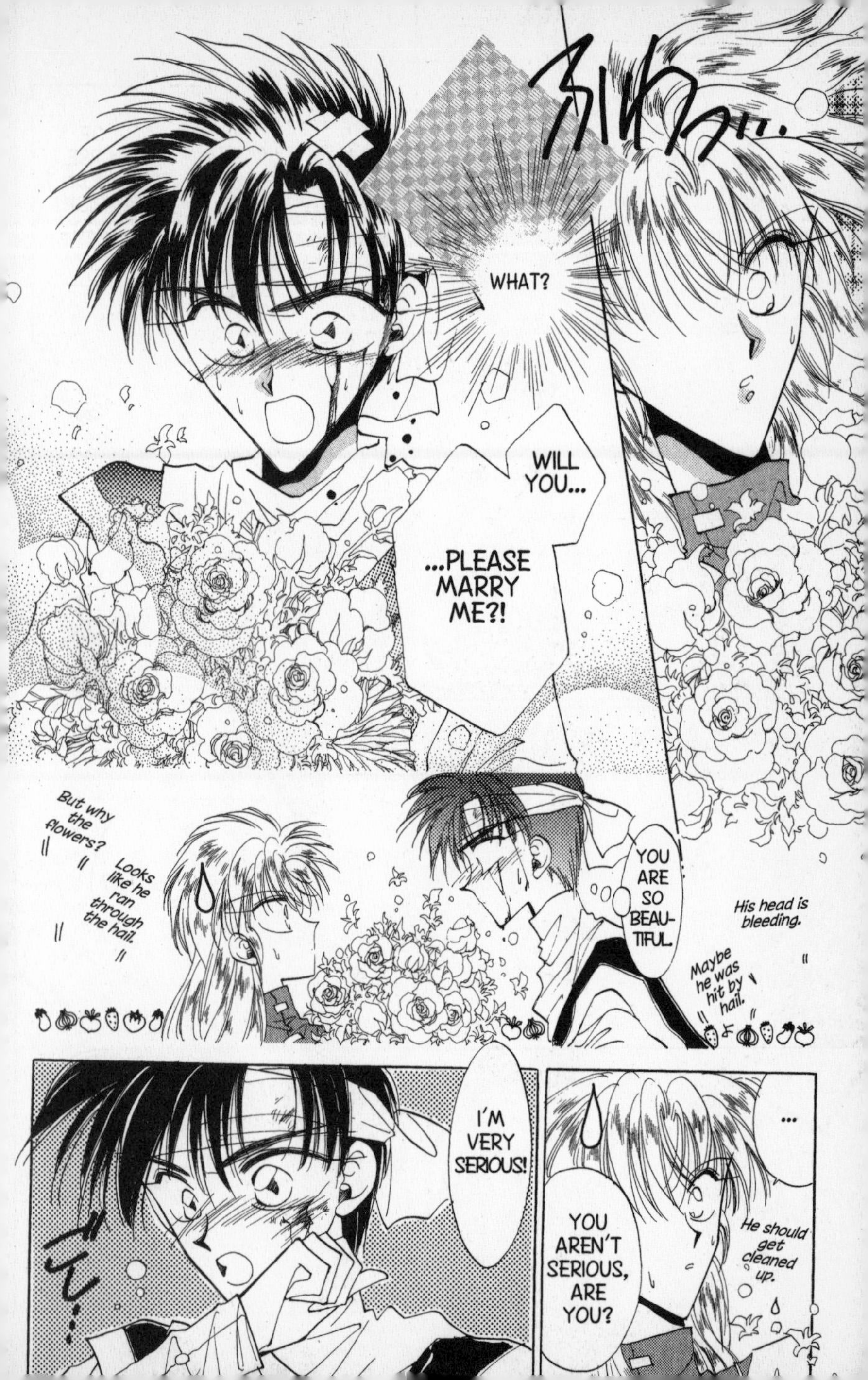
ふわっ...
WHAT?
WILL YOU...
...PLEASE MARRY ME?!
His head is bleeding.
YOU ARE SO BEAU-TIFUL.
Maybe he was hit by hail.
But why the flowers?
Looks like he ran through the hail.
...
YOU AREN'T SERIOUS, ARE YOU?
He should get cleaned up.
I'M VERY SERIOUS!

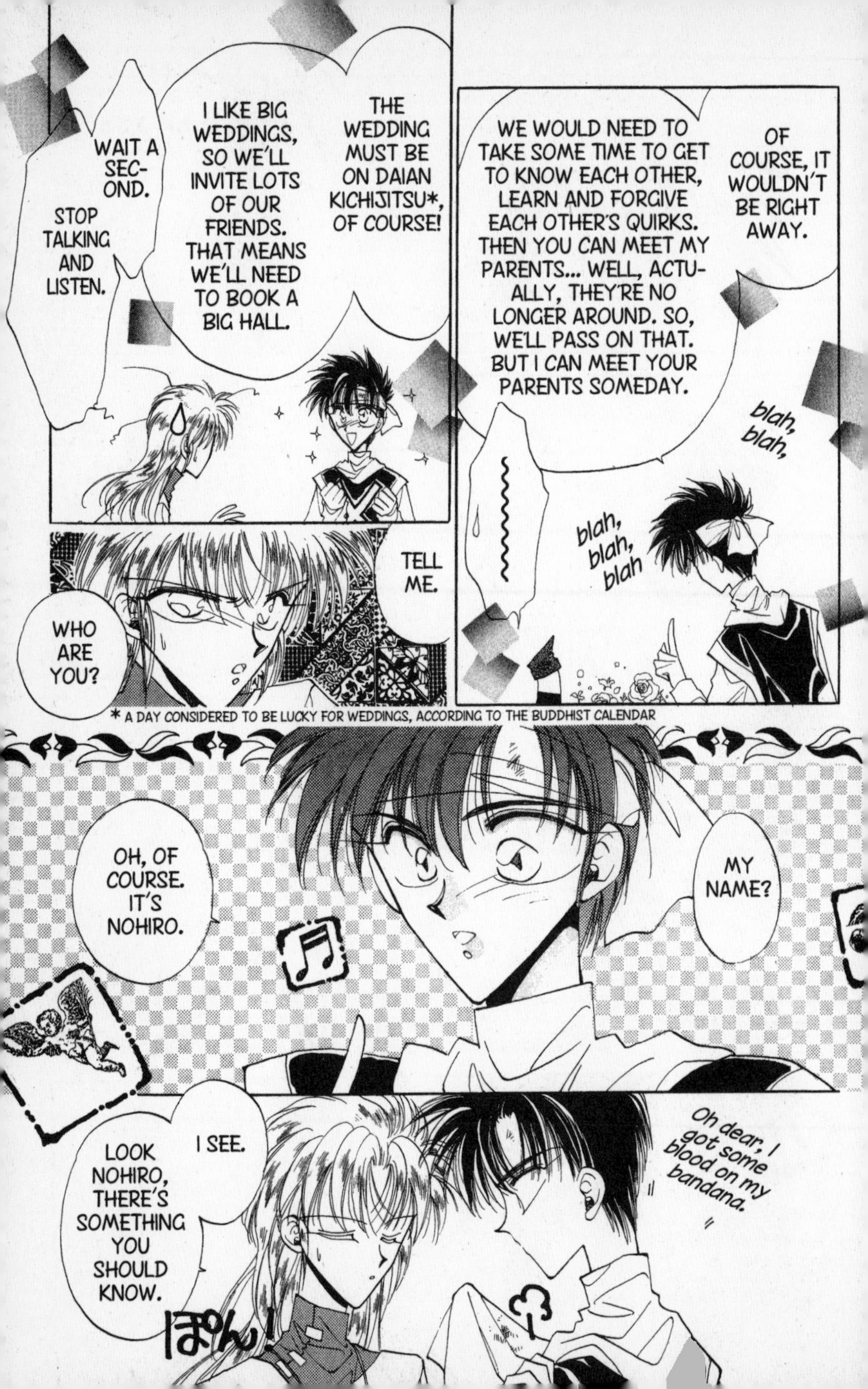
THE WEDDING MUST BE ON DAIAN KICHIJITSU*, OF COURSE!
I LIKE BIG WEDDINGS, SO WE'LL INVITE LOTS OF OUR FRIENDS. THAT MEANS WE'LL NEED TO BOOK A BIG HALL.
WAIT A SEC-OND.
STOP TALKING AND LISTEN.
OF COURSE, IT WOULDN'T BE RIGHT AWAY.
WE WOULD NEED TO TAKE SOME TIME TO GET TO KNOW EACH OTHER, LEARN AND FORGIVE EACH OTHER'S QUIRKS. THEN YOU CAN MEET MY PARENTS... WELL, ACTU-ALLY, THEY'RE NO LONGER AROUND. SO, WE'LL PASS ON THAT. BUT I CAN MEET YOUR PARENTS SOMEDAY.
blah, blah,
blah, blah, blah
TELL ME.
WHO ARE YOU?
MY NAME?
OH, OF COURSE. IT'S NOHIRO.
Oh dear, I got some blood on my bandana.
I SEE.
LOOK NOHIRO, THERE'S SOMETHING YOU SHOULD KNOW.
ぽん!

* A DAY CONSIDERED TO BE LUCKY FOR WEDDINGS, ACCORDING TO THE BUDDHIST CALENDAR

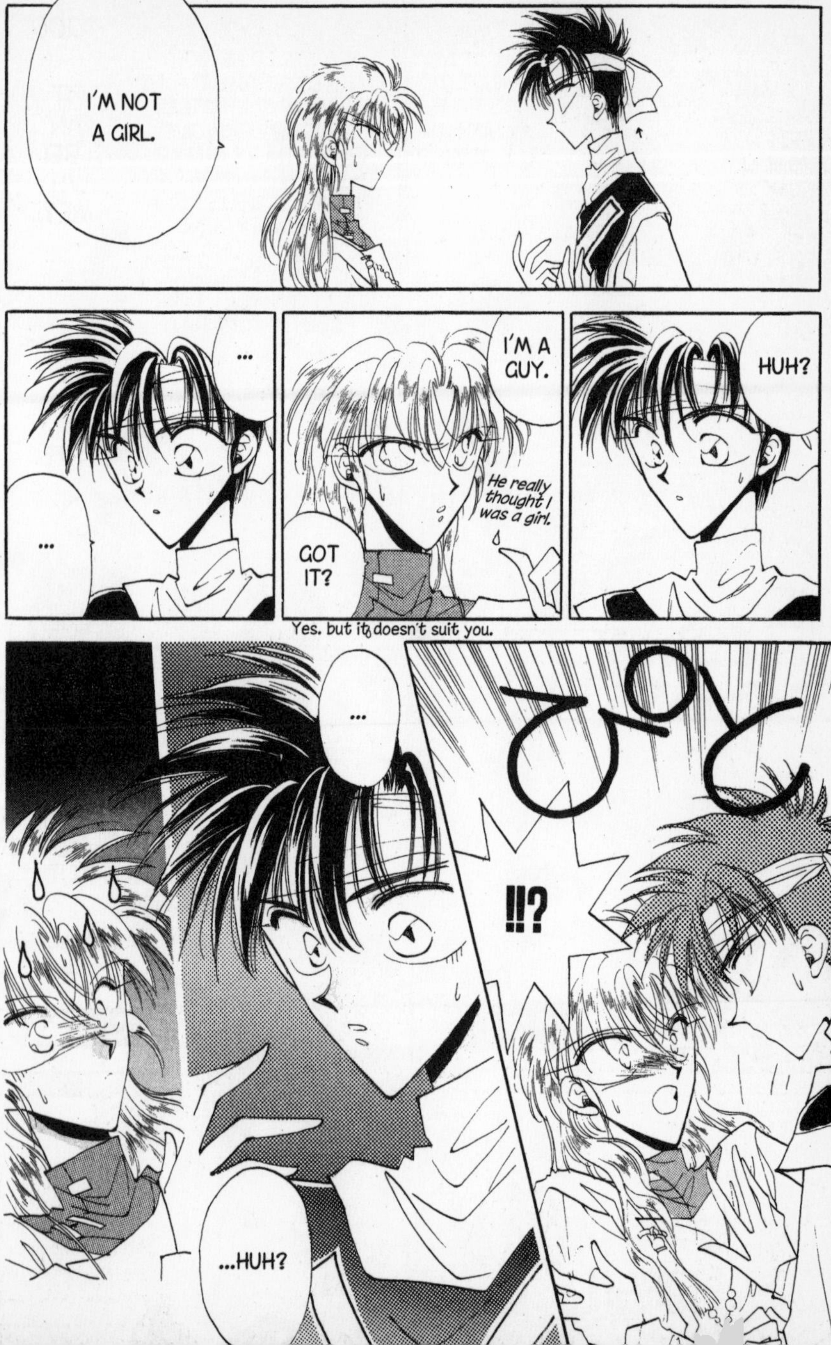
I'M NOT A GIRL.
HUH?
I'M A GUY.
GOT IT?
He really thought I was a girl.
...
...
Yes. but it doesn't suit you.
!!?
...
...HUH?

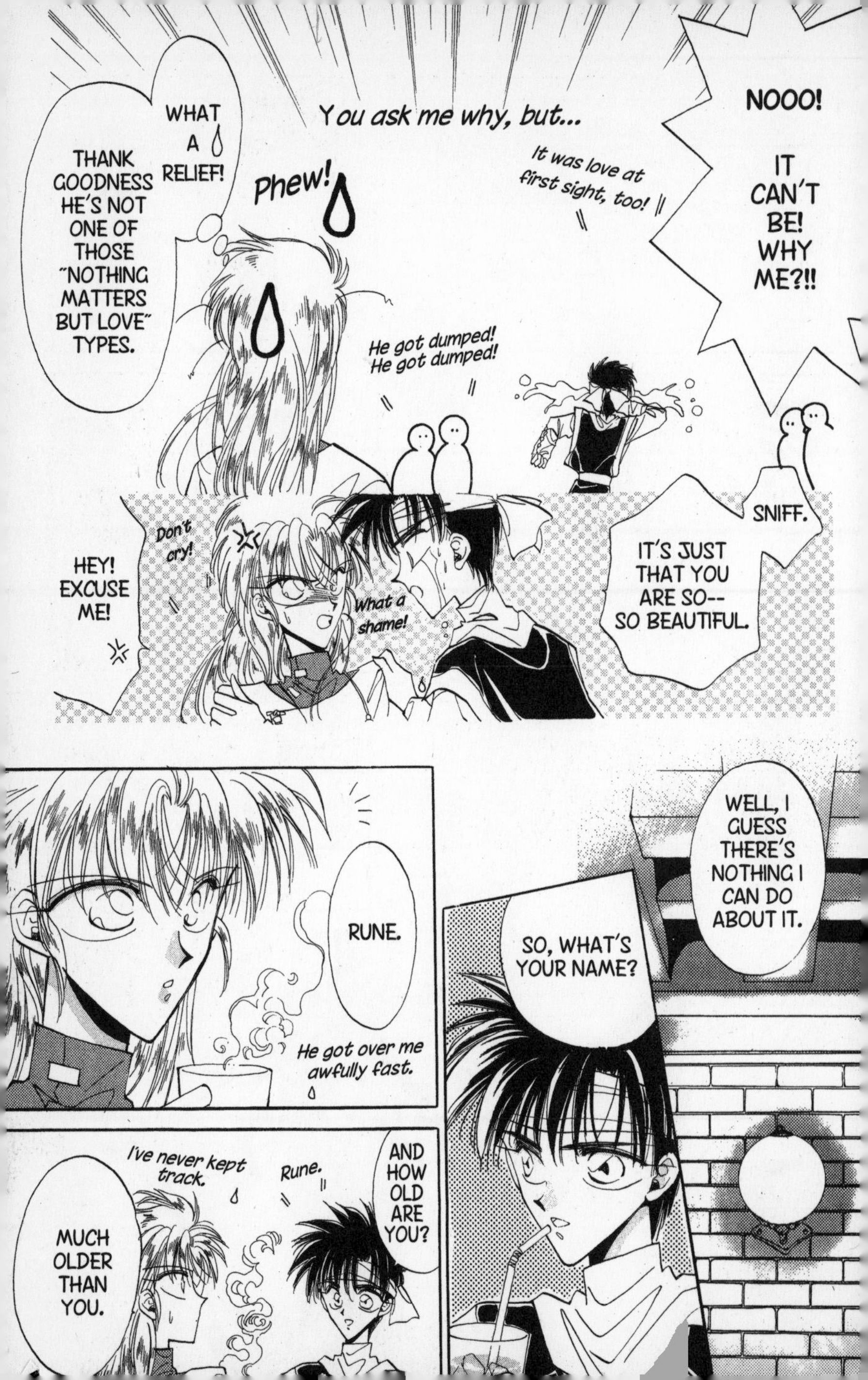
NOOO!
IT CAN'T BE! WHY ME?!!
It was love at first sight, too!
You ask me why, but...
Phew!
WHAT A RELIEF!
THANK GOODNESS HE'S NOT ONE OF THOSE "NOTHING MATTERS BUT LOVE" TYPES.
He got dumped! He got dumped!
SNIFF.
IT'S JUST THAT YOU ARE SO-- SO BEAUTIFUL.
What a shame!
Don't cry!
HEY! EXCUSE ME!
WELL, I GUESS THERE'S NOTHING I CAN DO ABOUT IT.
SO, WHAT'S YOUR NAME?
RUNE.
He got over me awfully fast.
AND HOW OLD ARE YOU?
Rune.
I've never kept track.
MUCH OLDER THAN YOU.

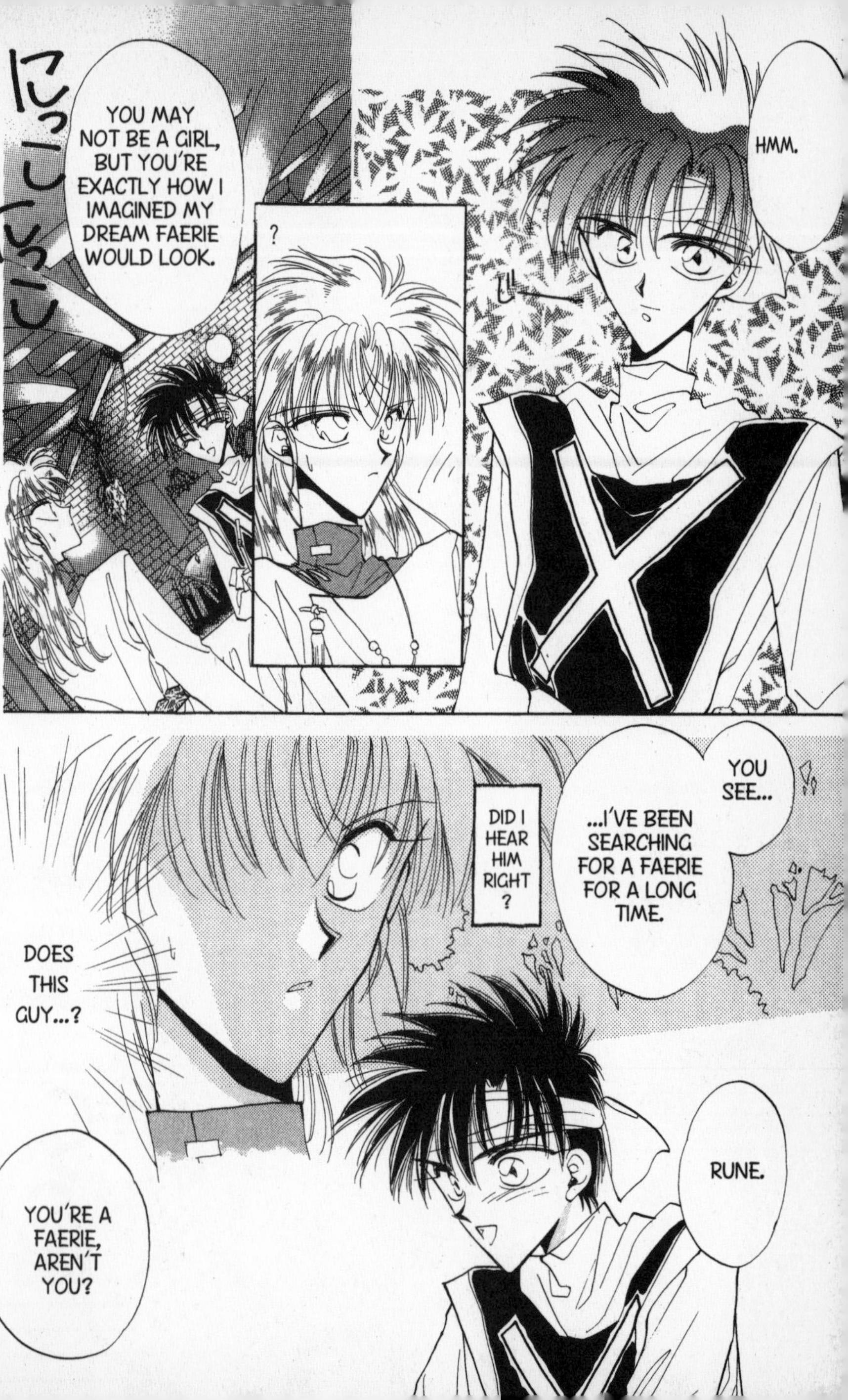
HMM.
?
YOU MAY NOT BE A GIRL, BUT YOU'RE EXACTLY HOW I IMAGINED MY DREAM FAERIE WOULD LOOK.
YOU SEE...
...I'VE BEEN SEARCHING FOR A FAERIE FOR A LONG TIME.
DID I HEAR HIM RIGHT?
DOES THIS GUY...?
RUNE.
YOU'RE A FAERIE, AREN'T YOU?

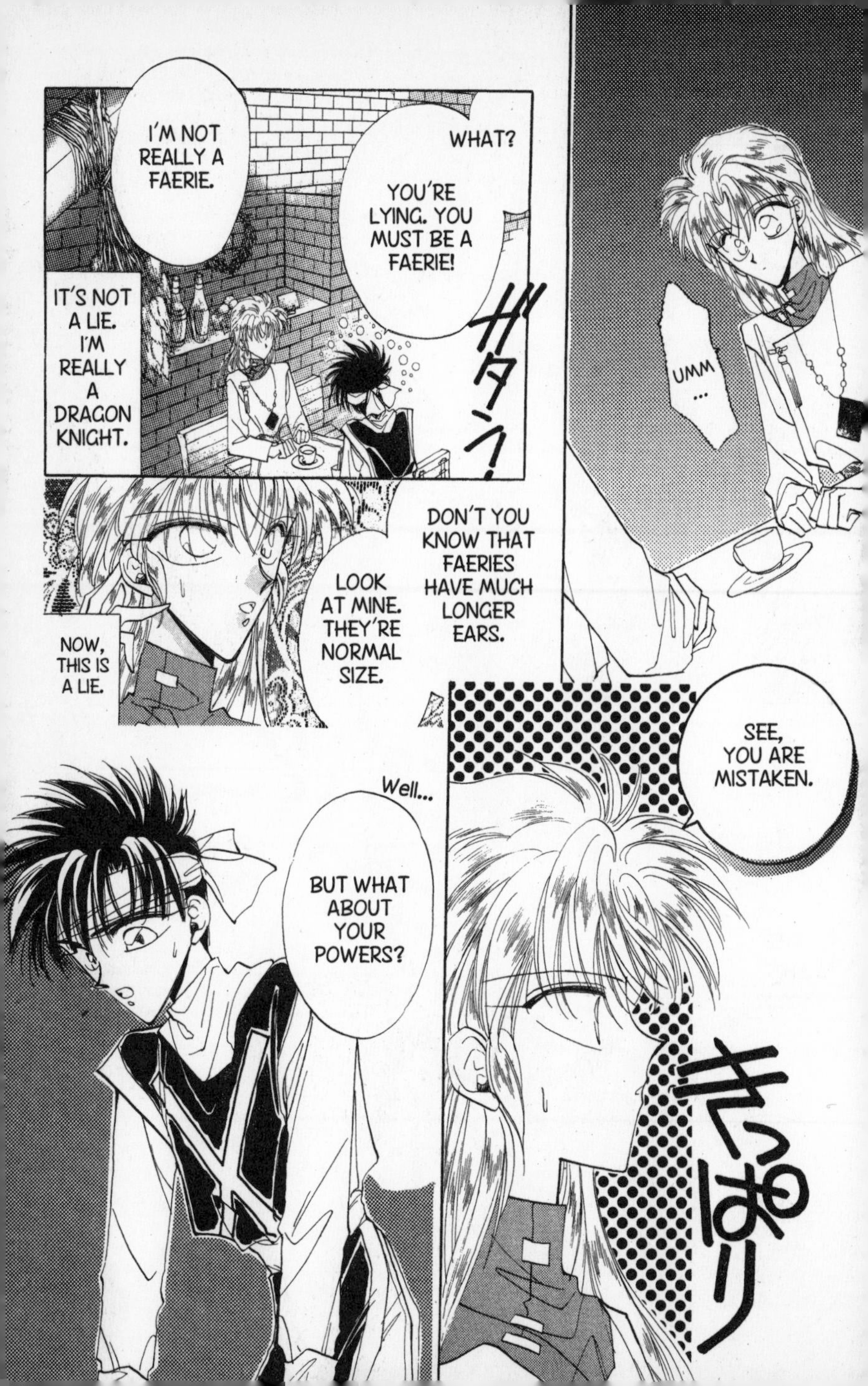
UMM...
I'M NOT REALLY A FAERIE.
WHAT?
YOU'RE LYING. YOU MUST BE A FAERIE!
ガタン!
IT'S NOT A LIE. I'M REALLY A DRAGON KNIGHT.
DON'T YOU KNOW THAT FAERIES HAVE MUCH LONGER EARS.
LOOK AT MINE. THEY'RE NORMAL SIZE.
NOW, THIS IS A LIE.
SEE, YOU ARE MISTAKEN.
きっぱり
Well...
BUT WHAT ABOUT YOUR POWERS?

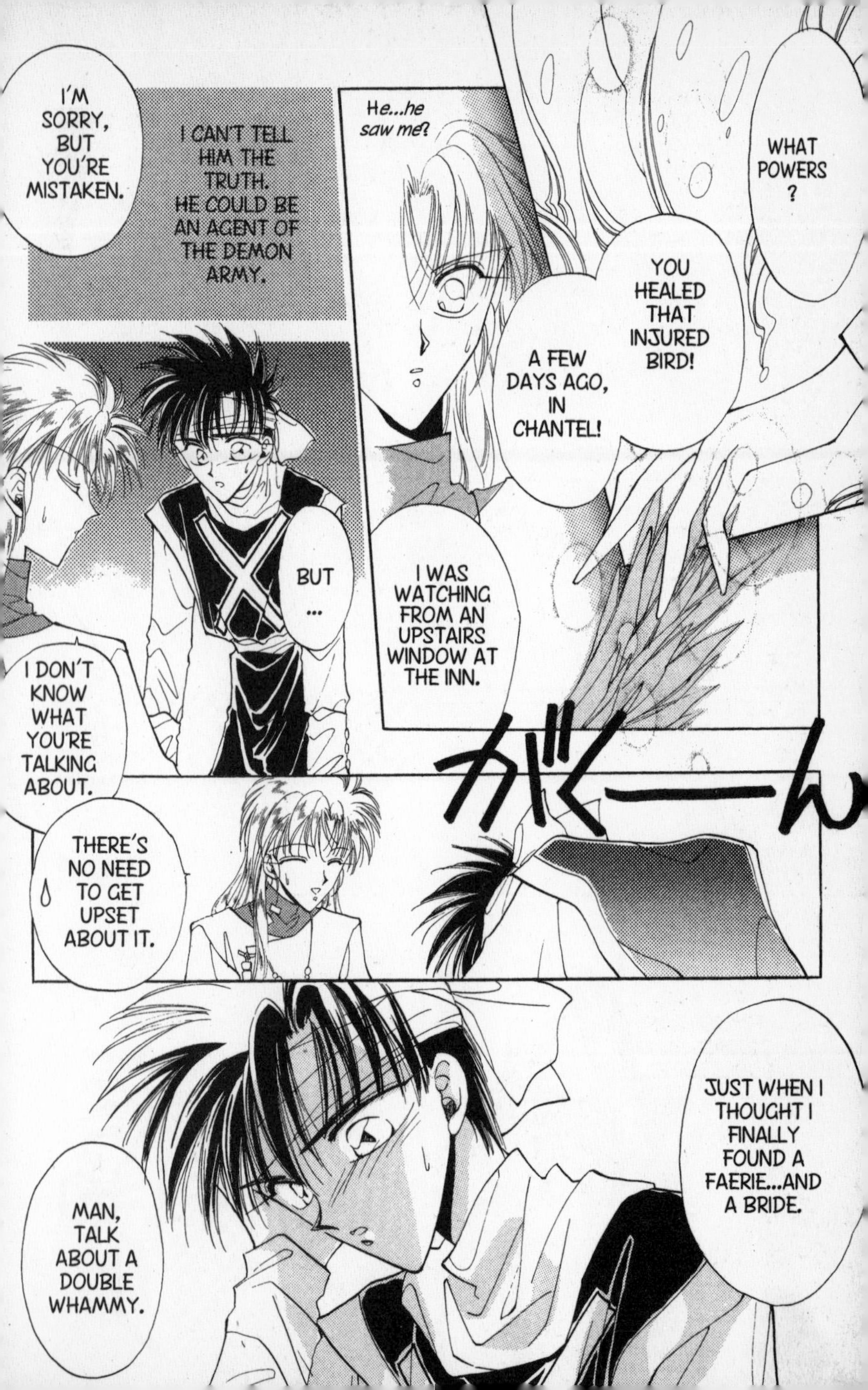
WHAT POWERS ?
YOU HEALED THAT INJURED BIRD!
A FEW DAYS AGO, IN CHANTEL!
I WAS WATCHING FROM AN UPSTAIRS WINDOW AT THE INN.
He...he saw me?
I'M SORRY, BUT YOU'RE MISTAKEN.
I CAN'T TELL HIM THE TRUTH. HE COULD BE AN AGENT OF THE DEMON ARMY.
BUT ...
I DON'T KNOW WHAT YOU'RE TALKING ABOUT.
がくーん
THERE'S NO NEED TO GET UPSET ABOUT IT.
JUST WHEN I THOUGHT I FINALLY FOUND A FAERIE...AND A BRIDE.
MAN, TALK ABOUT A DOUBLE WHAMMY.

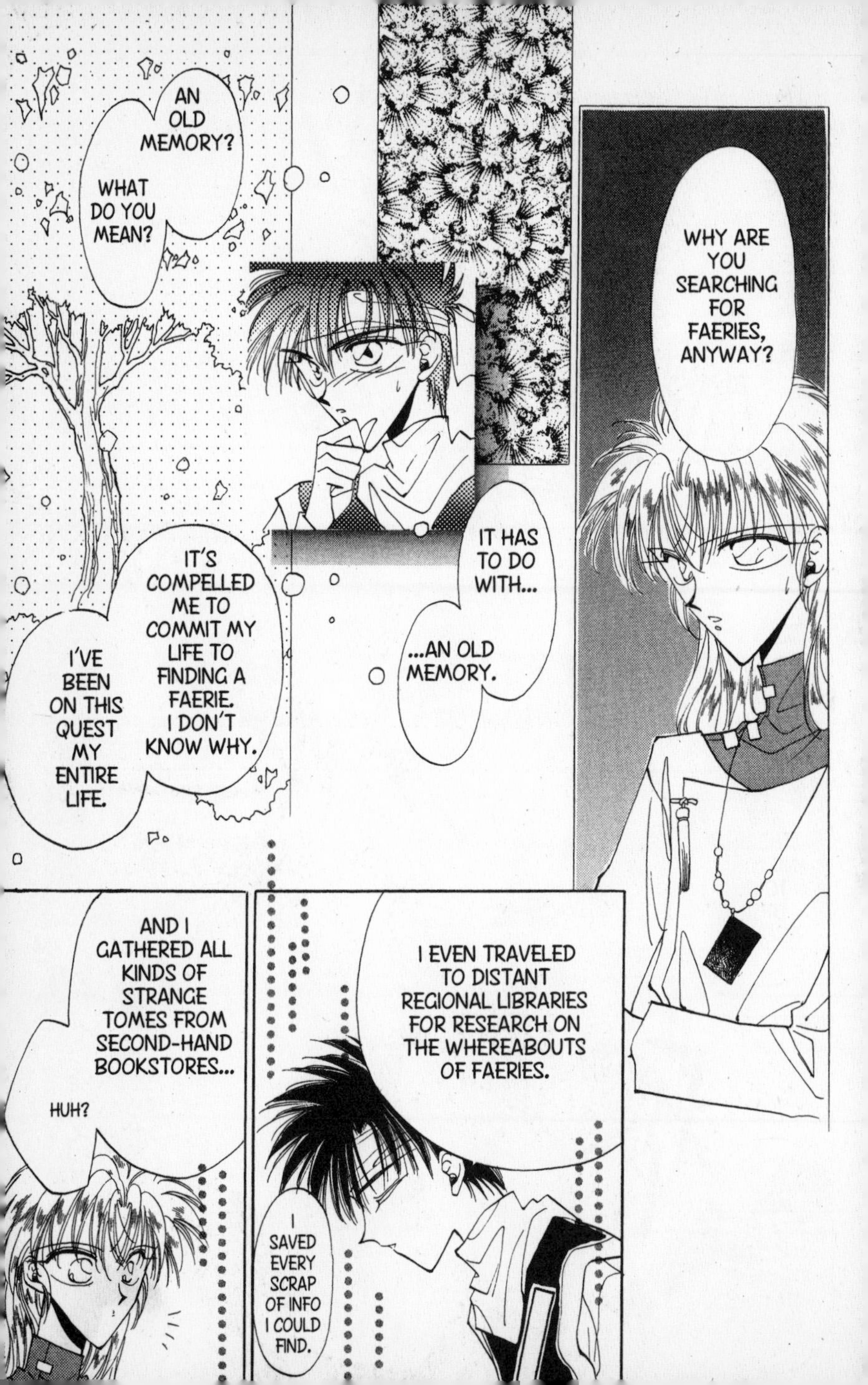
WHY ARE YOU SEARCHING FOR FAERIES, ANYWAY?
IT HAS TO DO WITH...
...AN OLD MEMORY.
AN OLD MEMORY?
WHAT DO YOU MEAN?
IT'S COMPELLED ME TO COMMIT MY LIFE TO FINDING A FAERIE. I DON'T KNOW WHY.
I'VE BEEN ON THIS QUEST MY ENTIRE LIFE.
I EVEN TRAVELED TO DISTANT REGIONAL LIBRARIES FOR RESEARCH ON THE WHEREABOUTS OF FAERIES.
I SAVED EVERY SCRAP OF INFO I COULD FIND.
AND I GATHERED ALL KINDS OF STRANGE TOMES FROM SECOND-HAND BOOKSTORES...
HUH?

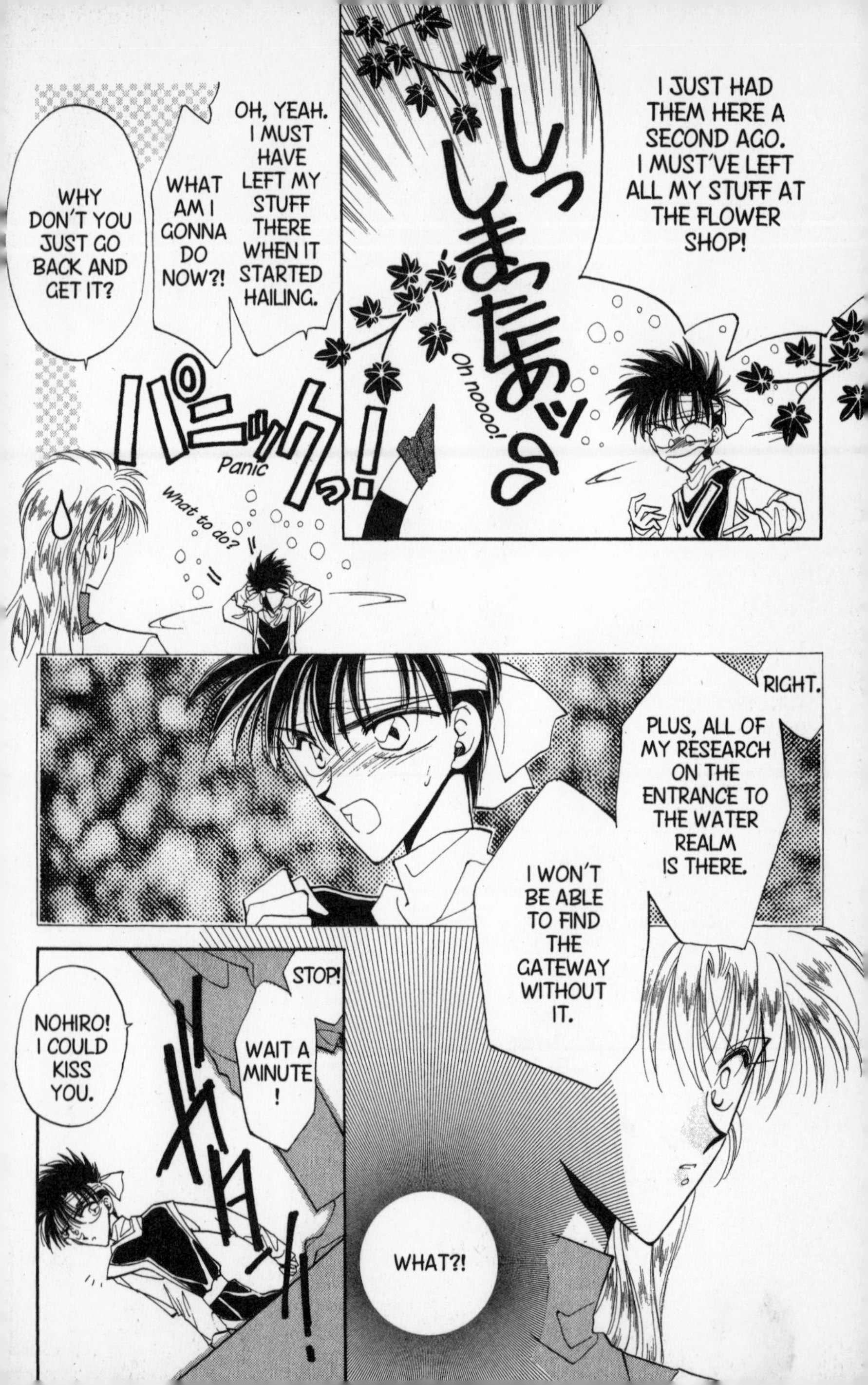
I JUST HAD THEM HERE A SECOND AGO. I MUST'VE LEFT ALL MY STUFF AT THE FLOWER SHOP!
しっしまったあッ
Oh noooo!
OH, YEAH. I MUST HAVE LEFT MY STUFF THERE WHEN IT STARTED HAILING.
WHAT AM I GONNA DO NOW?!
WHY DON'T YOU JUST GO BACK AND GET IT?
パニックっ!
Panic
What to do?
RIGHT.
PLUS, ALL OF MY RESEARCH ON THE ENTRANCE TO THE WATER REALM IS THERE.
I WON'T BE ABLE TO FIND THE GATEWAY WITHOUT IT.
WHAT?!
STOP!
WAIT A MINUTE!
NOHIRO! I COULD KISS YOU.

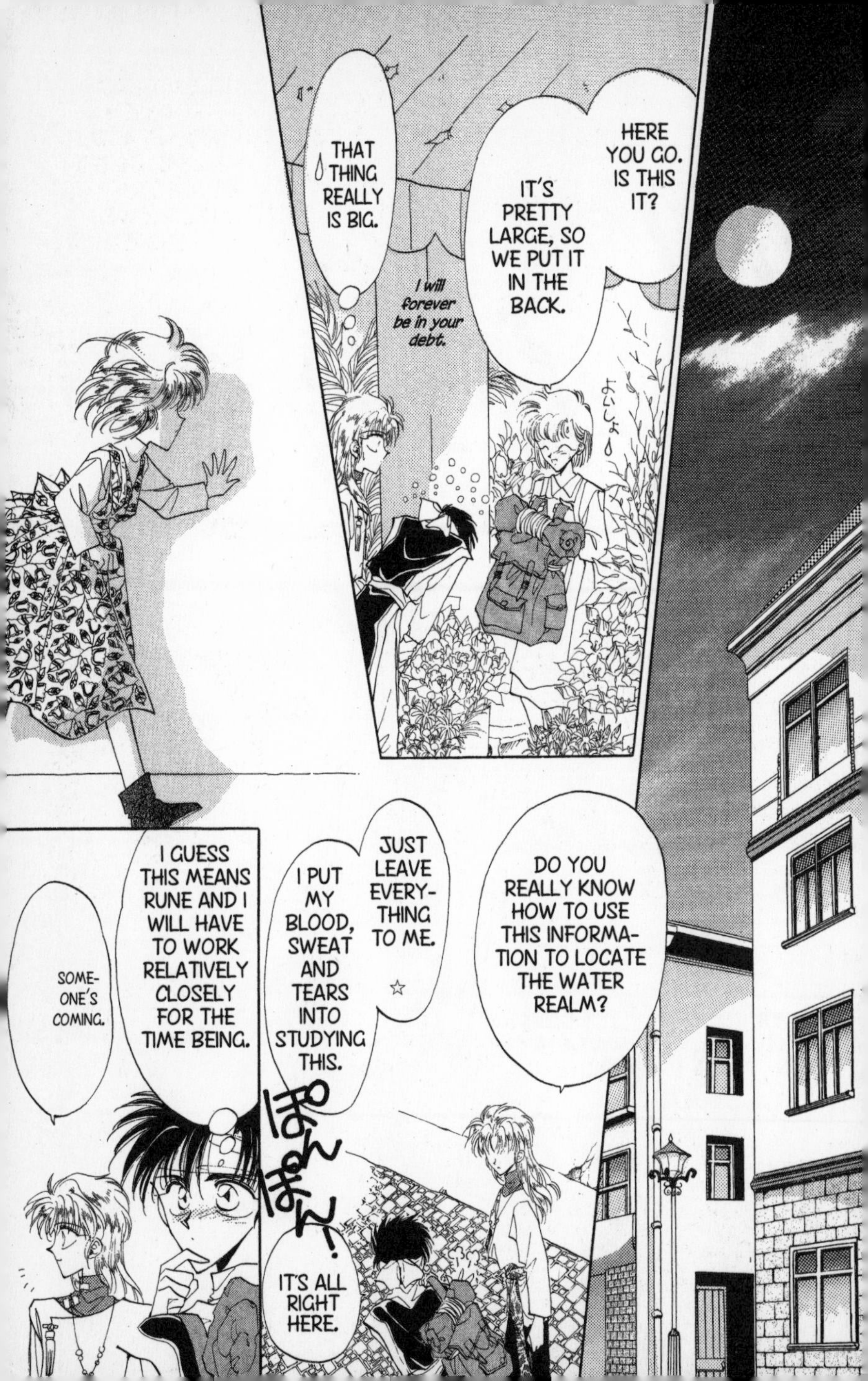
HERE YOU GO. IS THIS IT?
IT'S PRETTY LARGE, SO WE PUT IT IN THE BACK.
よいしょ
I will forever be in your debt.
THAT THING REALLY IS BIG.
DO YOU REALLY KNOW HOW TO USE THIS INFORMATION TO LOCATE THE WATER REALM?
JUST LEAVE EVERYTHING TO ME. ☆
I PUT MY BLOOD, SWEAT AND TEARS INTO STUDYING THIS.
ぽんぽん!
IT'S ALL RIGHT HERE.
I GUESS THIS MEANS RUNE AND I WILL HAVE TO WORK RELATIVELY CLOSELY FOR THE TIME BEING.
SOMEONE'S COMING.

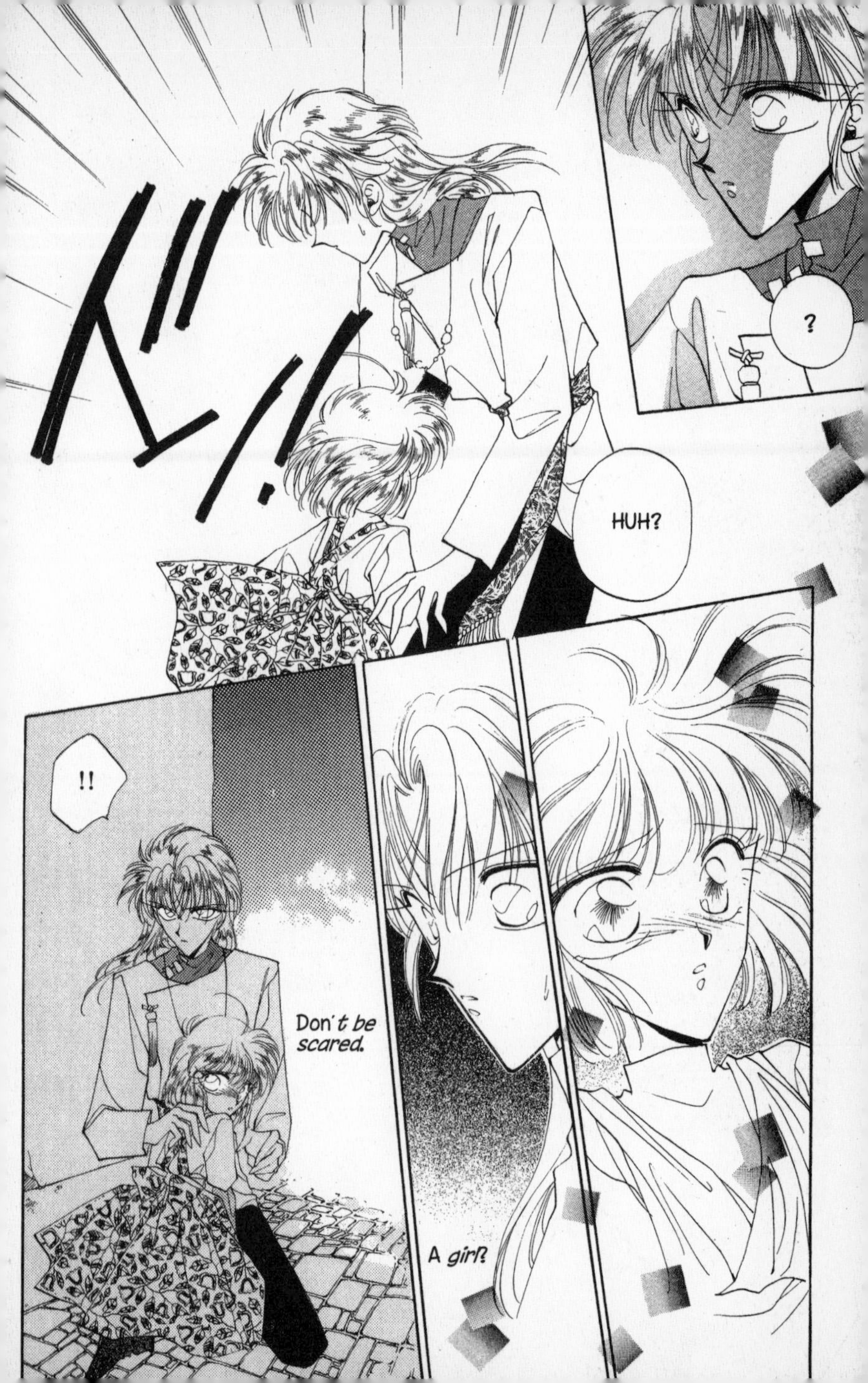
?
HUH?
A girl?
!!
Don't be scared.

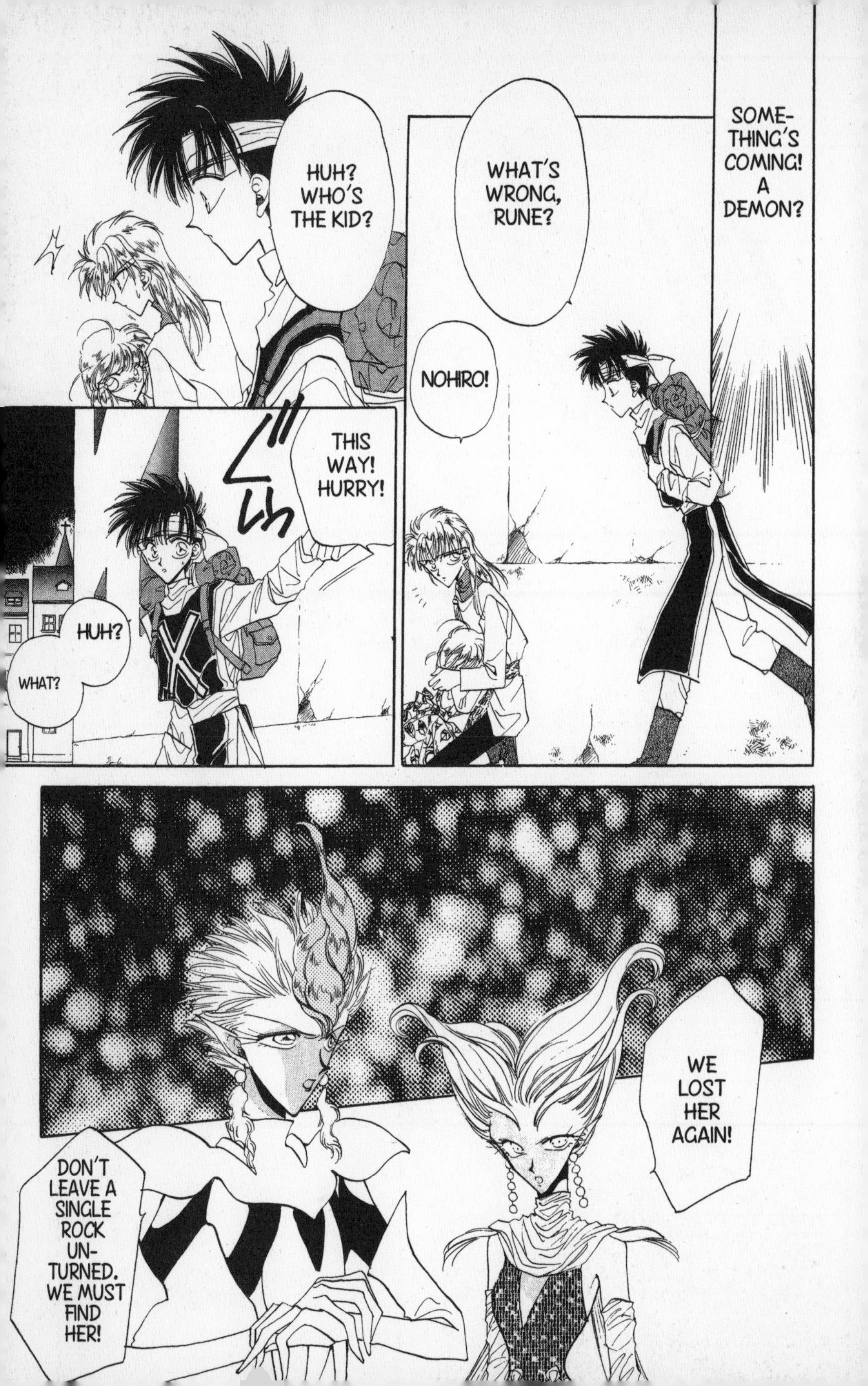
SOME-THING'S COMING! A DEMON?
WHAT'S WRONG, RUNE?
NOHIRO!
HUH? WHO'S THE KID?
THIS WAY! HURRY!
HUH?
WHAT?
WE LOST HER AGAIN!
DON'T LEAVE A SINGLE ROCK UN-TURNED. WE MUST FIND HER!

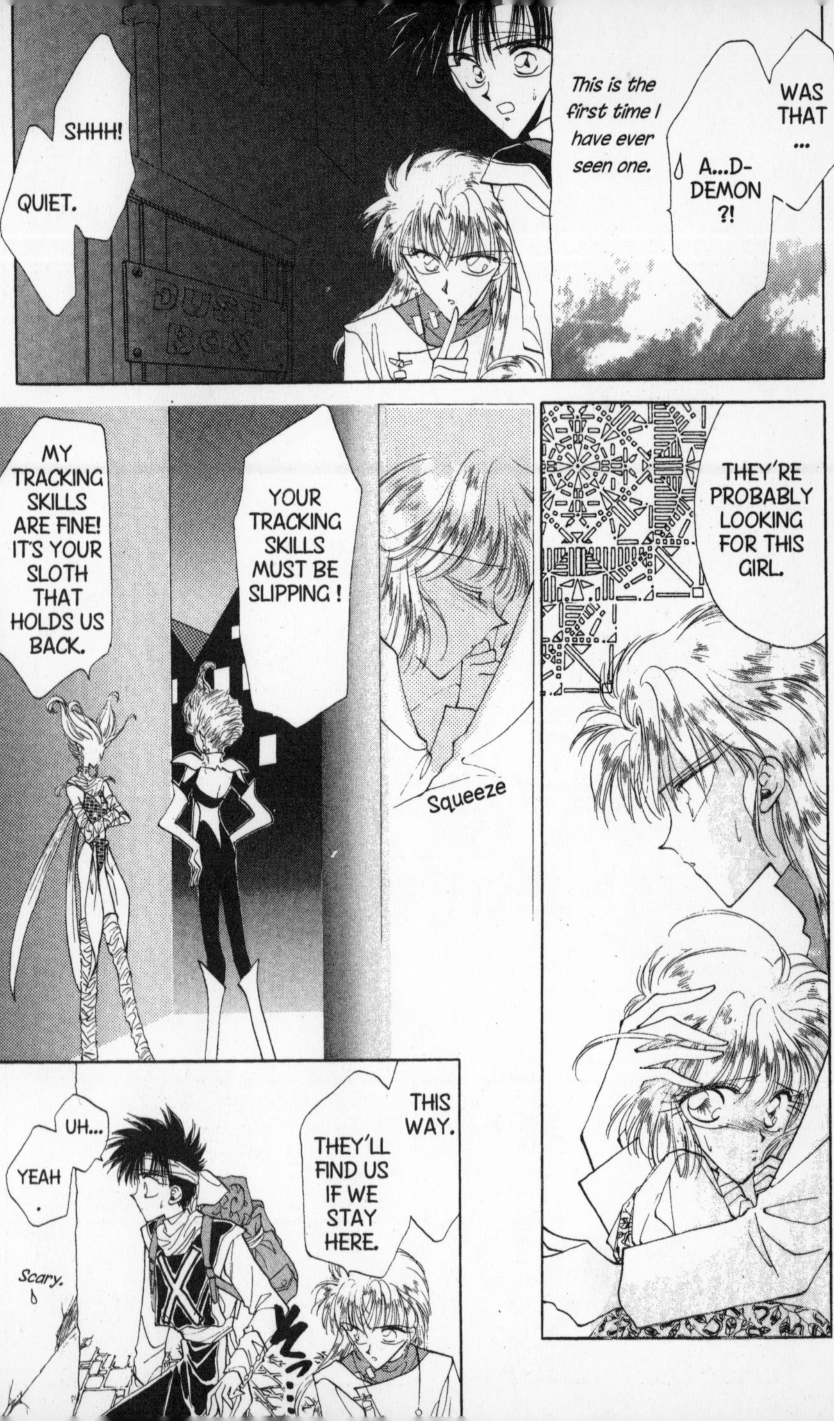
WAS THAT ... A...D-DEMON ?!
This is the first time I have ever seen one.
SHHH!
QUIET.
THEY'RE PROBABLY LOOKING FOR THIS GIRL.
Squeeze
YOUR TRACKING SKILLS MUST BE SLIPPING !
MY TRACKING SKILLS ARE FINE! IT'S YOUR SLOTH THAT HOLDS US BACK.
THIS WAY.
THEY'LL FIND US IF WE STAY HERE.
UH...
YEAH.
Scary.

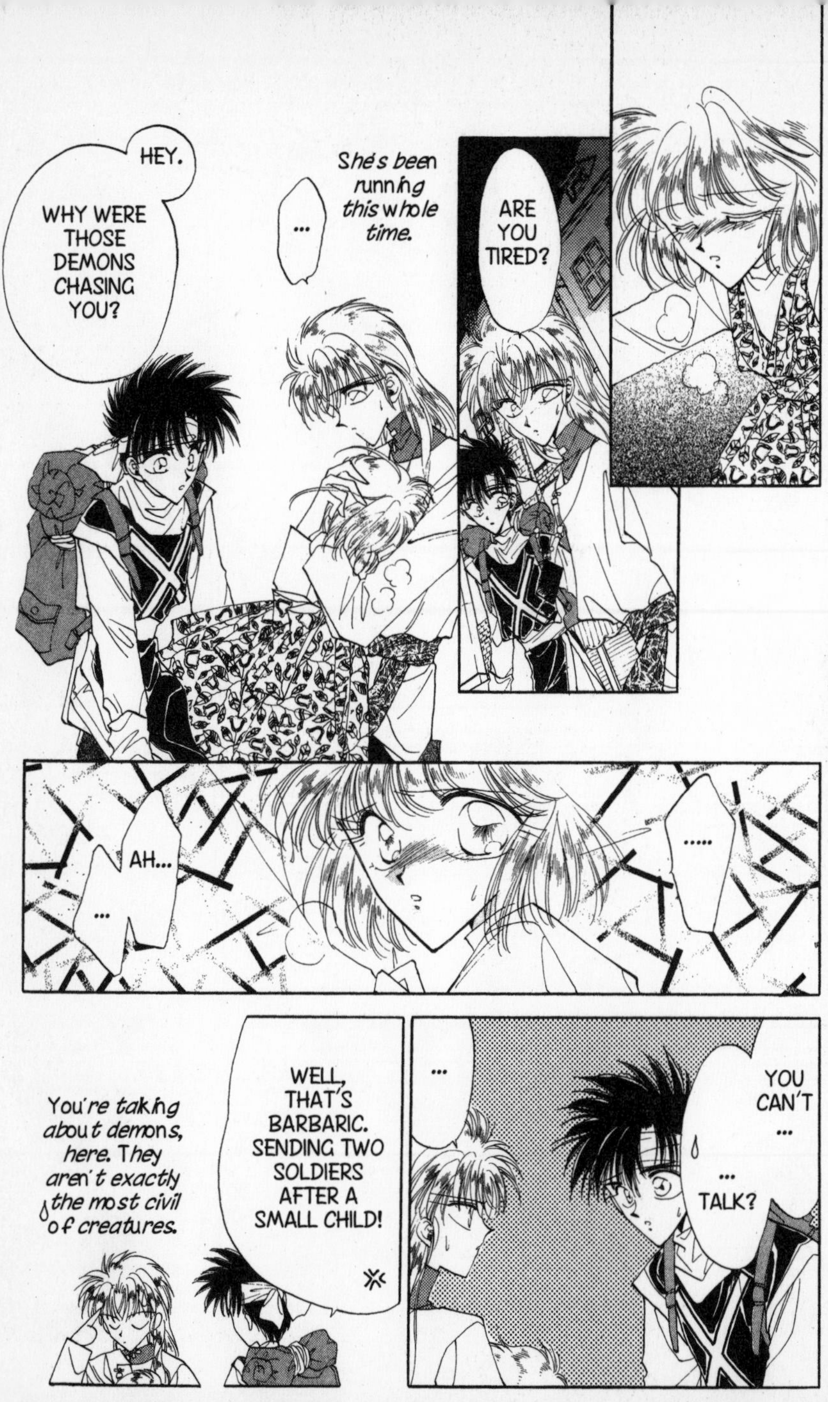
ARE YOU TIRED?
She's been running this whole time.
...
HEY.
WHY WERE THOSE DEMONS CHASING YOU?
......
AH...
...
YOU CAN'T ... ... TALK?
...
WELL, THAT'S BARBARIC. SENDING TWO SOLDIERS AFTER A SMALL CHILD!
You're taking about demons, here. They aren't exactly the most civil of creatures.

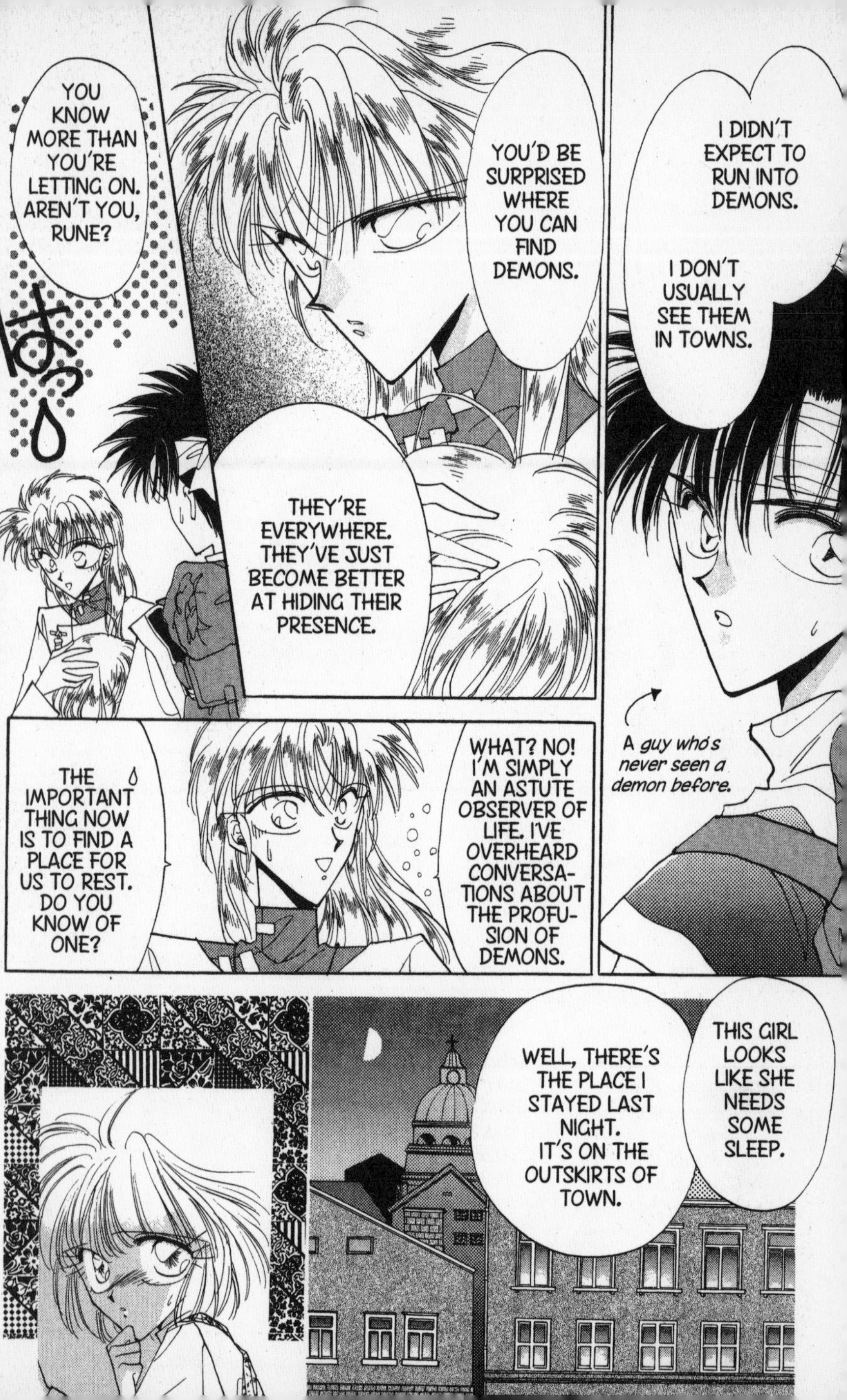
I DIDN'T EXPECT TO RUN INTO DEMONS.
I DON'T USUALLY SEE THEM IN TOWNS.
A guy who's never seen a demon before.
YOU'D BE SURPRISED WHERE YOU CAN FIND DEMONS.
THEY'RE EVERYWHERE. THEY'VE JUST BECOME BETTER AT HIDING THEIR PRESENCE.
YOU KNOW MORE THAN YOU'RE LETTING ON. AREN'T YOU, RUNE?
はっ
WHAT? NO! I'M SIMPLY AN ASTUTE OBSERVER OF LIFE. I'VE OVERHEARD CONVERSA-TIONS ABOUT THE PROFU-SION OF DEMONS.
THE IMPORTANT THING NOW IS TO FIND A PLACE FOR US TO REST. DO YOU KNOW OF ONE?
THIS GIRL LOOKS LIKE SHE NEEDS SOME SLEEP.
WELL, THERE'S THE PLACE I STAYED LAST NIGHT. IT'S ON THE OUTSKIRTS OF TOWN.

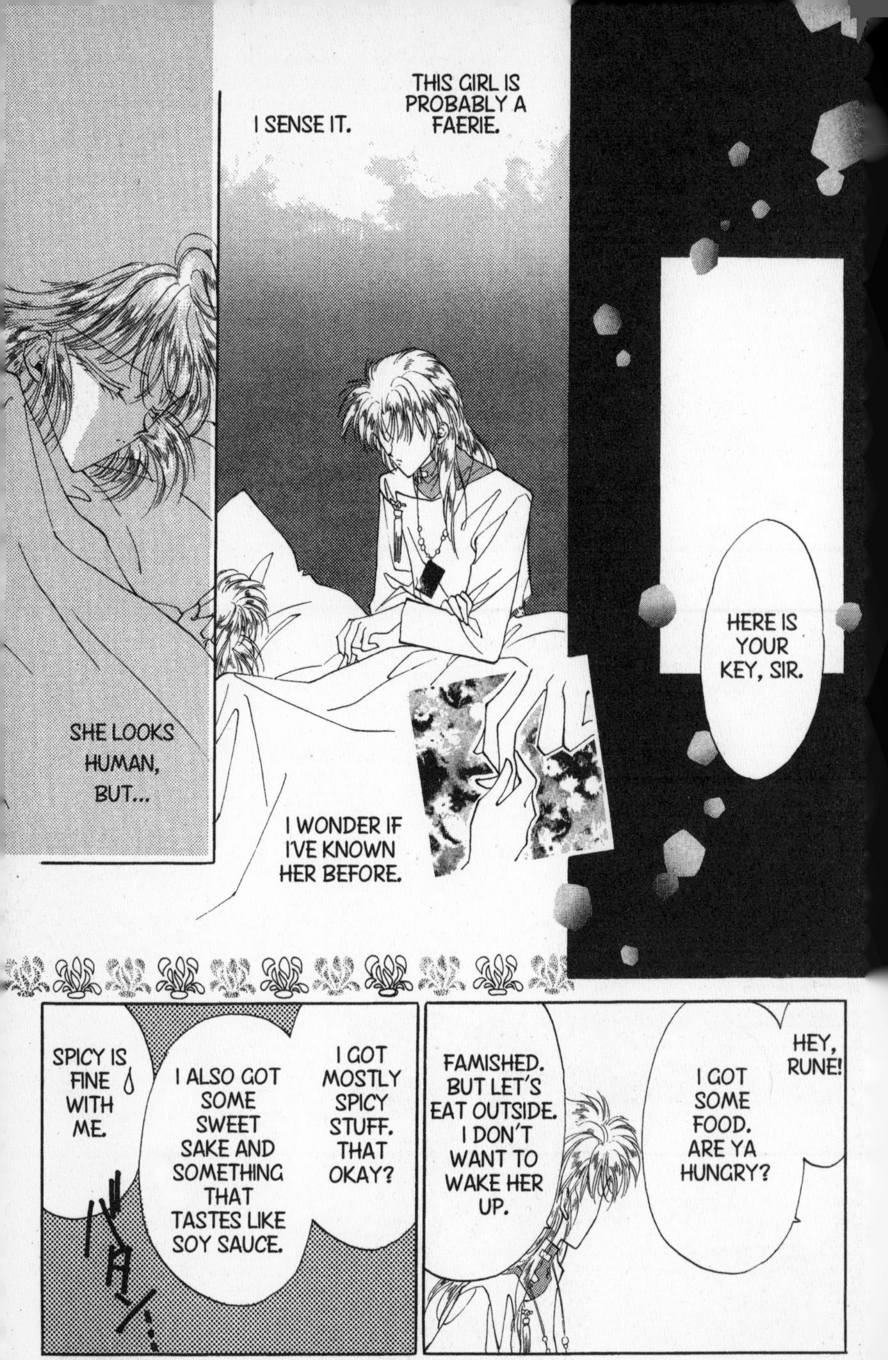
HERE IS YOUR KEY, SIR.
THIS GIRL IS PROBABLY A FAERIE.
I SENSE IT.
I WONDER IF I'VE KNOWN HER BEFORE.
SHE LOOKS HUMAN, BUT...
HEY, RUNE!
I GOT SOME FOOD. ARE YA HUNGRY?
FAMISHED. BUT LET'S EAT OUTSIDE. I DON'T WANT TO WAKE HER UP.
I GOT MOSTLY SPICY STUFF. THAT OKAY?
I ALSO GOT SOME SWEET SAKE AND SOMETHING THAT TASTES LIKE SOY SAUCE.
SPICY IS FINE WITH ME.

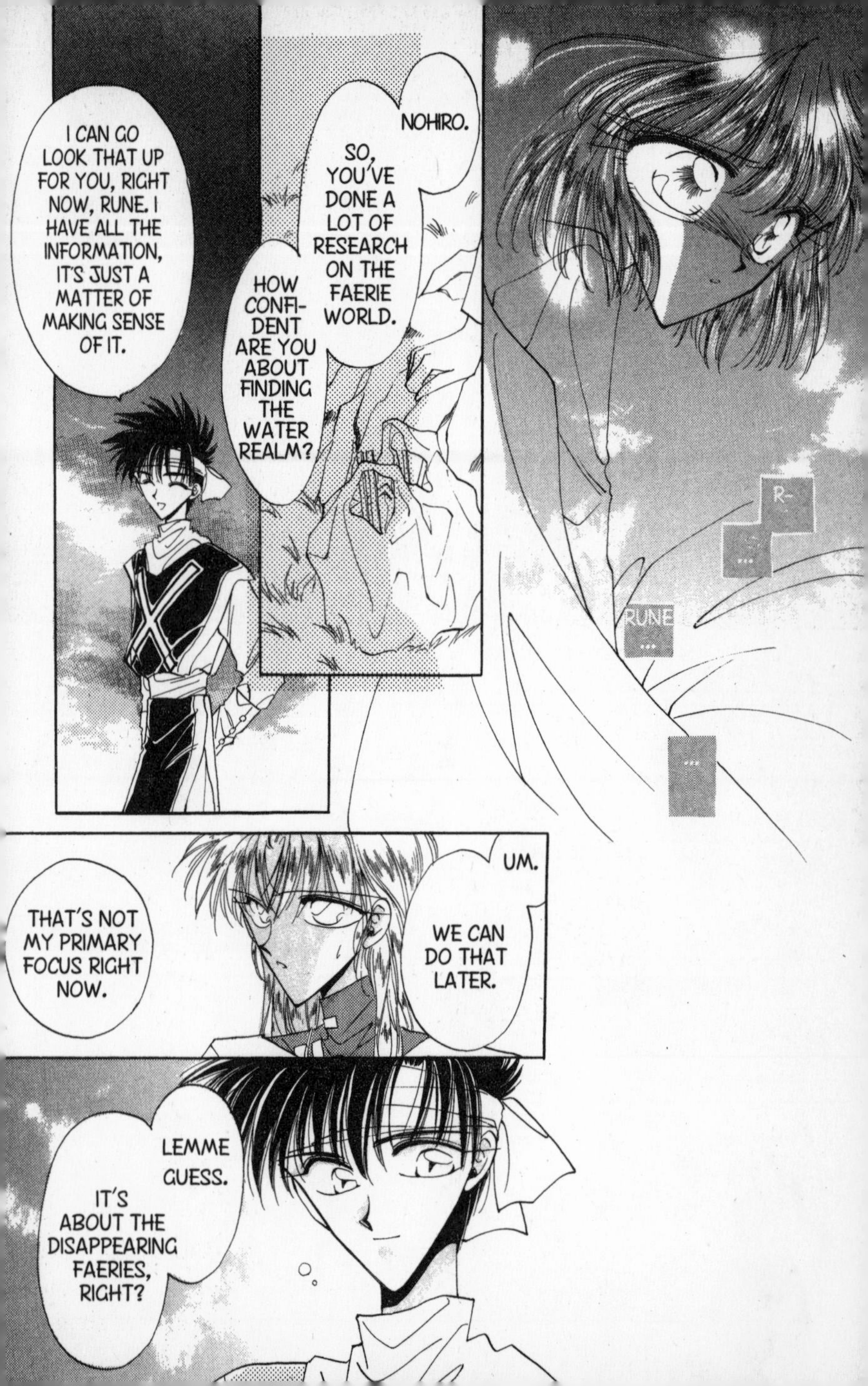
NOHIRO.
SO, YOU'VE DONE A LOT OF RESEARCH ON THE FAERIE WORLD.
HOW CONFIDENT ARE YOU ABOUT FINDING THE WATER REALM?
I CAN GO LOOK THAT UP FOR YOU, RIGHT NOW, RUNE. I HAVE ALL THE INFORMATION, IT'S JUST A MATTER OF MAKING SENSE OF IT.
R-
...
...
RUNE ...
...
UM.
WE CAN DO THAT LATER.
THAT'S NOT MY PRIMARY FOCUS RIGHT NOW.
LEMME GUESS.
IT'S ABOUT THE DISAPPEARING FAERIES, RIGHT?

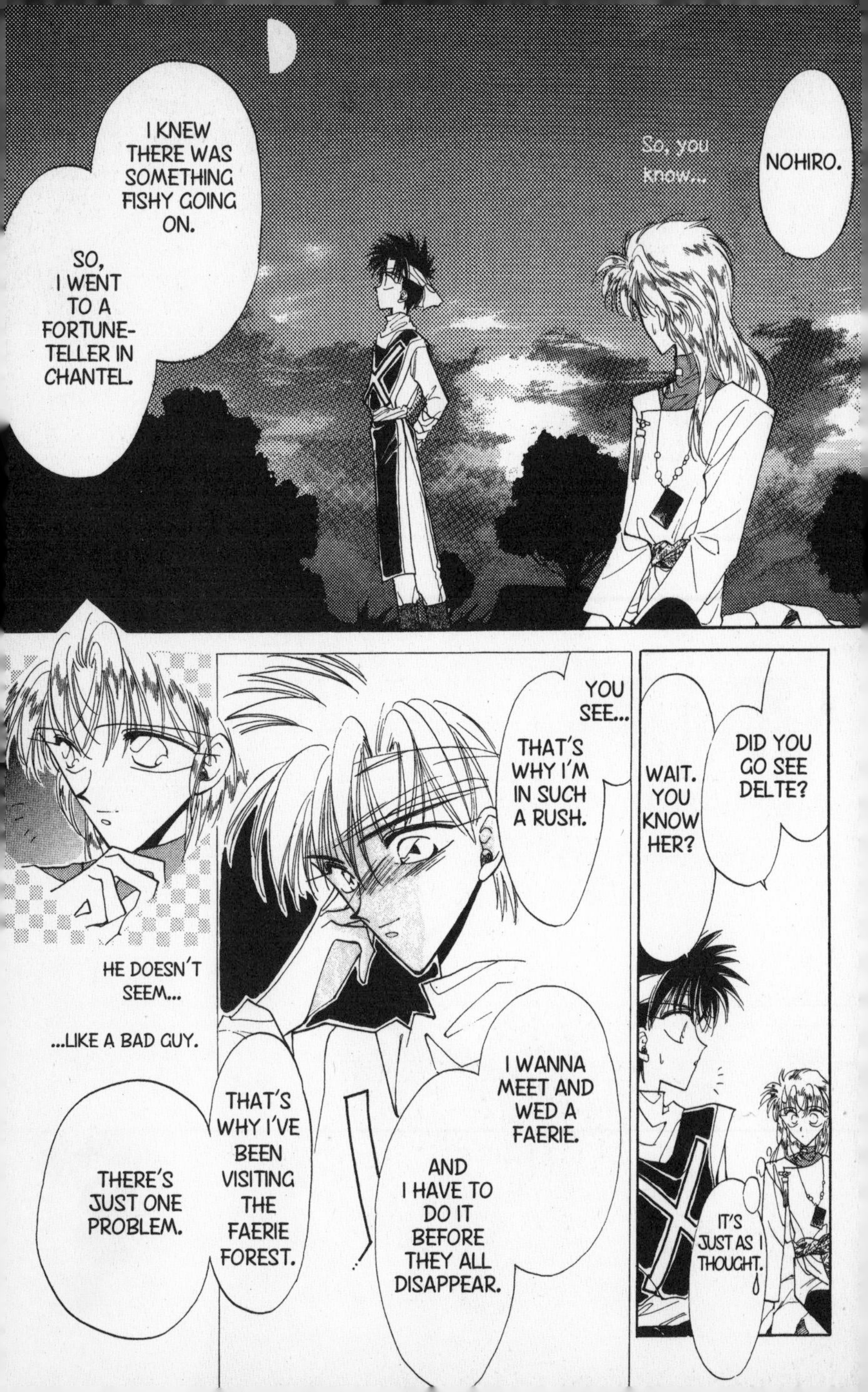
NOHIRO.
So, you know...
I KNEW THERE WAS SOMETHING FISHY GOING ON.
SO, I WENT TO A FORTUNE-TELLER IN CHANTEL.
DID YOU GO SEE DELTE?
WAIT. YOU KNOW HER?
IT'S JUST AS I THOUGHT.
YOU SEE...
THAT'S WHY I'M IN SUCH A RUSH.
I WANNA MEET AND WED A FAERIE.
AND I HAVE TO DO IT BEFORE THEY ALL DISAPPEAR.
THAT'S WHY I'VE BEEN VISITING THE FAERIE FOREST.
THERE'S JUST ONE PROBLEM.
HE DOESN'T SEEM...
...LIKE A BAD GUY.

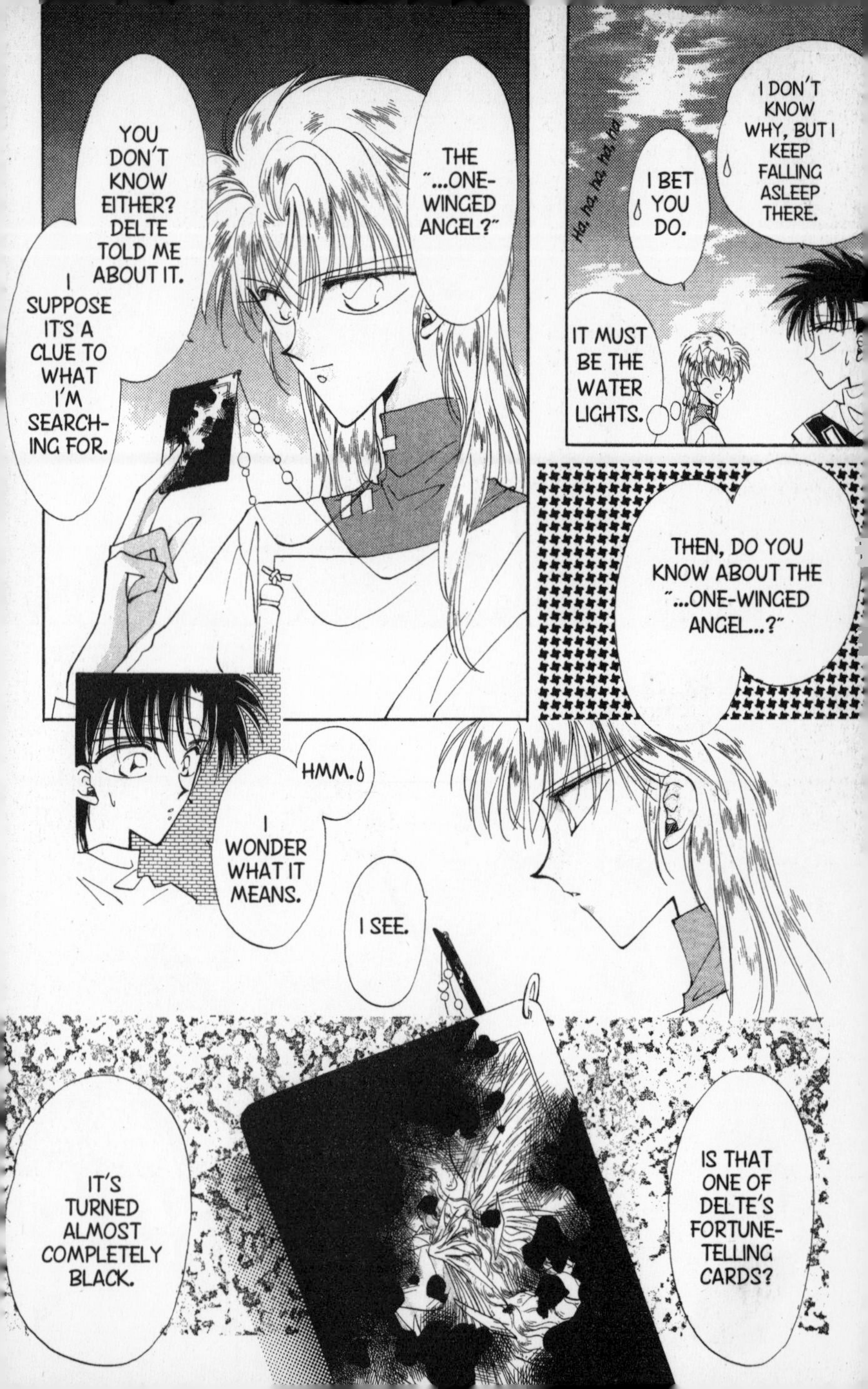
I DON'T KNOW WHY, BUT I KEEP FALLING ASLEEP THERE.
Ha, ha, ha, ha, ha
I BET YOU DO.
IT MUST BE THE WATER LIGHTS.
THEN, DO YOU KNOW ABOUT THE "...ONE-WINGED ANGEL...?"
THE "...ONE-WINGED ANGEL?"
YOU DON'T KNOW EITHER? DELTE TOLD ME ABOUT IT.
I SUPPOSE IT'S A CLUE TO WHAT I'M SEARCHING FOR.
HMM.
I WONDER WHAT IT MEANS.
I SEE.
IS THAT ONE OF DELTE'S FORTUNE-TELLING CARDS?
IT'S TURNED ALMOST COMPLETELY BLACK.

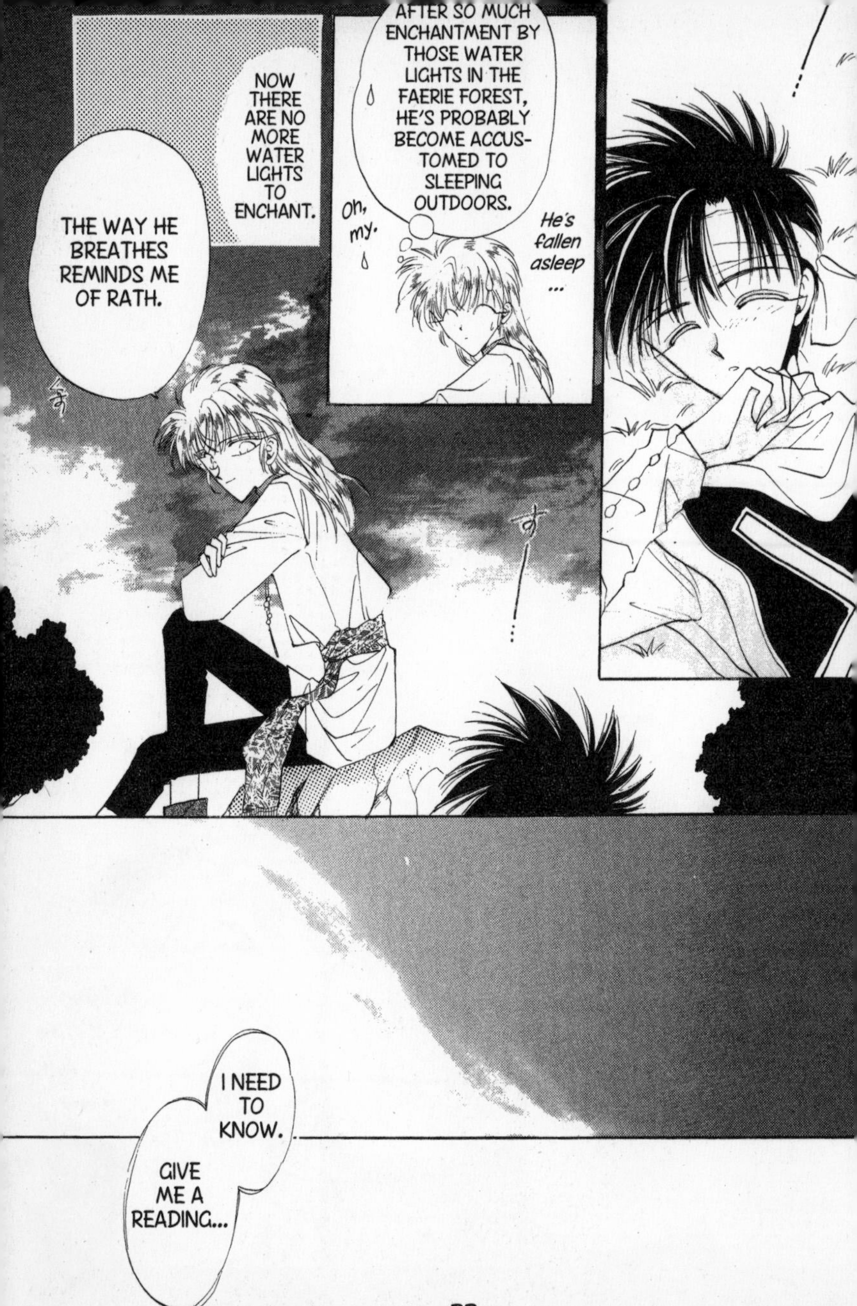
He's fallen asleep...
AFTER SO MUCH ENCHANTMENT BY THOSE WATER LIGHTS IN THE FAERIE FOREST, HE'S PROBABLY BECOME ACCUSTOMED TO SLEEPING OUTDOORS.
Oh, my.
NOW THERE ARE NO MORE WATER LIGHTS TO ENCHANT.
THE WAY HE BREATHES REMINDS ME OF RATH.
I NEED TO KNOW.
GIVE ME A READING...

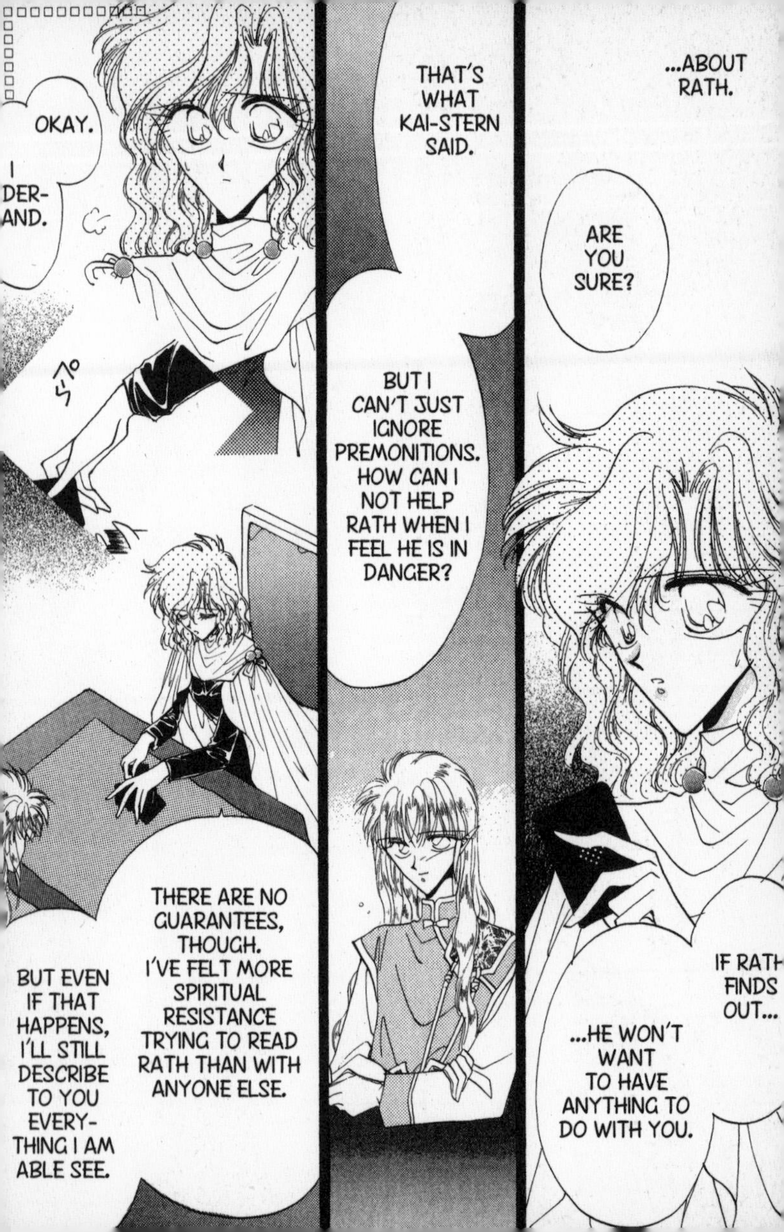
...ABOUT RATH.
ARE YOU SURE?
IF RATH FINDS OUT...
...HE WON'T WANT TO HAVE ANYTHING TO DO WITH YOU.
THAT'S WHAT KAI-STERN SAID.
BUT I CAN'T JUST IGNORE PREMONITIONS. HOW CAN I NOT HELP RATH WHEN I FEEL HE IS IN DANGER?
OKAY.
I
DER-
AND.
THERE ARE NO GUARANTEES, THOUGH. I'VE FELT MORE SPIRITUAL RESISTANCE TRYING TO READ RATH THAN WITH ANYONE ELSE.
BUT EVEN IF THAT HAPPENS, I'LL STILL DESCRIBE TO YOU EVERY-THING I AM ABLE SEE.

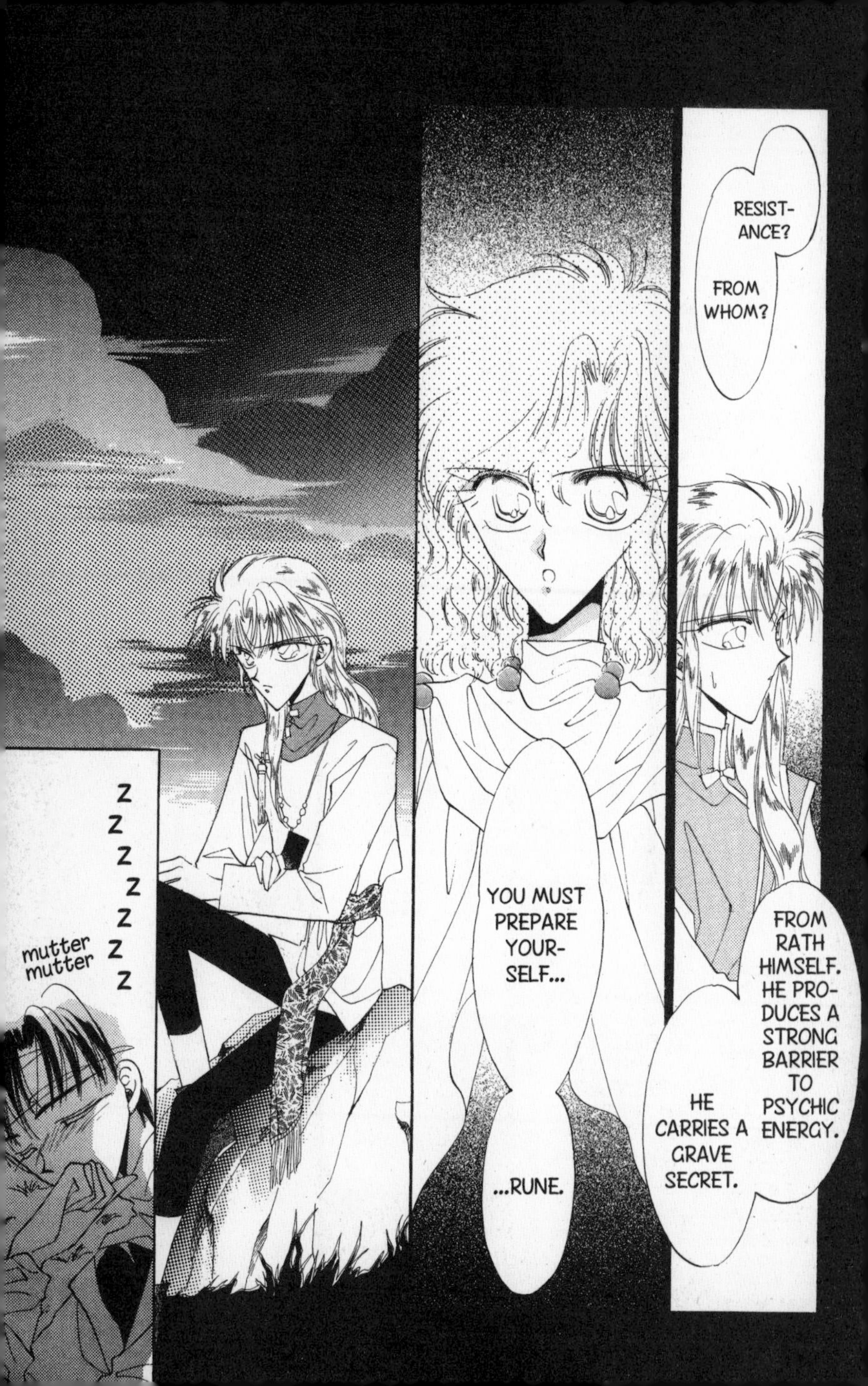
RESIST-ANCE? FROM WHOM?
FROM RATH HIMSELF. HE PRO-DUCES A STRONG BARRIER TO PSYCHIC ENERGY.
HE CARRIES A GRAVE SECRET.
YOU MUST PREPARE YOUR-SELF...
...RUNE.
Z Z Z Z Z Z Z
mutter mutter

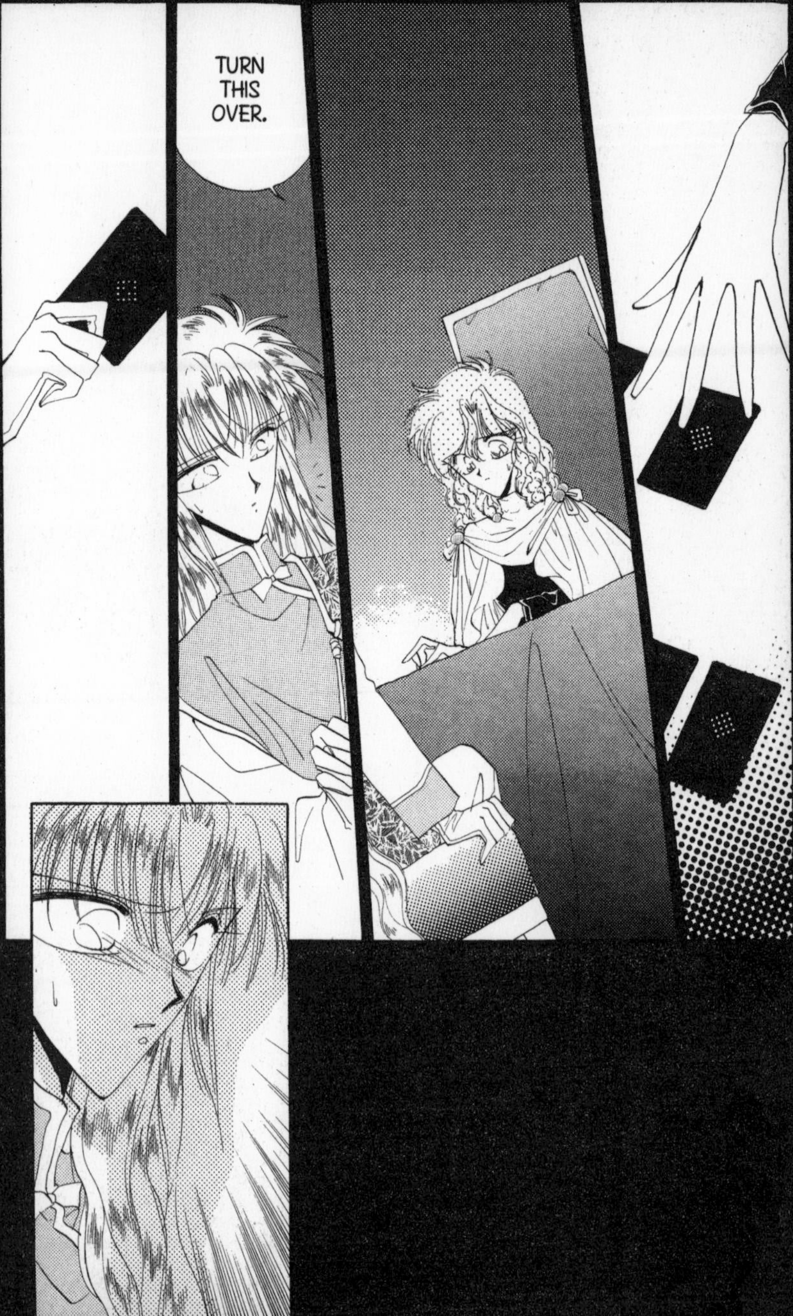
TURN THIS OVER.

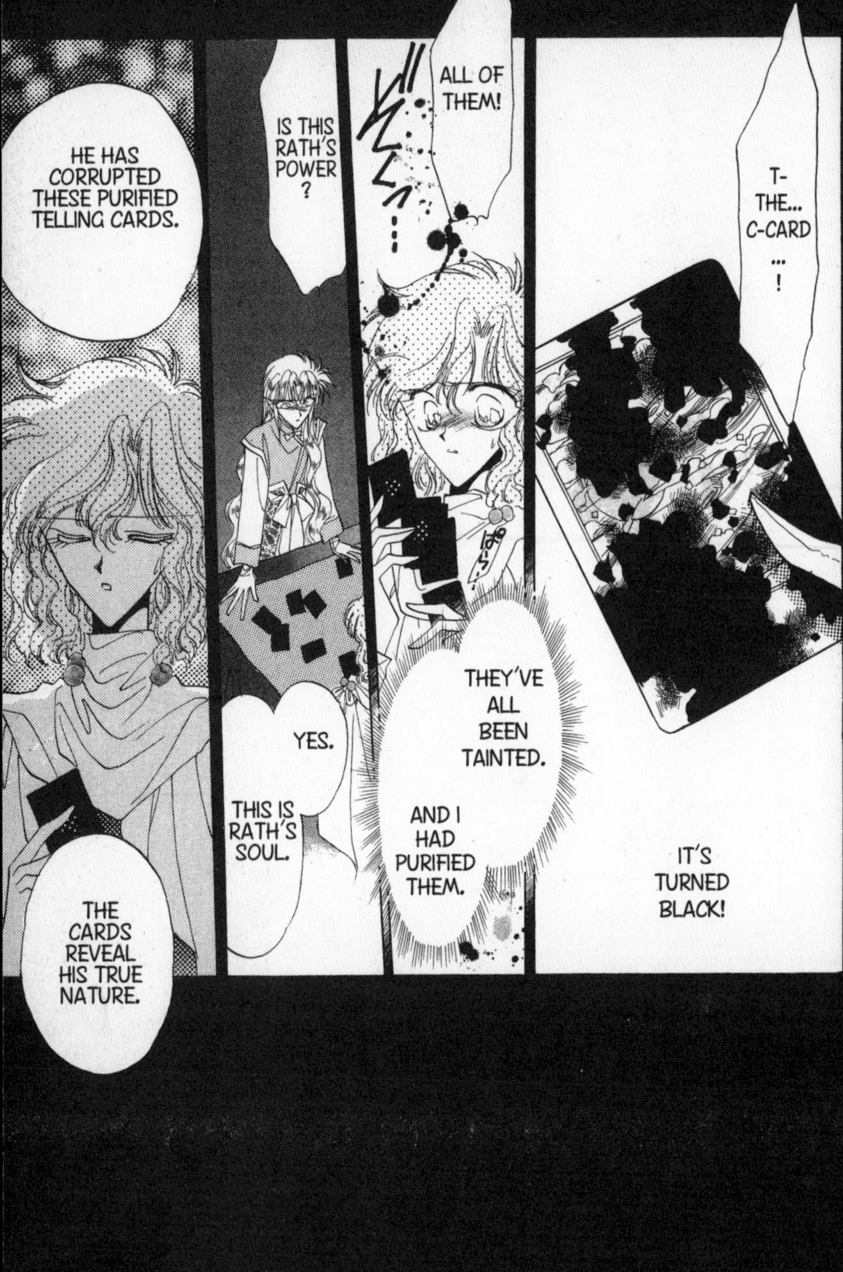
T- THE... C-CARD ...!
IT'S TURNED BLACK!
ALL OF THEM!
THEY'VE ALL BEEN TAINTED.
AND I HAD PURIFIED THEM.
IS THIS RATH'S POWER?
YES.
THIS IS RATH'S SOUL.
HE HAS CORRUPTED THESE PURIFIED TELLING CARDS.
THE CARDS REVEAL HIS TRUE NATURE.

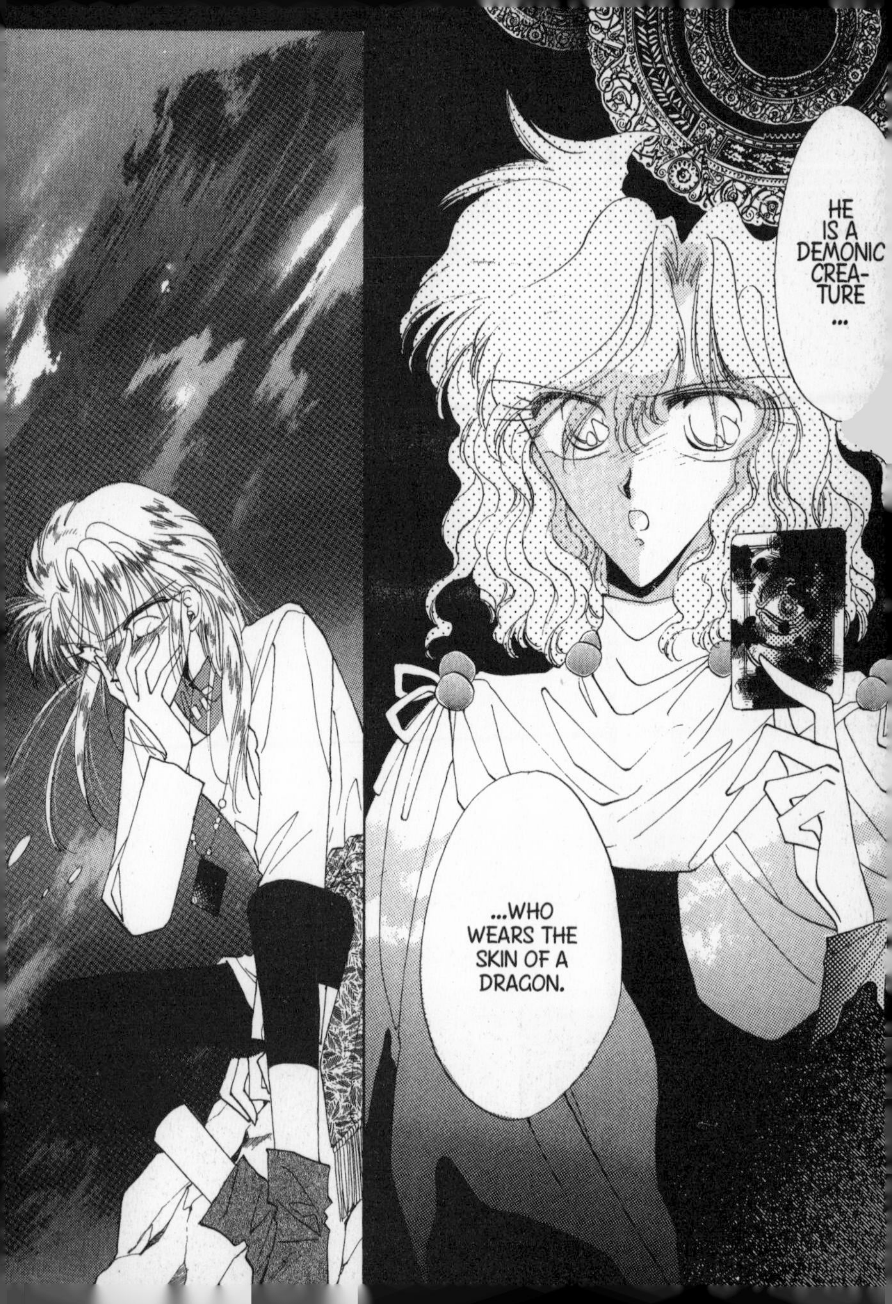
HE IS A DEMONIC CREATURE...
...WHO WEARS THE SKIN OF A DRAGON.

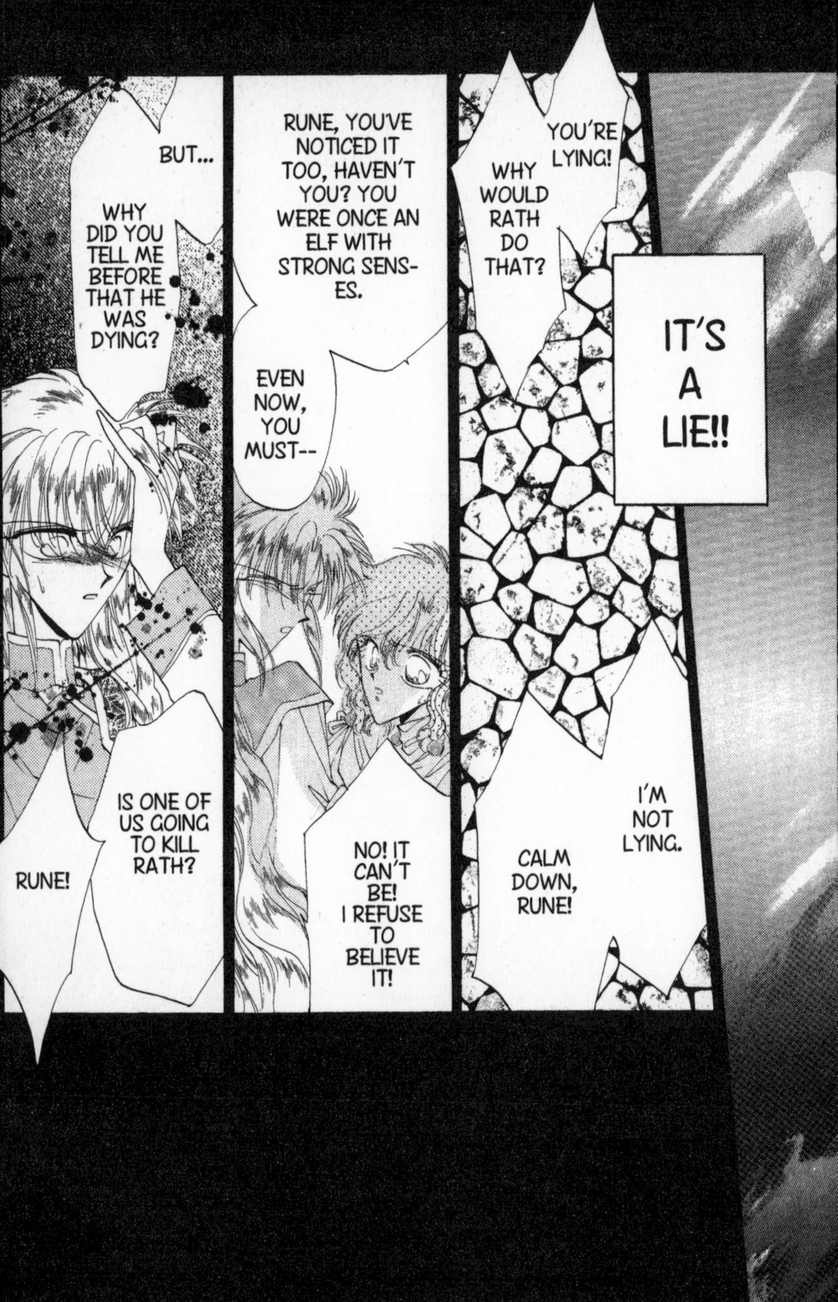
IT'S A LIE!!
YOU'RE LYING!
WHY WOULD RATH DO THAT?
I'M NOT LYING.
CALM DOWN, RUNE!
RUNE, YOU'VE NOTICED IT TOO, HAVEN'T YOU? YOU WERE ONCE AN ELF WITH STRONG SENS-ES.
EVEN NOW, YOU MUST--
NO! IT CAN'T BE! I REFUSE TO BELIEVE IT!
BUT...
WHY DID YOU TELL ME BEFORE THAT HE WAS DYING?
IS ONE OF US GOING TO KILL RATH?
RUNE!

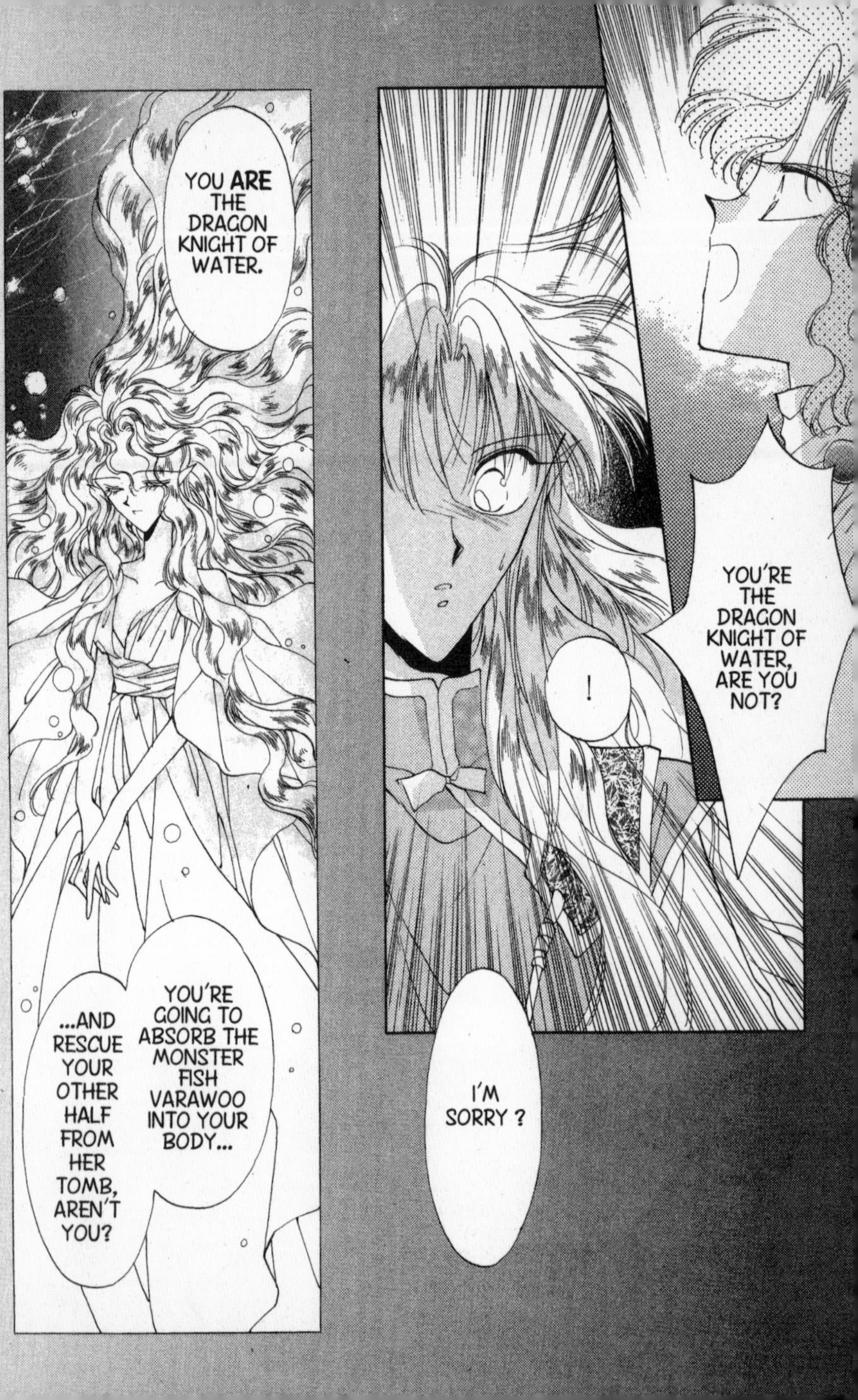
YOU'RE THE DRAGON KNIGHT OF WATER, ARE YOU NOT?
!
I'M SORRY ?
YOU **ARE** THE DRAGON KNIGHT OF WATER.
YOU'RE GOING TO ABSORB THE MONSTER FISH VARAWOO INTO YOUR BODY...
...AND RESCUE YOUR OTHER HALF FROM HER TOMB, AREN'T YOU?

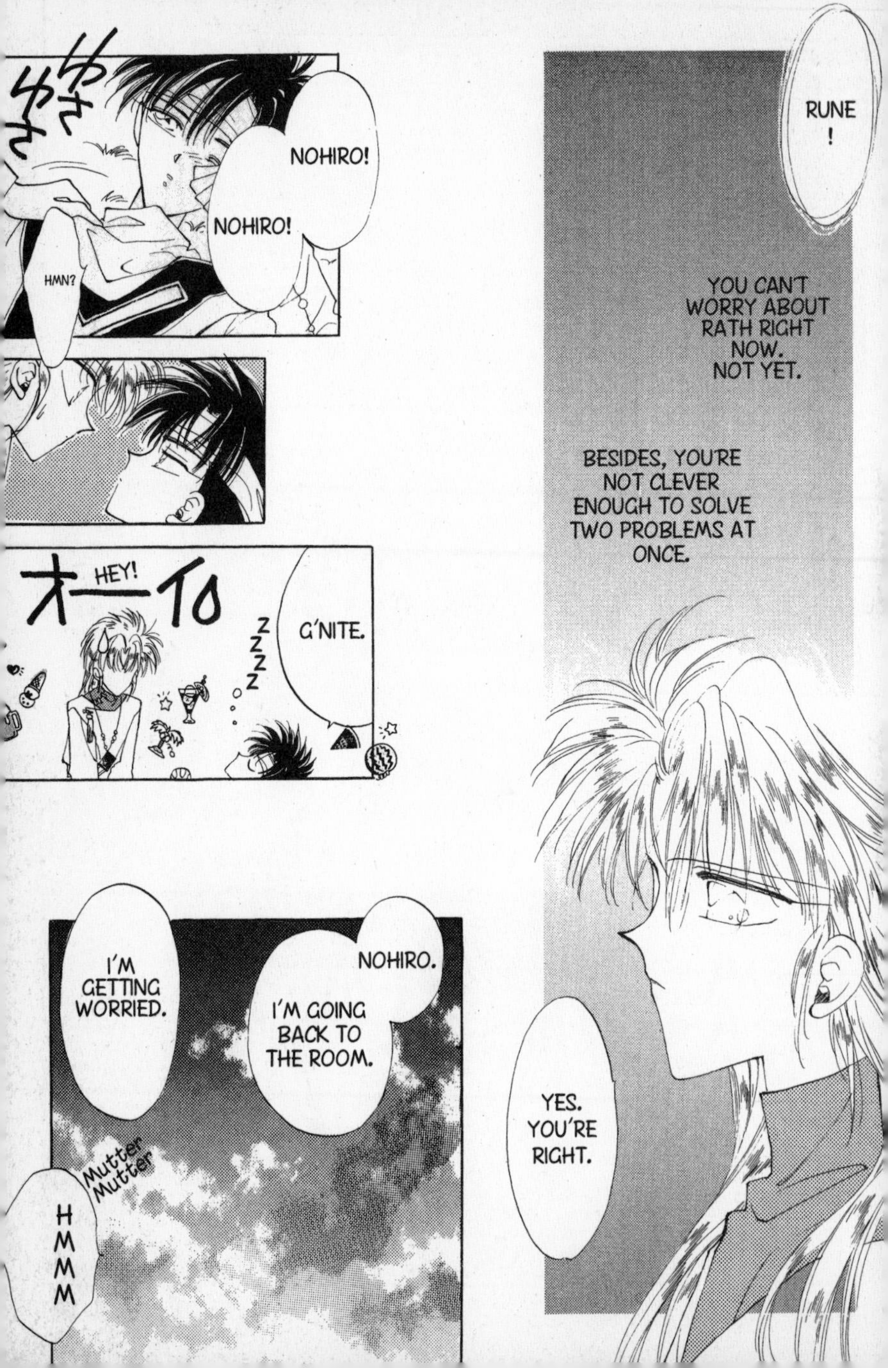
RUNE!
YOU CAN'T WORRY ABOUT RATH RIGHT NOW. NOT YET.
BESIDES, YOU'RE NOT CLEVER ENOUGH TO SOLVE TWO PROBLEMS AT ONCE.
YES. YOU'RE RIGHT.
ゆさゆさ
NOHIRO!
NOHIRO!
HMN?
HEY!
オーイ
G'NITE.
ZZZZ
NOHIRO.
I'M GOING BACK TO THE ROOM.
I'M GETTING WORRIED.
Mutter Mutter
HMMM

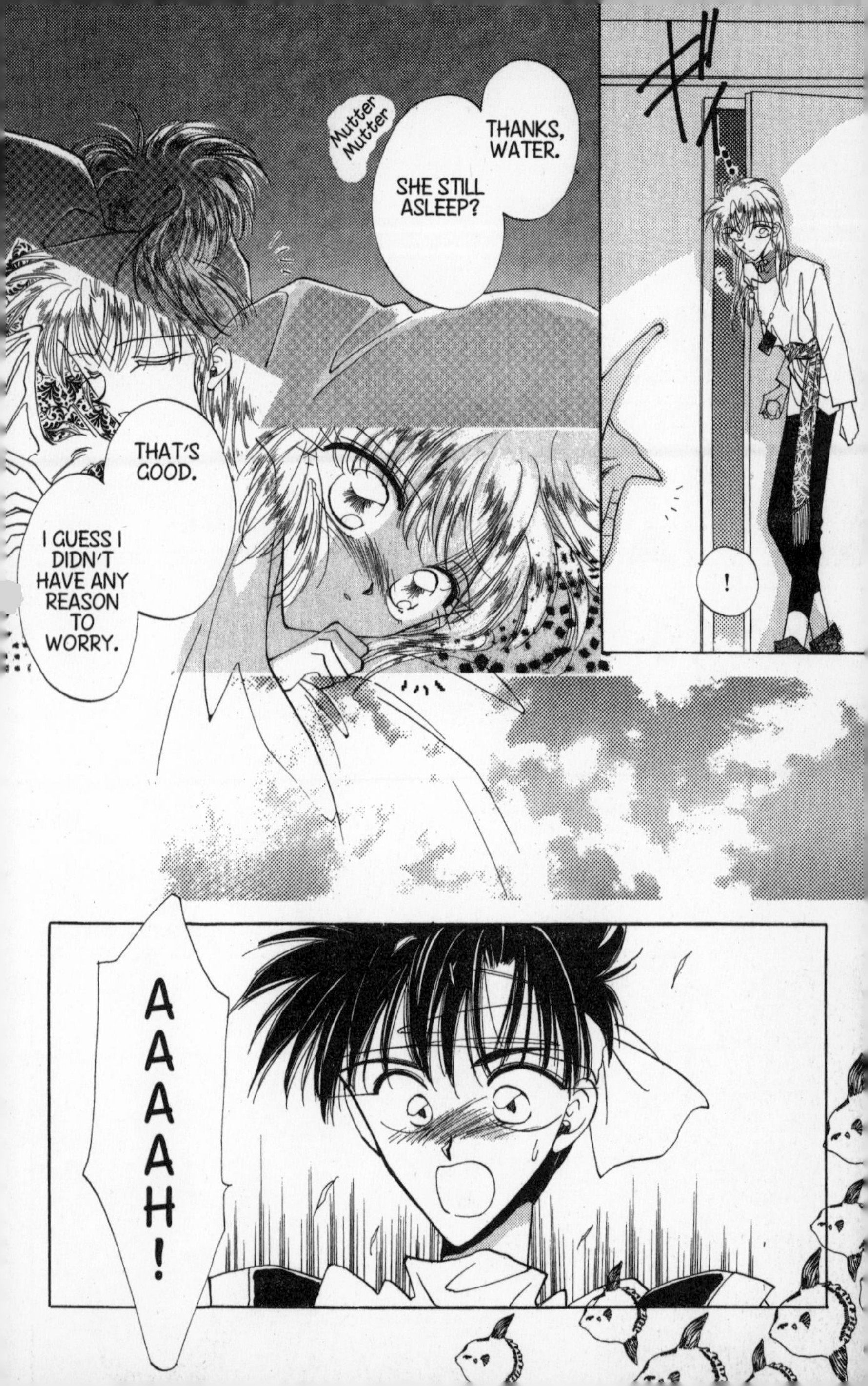
!
THANKS, WATER.
SHE STILL ASLEEP?
Mutter Mutter
THAT'S GOOD.
I GUESS I DIDN'T HAVE ANY REASON TO WORRY.
AAAAH!

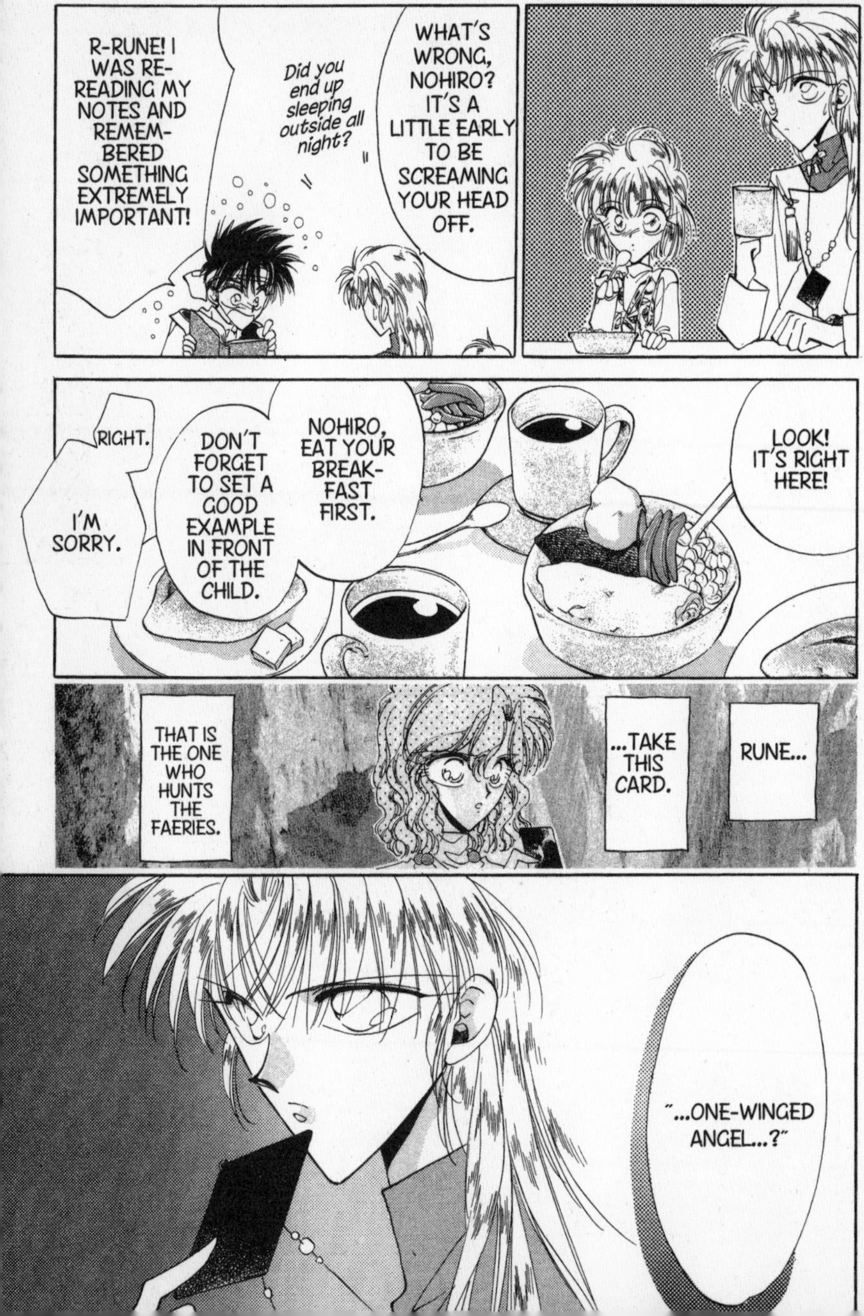
WHAT'S WRONG, NOHIRO? IT'S A LITTLE EARLY TO BE SCREAMING YOUR HEAD OFF.
Did you end up sleeping outside all night?
R-RUNE! I WAS RE-READING MY NOTES AND REMEMBERED SOMETHING EXTREMELY IMPORTANT!
LOOK! IT'S RIGHT HERE!
NOHIRO, EAT YOUR BREAKFAST FIRST.
DON'T FORGET TO SET A GOOD EXAMPLE IN FRONT OF THE CHILD.
RIGHT.
I'M SORRY.
RUNE...
...TAKE THIS CARD.
THAT IS THE ONE WHO HUNTS THE FAERIES.
"...ONE-WINGED ANGEL...?"

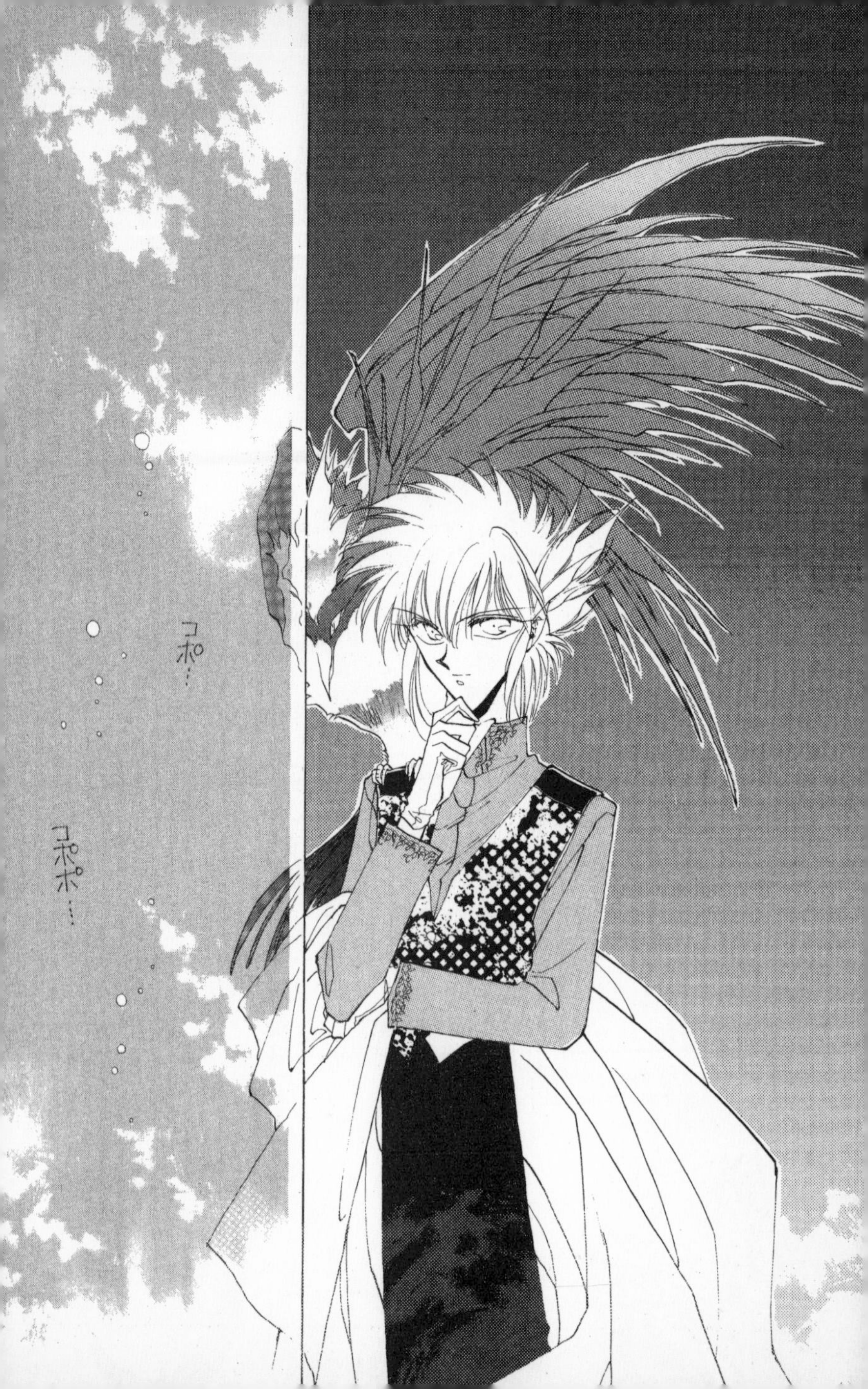
コポ…
コポポ…

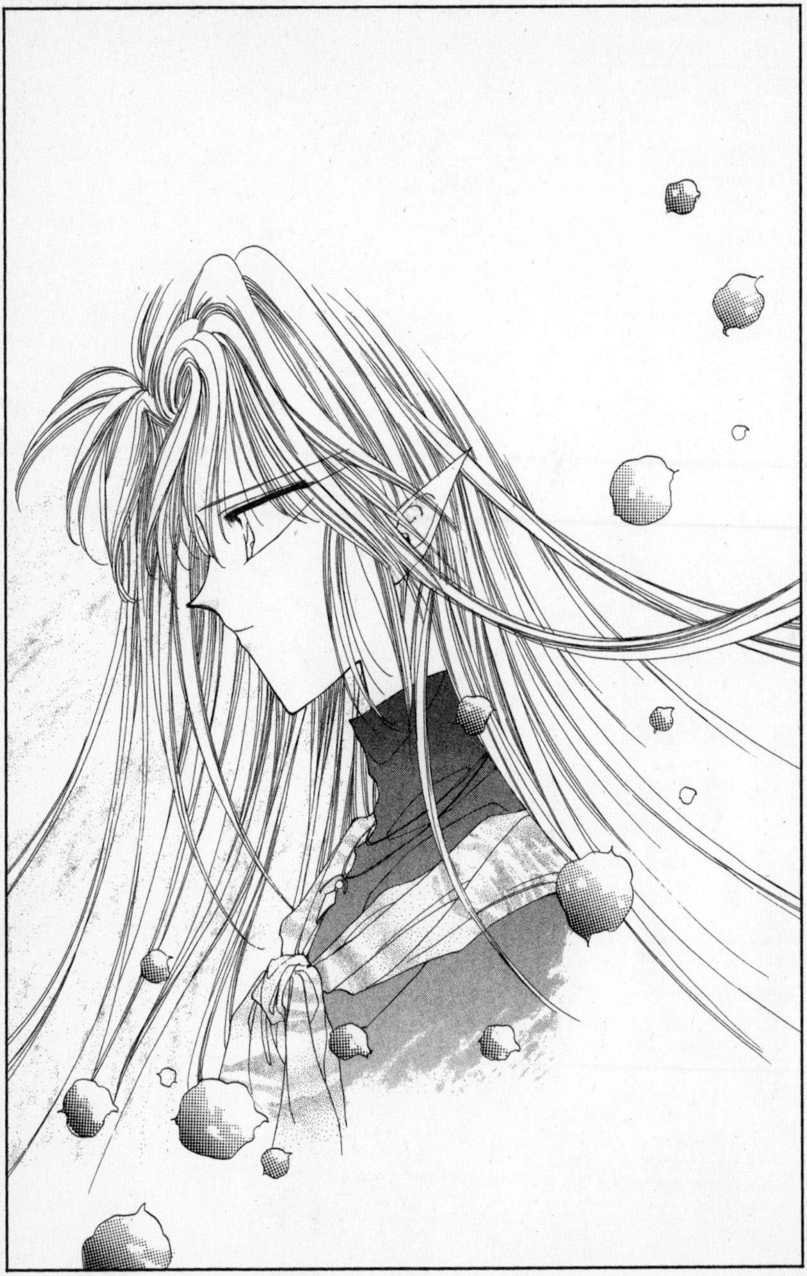

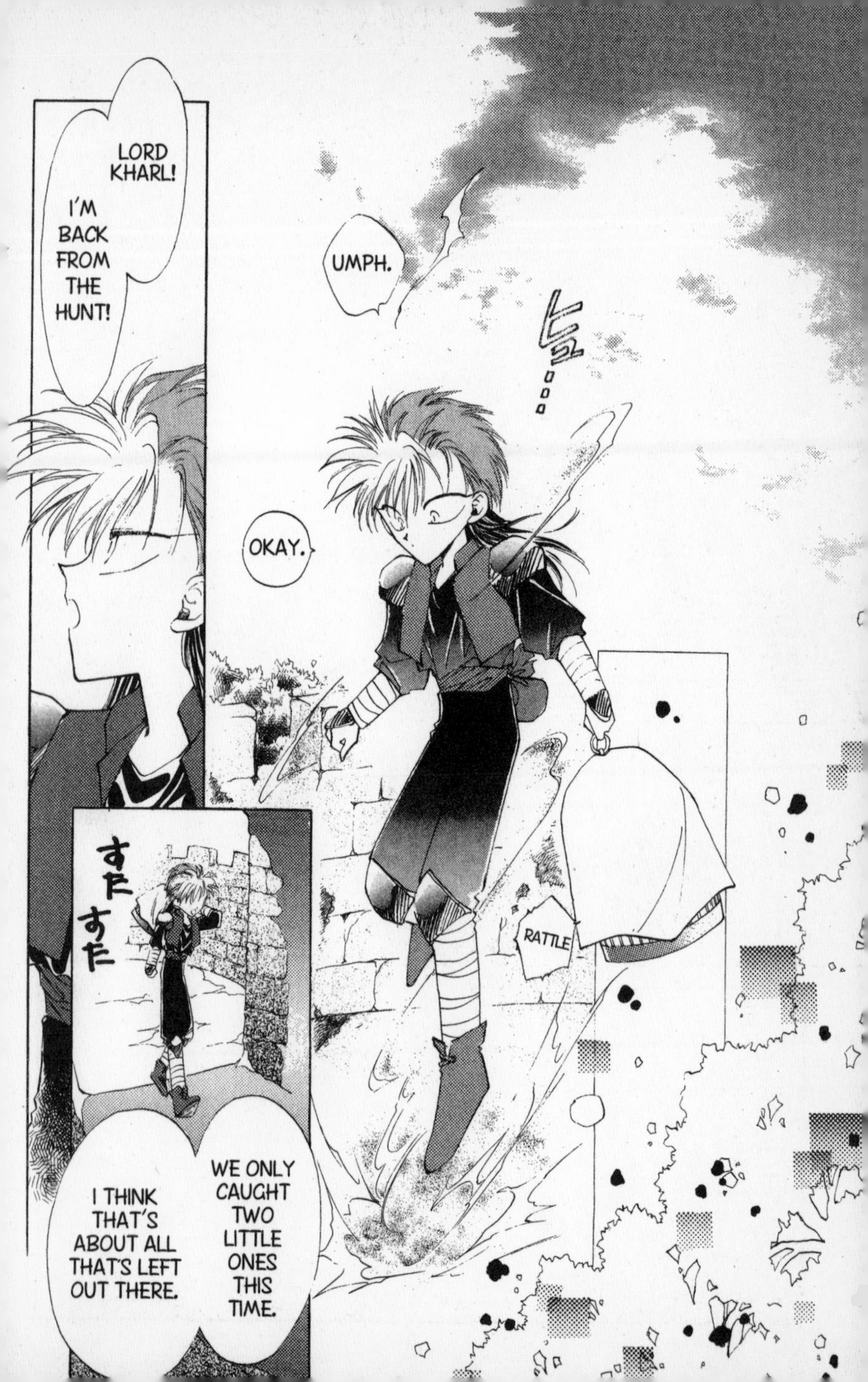
ヒュ...
UMPH.
OKAY.
RATTLE
LORD KHARL! I'M BACK FROM THE HUNT!
すたすた
WE ONLY CAUGHT TWO LITTLE ONES THIS TIME.
I THINK THAT'S ABOUT ALL THAT'S LEFT OUT THERE.

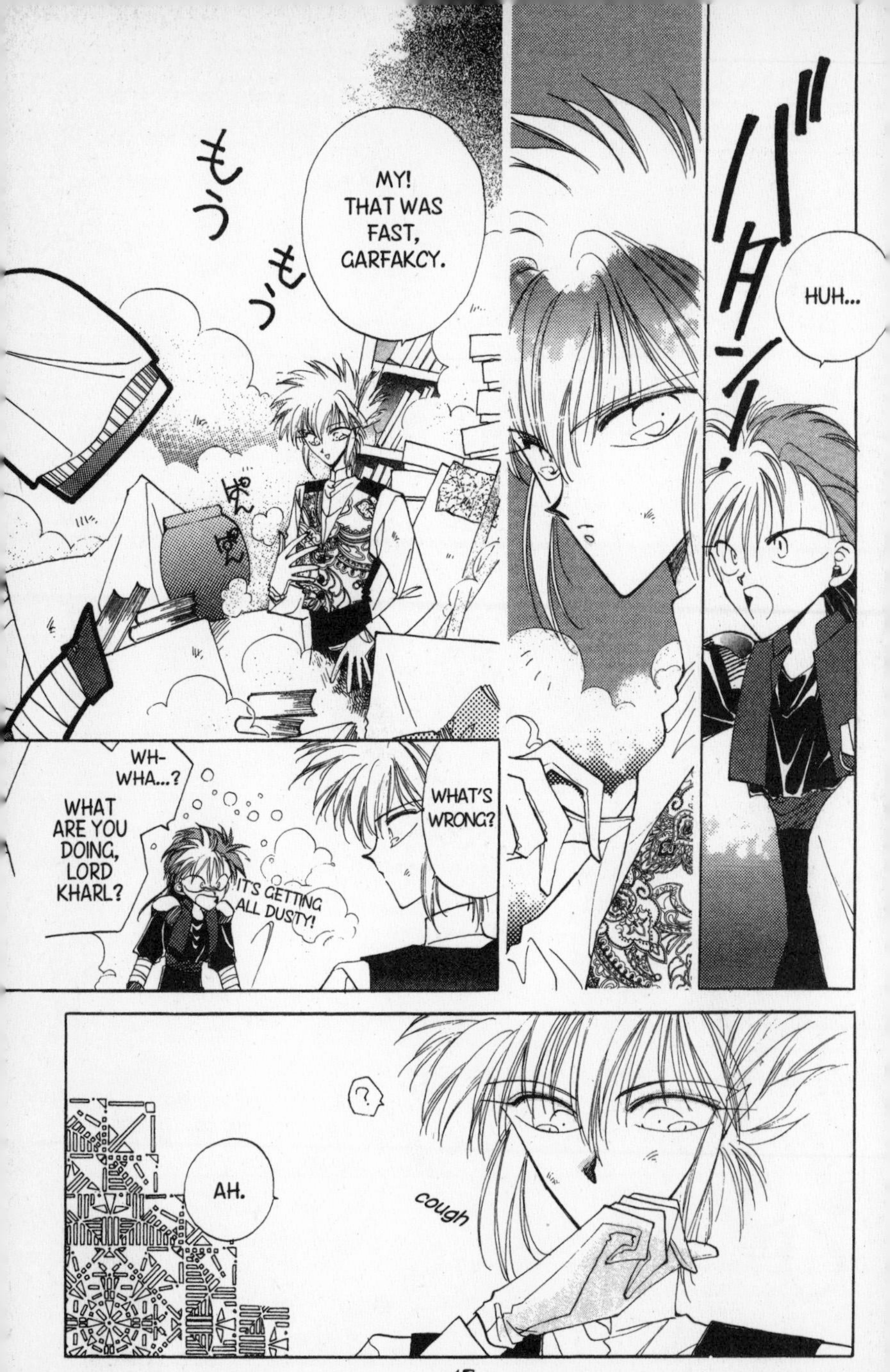
バタン!!
HUH...
MY! THAT WAS FAST, GARFAKCY.
もうもう
ぽんぽん
WHAT'S WRONG?
WH- WHA...?
WHAT ARE YOU DOING, LORD KHARL?
IT'S GETTING ALL DUSTY!
?
cough
AH.

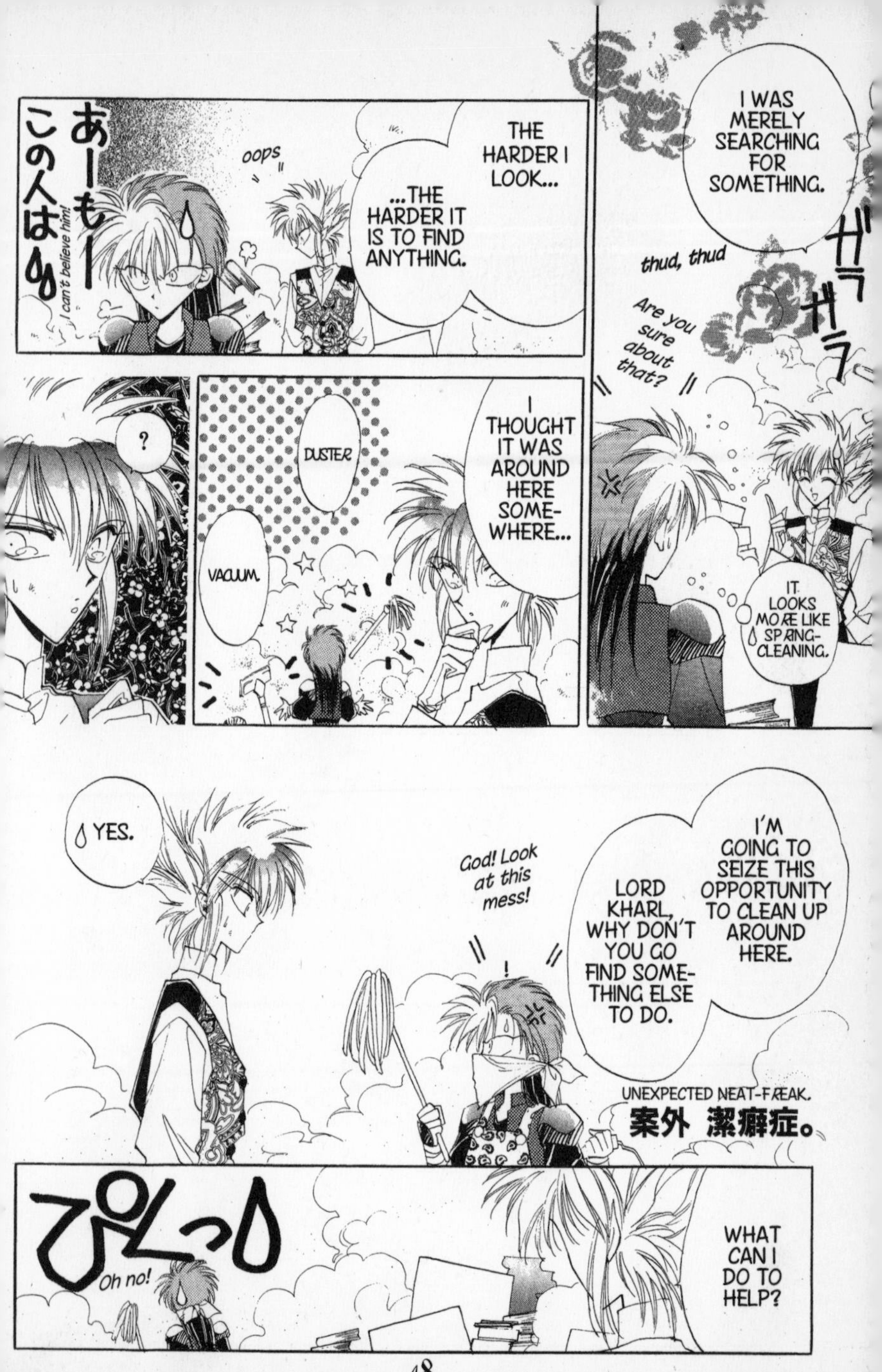

I WAS MERELY SEARCHING FOR SOMETHING.
ガラガラ
thud, thud
Are you sure about that?
IT LOOKS MORE LIKE SPRING-CLEANING.
THE HARDER I LOOK...
...THE HARDER IT IS TO FIND ANYTHING.
oops
あーもーこの人は
I can't believe him!
I THOUGHT IT WAS AROUND HERE SOMEWHERE...
DUSTER
VACUUM
?
I'M GOING TO SEIZE THIS OPPORTUNITY TO CLEAN UP AROUND HERE.
LORD KHARL, WHY DON'T YOU GO FIND SOMETHING ELSE TO DO.
God! Look at this mess!
YES.
UNEXPECTED NEAT-FREAK.
案外 潔癖症。
WHAT CAN I DO TO HELP?
ぴくっ
Oh no!

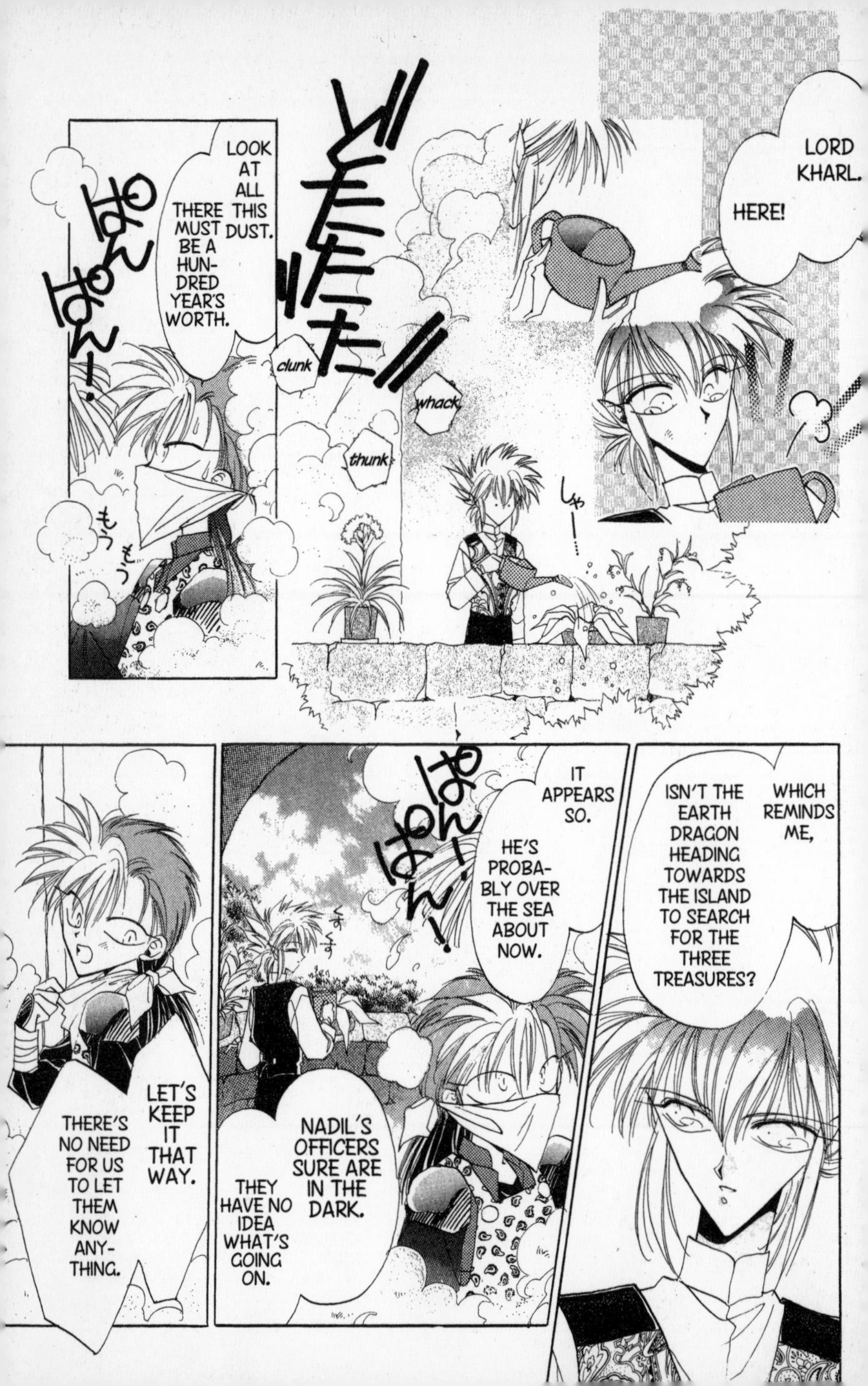
LORD KHARL.
HERE!
clunk
whack
thunk
LOOK AT ALL THIS DUST.
THERE MUST BE A HUN-DRED YEAR'S WORTH.
ぱんぱん!
WHICH REMINDS ME,
ISN'T THE EARTH DRAGON HEADING TOWARDS THE ISLAND TO SEARCH FOR THE THREE TREASURES?
IT APPEARS SO.
HE'S PROBA-BLY OVER THE SEA ABOUT NOW.
ぱんぱん!
NADIL'S OFFICERS SURE ARE IN THE DARK.
THEY HAVE NO IDEA WHAT'S GOING ON.
LET'S KEEP IT THAT WAY.
THERE'S NO NEED FOR US TO LET THEM KNOW ANY-THING.

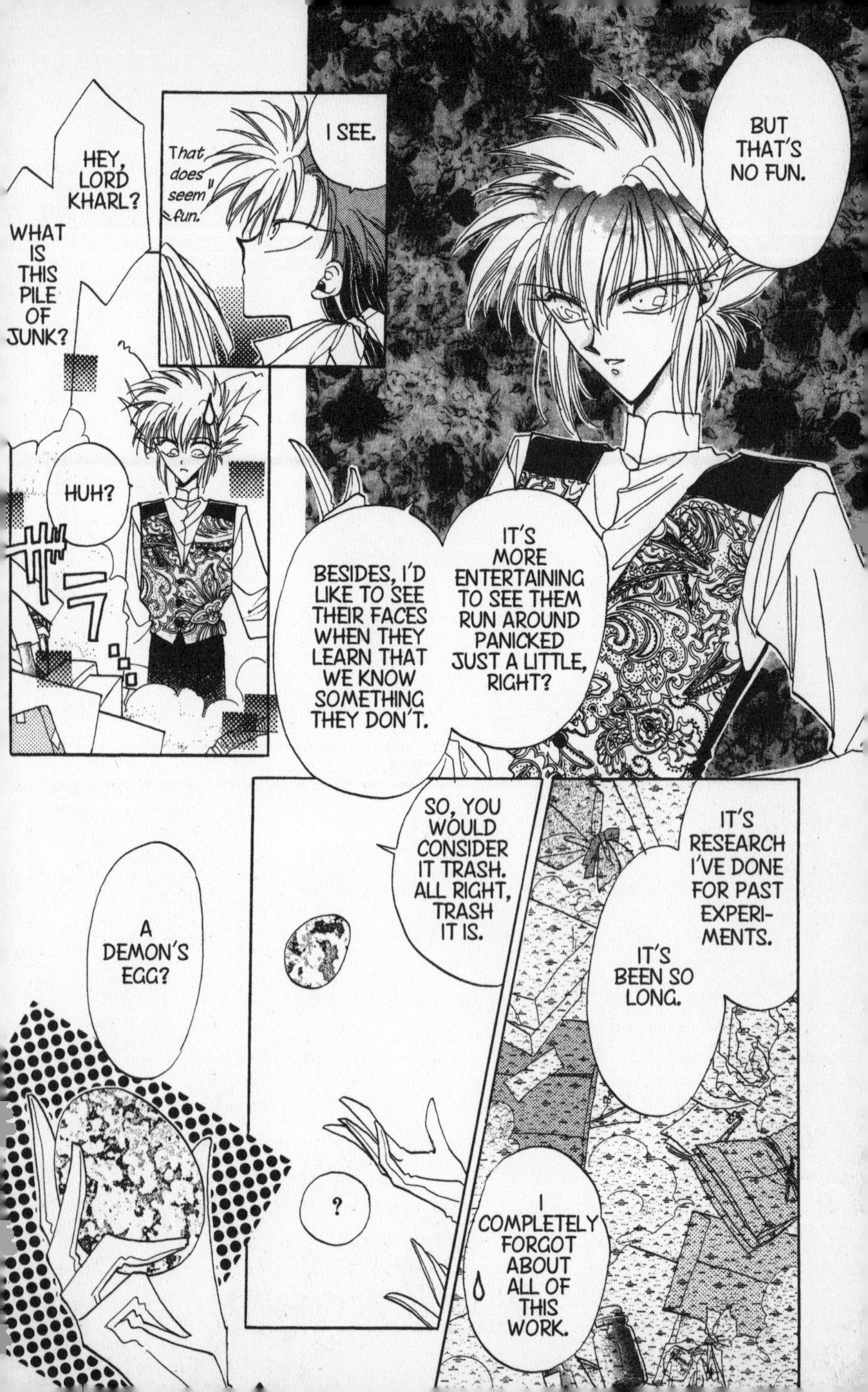
BUT THAT'S NO FUN.
IT'S MORE ENTERTAINING TO SEE THEM RUN AROUND PANICKED JUST A LITTLE, RIGHT?
BESIDES, I'D LIKE TO SEE THEIR FACES WHEN THEY LEARN THAT WE KNOW SOMETHING THEY DON'T.
I SEE.
That does seem fun.
HEY, LORD KHARL?
WHAT IS THIS PILE OF JUNK?
HUH?
IT'S RESEARCH I'VE DONE FOR PAST EXPERIMENTS.
IT'S BEEN SO LONG.
I COMPLETELY FORGOT ABOUT ALL OF THIS WORK.
SO, YOU WOULD CONSIDER IT TRASH. ALL RIGHT, TRASH IT IS.
?
A DEMON'S EGG?

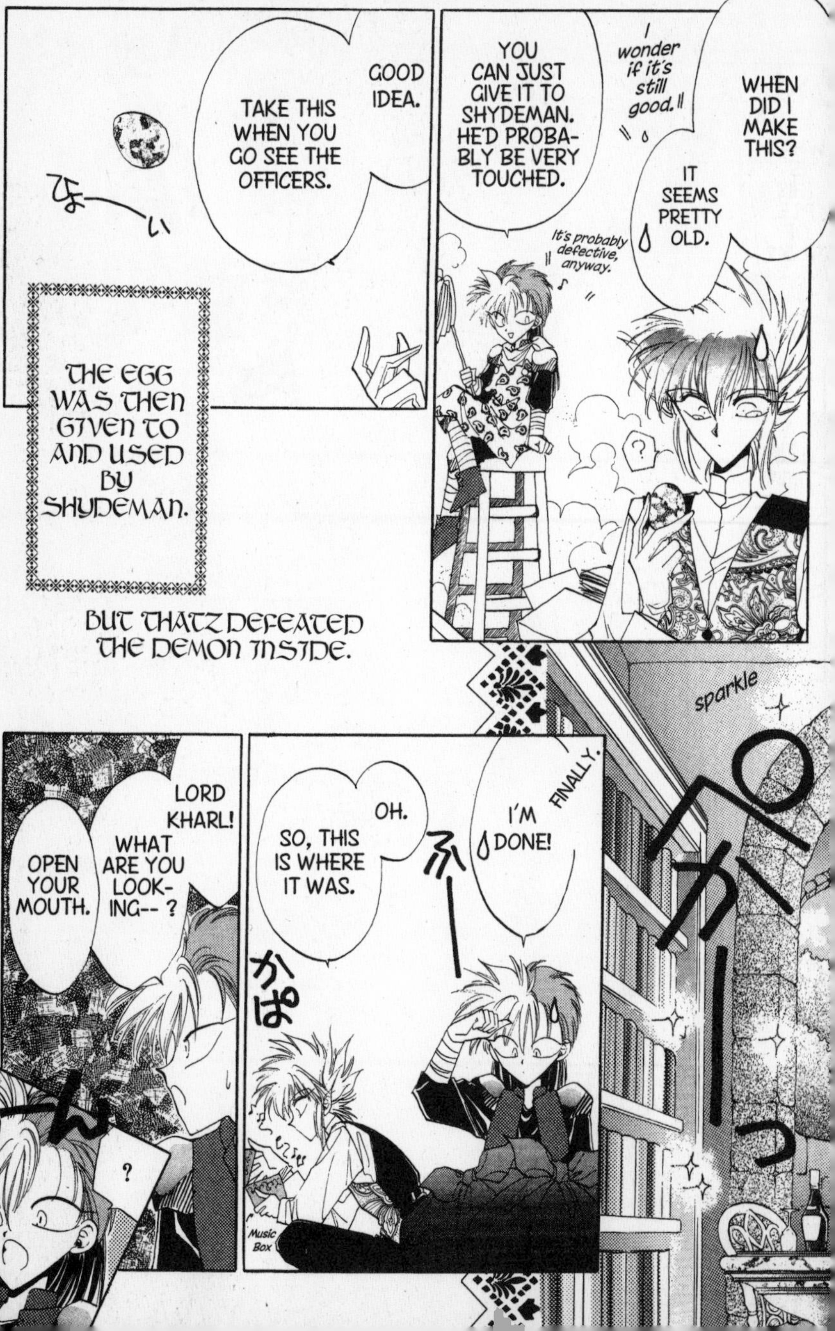
WHEN DID I MAKE THIS?
IT SEEMS PRETTY OLD.
I wonder if it's still good.
YOU CAN JUST GIVE IT TO SHYDEMAN. HE'D PROBABLY BE VERY TOUCHED.
It's probably defective, anyway.
?
GOOD IDEA.
TAKE THIS WHEN YOU GO SEE THE OFFICERS.
ひょーい
THE EGG WAS THEN GIVEN TO AND USED BY SHYDEMAN.
BUT THATZ DEFEATED THE DEMON INSIDE.
sparkle
ぺかーっ
FINALLY.
I'M DONE!
ふー
OH.
SO, THIS IS WHERE IT WAS.
かぱ
Music Box
LORD KHARL!
WHAT ARE YOU LOOKING-- ?
OPEN YOUR MOUTH.
あーん
?

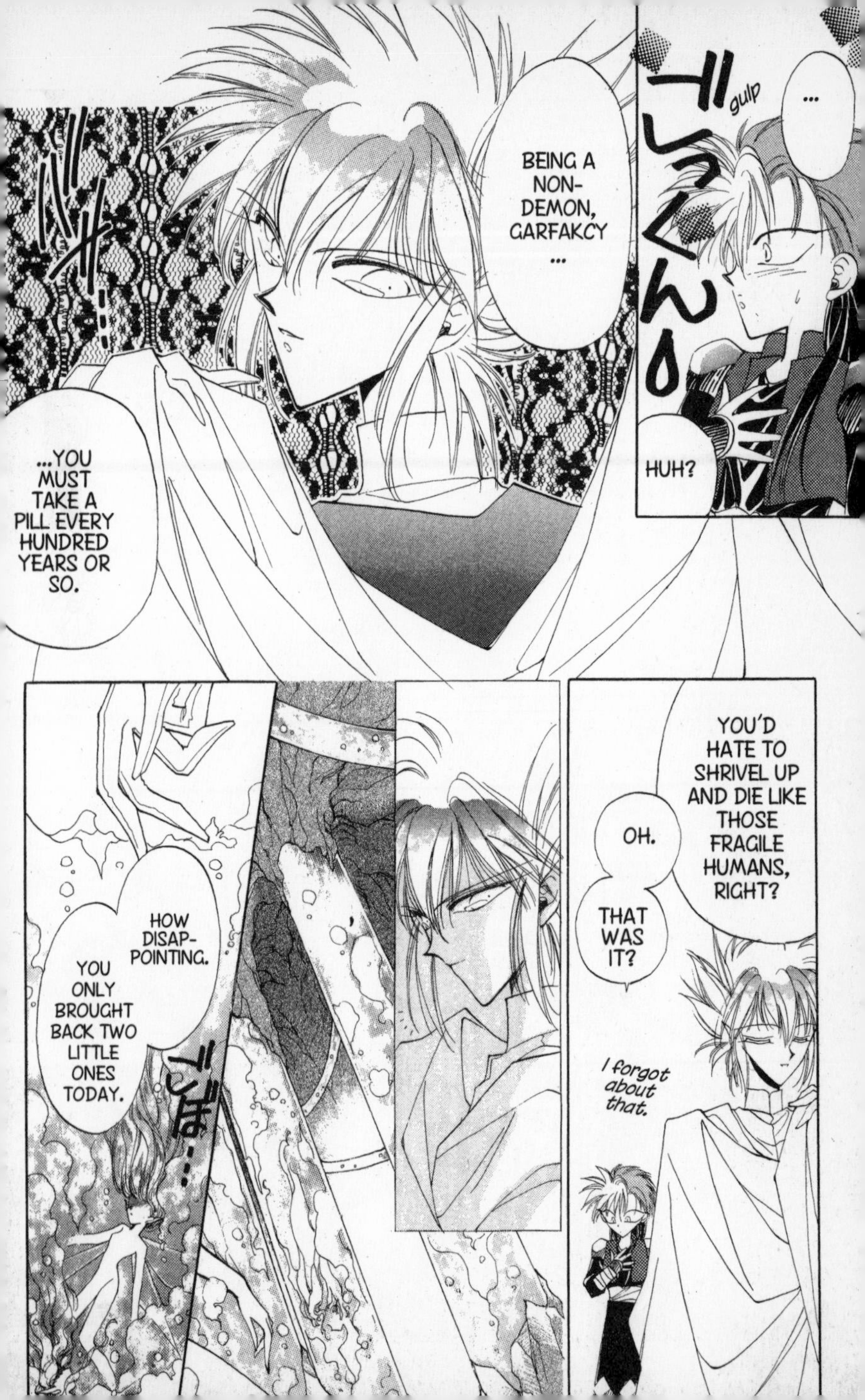
...
gulp
HUH?
BEING A NON-DEMON, GARFAKCY ...
...YOU MUST TAKE A PILL EVERY HUNDRED YEARS OR SO.
YOU'D HATE TO SHRIVEL UP AND DIE LIKE THOSE FRAGILE HUMANS, RIGHT?
OH.
THAT WAS IT?
I forgot about that.
HOW DISAPPOINTING.
YOU ONLY BROUGHT BACK TWO LITTLE ONES TODAY.

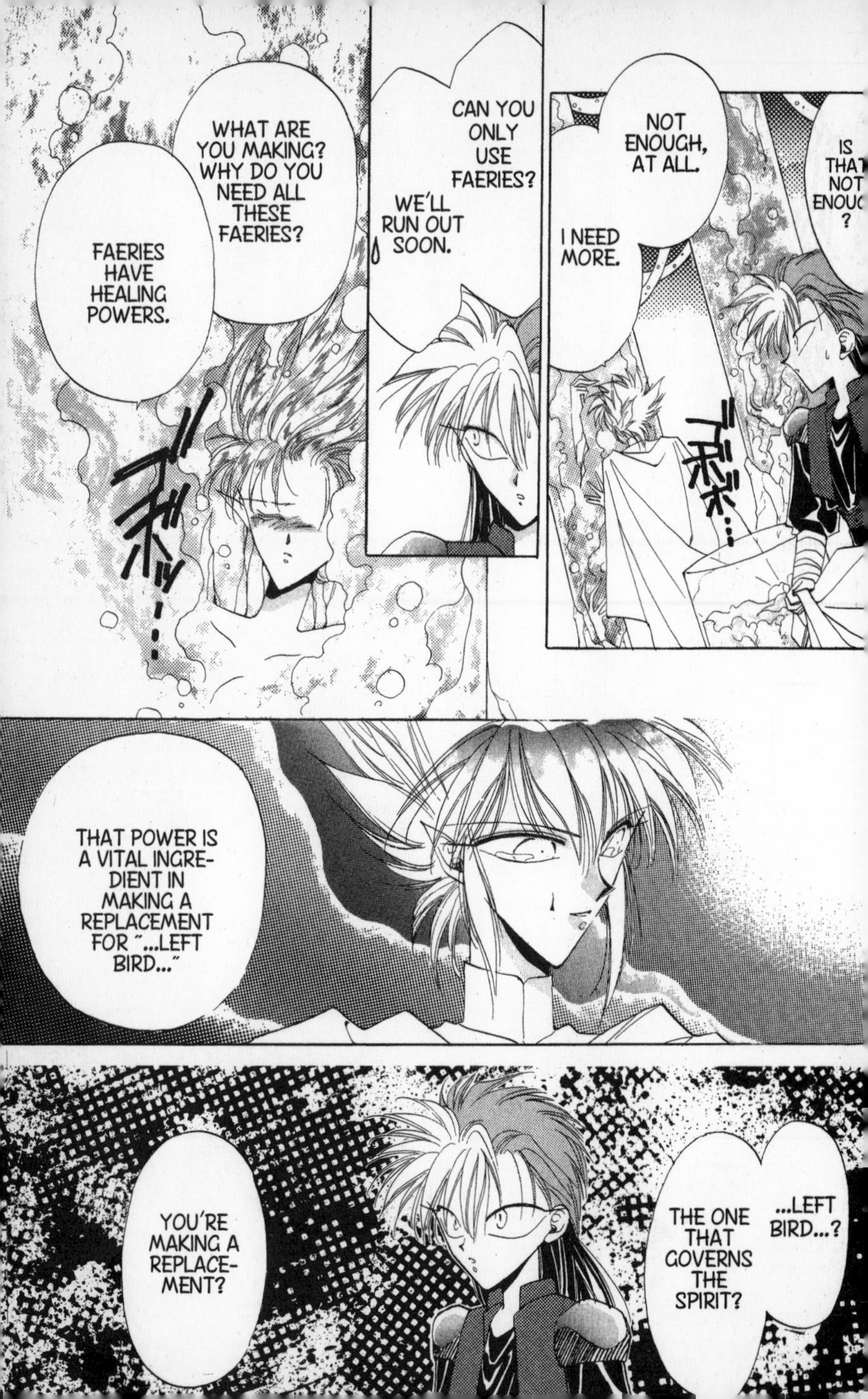
IS THAT NOT ENOUG ?
NOT ENOUGH, AT ALL.
I NEED MORE.
ゴボボ…
CAN YOU ONLY USE FAERIES?
WE'LL RUN OUT SOON.
WHAT ARE YOU MAKING? WHY DO YOU NEED ALL THESE FAERIES?
FAERIES HAVE HEALING POWERS.
ゴボッ…
THAT POWER IS A VITAL INGRE-DIENT IN MAKING A REPLACEMENT FOR "...LEFT BIRD..."
...LEFT BIRD...?
THE ONE THAT GOVERNS THE SPIRIT?
YOU'RE MAKING A REPLACE-MENT?

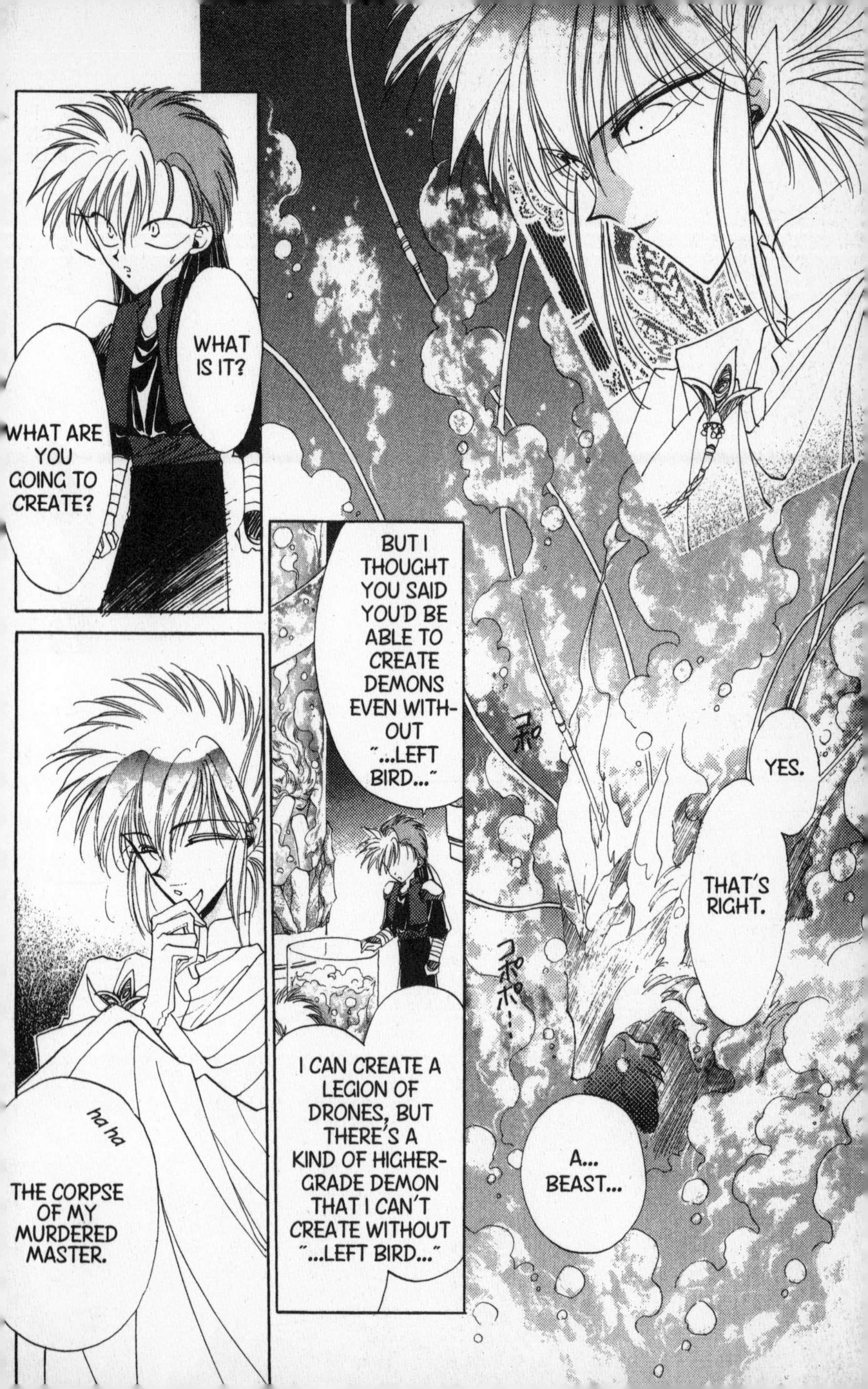
YES.
THAT'S RIGHT.
コポポ…
A... BEAST...
WHAT IS IT?
WHAT ARE YOU GOING TO CREATE?
BUT I THOUGHT YOU SAID YOU'D BE ABLE TO CREATE DEMONS EVEN WITH-OUT "...LEFT BIRD..."
I CAN CREATE A LEGION OF DRONES, BUT THERE'S A KIND OF HIGHER-GRADE DEMON THAT I CAN'T CREATE WITHOUT "...LEFT BIRD..."
ha ha
THE CORPSE OF MY MURDERED MASTER.

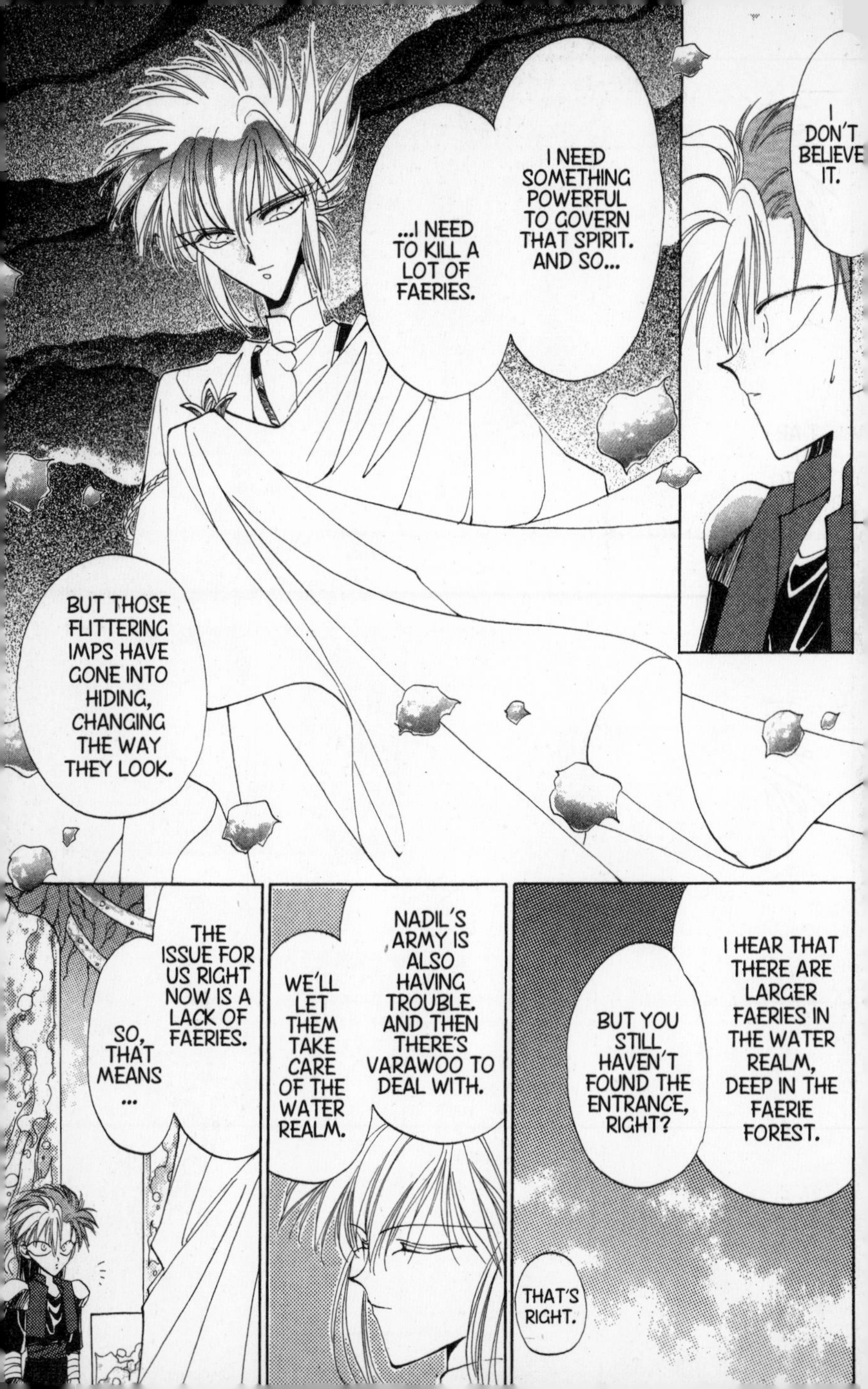
I DON'T BELIEVE IT.
I NEED SOMETHING POWERFUL TO GOVERN THAT SPIRIT. AND SO...
...I NEED TO KILL A LOT OF FAERIES.
BUT THOSE FLITTERING IMPS HAVE GONE INTO HIDING, CHANGING THE WAY THEY LOOK.
I HEAR THAT THERE ARE LARGER FAERIES IN THE WATER REALM, DEEP IN THE FAERIE FOREST.
BUT YOU STILL HAVEN'T FOUND THE ENTRANCE, RIGHT?
THAT'S RIGHT.
NADIL'S ARMY IS ALSO HAVING TROUBLE. AND THEN THERE'S VARAWOO TO DEAL WITH.
WE'LL LET THEM TAKE CARE OF THE WATER REALM.
THE ISSUE FOR US RIGHT NOW IS A LACK OF FAERIES.
SO, THAT MEANS ...

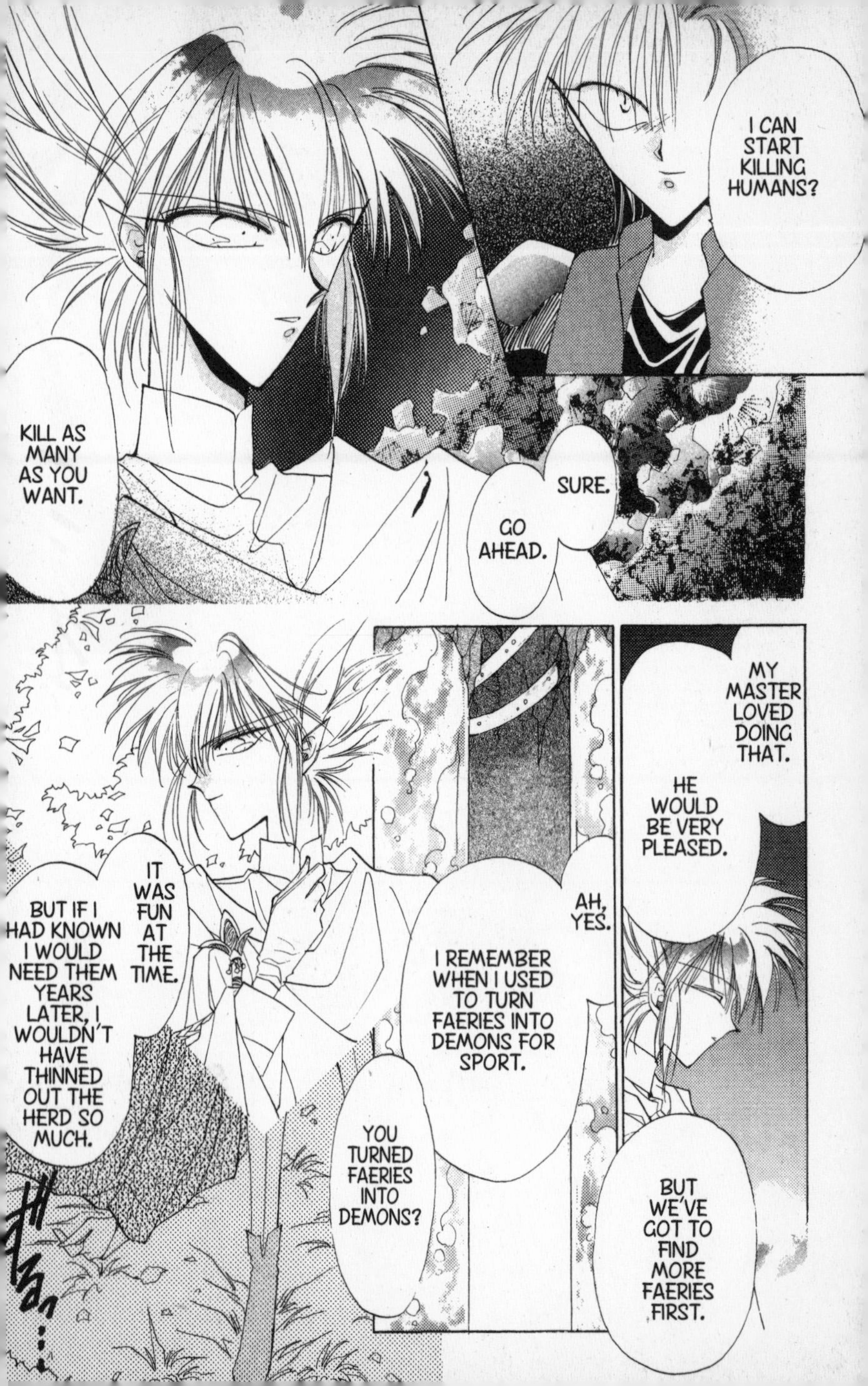
I CAN START KILLING HUMANS?
SURE.
GO AHEAD.
KILL AS MANY AS YOU WANT.
MY MASTER LOVED DOING THAT.
HE WOULD BE VERY PLEASED.
BUT WE'VE GOT TO FIND MORE FAERIES FIRST.
AH, YES.
I REMEMBER WHEN I USED TO TURN FAERIES INTO DEMONS FOR SPORT.
IT WAS FUN AT THE TIME.
BUT IF I HAD KNOWN I WOULD NEED THEM YEARS LATER, I WOULDN'T HAVE THINNED OUT THE HERD SO MUCH.
YOU TURNED FAERIES INTO DEMONS?

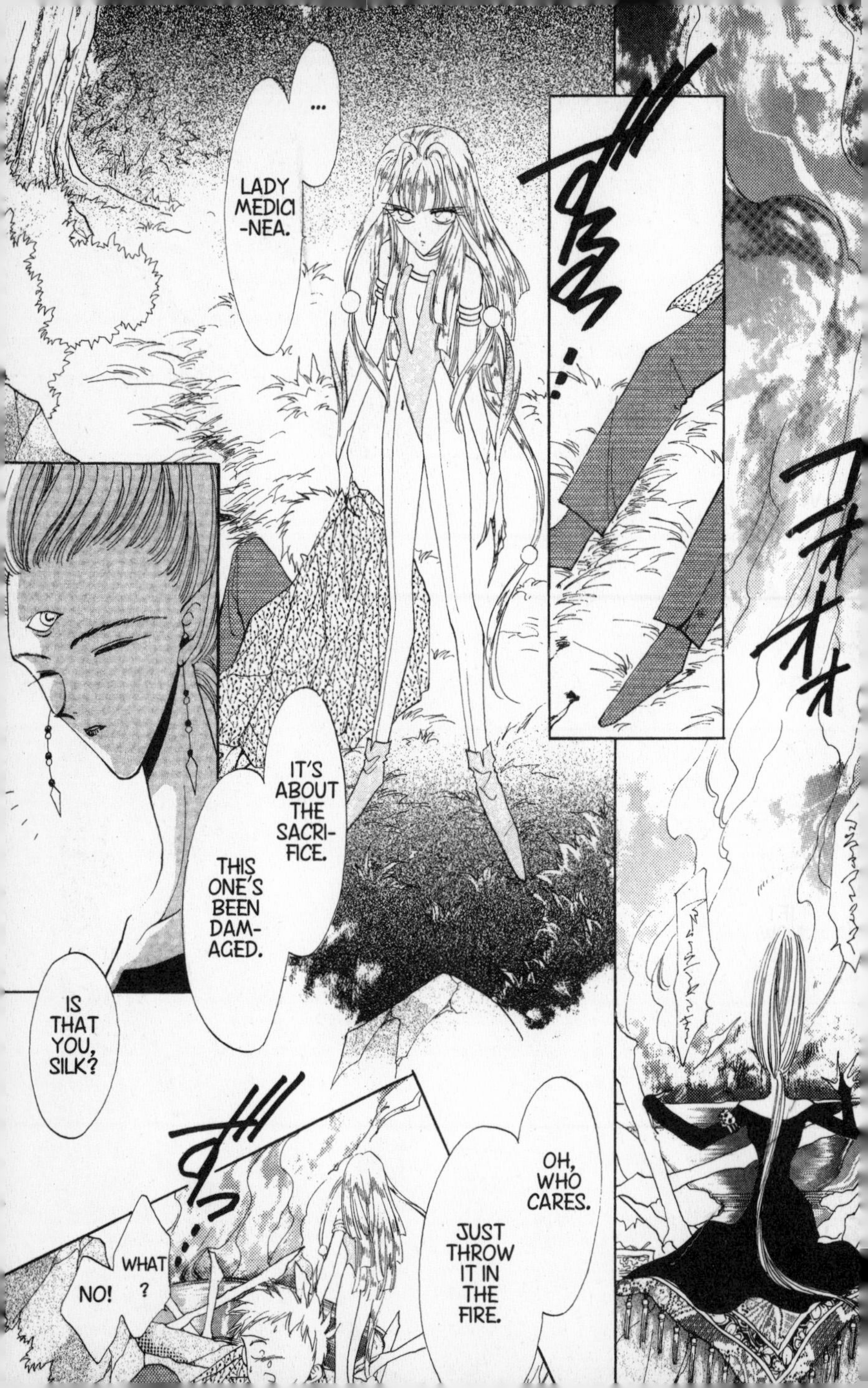
...
LADY MEDICI-NEA.
IT'S ABOUT THE SACRI-FICE.
THIS ONE'S BEEN DAM-AGED.
IS THAT YOU, SILK?
OH, WHO CARES.
JUST THROW IT IN THE FIRE.
WHAT ?
NO!

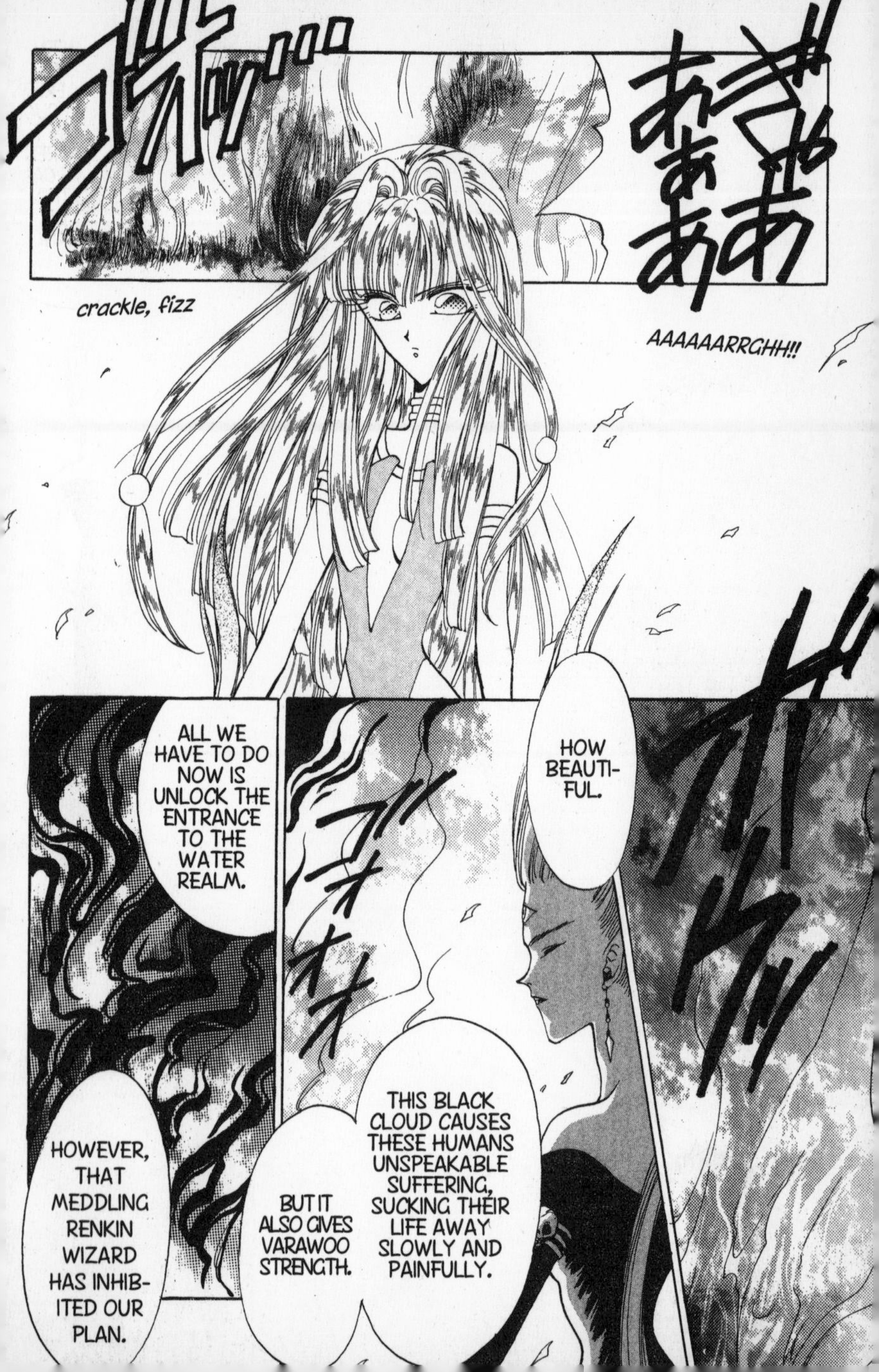
ぎゃあああああ!!
AAAAAARRGHH!!
crackle, fizz
HOW BEAUTIFUL.
THIS BLACK CLOUD CAUSES THESE HUMANS UNSPEAKABLE SUFFERING, SUCKING THEIR LIFE AWAY SLOWLY AND PAINFULLY.
BUT IT ALSO GIVES VARAWOO STRENGTH.
ALL WE HAVE TO DO NOW IS UNLOCK THE ENTRANCE TO THE WATER REALM.
HOWEVER, THAT MEDDLING RENKIN WIZARD HAS INHIBITED OUR PLAN.

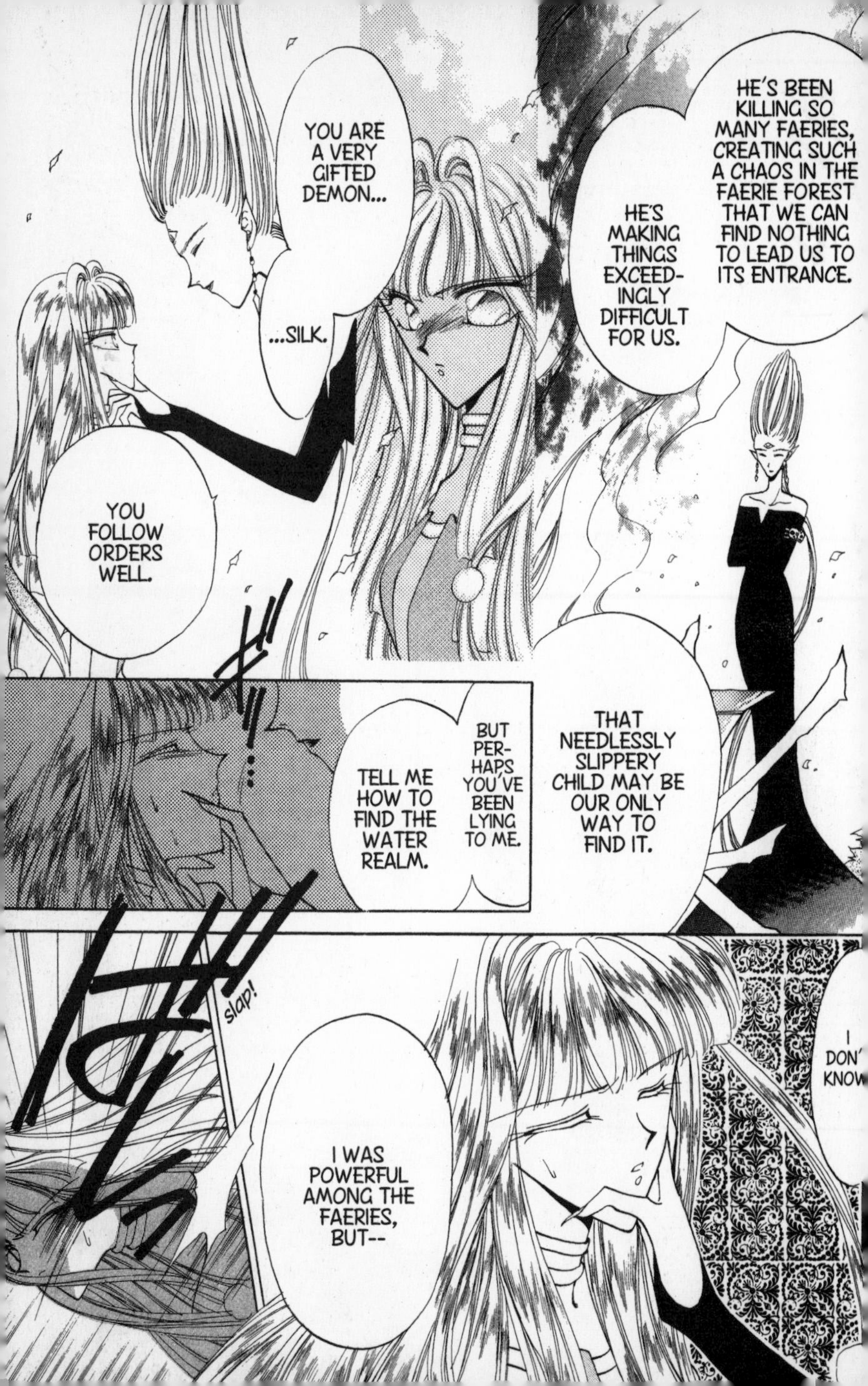
HE'S BEEN KILLING SO MANY FAERIES, CREATING SUCH A CHAOS IN THE FAERIE FOREST THAT WE CAN FIND NOTHING TO LEAD US TO ITS ENTRANCE.
HE'S MAKING THINGS EXCEEDINGLY DIFFICULT FOR US.
THAT NEEDLESSLY SLIPPERY CHILD MAY BE OUR ONLY WAY TO FIND IT.
YOU ARE A VERY GIFTED DEMON...
...SILK.
YOU FOLLOW ORDERS WELL.
BUT PERHAPS YOU'VE BEEN LYING TO ME.
TELL ME HOW TO FIND THE WATER REALM.
I DON' KNOW
I WAS POWERFUL AMONG THE FAERIES, BUT--
slap!

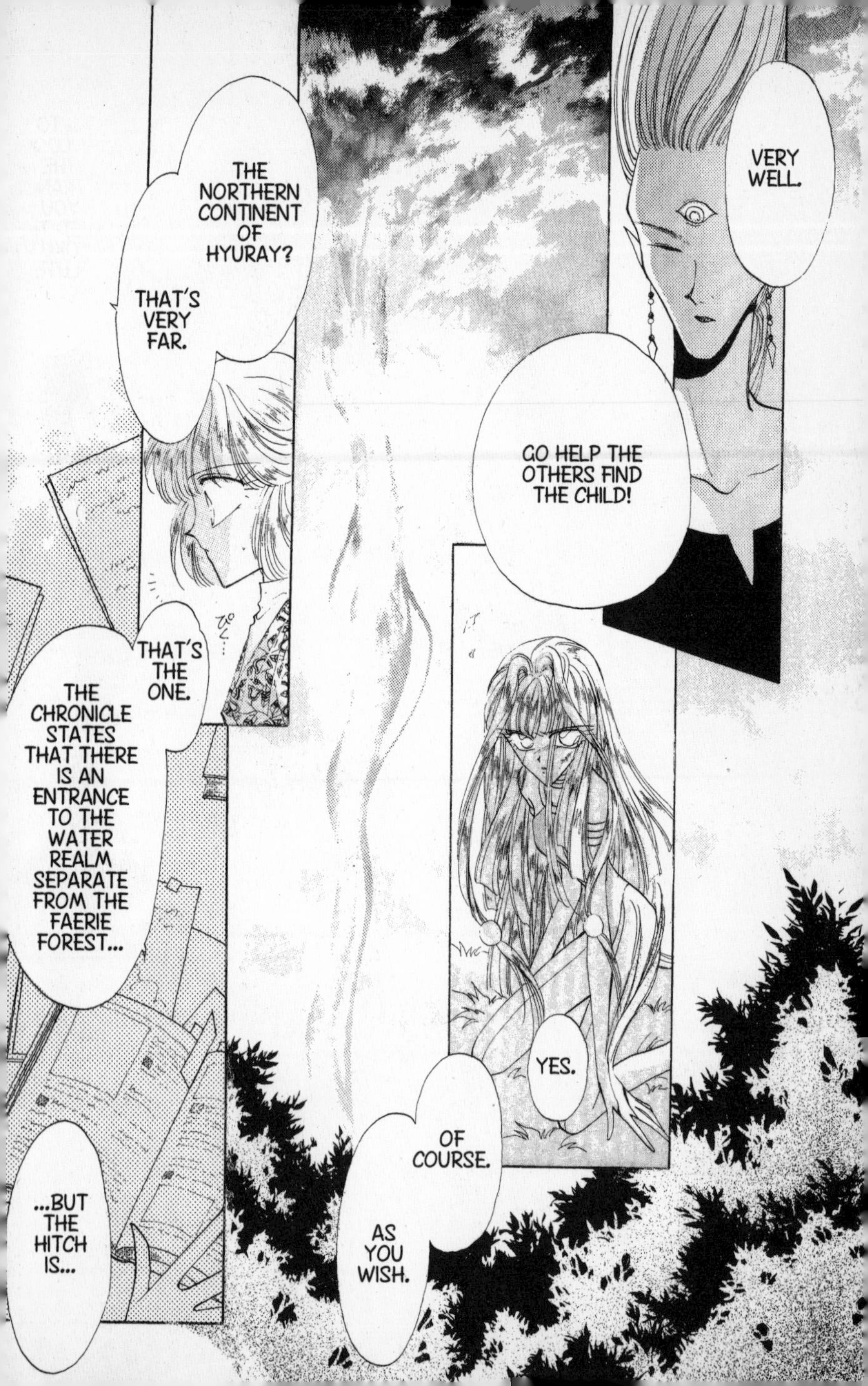
VERY WELL.
GO HELP THE OTHERS FIND THE CHILD!
YES.
OF COURSE.
AS YOU WISH.
THE NORTHERN CONTINENT OF HYURAY?
THAT'S VERY FAR.
THAT'S THE ONE.
THE CHRONICLE STATES THAT THERE IS AN ENTRANCE TO THE WATER REALM SEPARATE FROM THE FAERIE FOREST...
...BUT THE HITCH IS...

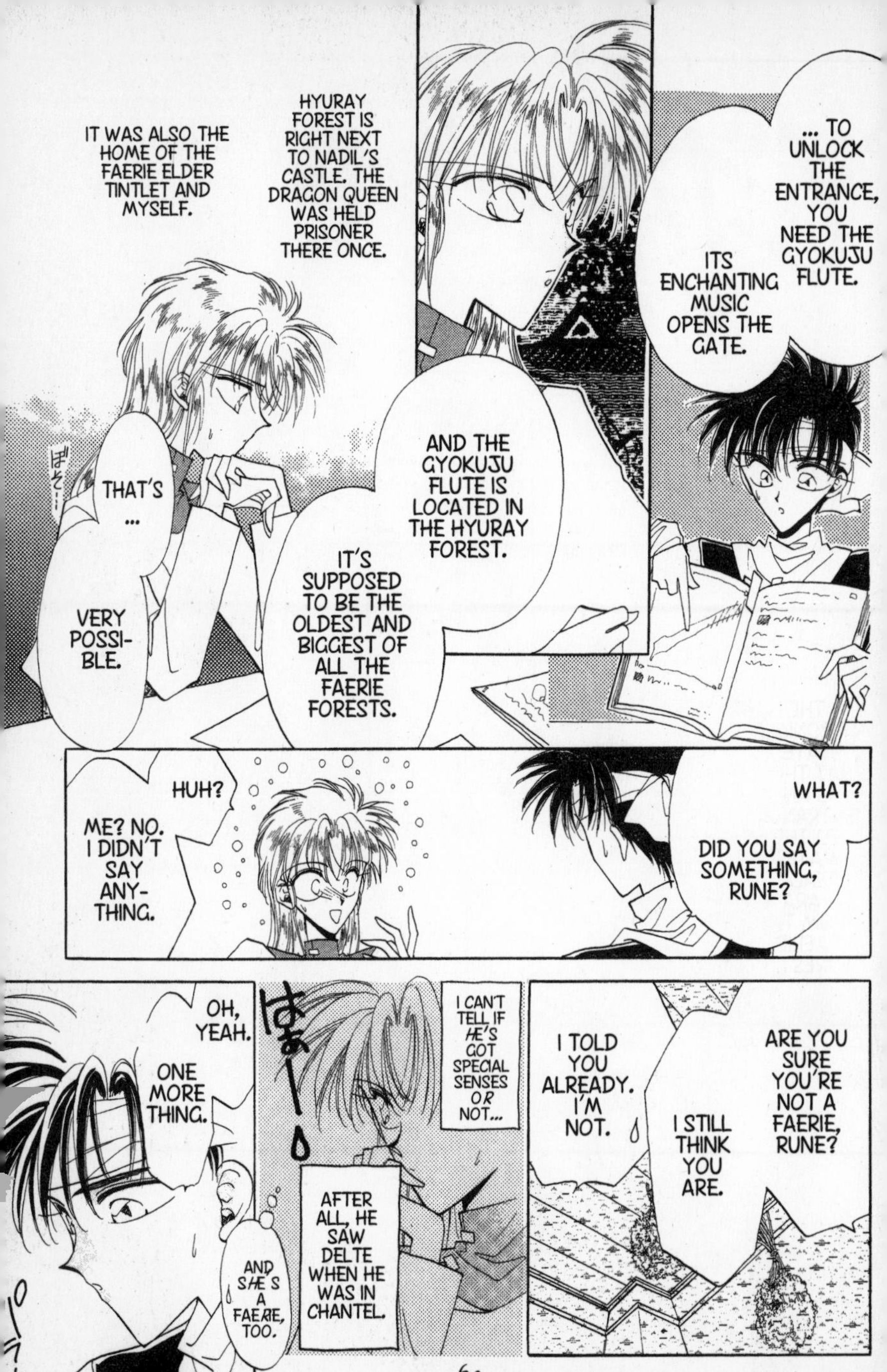
... TO UNLOCK THE ENTRANCE, YOU NEED THE GYOKUJU FLUTE.
ITS ENCHANTING MUSIC OPENS THE GATE.
AND THE GYOKUJU FLUTE IS LOCATED IN THE HYURAY FOREST.
IT'S SUPPOSED TO BE THE OLDEST AND BIGGEST OF ALL THE FAERIE FORESTS.
HYURAY FOREST IS RIGHT NEXT TO NADIL'S CASTLE. THE DRAGON QUEEN WAS HELD PRISONER THERE ONCE.
IT WAS ALSO THE HOME OF THE FAERIE ELDER TINTLET AND MYSELF.
ぼそ…
THAT'S ...
VERY POSSI-BLE.
WHAT?
DID YOU SAY SOMETHING, RUNE?
HUH?
ME? NO. I DIDN'T SAY ANY-THING.
ARE YOU SURE YOU'RE NOT A FAERIE, RUNE?
I STILL THINK YOU ARE.
I TOLD YOU ALREADY. I'M NOT.
I CAN'T TELL IF HE'S GOT SPECIAL SENSES OR NOT...
はぁー
AFTER ALL, HE SAW DELTE WHEN HE WAS IN CHANTEL.
OH, YEAH.
ONE MORE THING.
AND SHE'S A FAERIE, TOO.

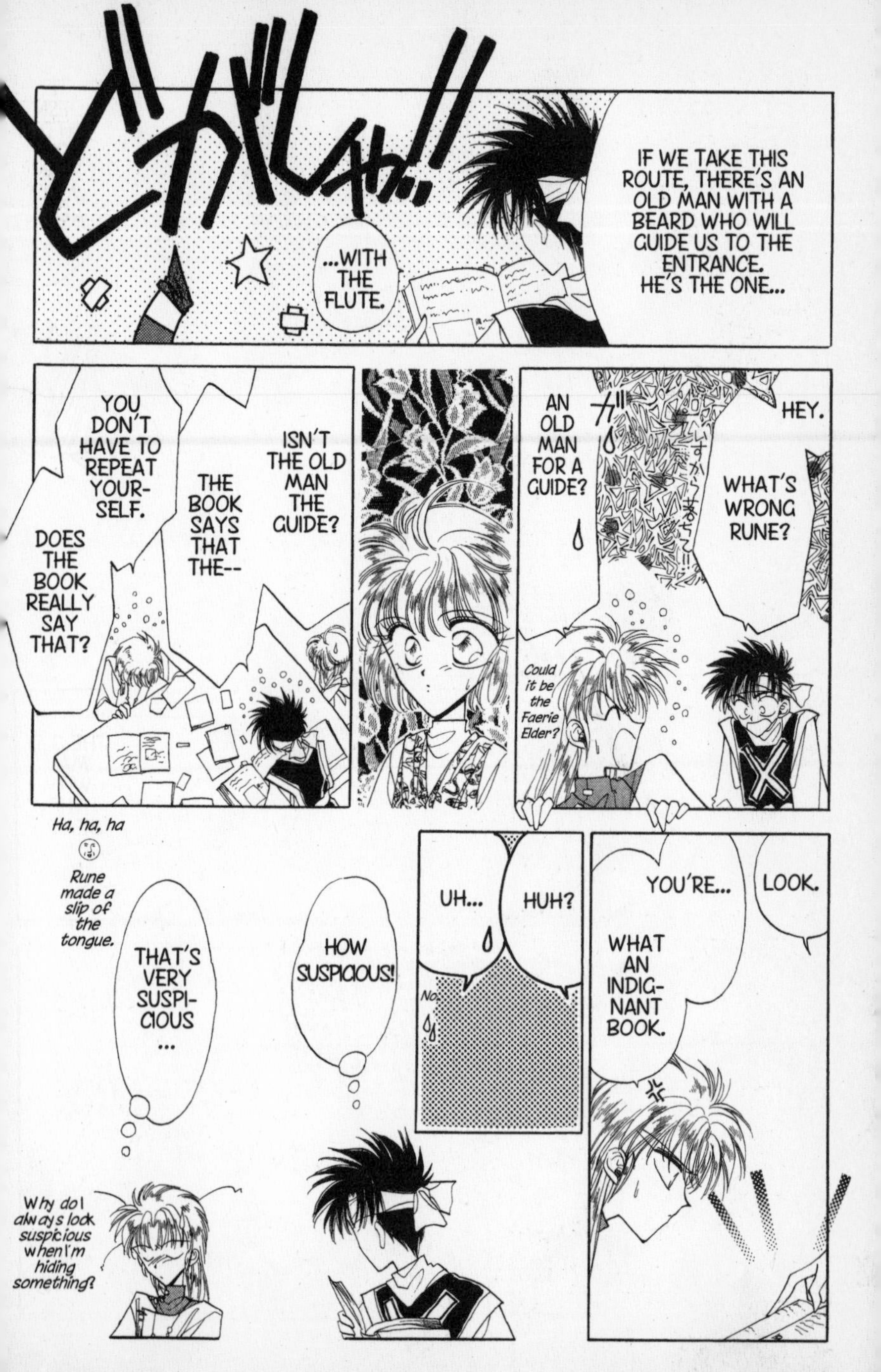
どがしゃ!!
IF WE TAKE THIS ROUTE, THERE'S AN OLD MAN WITH A BEARD WHO WILL GUIDE US TO THE ENTRANCE. HE'S THE ONE...
...WITH THE FLUTE.
HEY.
WHAT'S WRONG RUNE?
AN OLD MAN FOR A GUIDE?
Could it be the Faerie Elder?
ISN'T THE OLD MAN THE GUIDE?
THE BOOK SAYS THAT THE--
YOU DON'T HAVE TO REPEAT YOURSELF.
DOES THE BOOK REALLY SAY THAT?
LOOK.
YOU'RE...
WHAT AN INDIGNANT BOOK.
HUH?
UH...
No.
HOW SUSPICIOUS!
THAT'S VERY SUSPICIOUS...
Ha, ha, ha
Rune made a slip of the tongue.
Why do I always look suspicious when I'm hiding something?

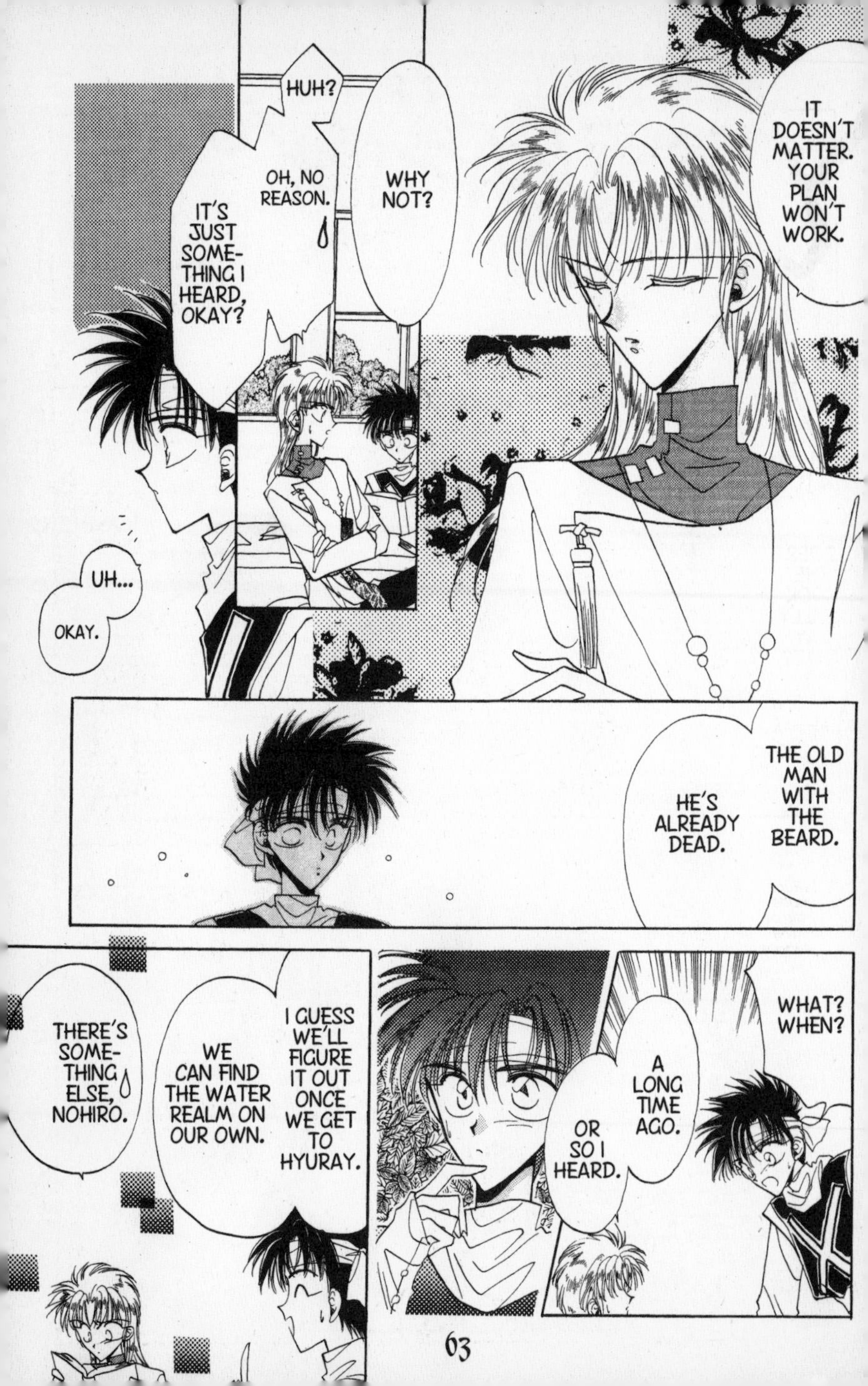
IT DOESN'T MATTER. YOUR PLAN WON'T WORK.
WHY NOT?
HUH?
OH, NO REASON.
IT'S JUST SOMETHING I HEARD, OKAY?
UH...
OKAY.
THE OLD MAN WITH THE BEARD.
HE'S ALREADY DEAD.
WHAT? WHEN?
A LONG TIME AGO.
OR SO I HEARD.
I GUESS WE'LL FIGURE IT OUT ONCE WE GET TO HYURAY.
WE CAN FIND THE WATER REALM ON OUR OWN.
THERE'S SOMETHING ELSE, NOHIRO.

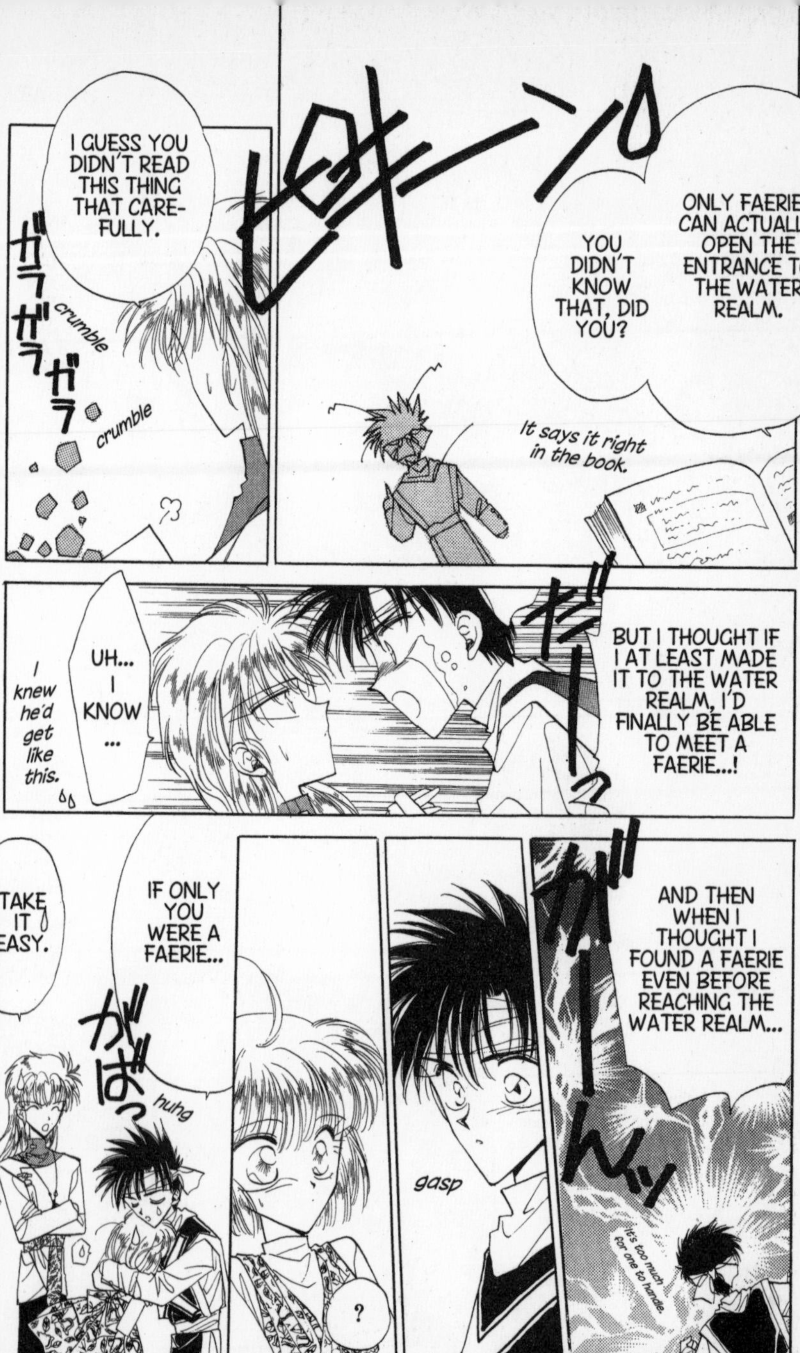

ONLY FAERIES CAN ACTUALLY OPEN THE ENTRANCE TO THE WATER REALM.
YOU DIDN'T KNOW THAT, DID YOU?
It says it right in the book.
I GUESS YOU DIDN'T READ THIS THING THAT CARE-FULLY.
ガラガラ
crumble
ガラ
crumble
BUT I THOUGHT IF I AT LEAST MADE IT TO THE WATER REALM, I'D FINALLY BE ABLE TO MEET A FAERIE...!
だーっ
UH... I KNOW ...
I knew he'd get like this.
AND THEN WHEN I THOUGHT I FOUND A FAERIE EVEN BEFORE REACHING THE WATER REALM...
がーん
It's too much for one to handle.
gasp
?
IF ONLY YOU WERE A FAERIE...
TAKE IT EASY.
がばっ
huhg

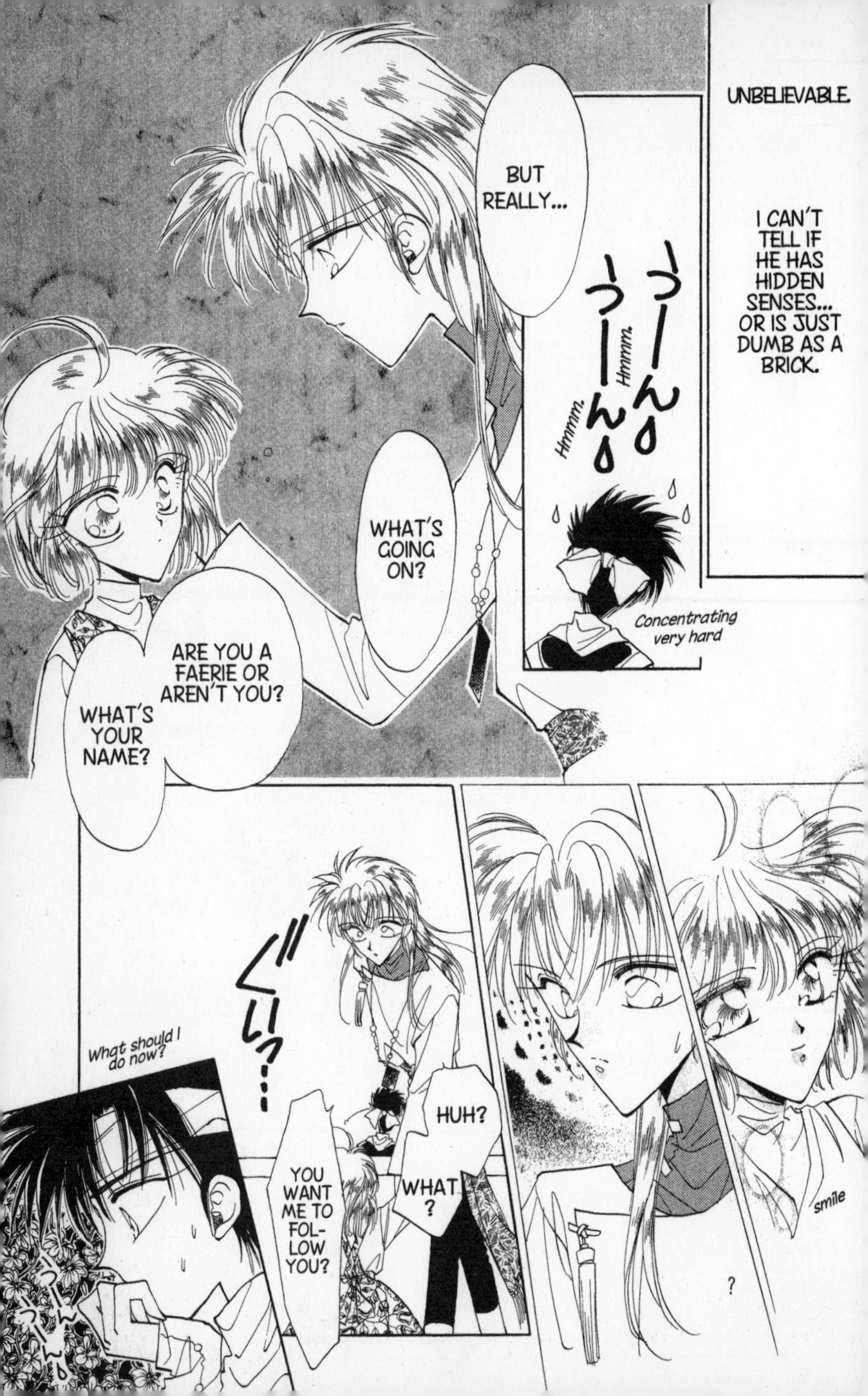
UNBELIEVABLE.
I CAN'T TELL IF HE HAS HIDDEN SENSES... OR IS JUST DUMB AS A BRICK.
うーん うーん
Hmmm.
Hmmm.
Concentrating very hard
BUT REALLY...
WHAT'S GOING ON?
ARE YOU A FAERIE OR AREN'T YOU?
WHAT'S YOUR NAME?
smile
?
ぐいっ...
HUH?
WHAT?
YOU WANT ME TO FOL-LOW YOU?
What should I do now?
うーんうーん

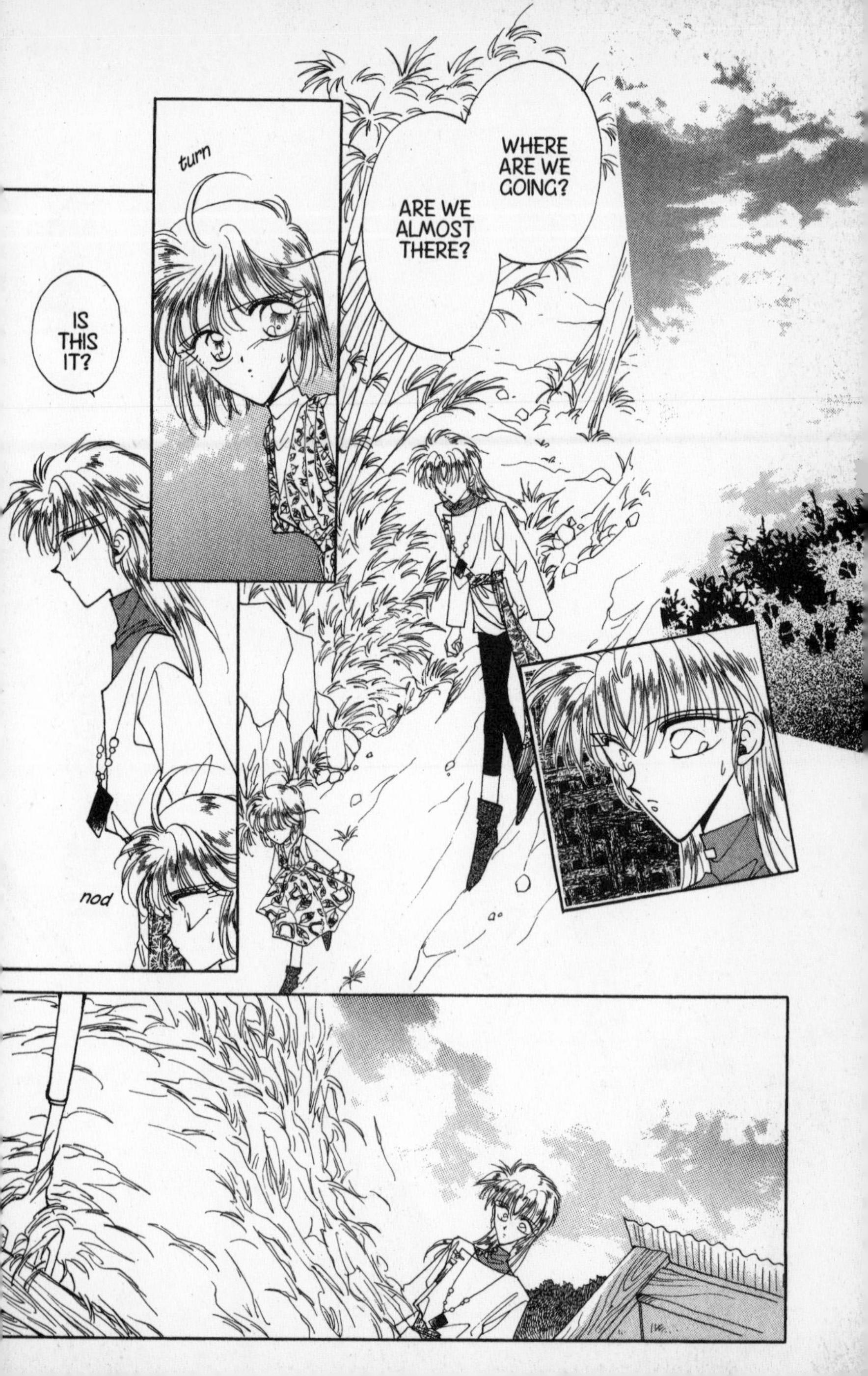
WHERE ARE WE GOING?
ARE WE ALMOST THERE?
turn
IS THIS IT?
nod

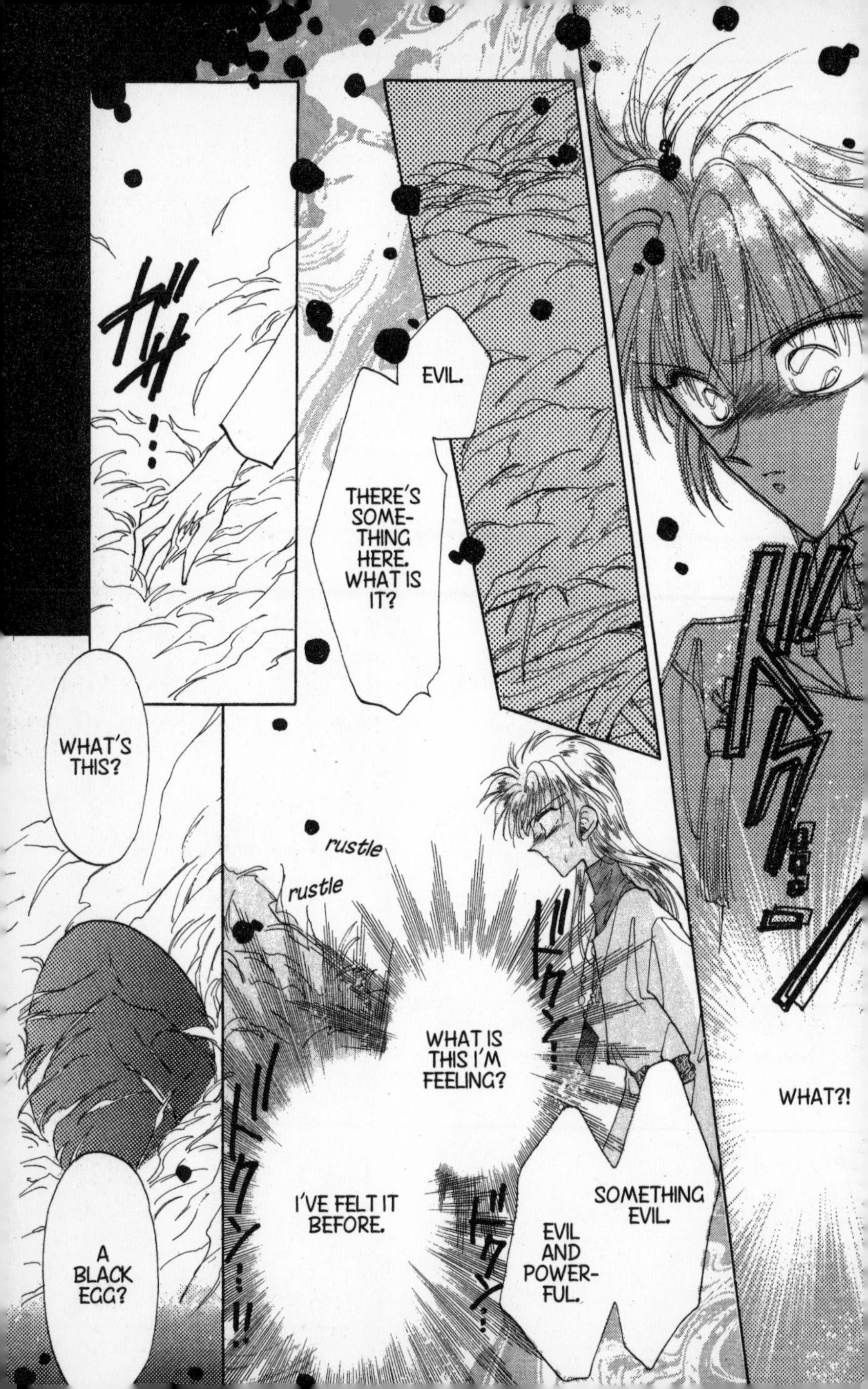
WHAT?!
EVIL.
THERE'S SOME-THING HERE. WHAT IS IT?
SOMETHING EVIL.
EVIL AND POWER-FUL.
WHAT IS THIS I'M FEELING?
I'VE FELT IT BEFORE.
rustle
rustle
WHAT'S THIS?
A BLACK EGG?

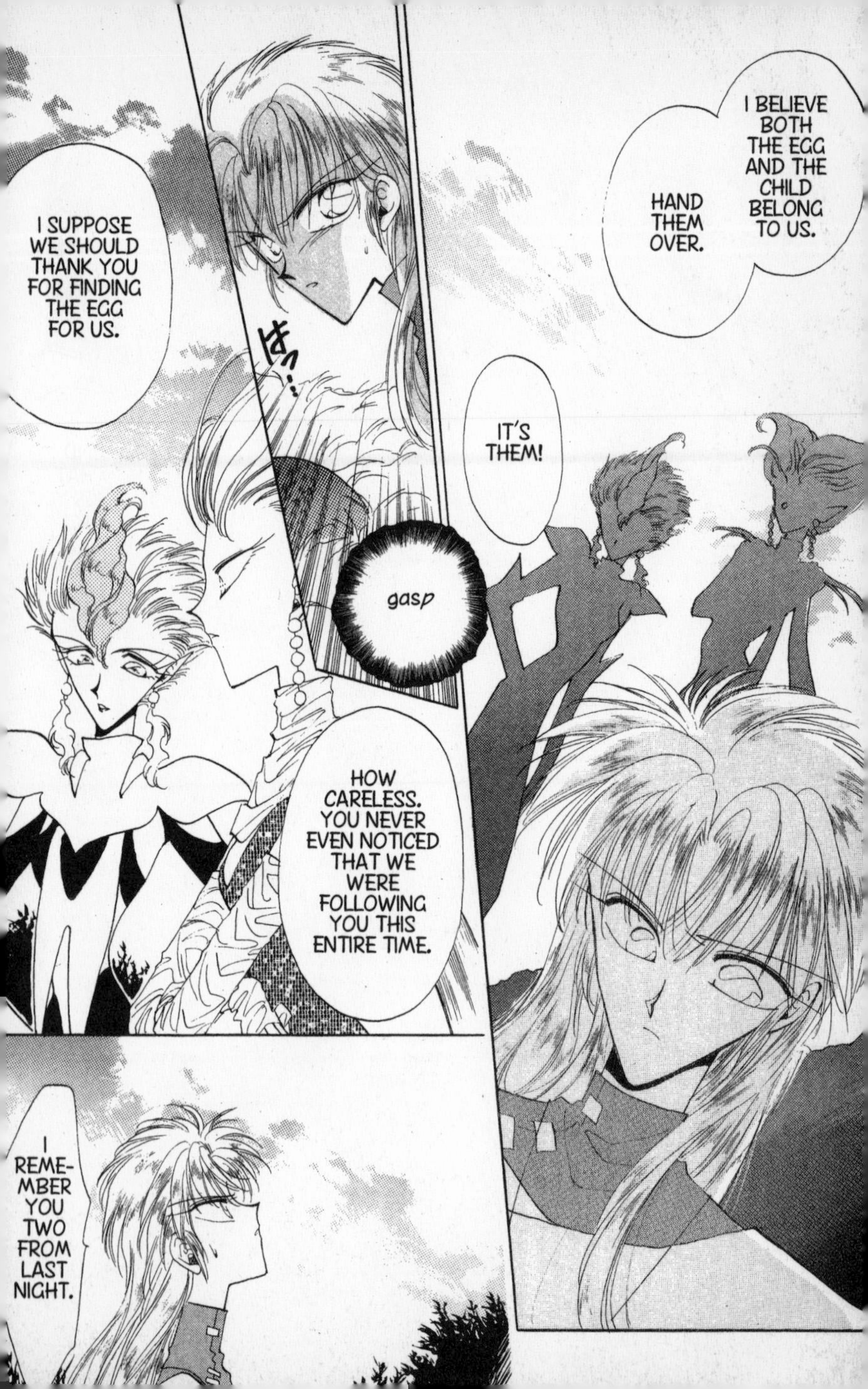
I BELIEVE BOTH THE EGG AND THE CHILD BELONG TO US.
HAND THEM OVER.
IT'S THEM!
はっ...
gasp
I SUPPOSE WE SHOULD THANK YOU FOR FINDING THE EGG FOR US.
HOW CARELESS. YOU NEVER EVEN NOTICED THAT WE WERE FOLLOWING YOU THIS ENTIRE TIME.
I REMEMBER YOU TWO FROM LAST NIGHT.

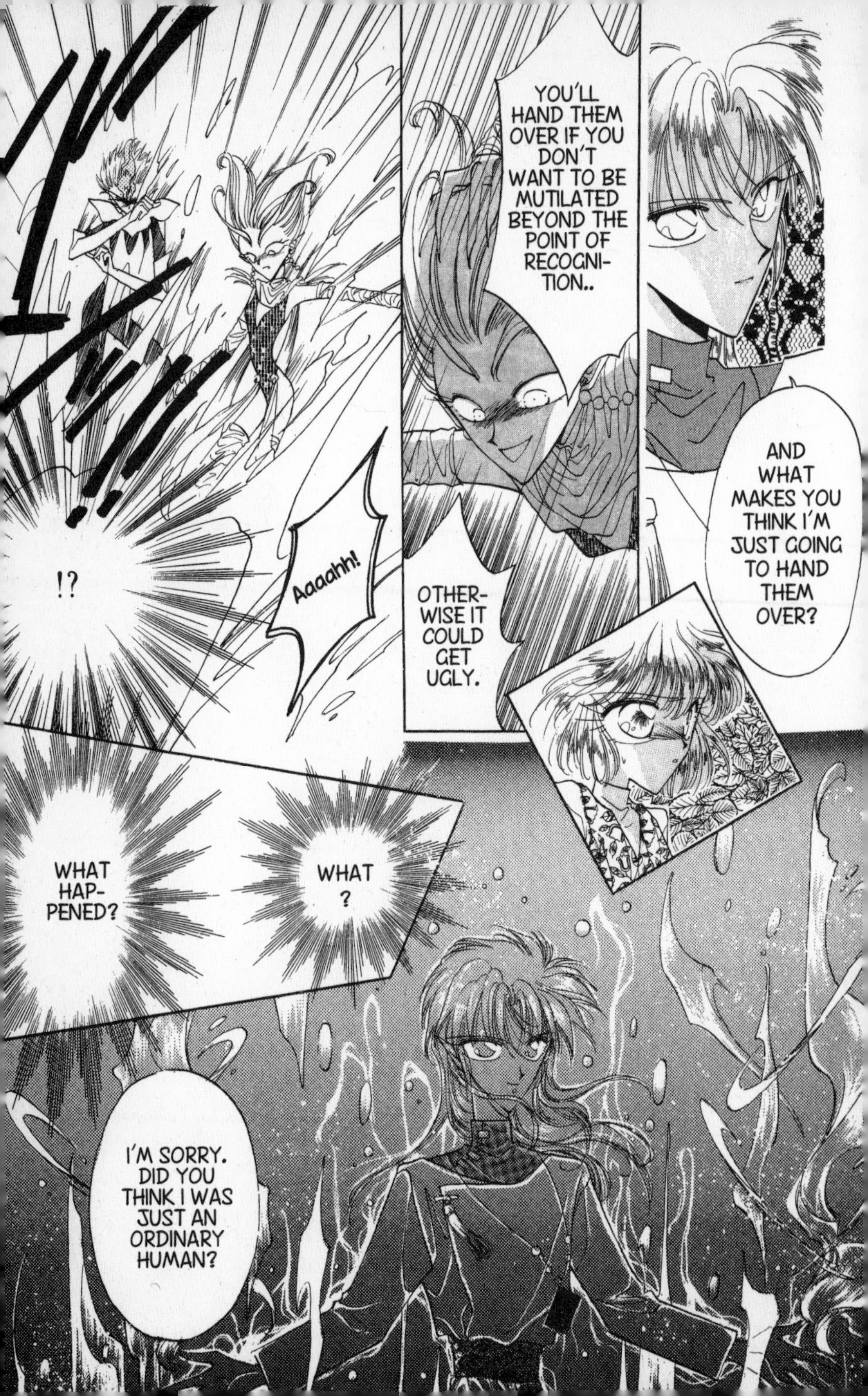
YOU'LL HAND THEM OVER IF YOU DON'T WANT TO BE MUTILATED BEYOND THE POINT OF RECOGNI-TION..
OTHER-WISE IT COULD GET UGLY.
AND WHAT MAKES YOU THINK I'M JUST GOING TO HAND THEM OVER?
Aaaahh!
!?
WHAT ?
WHAT HAP-PENED?
I'M SORRY. DID YOU THINK I WAS JUST AN ORDINARY HUMAN?

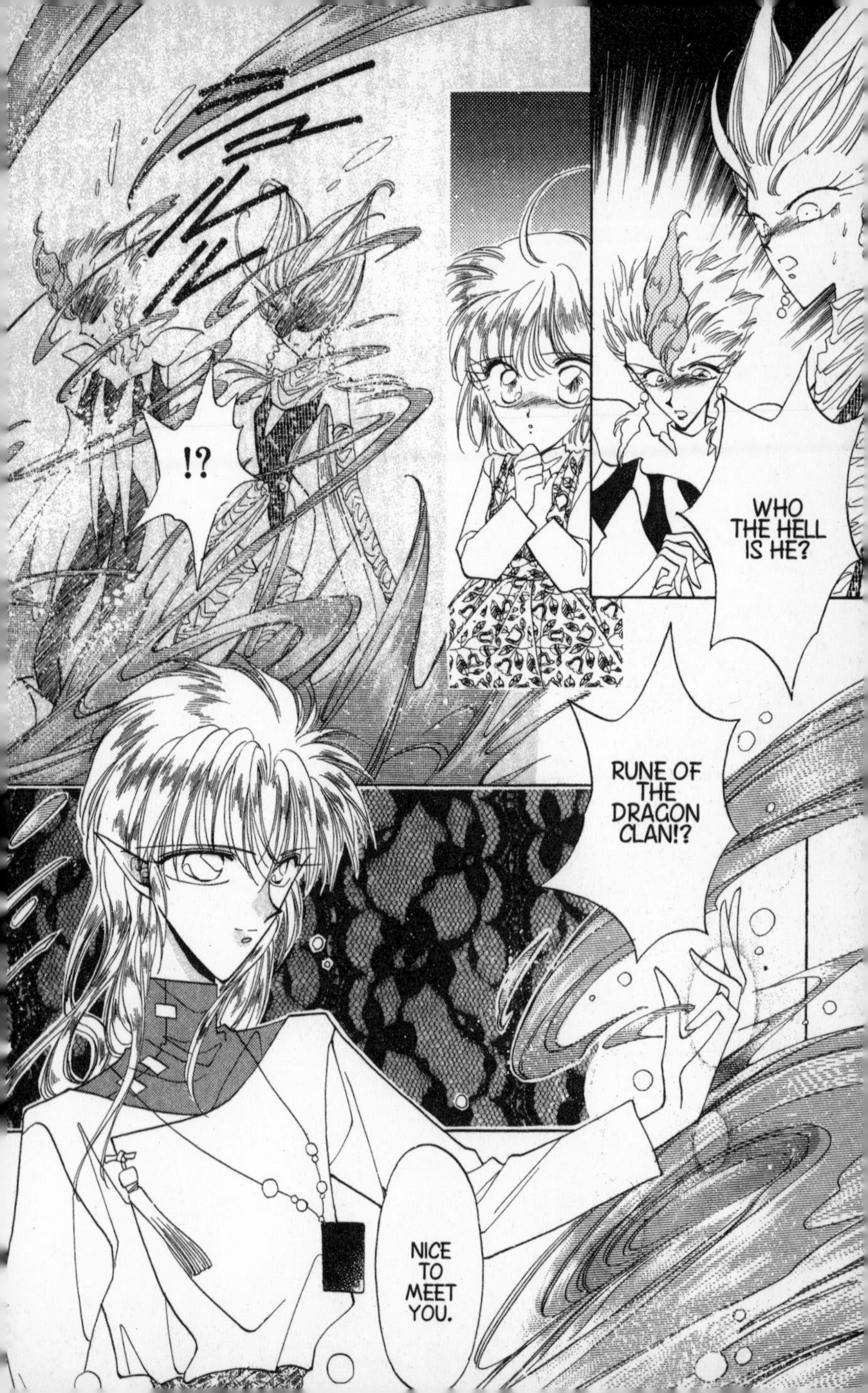
WHO THE HELL IS HE?
!?
RUNE OF THE DRAGON CLAN!?
NICE TO MEET YOU.

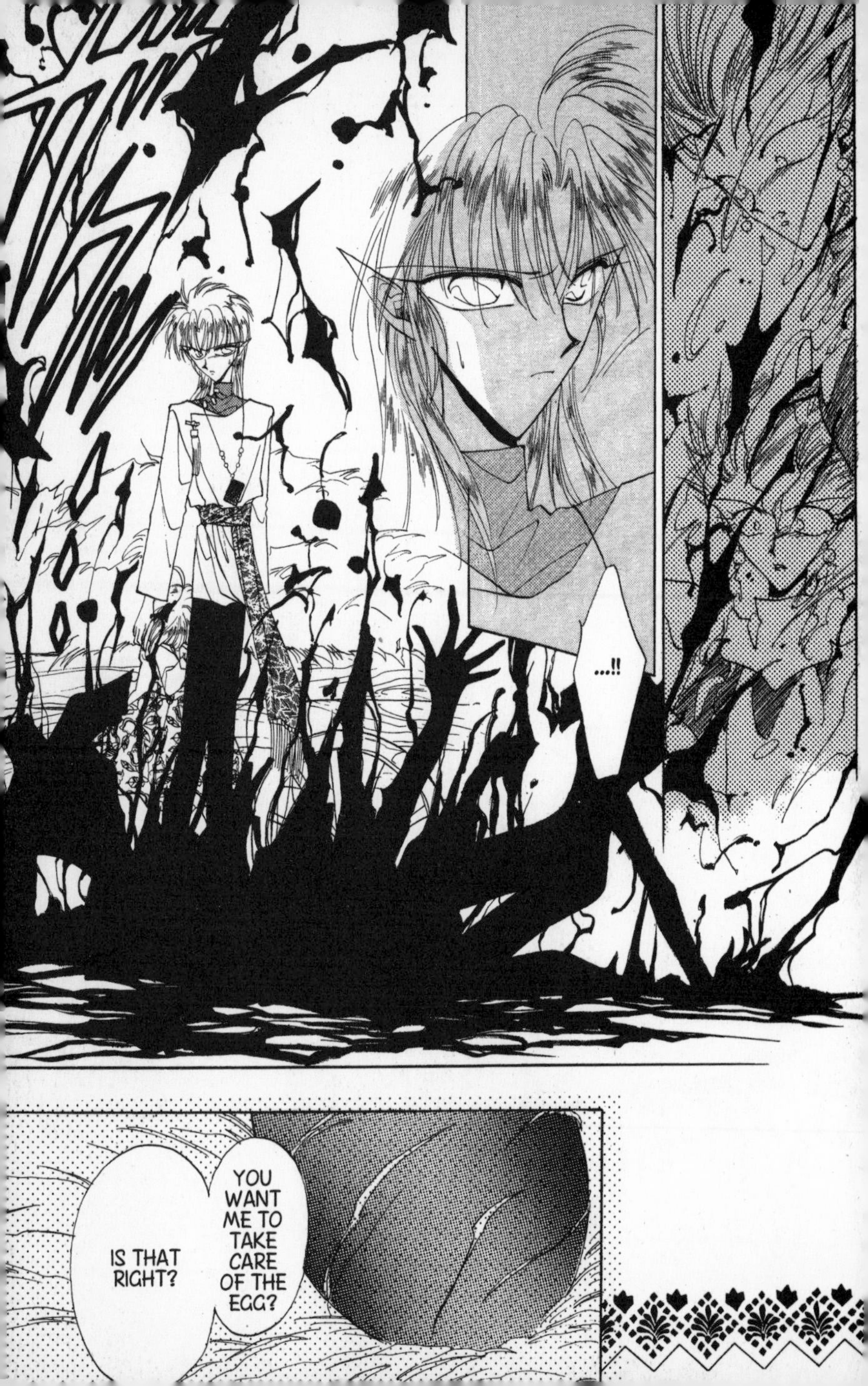
...!!
YOU WANT ME TO TAKE CARE OF THE EGG?
IS THAT RIGHT?

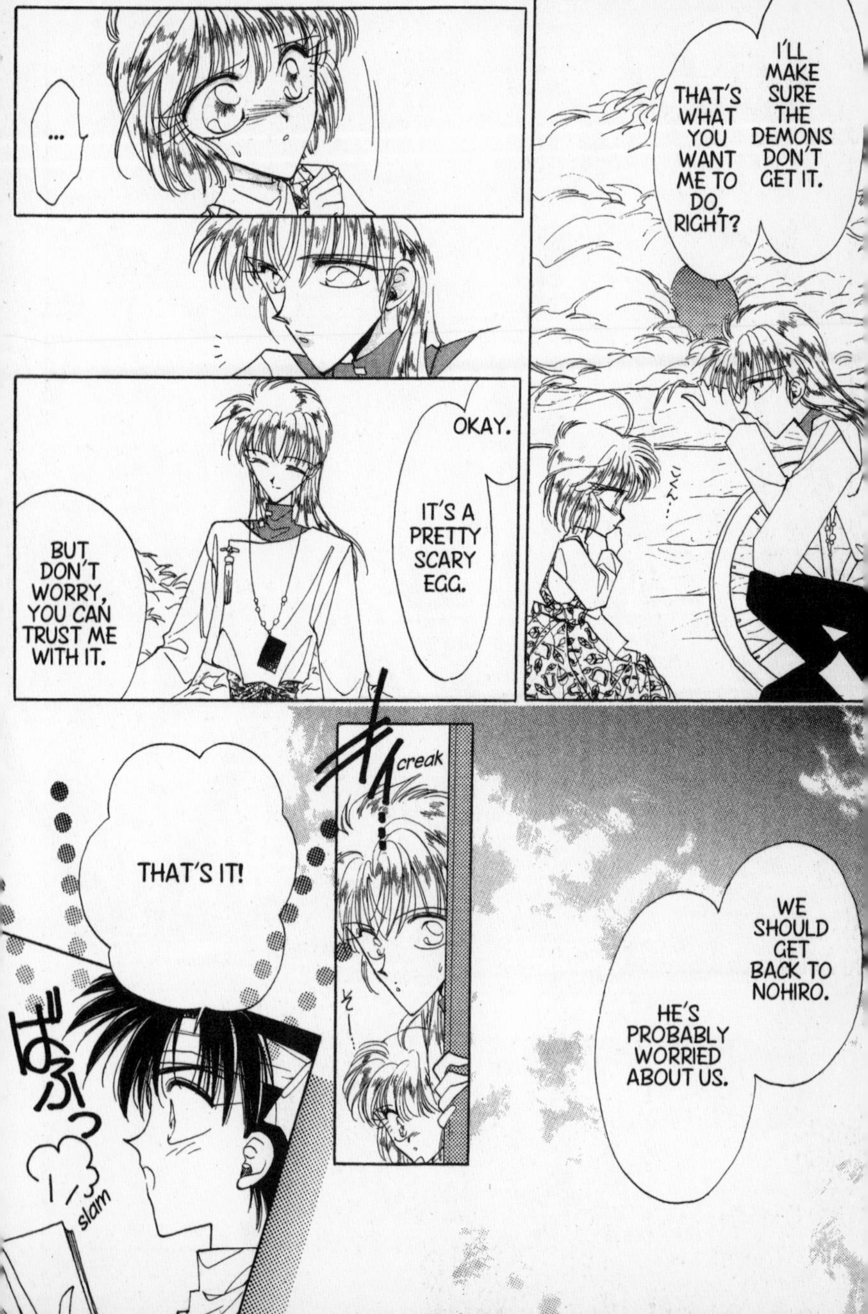
I'LL MAKE SURE THE DEMONS DON'T GET IT.
THAT'S WHAT YOU WANT ME TO DO, RIGHT?
...
OKAY.
IT'S A PRETTY SCARY EGG.
BUT DON'T WORRY, YOU CAN TRUST ME WITH IT.
WE SHOULD GET BACK TO NOHIRO.
HE'S PROBABLY WORRIED ABOUT US.
creak
THAT'S IT!
ぱふっ
slam

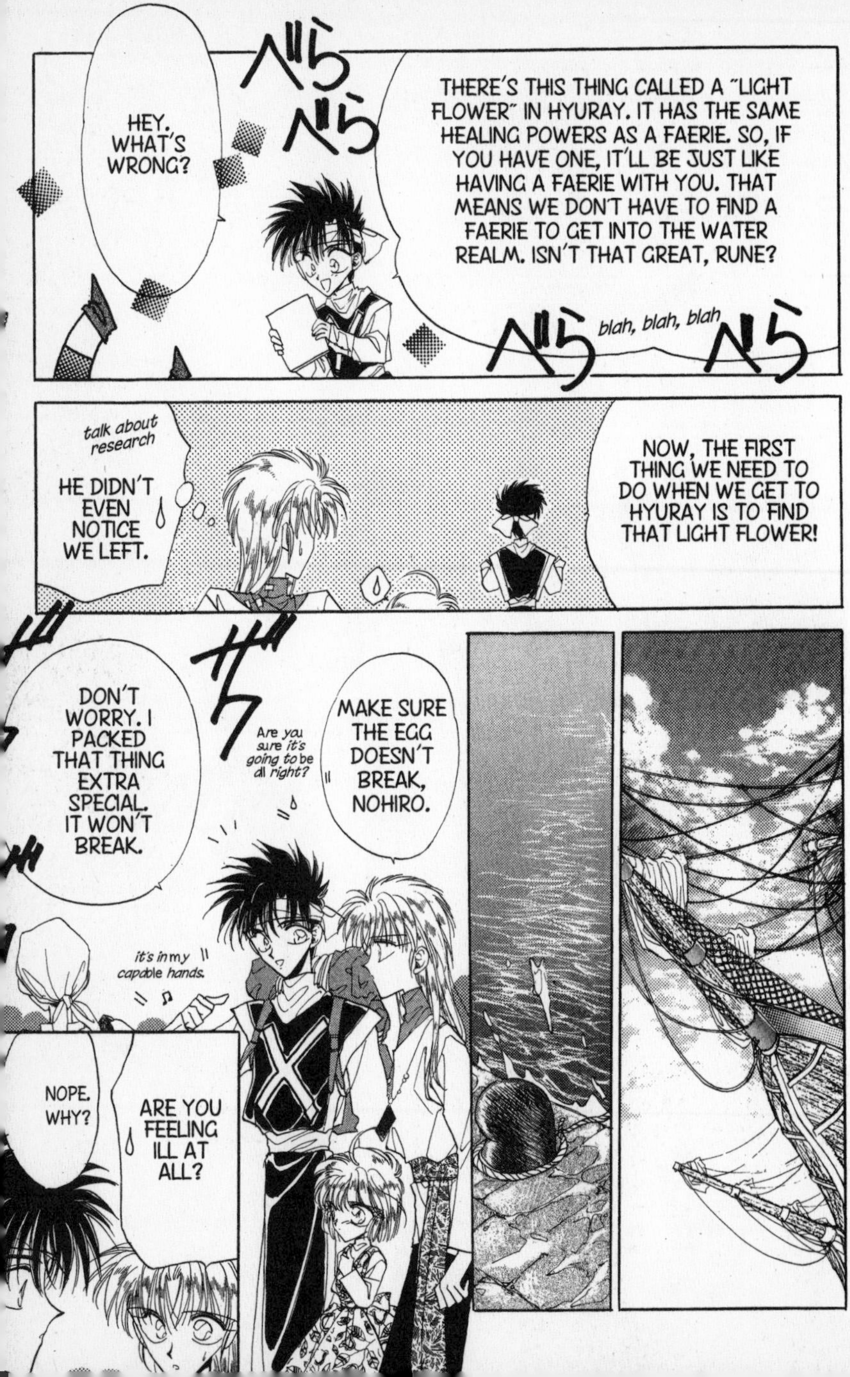
THERE'S THIS THING CALLED A "LIGHT FLOWER" IN HYURAY. IT HAS THE SAME HEALING POWERS AS A FAERIE. SO, IF YOU HAVE ONE, IT'LL BE JUST LIKE HAVING A FAERIE WITH YOU. THAT MEANS WE DON'T HAVE TO FIND A FAERIE TO GET INTO THE WATER REALM. ISN'T THAT GREAT, RUNE?
べら べら
べら blah, blah, blah べら
HEY. WHAT'S WRONG?
NOW, THE FIRST THING WE NEED TO DO WHEN WE GET TO HYURAY IS TO FIND THAT LIGHT FLOWER!
talk about research
HE DIDN'T EVEN NOTICE WE LEFT.
MAKE SURE THE EGG DOESN'T BREAK, NOHIRO.
Are you sure it's going to be all right?
DON'T WORRY. I PACKED THAT THING EXTRA SPECIAL. IT WON'T BREAK.
it's in my capable hands.
ARE YOU FEELING ILL AT ALL?
NOPE. WHY?

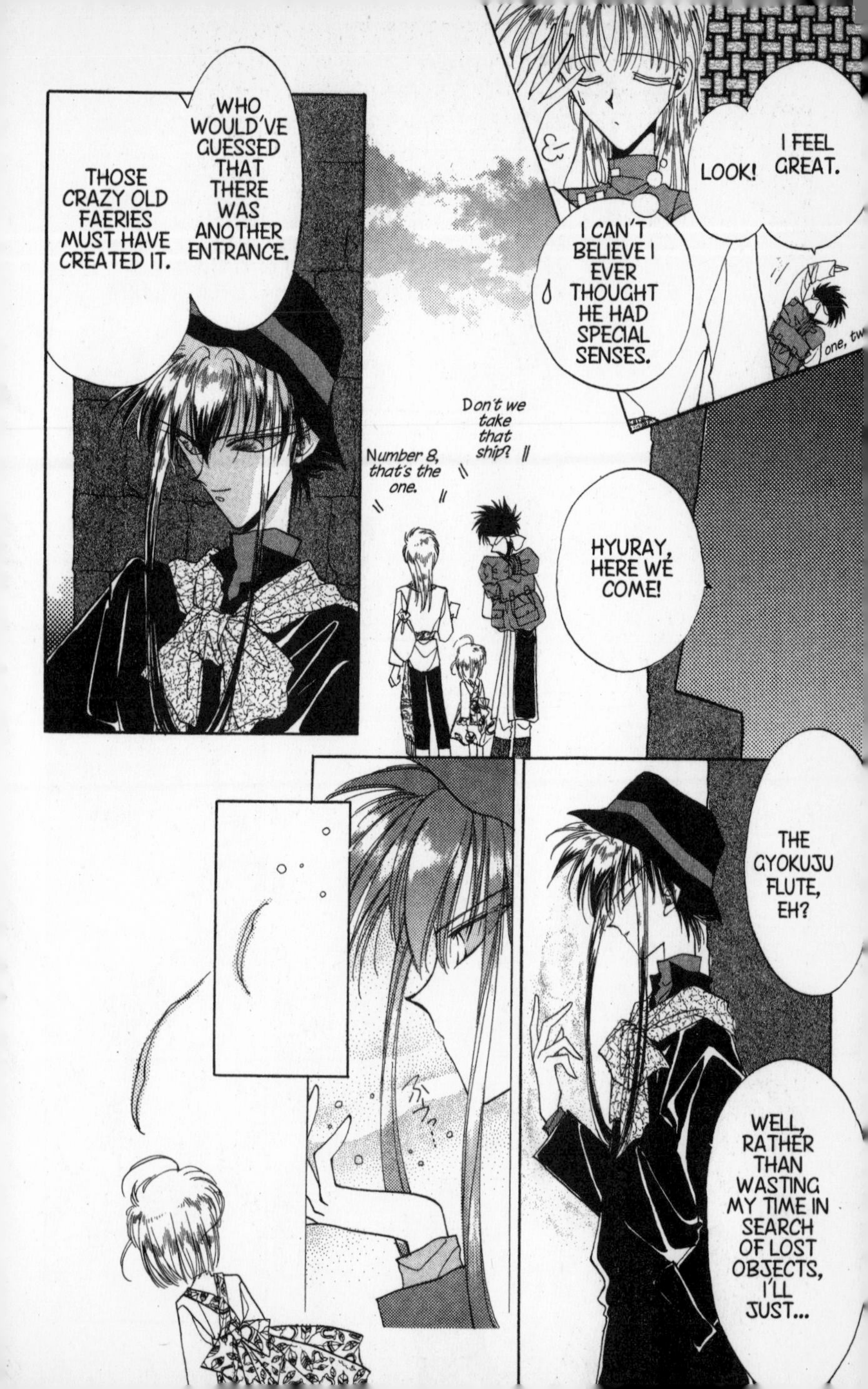

LOOK! I FEEL GREAT.
I CAN'T BELIEVE I EVER THOUGHT HE HAD SPECIAL SENSES.
one, tw
HYURAY, HERE WE COME!
Don't we take that ship?
Number 8, that's the one.
WHO WOULD'VE GUESSED THAT THERE WAS ANOTHER ENTRANCE.
THOSE CRAZY OLD FAERIES MUST HAVE CREATED IT.
THE GYOKUJU FLUTE, EH?
WELL, RATHER THAN WASTING MY TIME IN SEARCH OF LOST OBJECTS, I'LL JUST...

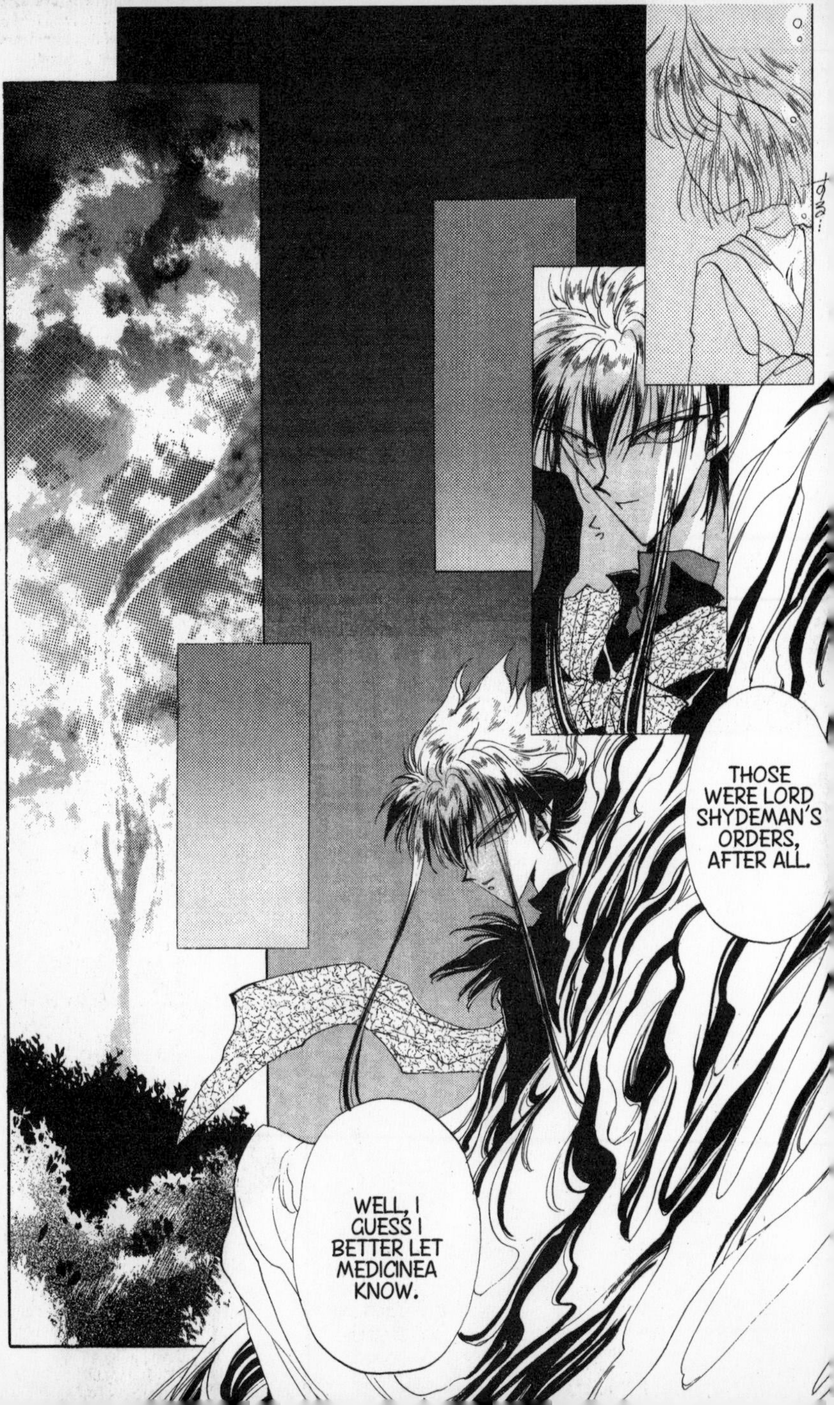
THOSE WERE LORD SHYDEMAN'S ORDERS, AFTER ALL.
WELL, I GUESS I BETTER LET MEDICINEA KNOW.

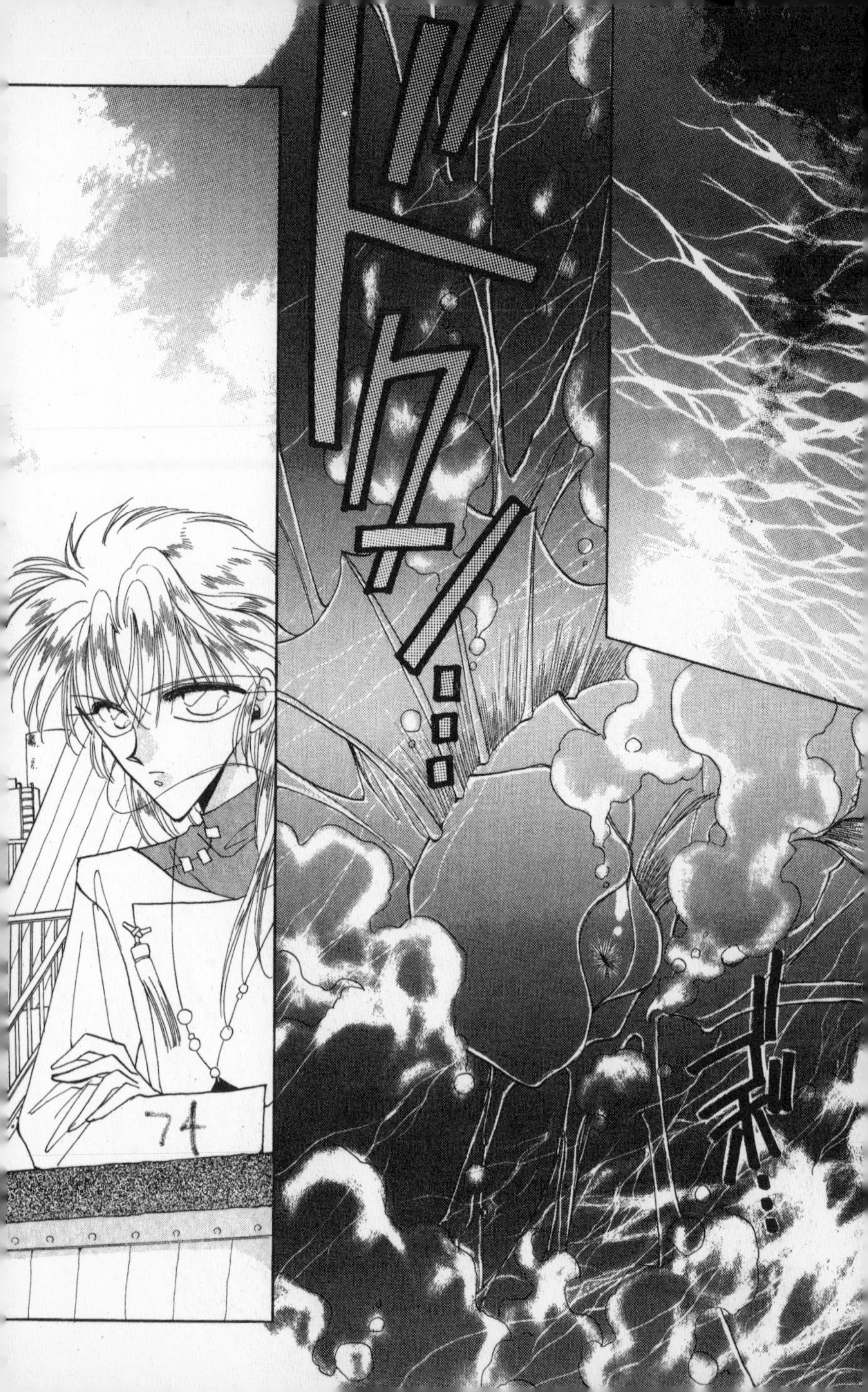
74

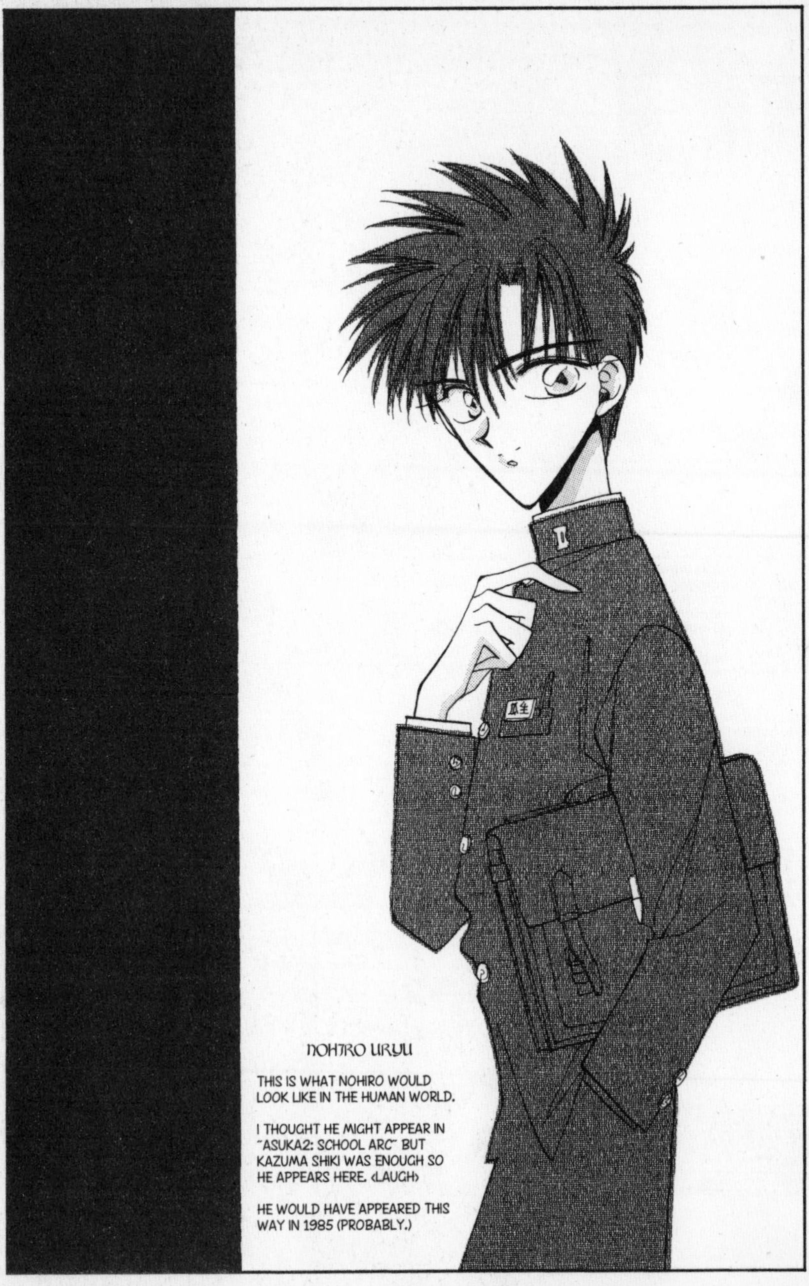
NOHIRO URYU
THIS IS WHAT NOHIRO WOULD LOOK LIKE IN THE HUMAN WORLD.
I THOUGHT HE MIGHT APPEAR IN "ASUKA2: SCHOOL ARC" BUT KAZUMA SHIKI WAS ENOUGH SO HE APPEARS HERE. <LAUGH>
HE WOULD HAVE APPEARED THIS WAY IN 1985 (PROBABLY.)

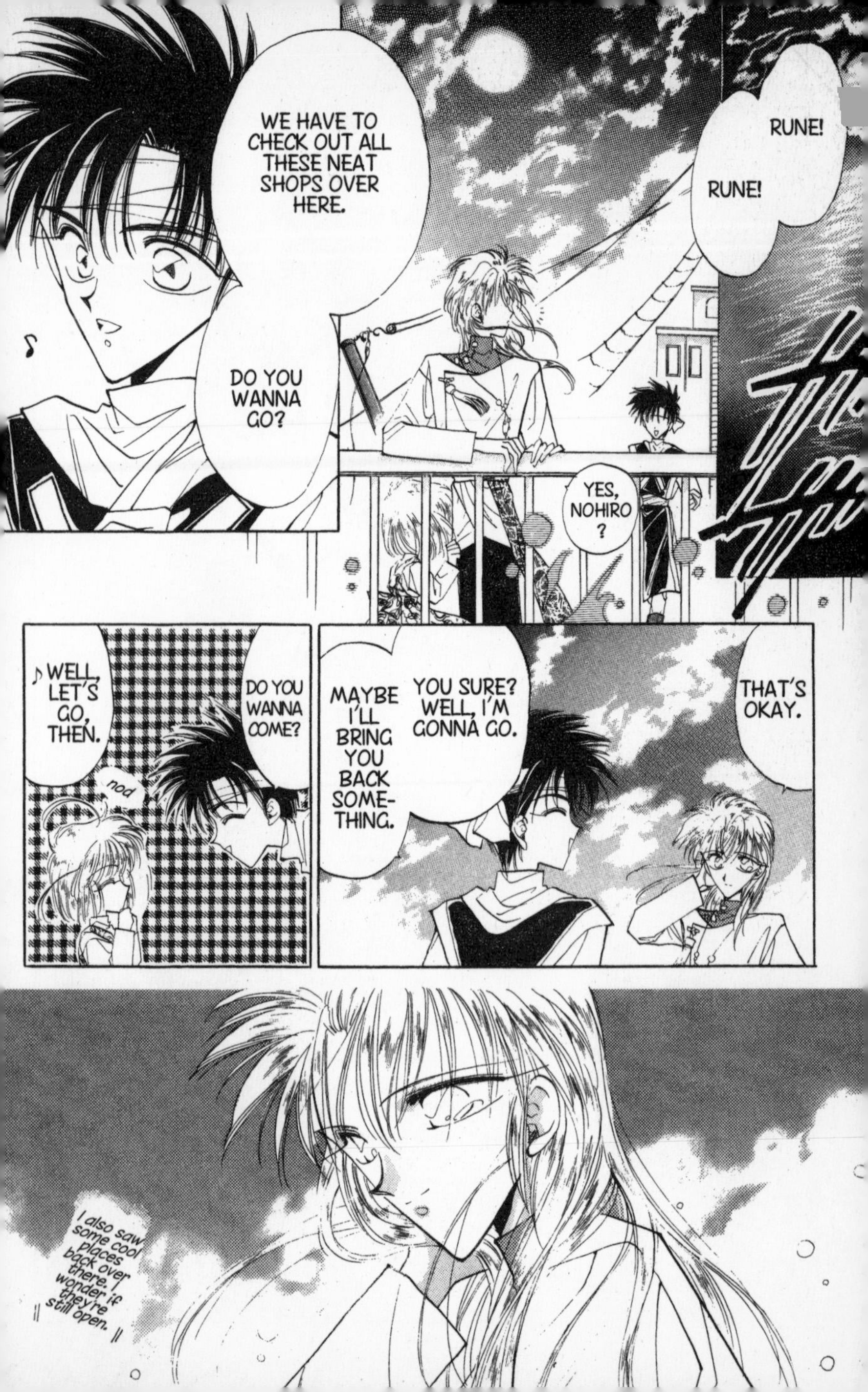
RUNE!
RUNE!
YES, NOHIRO?
WE HAVE TO CHECK OUT ALL THESE NEAT SHOPS OVER HERE.
DO YOU WANNA GO?
THAT'S OKAY.
YOU SURE? WELL, I'M GONNA GO.
MAYBE I'LL BRING YOU BACK SOME-THING.
DO YOU WANNA COME?
nod
♪ WELL, LET'S GO, THEN.
I also saw some cool places back over there. I wonder if they're still open.

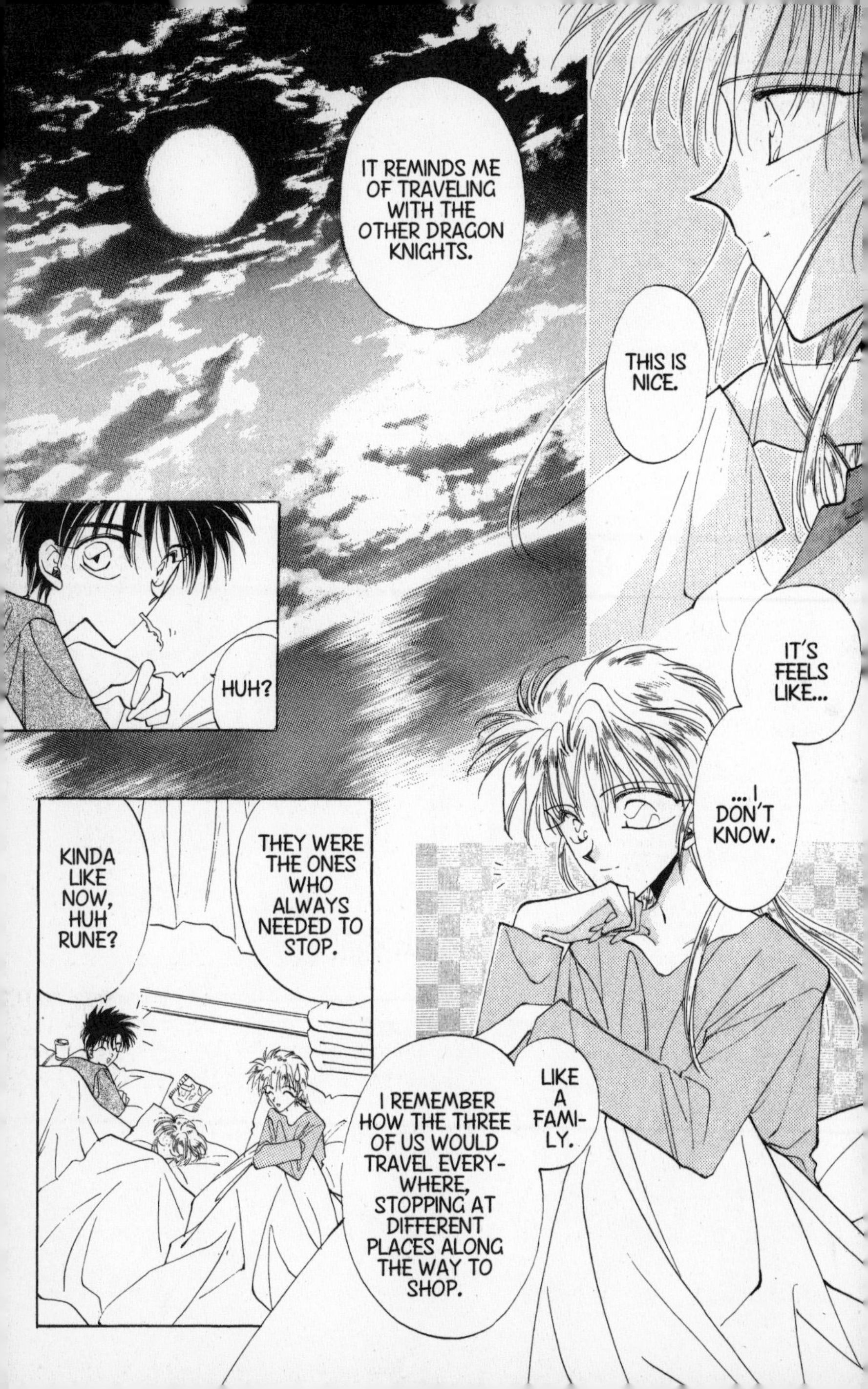
THIS IS NICE.
IT REMINDS ME OF TRAVELING WITH THE OTHER DRAGON KNIGHTS.
HUH?
IT'S FEELS LIKE...
... I DON'T KNOW.
LIKE A FAMI-LY.
I REMEMBER HOW THE THREE OF US WOULD TRAVEL EVERY-WHERE, STOPPING AT DIFFERENT PLACES ALONG THE WAY TO SHOP.
THEY WERE THE ONES WHO ALWAYS NEEDED TO STOP.
KINDA LIKE NOW, HUH RUNE?

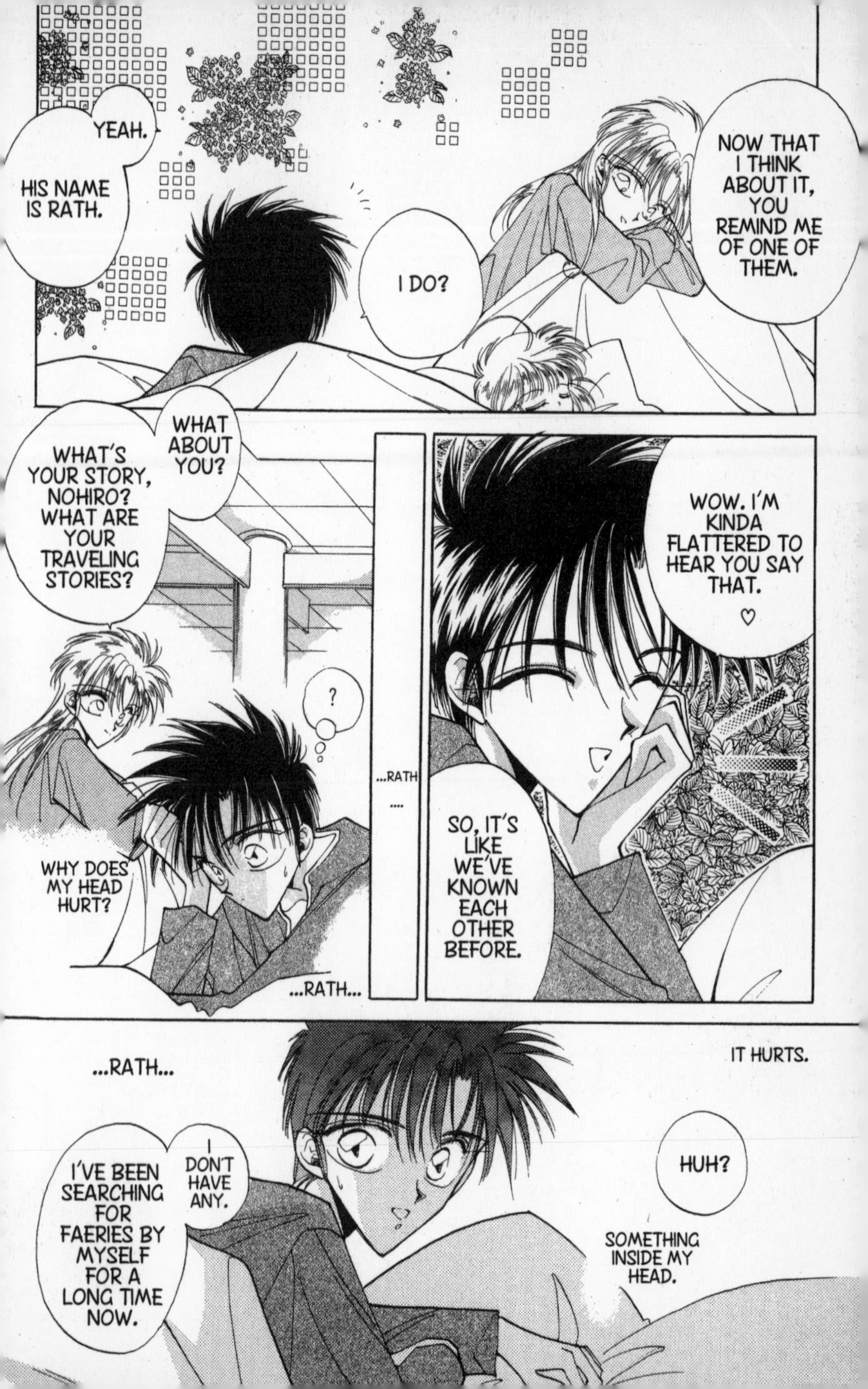
NOW THAT I THINK ABOUT IT, YOU REMIND ME OF ONE OF THEM.
I DO?
YEAH.
HIS NAME IS RATH.
WOW. I'M KINDA FLATTERED TO HEAR YOU SAY THAT. ♡
SO, IT'S LIKE WE'VE KNOWN EACH OTHER BEFORE.
...RATH ....
WHAT ABOUT YOU?
WHAT'S YOUR STORY, NOHIRO? WHAT ARE YOUR TRAVELING STORIES?
?
WHY DOES MY HEAD HURT?
...RATH...
IT HURTS.
HUH?
SOMETHING INSIDE MY HEAD.
...RATH...
I DON'T HAVE ANY.
I'VE BEEN SEARCHING FOR FAERIES BY MYSELF FOR A LONG TIME NOW.

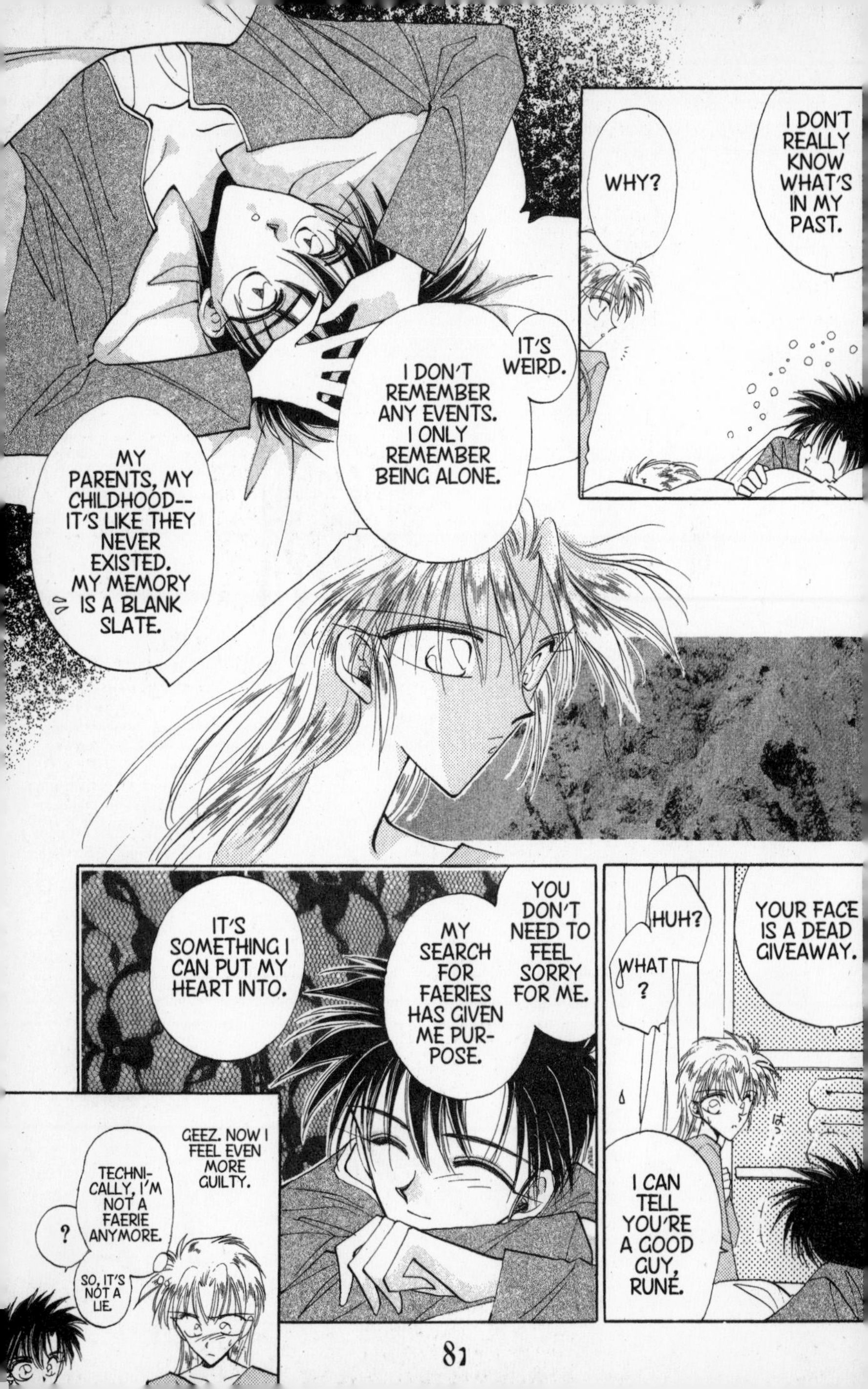

I DON'T REALLY KNOW WHAT'S IN MY PAST.
WHY?
IT'S WEIRD.
I DON'T REMEMBER ANY EVENTS. I ONLY REMEMBER BEING ALONE.
MY PARENTS, MY CHILDHOOD-- IT'S LIKE THEY NEVER EXISTED. MY MEMORY IS A BLANK SLATE.
YOUR FACE IS A DEAD GIVEAWAY.
HUH?
WHAT?
I CAN TELL YOU'RE A GOOD GUY, RUNE.
YOU DON'T NEED TO FEEL SORRY FOR ME.
MY SEARCH FOR FAERIES HAS GIVEN ME PURPOSE.
IT'S SOMETHING I CAN PUT MY HEART INTO.
GEEZ. NOW I FEEL EVEN MORE GUILTY.
TECHNICALLY, I'M NOT A FAERIE ANYMORE.
?
SO, IT'S NOT A LIE.

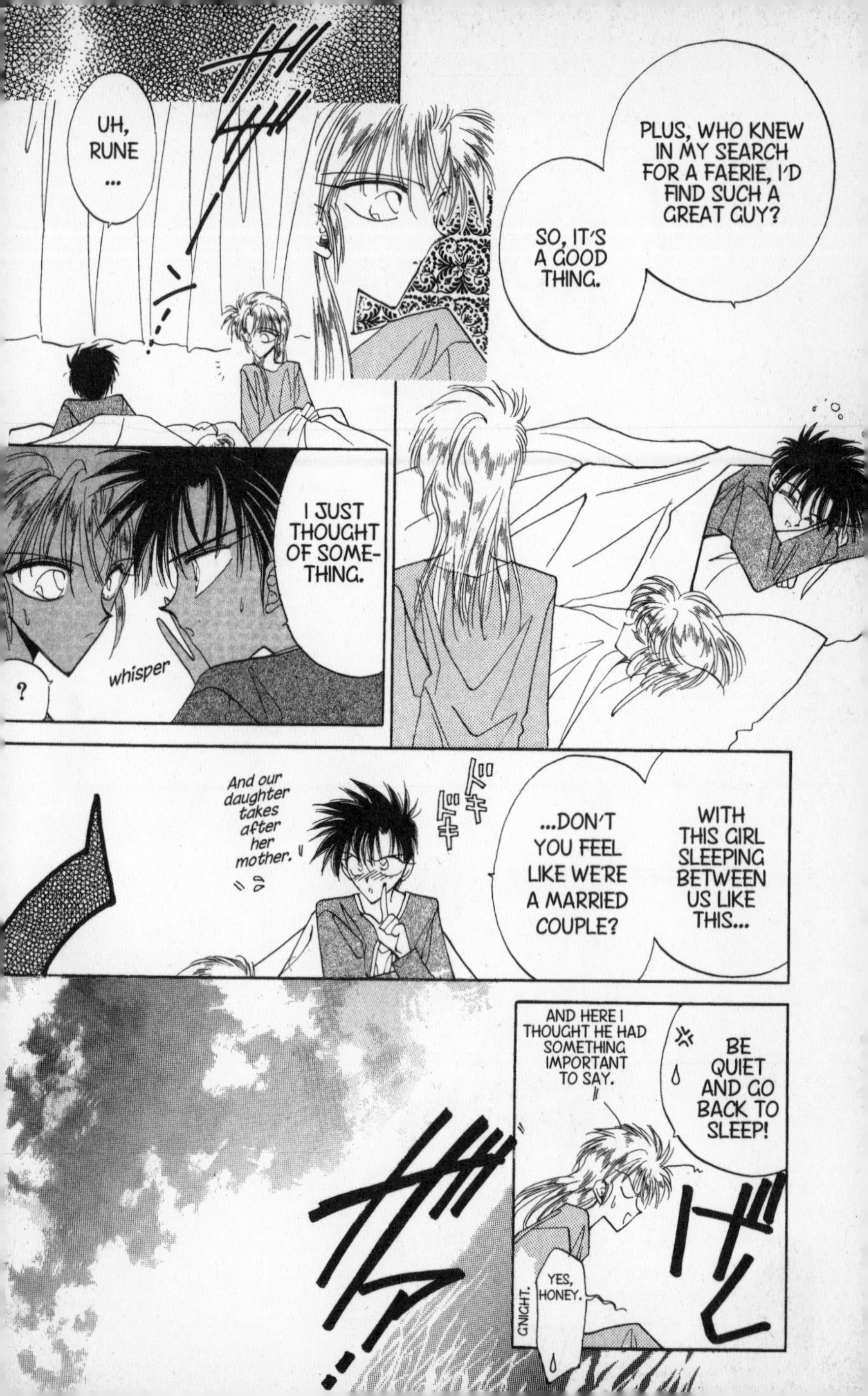
PLUS, WHO KNEW IN MY SEARCH FOR A FAERIE, I'D FIND SUCH A GREAT GUY?
SO, IT'S A GOOD THING.
UH, RUNE ...
I JUST THOUGHT OF SOME-THING.
whisper
?
WITH THIS GIRL SLEEPING BETWEEN US LIKE THIS...
...DON'T YOU FEEL LIKE WE'RE A MARRIED COUPLE?
And our daughter takes after her mother.
BE QUIET AND GO BACK TO SLEEP!
AND HERE I THOUGHT HE HAD SOMETHING IMPORTANT TO SAY.
YES, HONEY.
G'NIGHT.

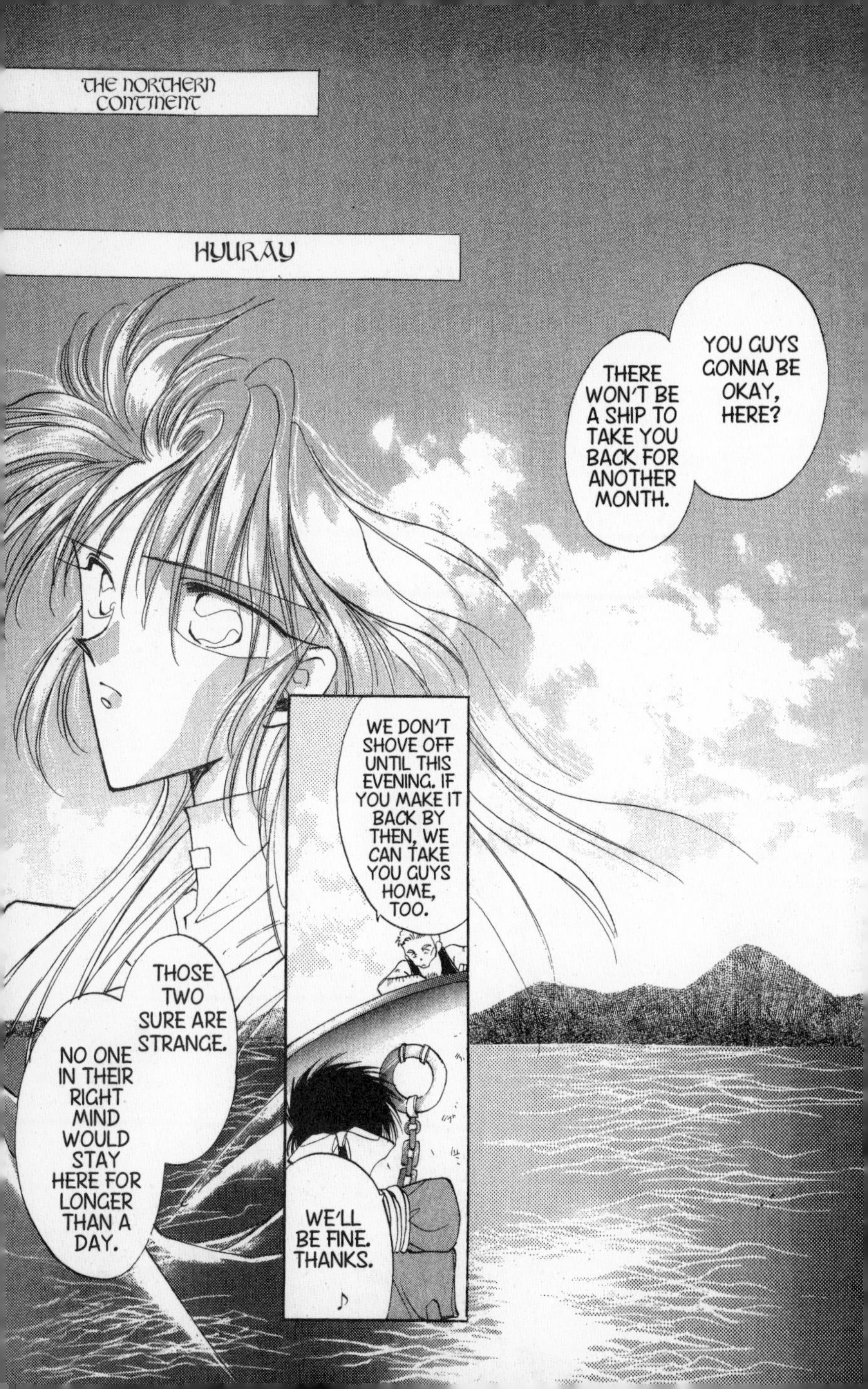
THE NORTHERN CONTINENT
HYURAY
YOU GUYS GONNA BE OKAY, HERE?
THERE WON'T BE A SHIP TO TAKE YOU BACK FOR ANOTHER MONTH.
WE DON'T SHOVE OFF UNTIL THIS EVENING. IF YOU MAKE IT BACK BY THEN, WE CAN TAKE YOU GUYS HOME, TOO.
WE'LL BE FINE. THANKS. ♪
THOSE TWO SURE ARE STRANGE.
NO ONE IN THEIR RIGHT MIND WOULD STAY HERE FOR LONGER THAN A DAY.

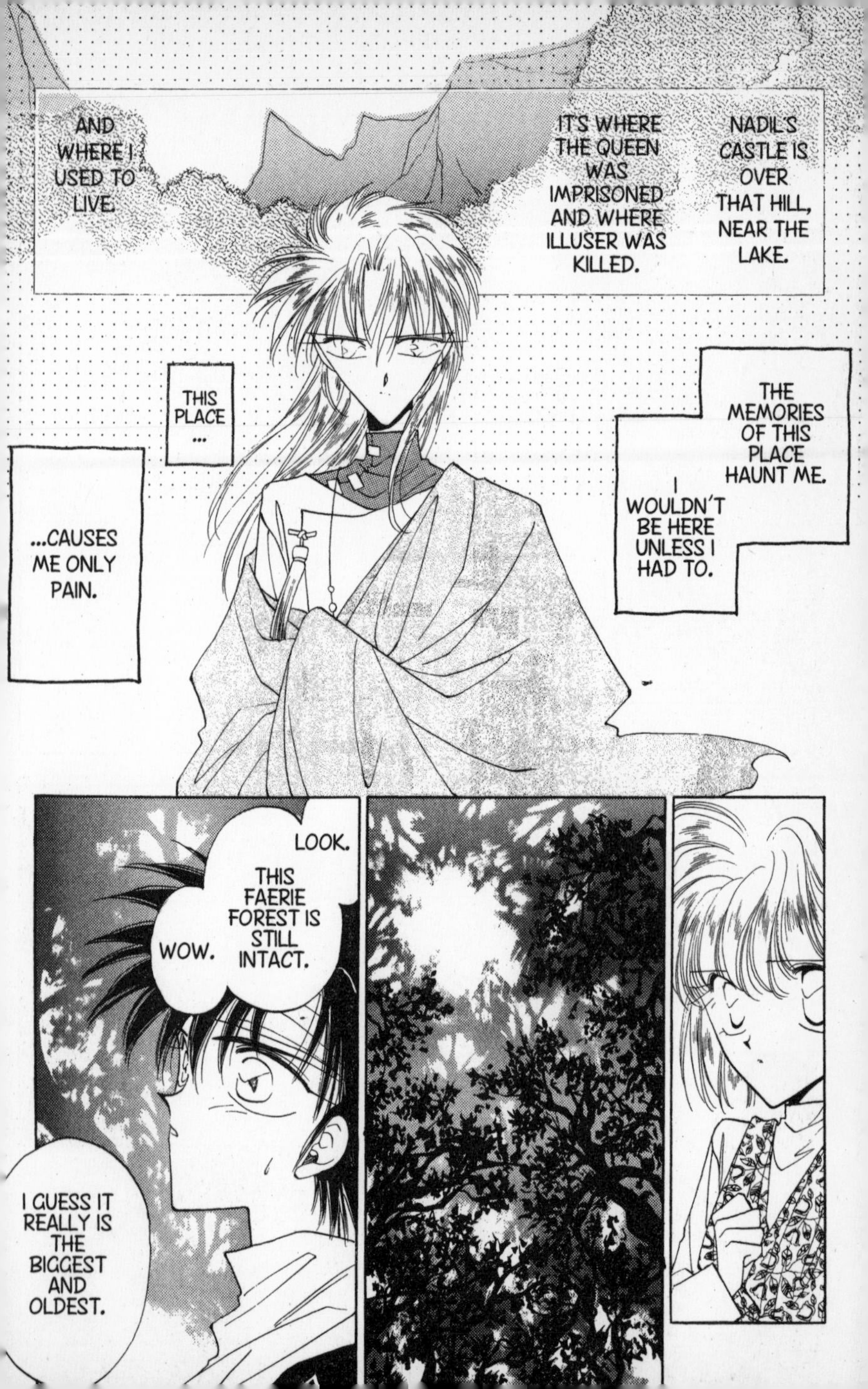
NADIL'S CASTLE IS OVER THAT HILL, NEAR THE LAKE.
IT'S WHERE THE QUEEN WAS IMPRISONED AND WHERE ILLUSER WAS KILLED.
AND WHERE I USED TO LIVE.
THE MEMORIES OF THIS PLACE HAUNT ME.
I WOULDN'T BE HERE UNLESS I HAD TO.
THIS PLACE...
...CAUSES ME ONLY PAIN.
LOOK.
THIS FAERIE FOREST IS STILL INTACT.
WOW.
I GUESS IT REALLY IS THE BIGGEST AND OLDEST.

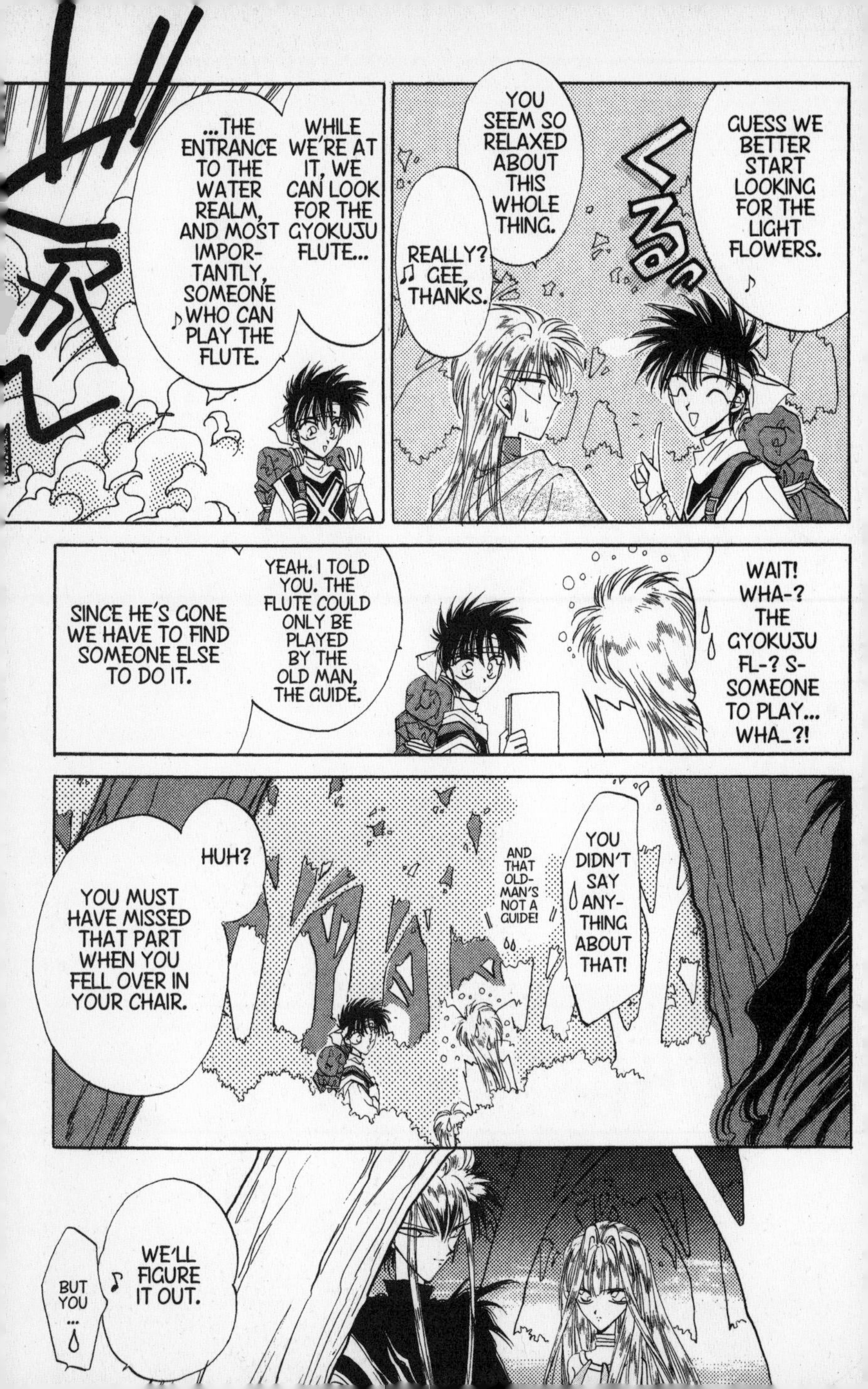
GUESS WE BETTER START LOOKING FOR THE LIGHT FLOWERS. ♪
YOU SEEM SO RELAXED ABOUT THIS WHOLE THING.
REALLY? ♫ GEE, THANKS.
WHILE WE'RE AT IT, WE CAN LOOK FOR THE GYOKUJU FLUTE...
...THE ENTRANCE TO THE WATER REALM, AND MOST IMPORTANTLY, SOMEONE ♪ WHO CAN PLAY THE FLUTE.
WAIT! WHA-? THE GYOKUJU FL-? S-SOMEONE TO PLAY... WHA_?!
YEAH. I TOLD YOU. THE FLUTE COULD ONLY BE PLAYED BY THE OLD MAN, THE GUIDE.
SINCE HE'S GONE WE HAVE TO FIND SOMEONE ELSE TO DO IT.
YOU DIDN'T SAY ANYTHING ABOUT THAT!
AND THAT OLD-MAN'S NOT A GUIDE!
HUH?
YOU MUST HAVE MISSED THAT PART WHEN YOU FELL OVER IN YOUR CHAIR.
♪ WE'LL FIGURE IT OUT.
BUT YOU...

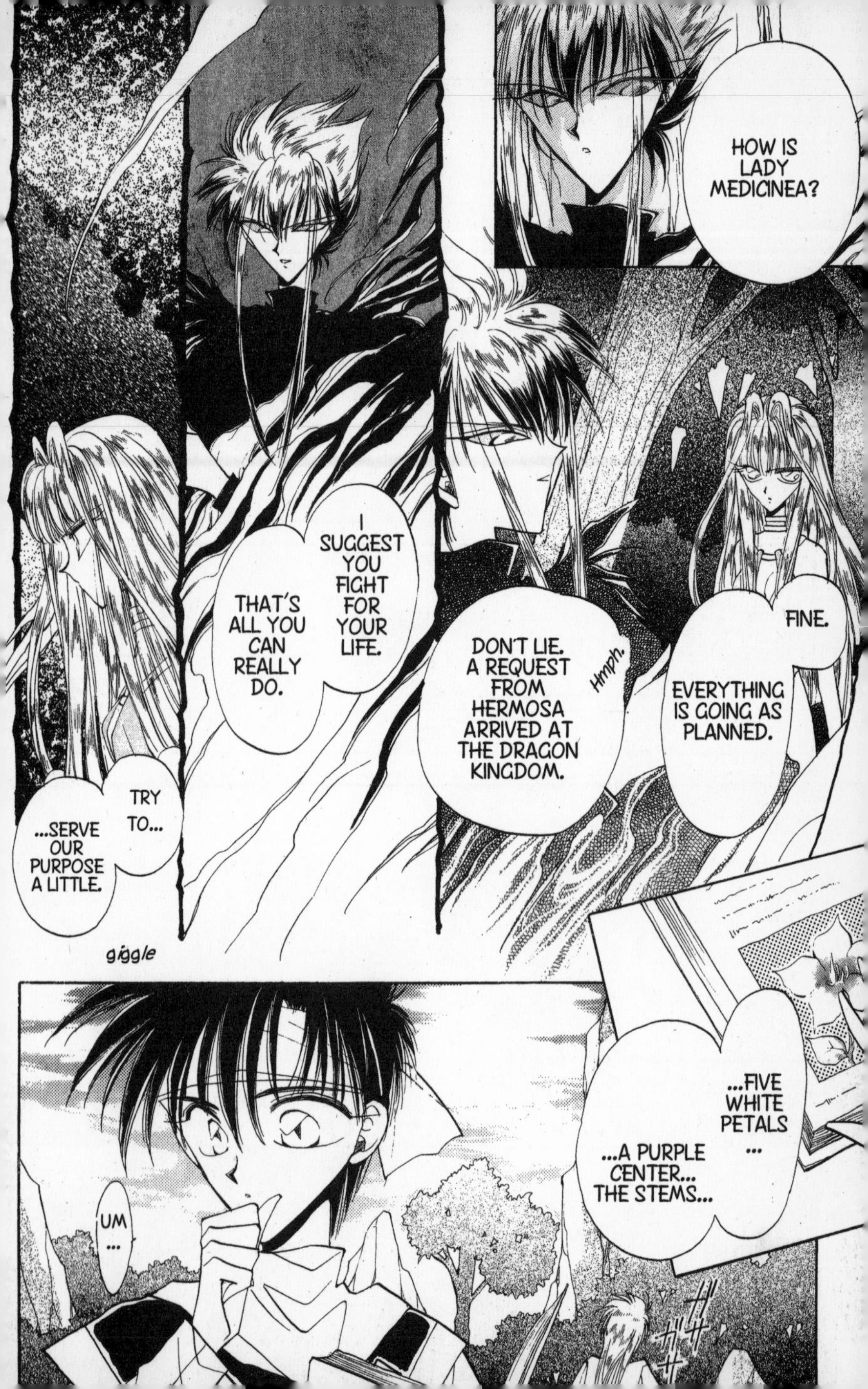
HOW IS LADY MEDICINEA?
FINE.
EVERYTHING IS GOING AS PLANNED.
Hmph.
DON'T LIE. A REQUEST FROM HERMOSA ARRIVED AT THE DRAGON KINGDOM.
I SUGGEST YOU FIGHT FOR YOUR LIFE.
THAT'S ALL YOU CAN REALLY DO.
TRY TO...
...SERVE OUR PURPOSE A LITTLE.
giggle
...FIVE WHITE PETALS ...
...A PURPLE CENTER... THE STEMS...
UM ...

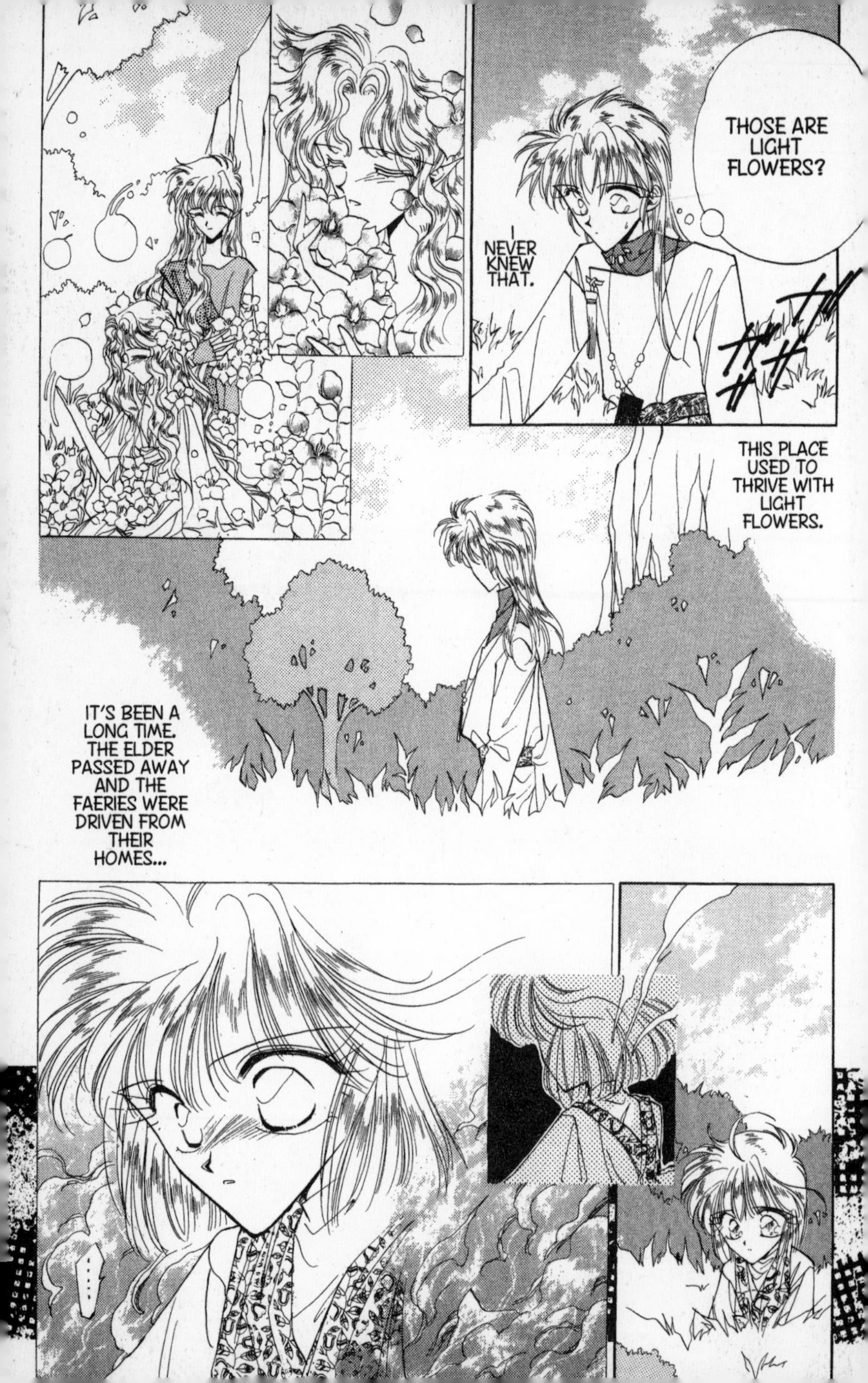
THOSE ARE LIGHT FLOWERS?
I NEVER KNEW THAT.
THIS PLACE USED TO THRIVE WITH LIGHT FLOWERS.
IT'S BEEN A LONG TIME. THE ELDER PASSED AWAY AND THE FAERIES WERE DRIVEN FROM THEIR HOMES...
.....

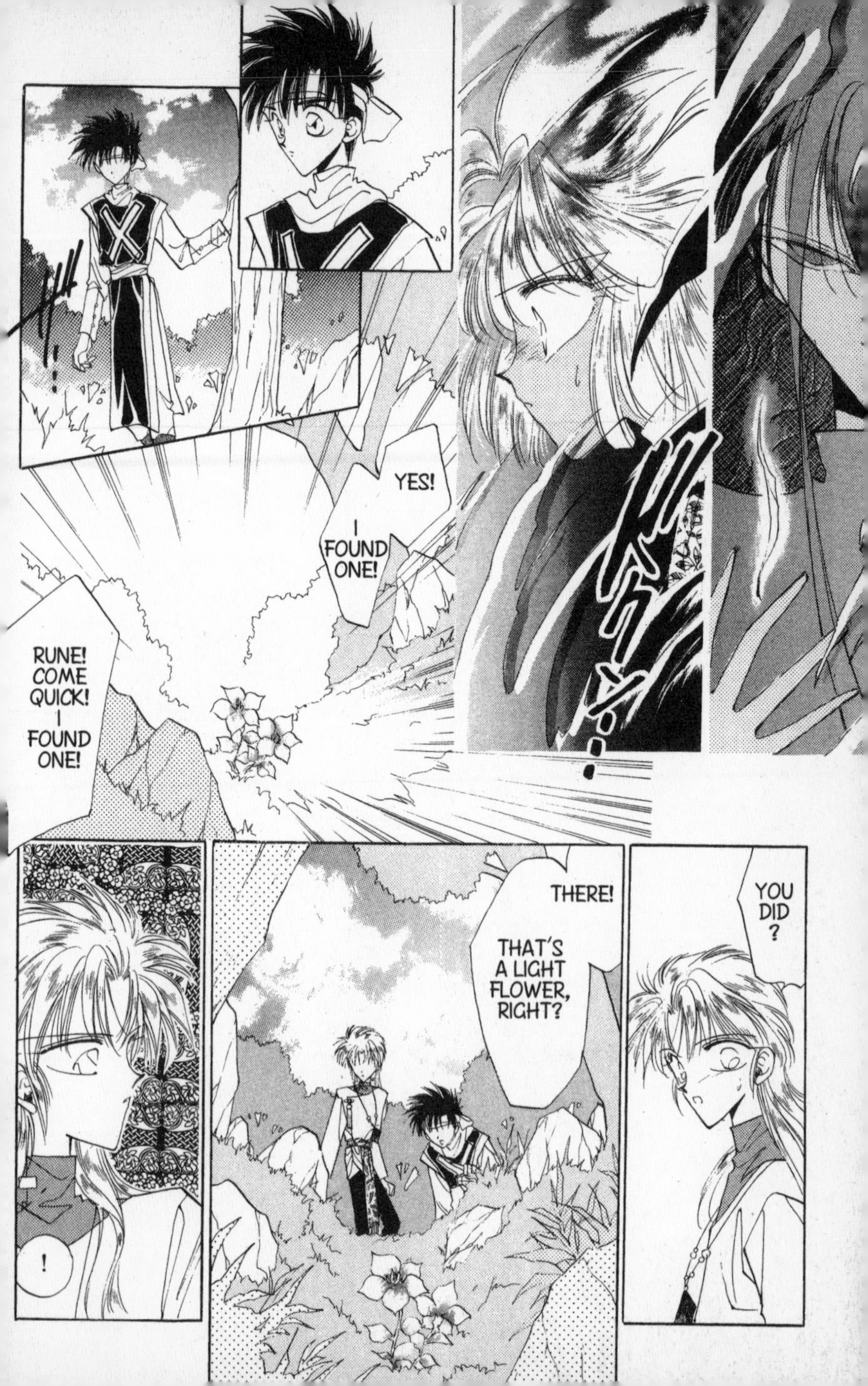
YES!
I FOUND ONE!
RUNE! COME QUICK! I FOUND ONE!
YOU DID?
THERE!
THAT'S A LIGHT FLOWER, RIGHT?
!

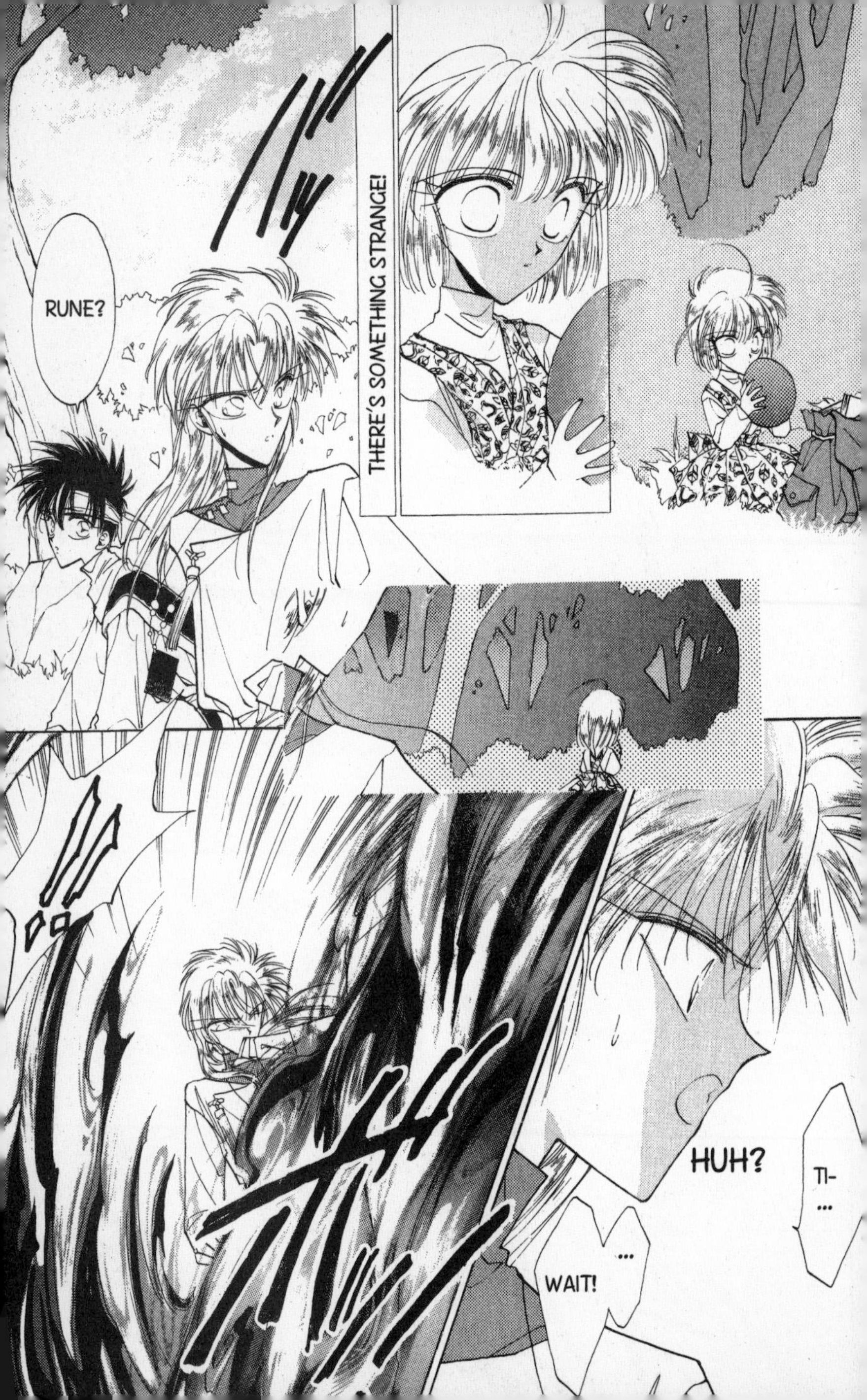
THERE'S SOMETHING STRANGE!
RUNE?
TI-...
HUH?
... WAIT!

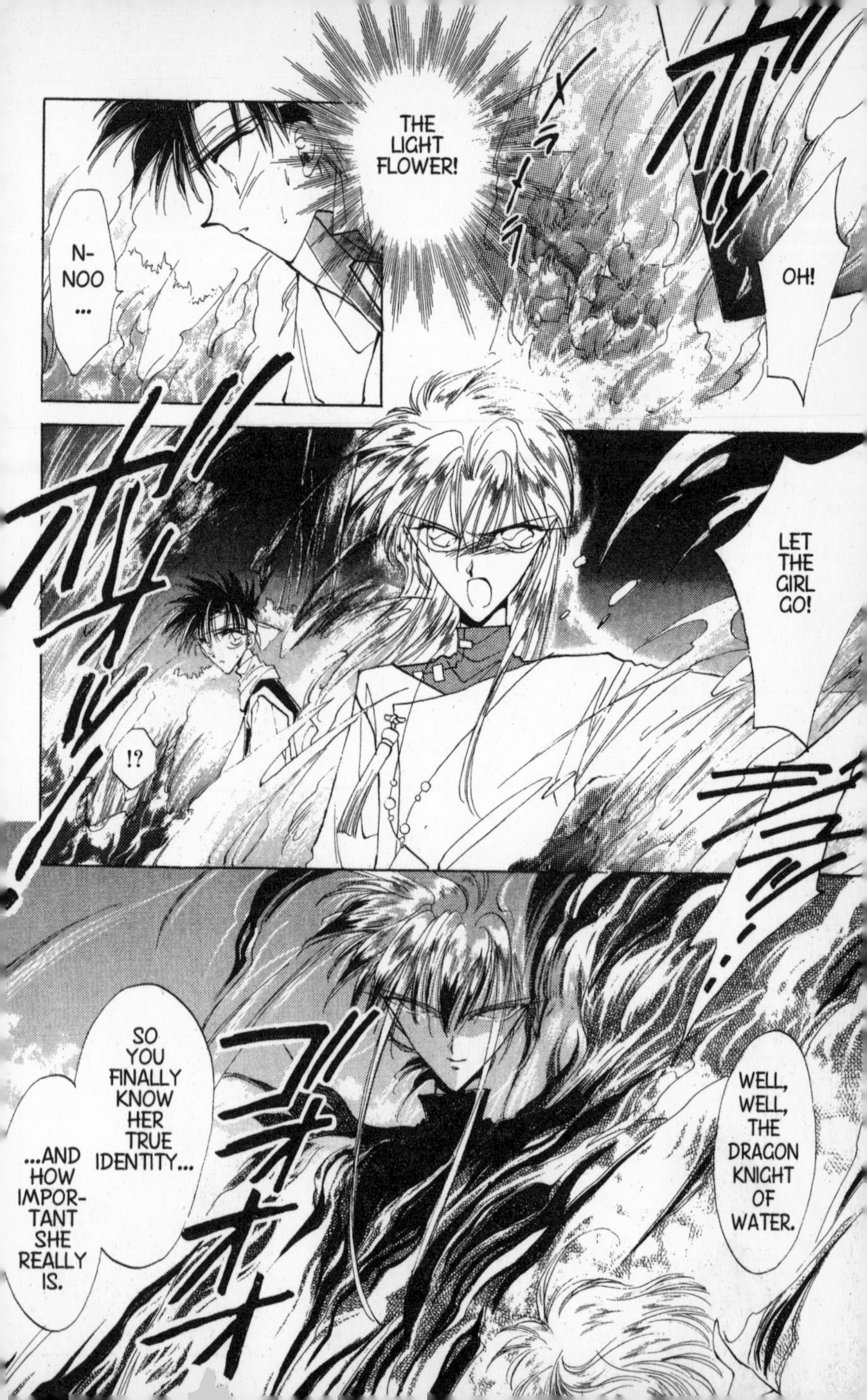

OH!
THE LIGHT FLOWER!
N-NOO ...
LET THE GIRL GO!
!?
WELL, WELL, THE DRAGON KNIGHT OF WATER.
SO YOU FINALLY KNOW HER TRUE IDENTITY...
...AND HOW IMPORTANT SHE REALLY IS.

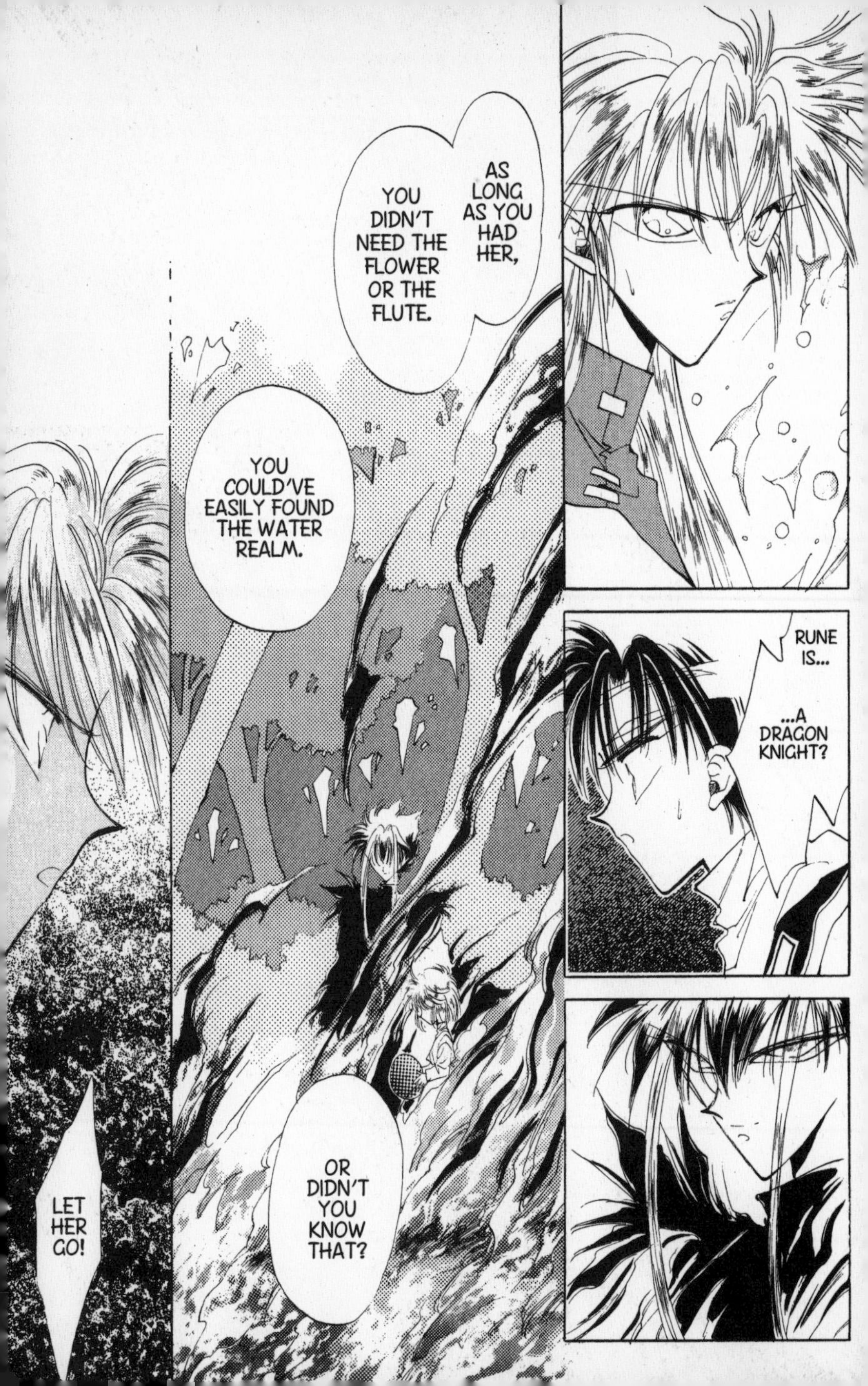
AS LONG AS YOU HAD HER,
YOU DIDN'T NEED THE FLOWER OR THE FLUTE.
YOU COULD'VE EASILY FOUND THE WATER REALM.
OR DIDN'T YOU KNOW THAT?
RUNE IS...
...A DRAGON KNIGHT?
LET HER GO!

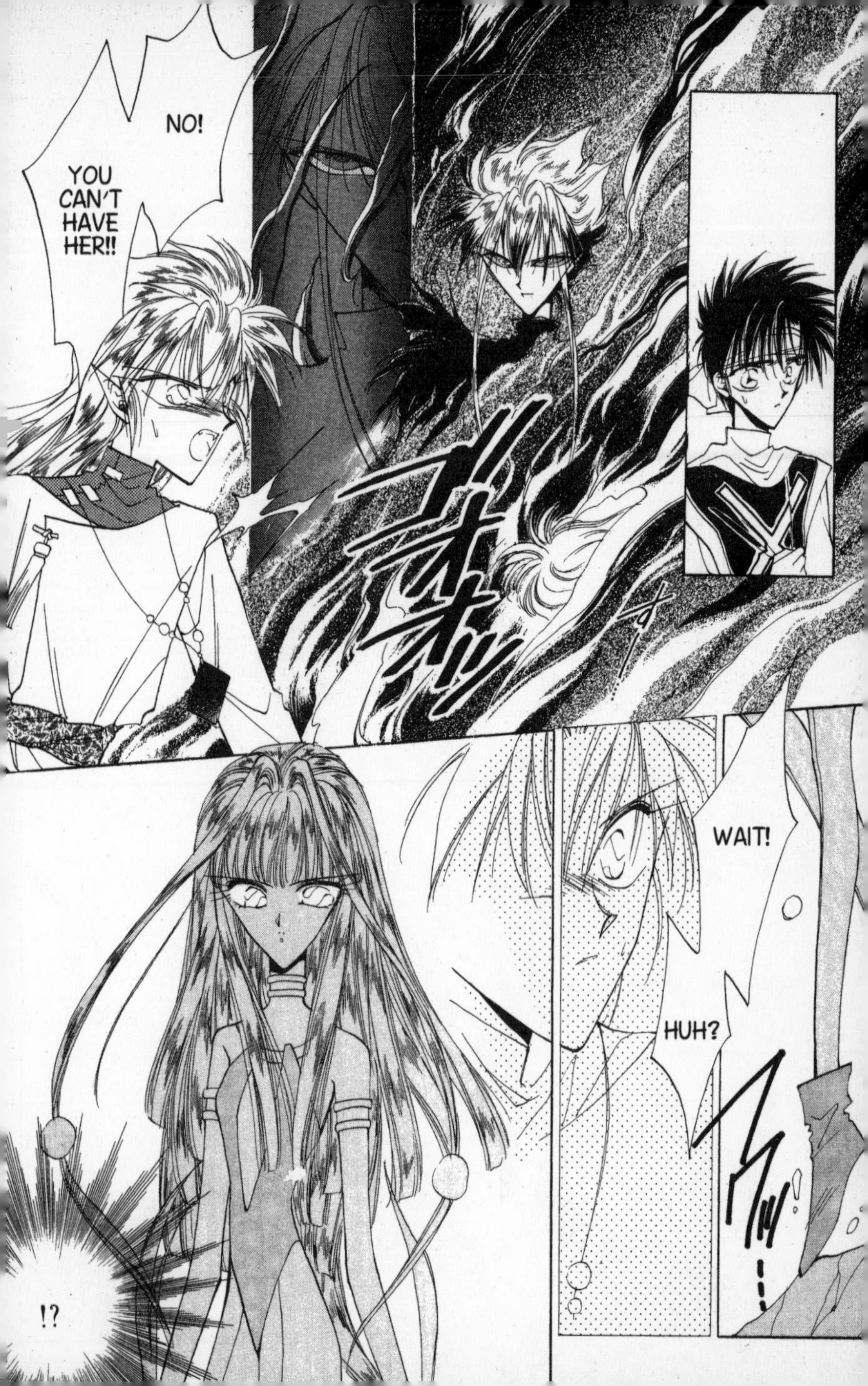
NO!
YOU CAN'T HAVE HER!!
WAIT!
HUH?
!?

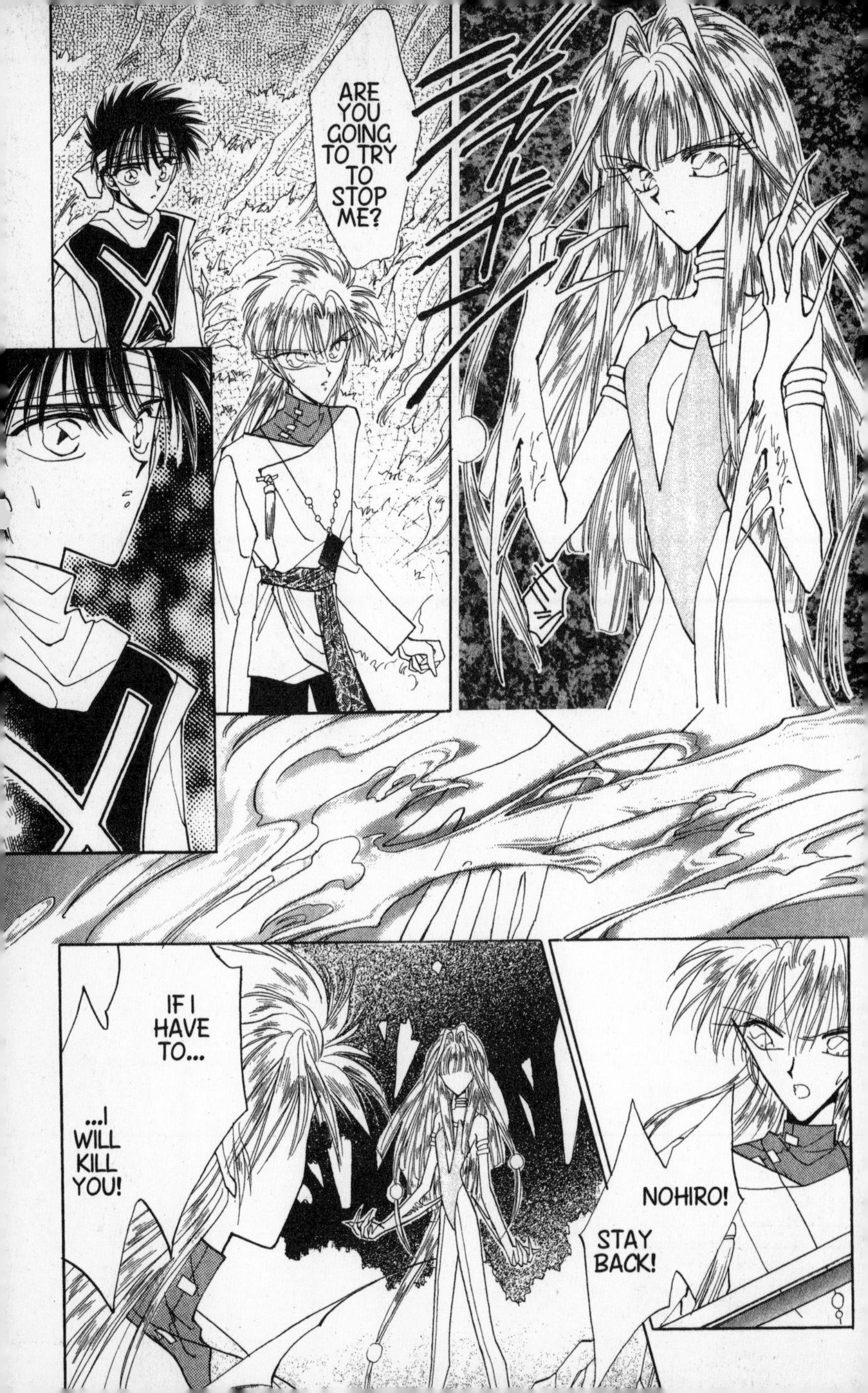
ARE YOU GOING TO TRY TO STOP ME?
NOHIRO!
STAY BACK!
IF I HAVE TO...
...I WILL KILL YOU!

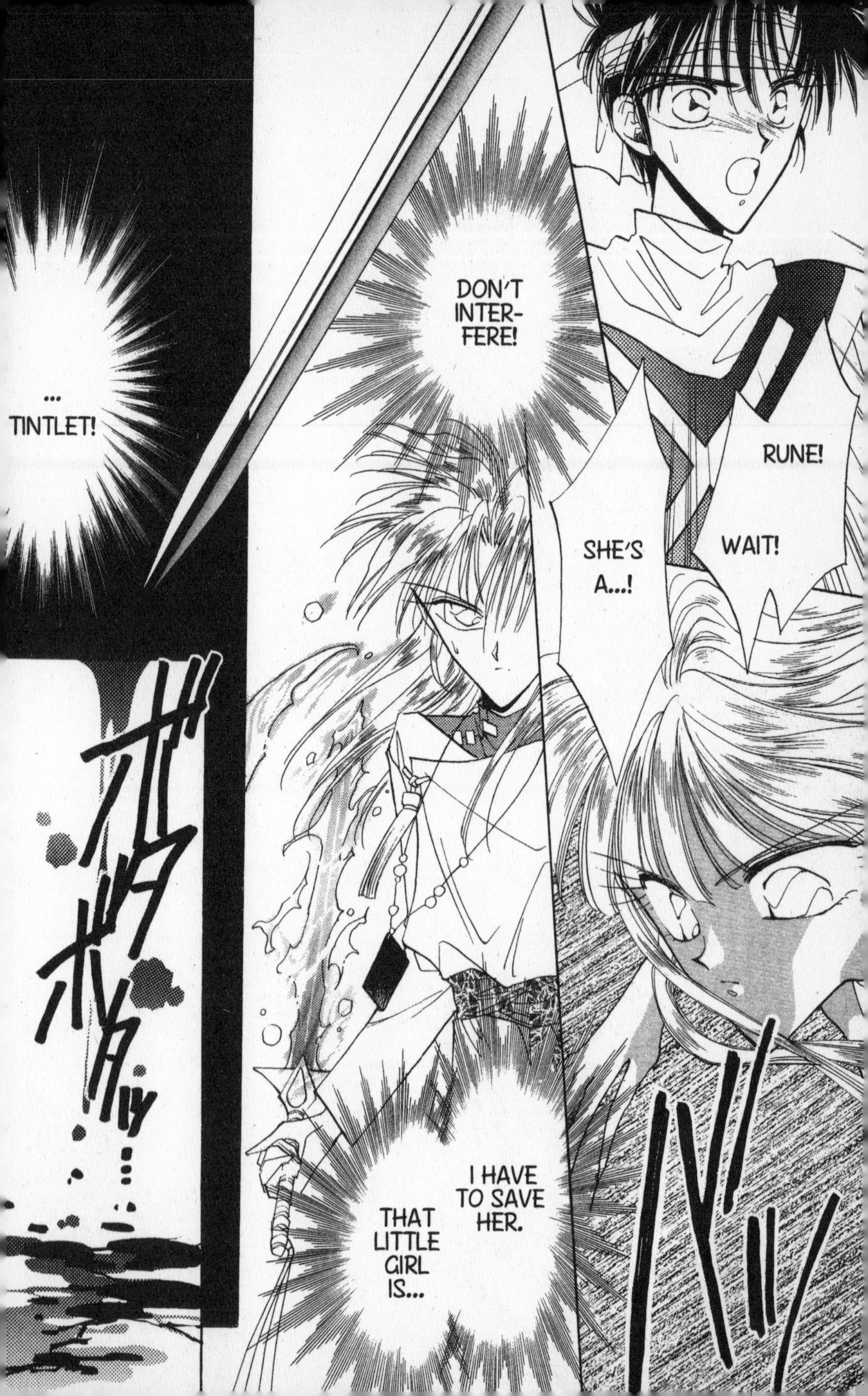
RUNE!
WAIT!
SHE'S A...!
DON'T INTERFERE!
I HAVE TO SAVE HER.
THAT LITTLE GIRL IS...
... TINTLET!

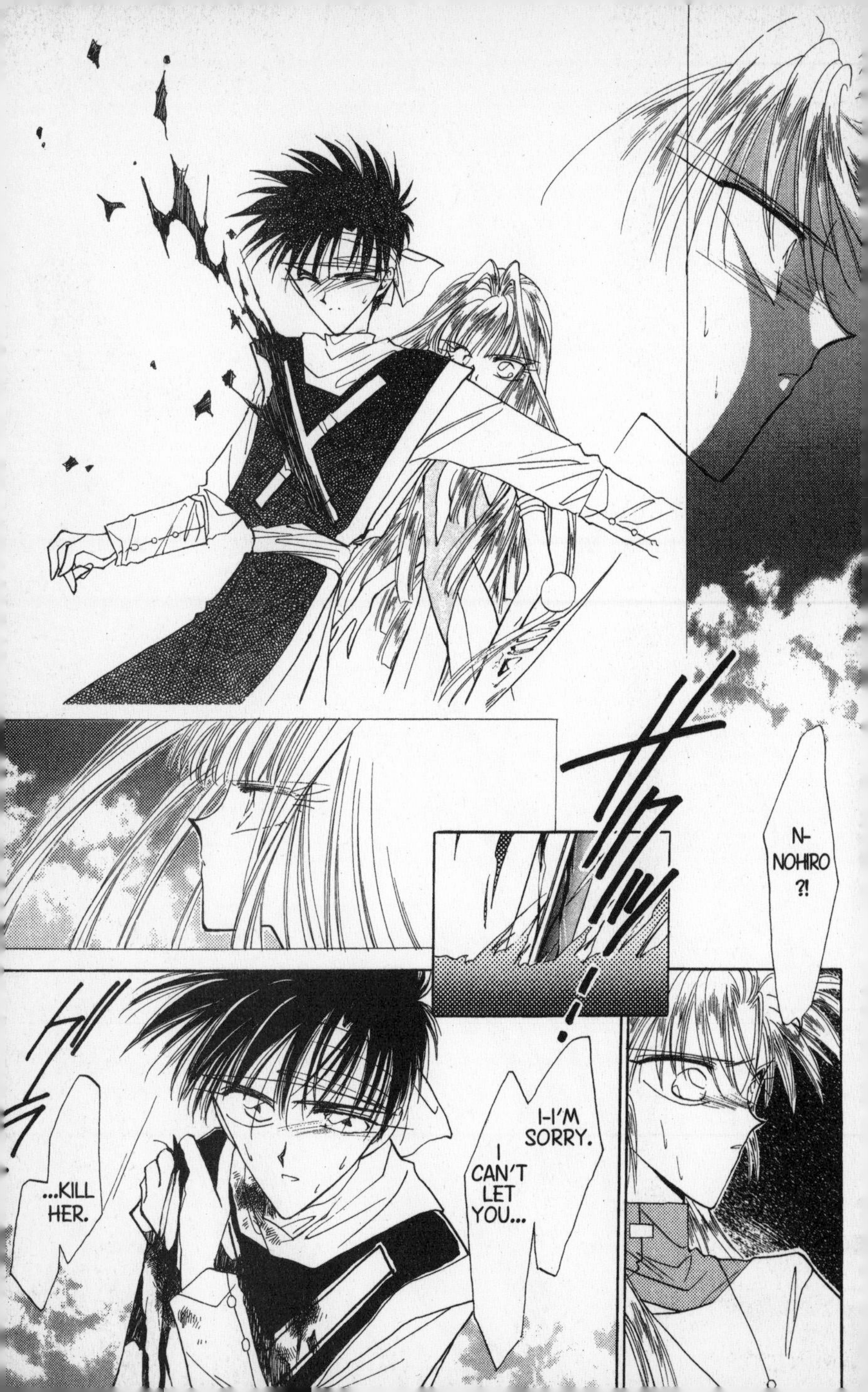
N-NOHIRO ?!
I-I'M SORRY.
I CAN'T LET YOU...
...KILL HER.

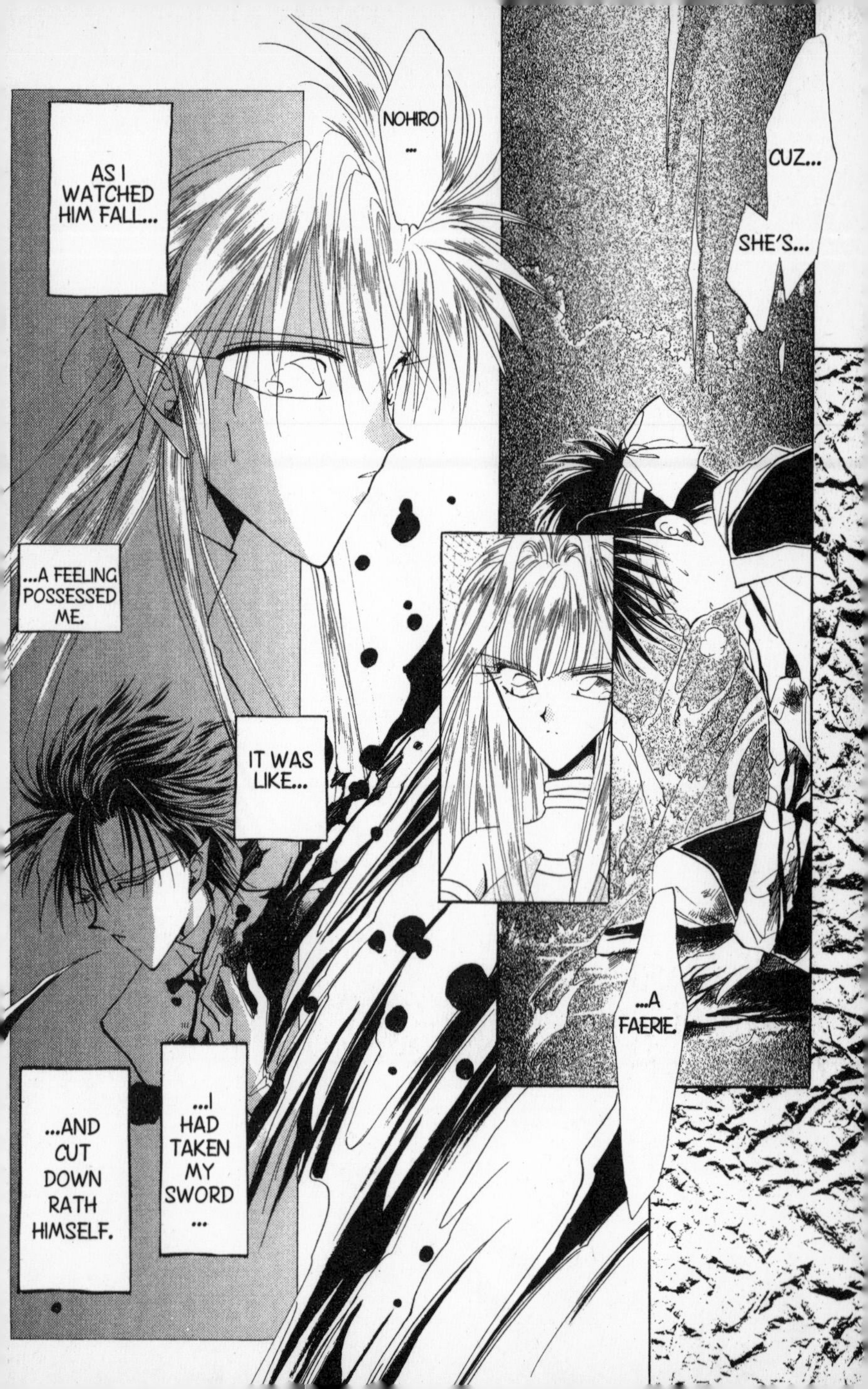
CUZ...
SHE'S...
...A FAERIE.
NOHIRO ...
AS I WATCHED HIM FALL...
...A FEELING POSSESSED ME.
IT WAS LIKE...
...I HAD TAKEN MY SWORD ...
...AND CUT DOWN RATH HIMSELF.

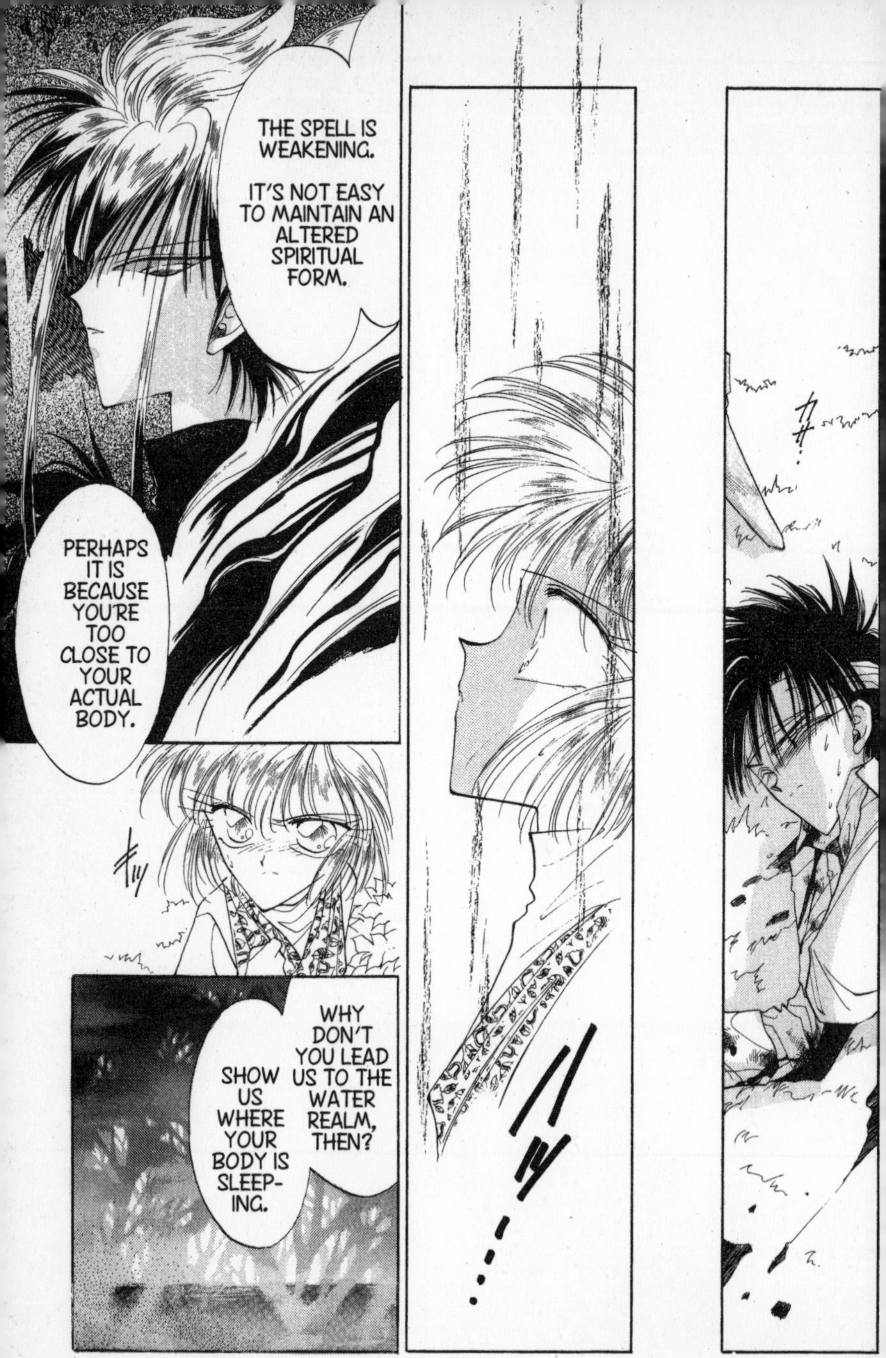
THE SPELL IS WEAKENING.
IT'S NOT EASY TO MAINTAIN AN ALTERED SPIRITUAL FORM.
PERHAPS IT IS BECAUSE YOU'RE TOO CLOSE TO YOUR ACTUAL BODY.
WHY DON'T YOU LEAD US TO THE WATER REALM, THEN?
SHOW US WHERE YOUR BODY IS SLEEP-ING.

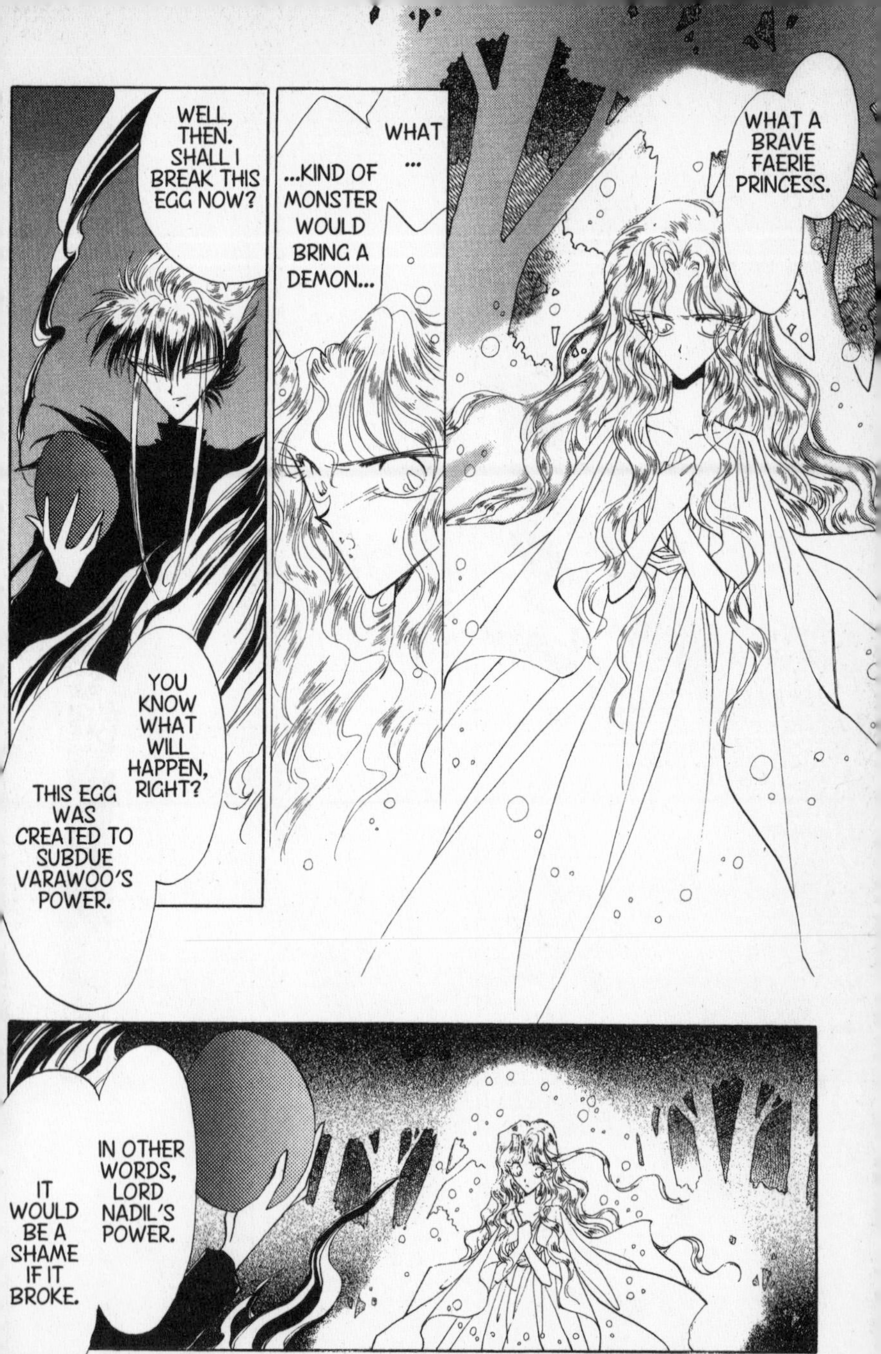
WHAT A BRAVE FAERIE PRINCESS.
WHAT ...
...KIND OF MONSTER WOULD BRING A DEMON...
WELL, THEN. SHALL I BREAK THIS EGG NOW?
YOU KNOW WHAT WILL HAPPEN, RIGHT?
THIS EGG WAS CREATED TO SUBDUE VARAWOO'S POWER.
IN OTHER WORDS, LORD NADIL'S POWER.
IT WOULD BE A SHAME IF IT BROKE.

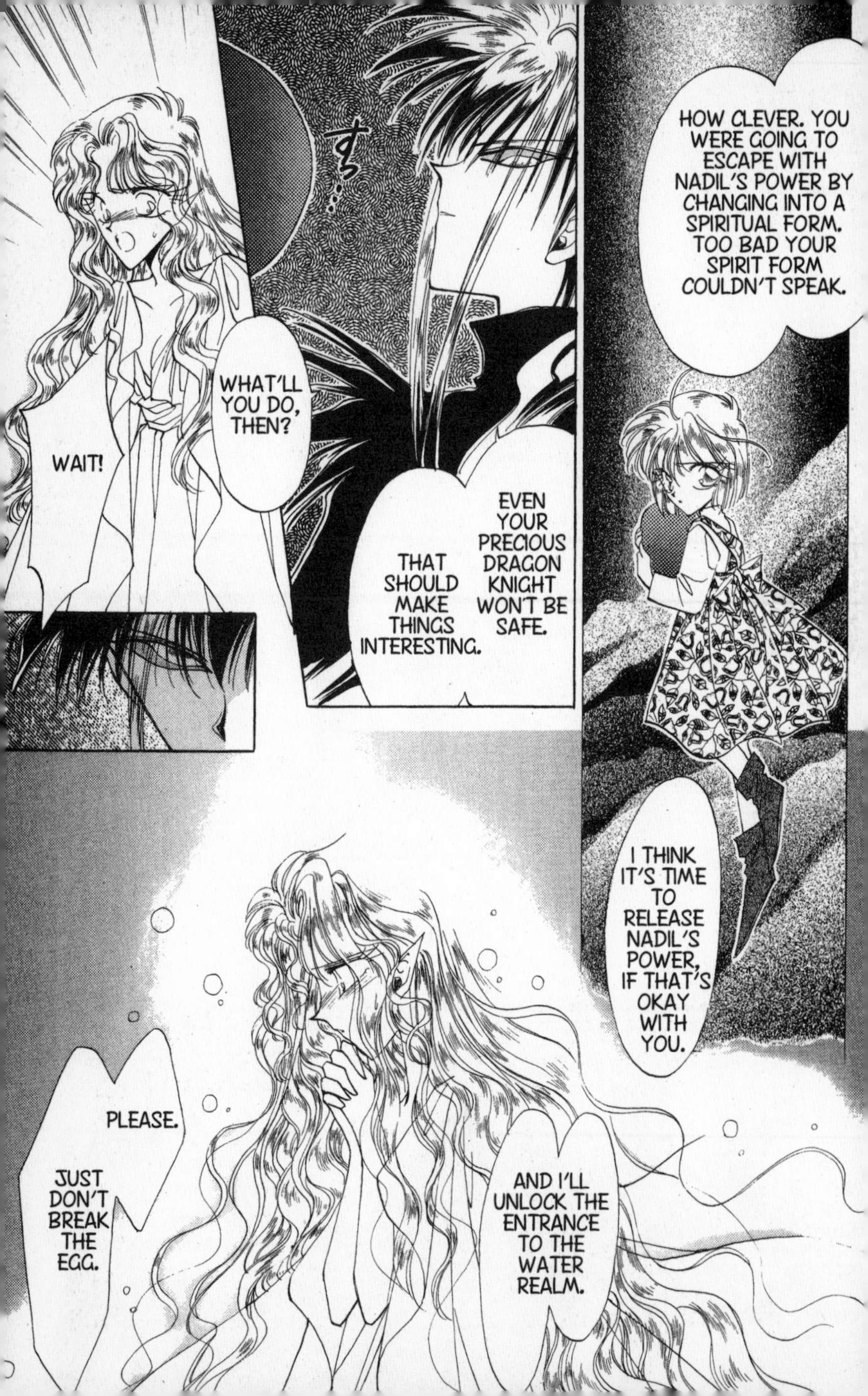
HOW CLEVER. YOU WERE GOING TO ESCAPE WITH NADIL'S POWER BY CHANGING INTO A SPIRITUAL FORM. TOO BAD YOUR SPIRIT FORM COULDN'T SPEAK.
I THINK IT'S TIME TO RELEASE NADIL'S POWER, IF THAT'S OKAY WITH YOU.
WHAT'LL YOU DO, THEN?
EVEN YOUR PRECIOUS DRAGON KNIGHT WON'T BE SAFE.
THAT SHOULD MAKE THINGS INTERESTING.
WAIT!
AND I'LL UNLOCK THE ENTRANCE TO THE WATER REALM.
PLEASE.
JUST DON'T BREAK THE EGG.

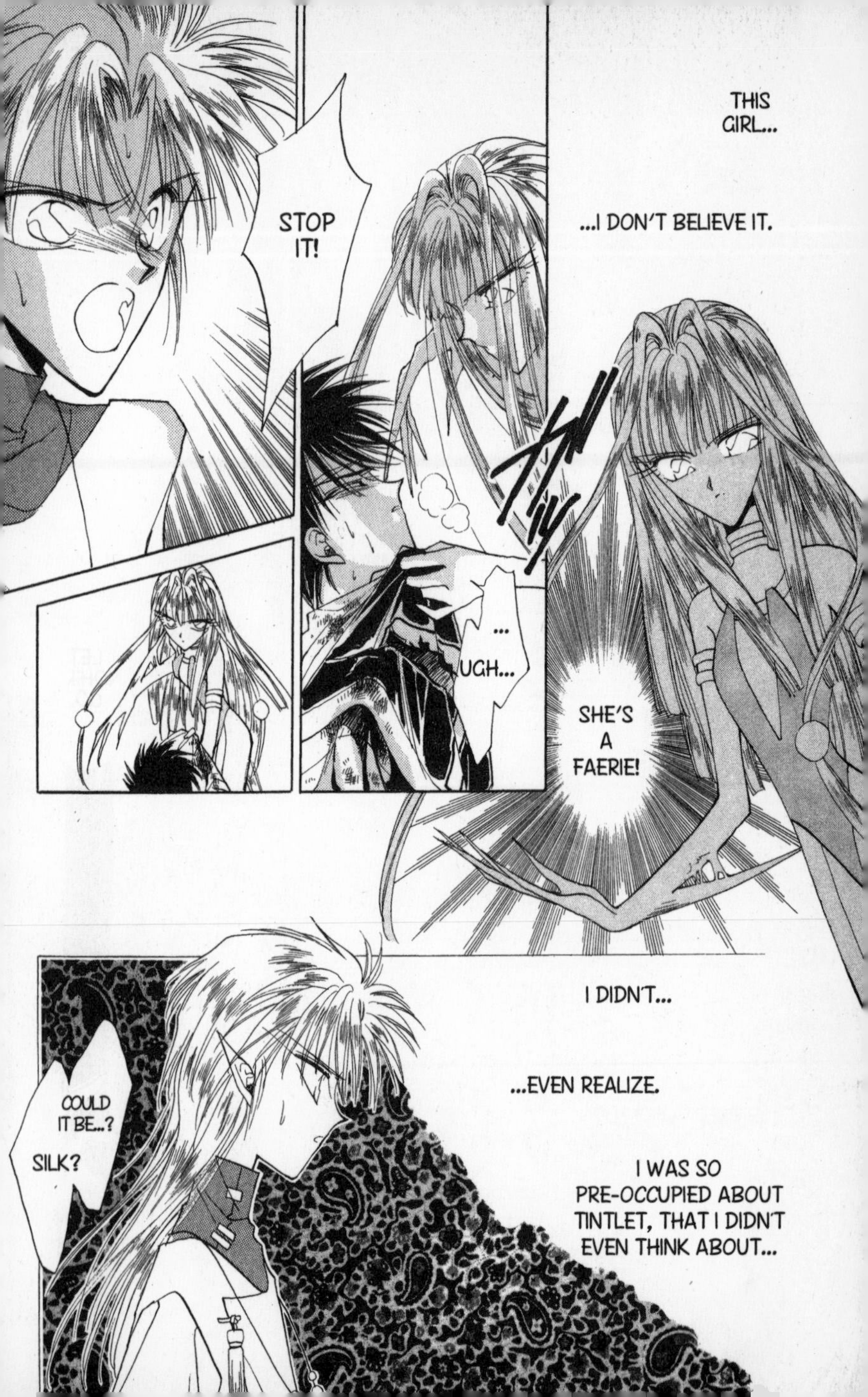
THIS GIRL...
...I DON'T BELIEVE IT.
STOP IT!
...
UGH...
SHE'S A FAERIE!
I DIDN'T...
...EVEN REALIZE.
I WAS SO PRE-OCCUPIED ABOUT TINTLET, THAT I DIDN'T EVEN THINK ABOUT...
COULD IT BE...?
SILK?

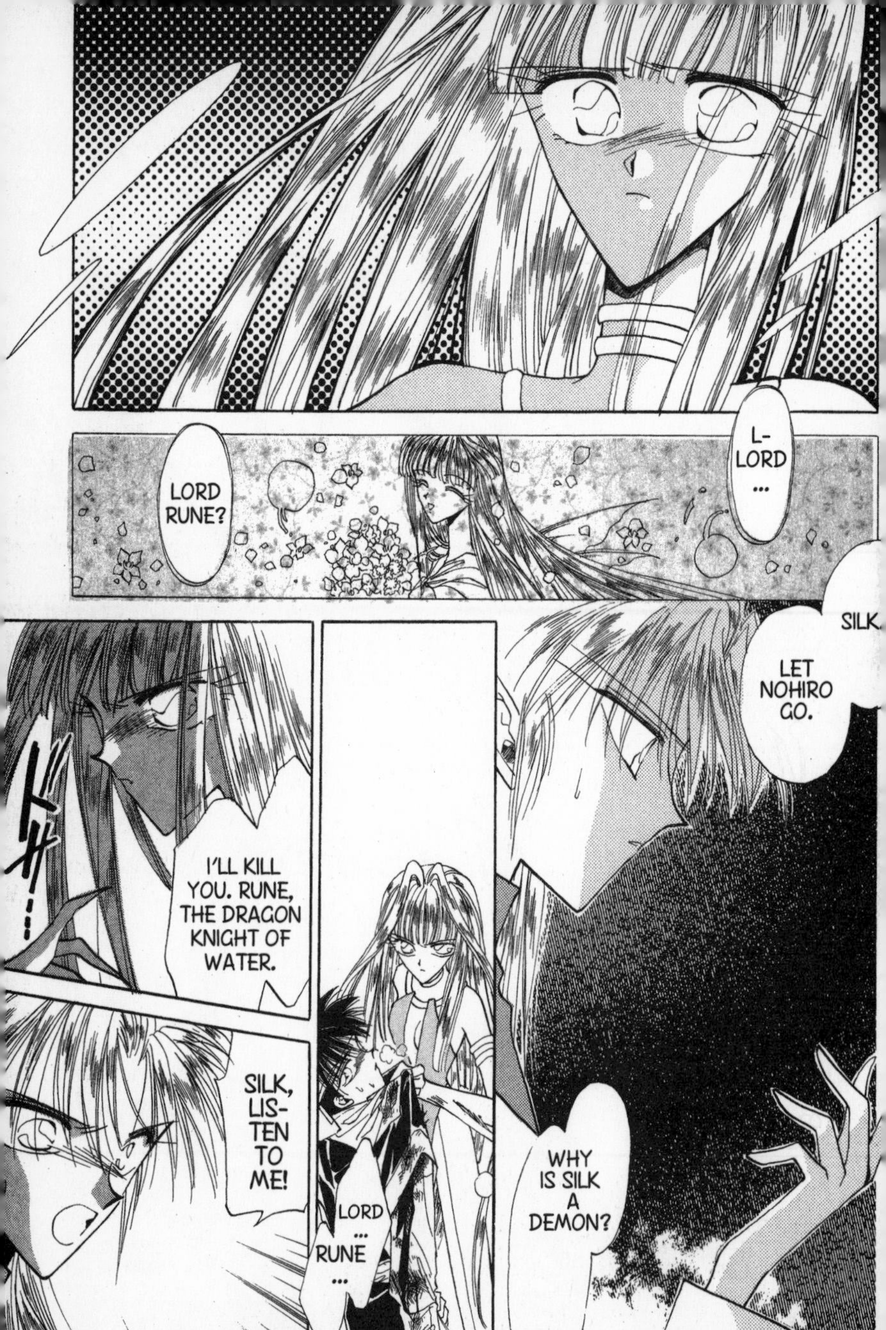
L-LORD...
LORD RUNE?
SILK.
LET NOHIRO GO.
WHY IS SILK A DEMON?
LORD... RUNE...
I'LL KILL YOU. RUNE, THE DRAGON KNIGHT OF WATER.
SILK, LIS-TEN TO ME!

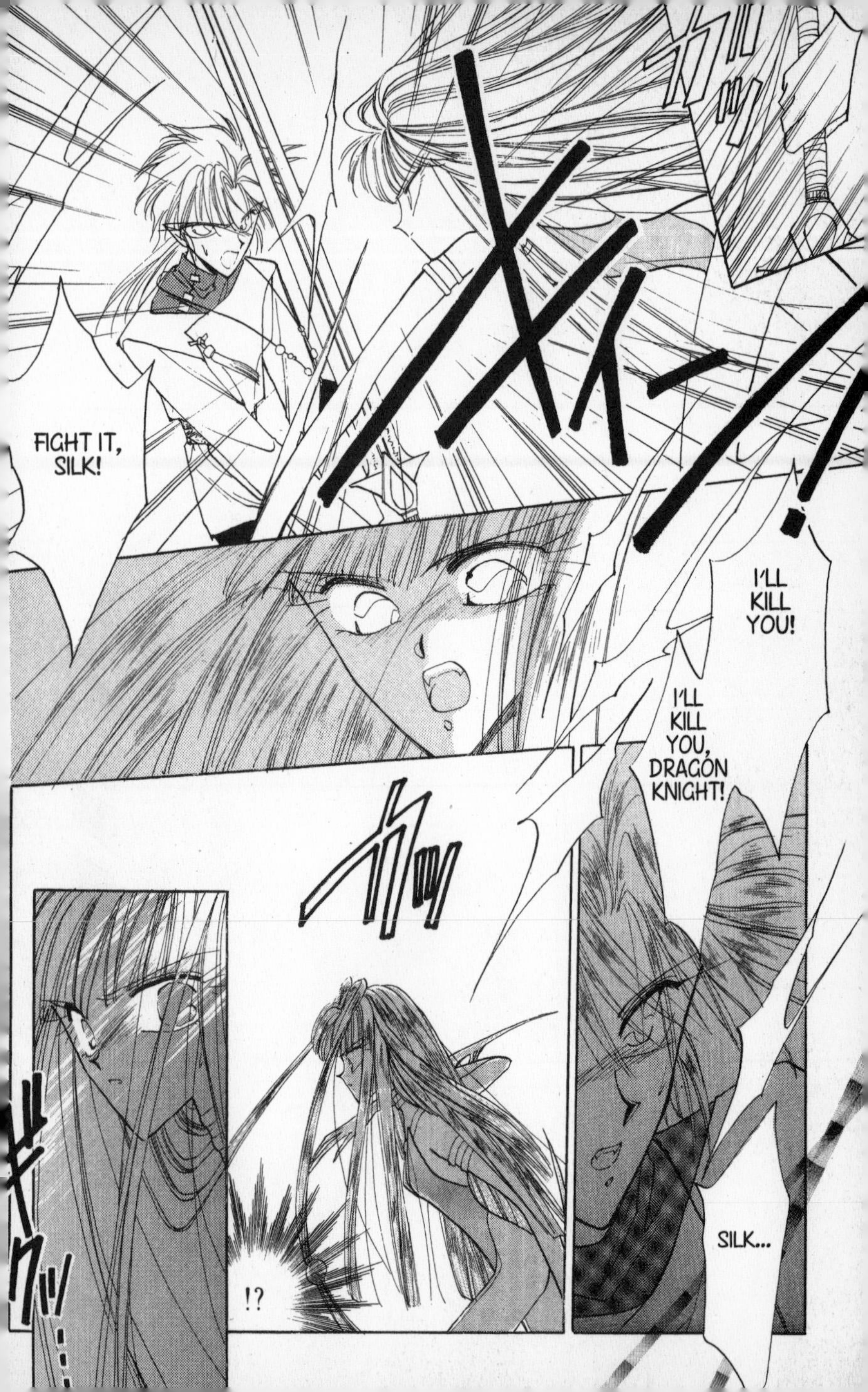
FIGHT IT, SILK!
I'LL KILL YOU!
I'LL KILL YOU, DRAGON KNIGHT!
SILK...
!?

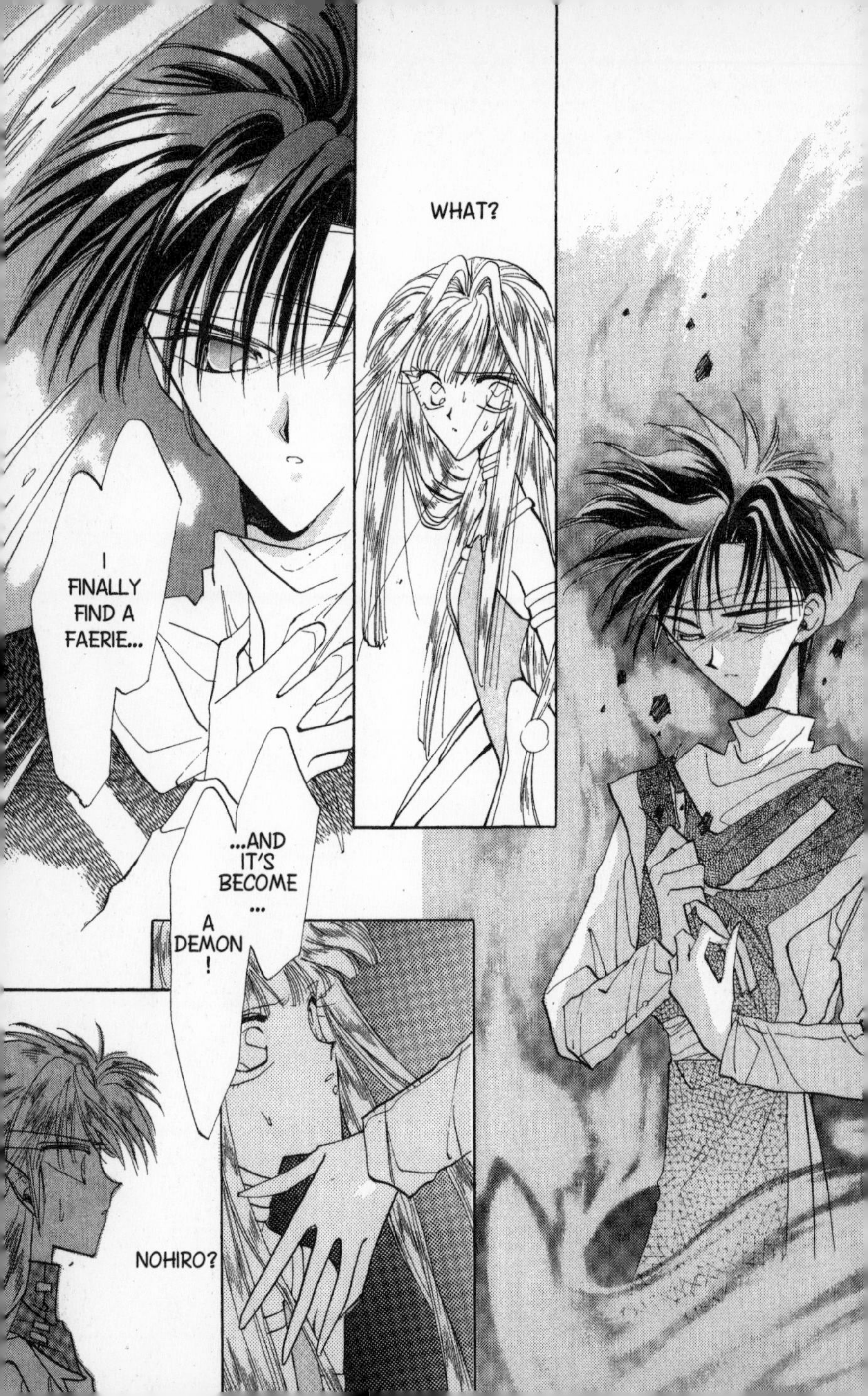
WHAT?
I FINALLY FIND A FAERIE...
...AND IT'S BECOME ... A DEMON!
NOHIRO?

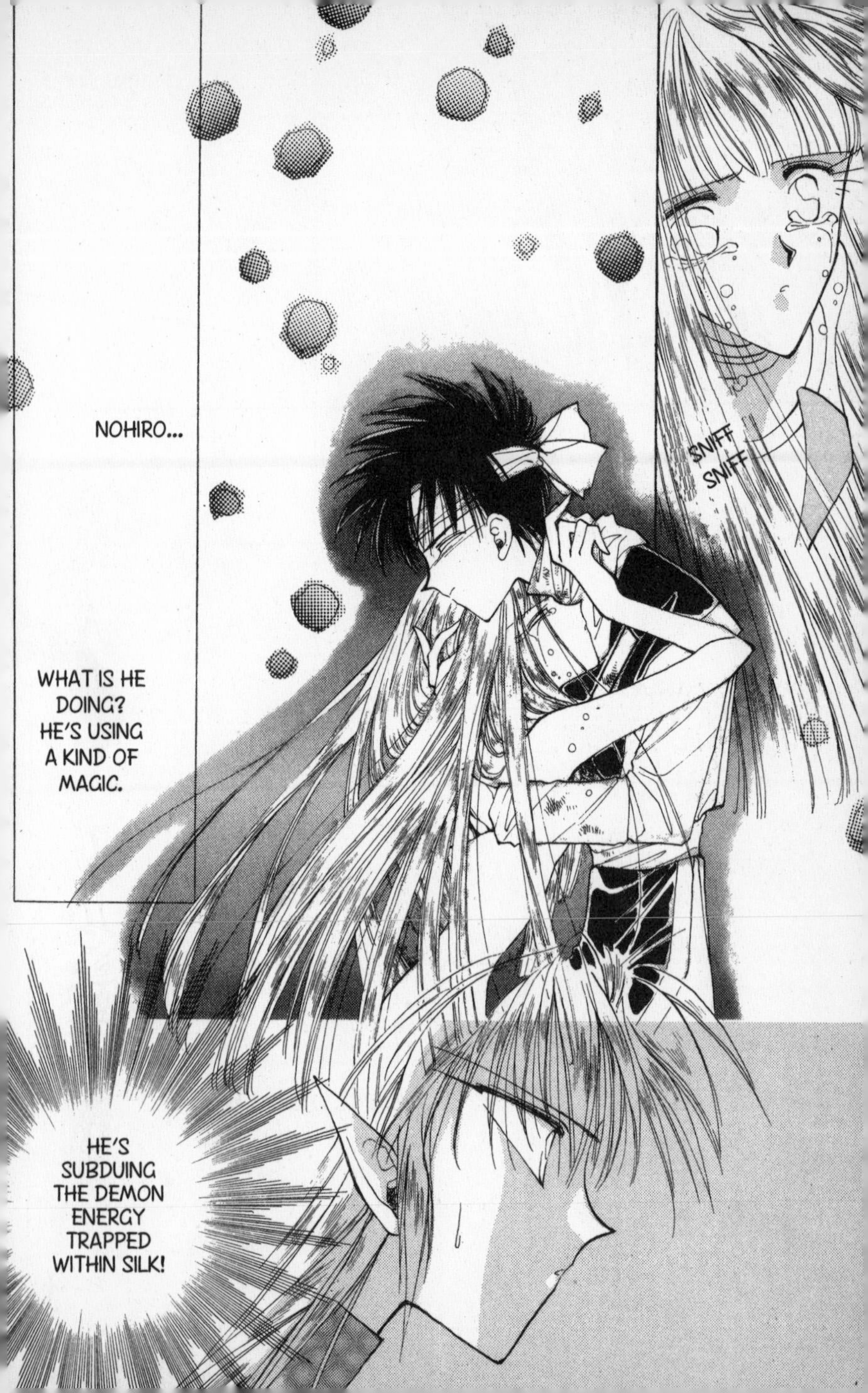
SNIFF
SNIFF
NOHIRO...
WHAT IS HE DOING? HE'S USING A KIND OF MAGIC.
HE'S SUBDUING THE DEMON ENERGY TRAPPED WITHIN SILK!

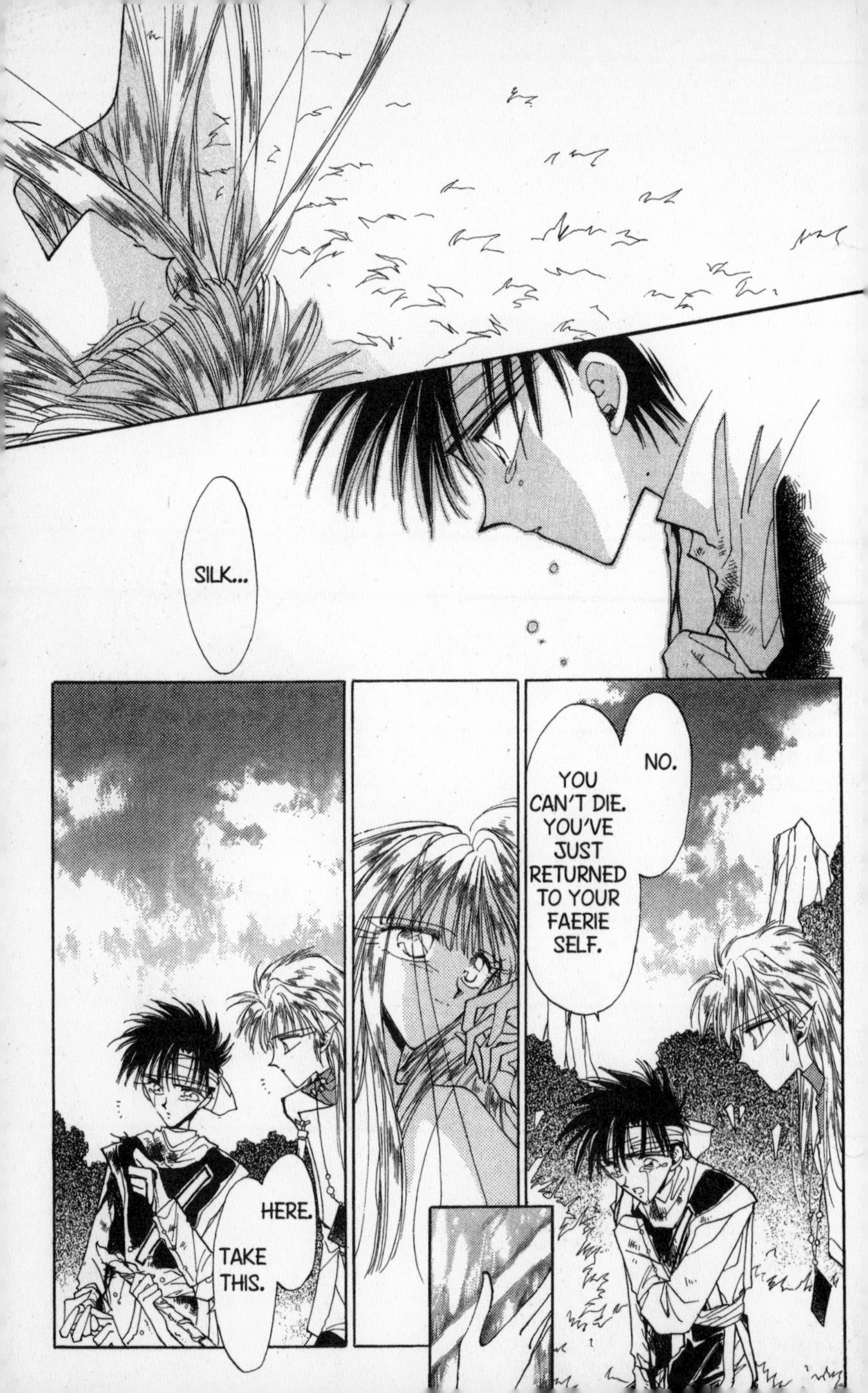
SILK...
NO.
YOU CAN'T DIE. YOU'VE JUST RETURNED TO YOUR FAERIE SELF.
HERE.
TAKE THIS.

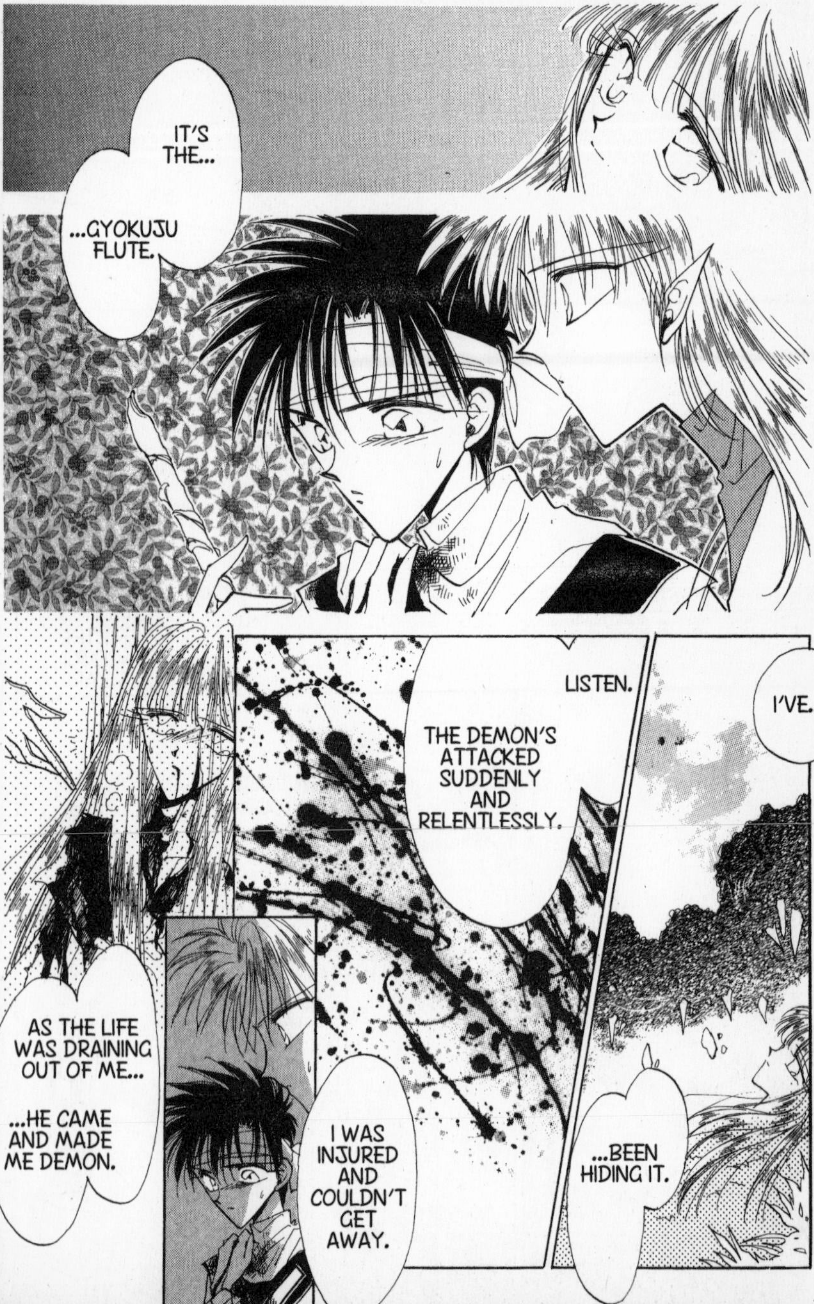
IT'S THE...
...GYOKUJU FLUTE.
I'VE...
...BEEN HIDING IT.
LISTEN.
THE DEMON'S ATTACKED SUDDENLY AND RELENTLESSLY.
I WAS INJURED AND COULDN'T GET AWAY.
AS THE LIFE WAS DRAINING OUT OF ME...
...HE CAME AND MADE ME DEMON.

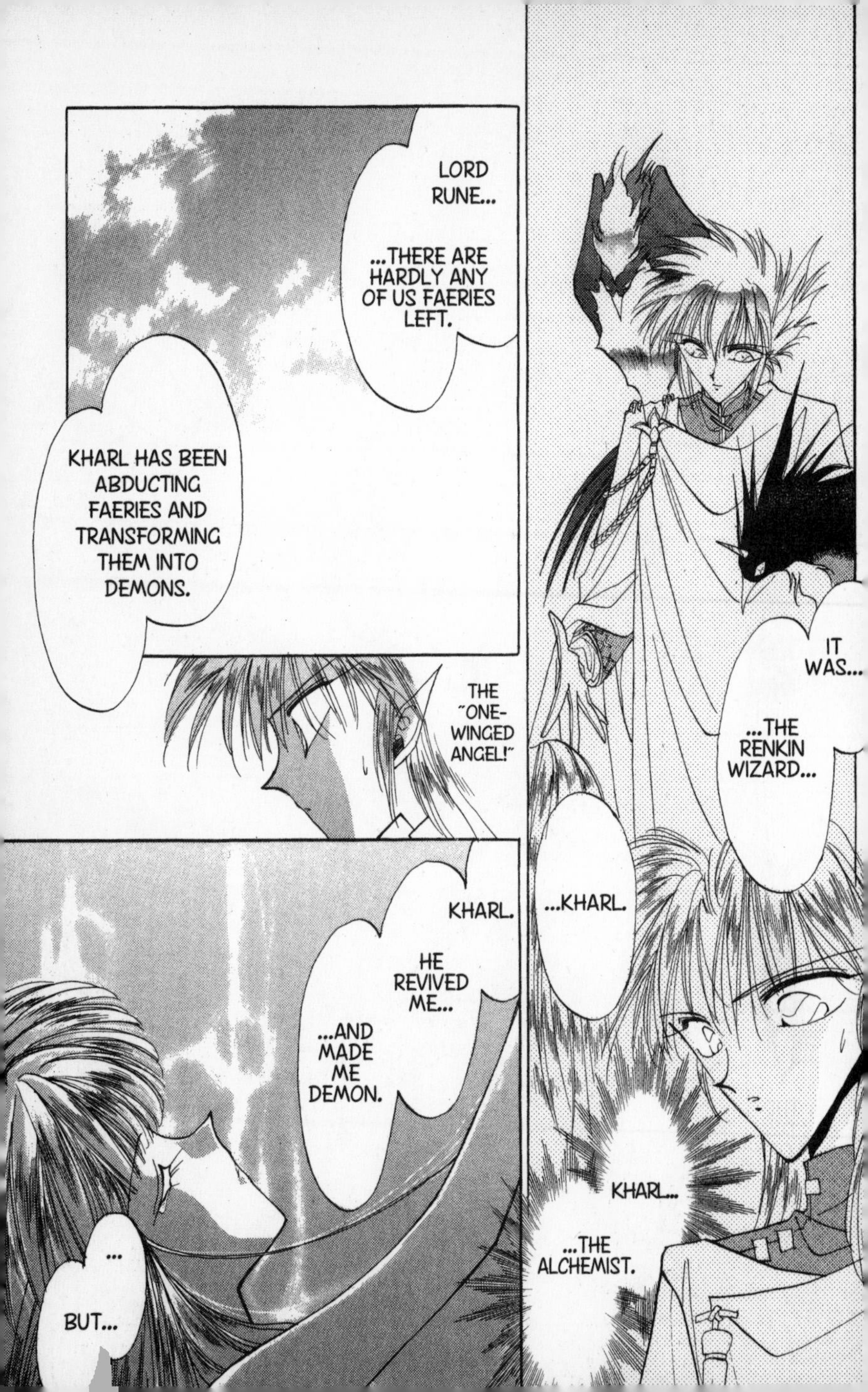
IT WAS...
...THE RENKIN WIZARD...
...KHARL.
KHARL...
...THE ALCHEMIST.
LORD RUNE...
...THERE ARE HARDLY ANY OF US FAERIES LEFT.
KHARL HAS BEEN ABDUCTING FAERIES AND TRANSFORMING THEM INTO DEMONS.
THE "ONE-WINGED ANGEL!"
KHARL.
HE REVIVED ME...
...AND MADE ME DEMON.
...
BUT...

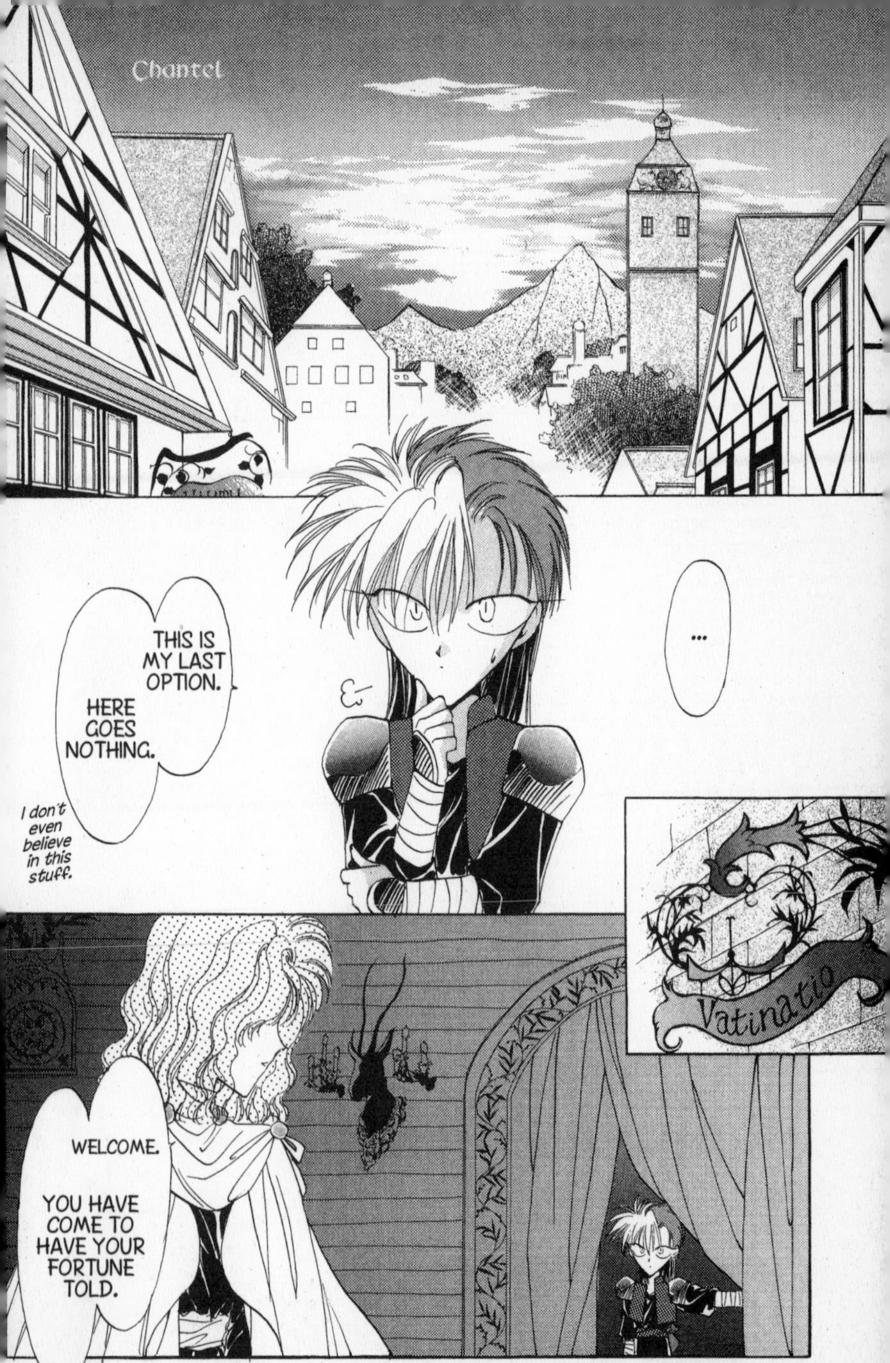
...
THIS IS MY LAST OPTION.
HERE GOES NOTHING.
I don't even believe in this stuff.
Vatinatio
WELCOME.
YOU HAVE COME TO HAVE YOUR FORTUNE TOLD.

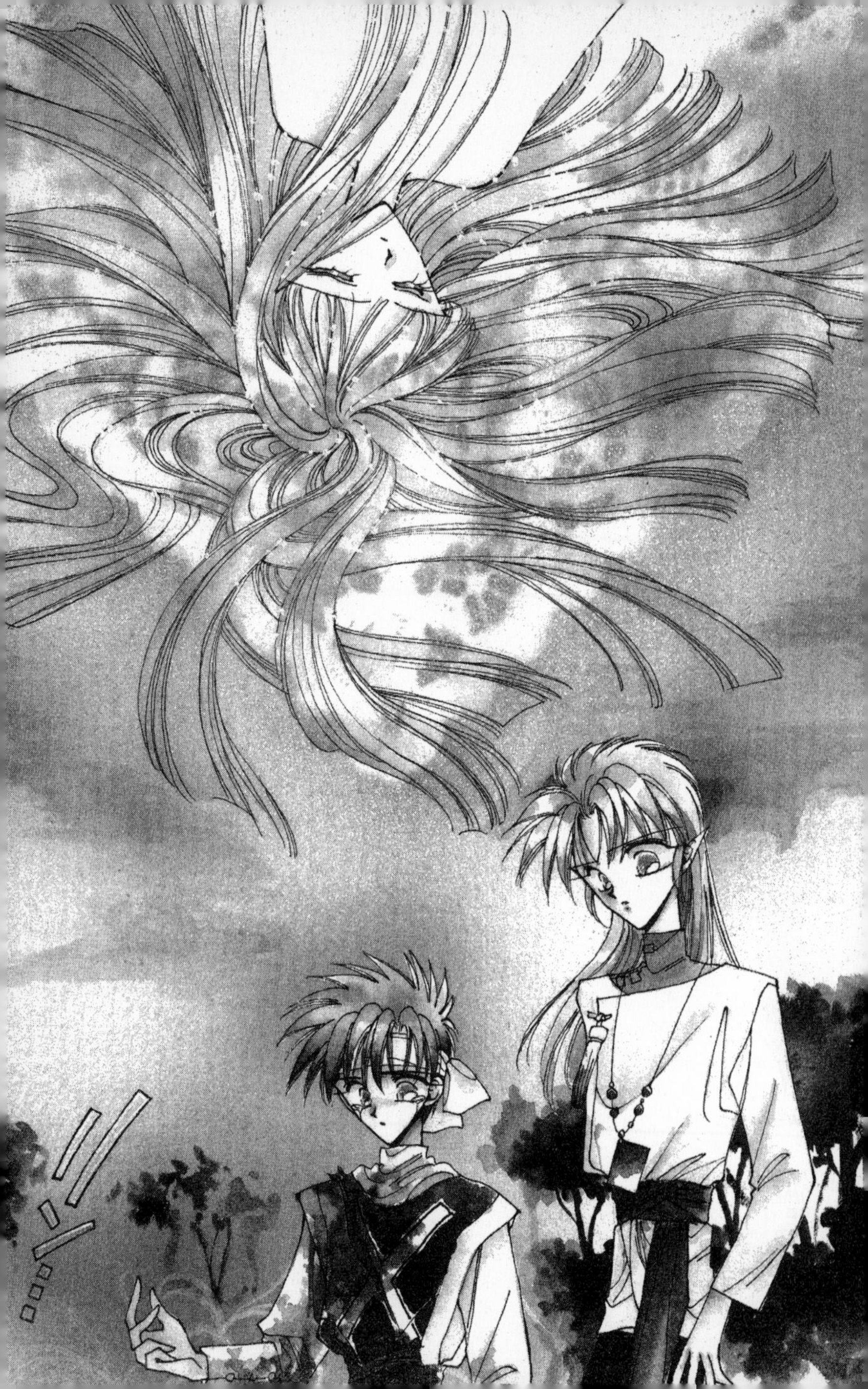

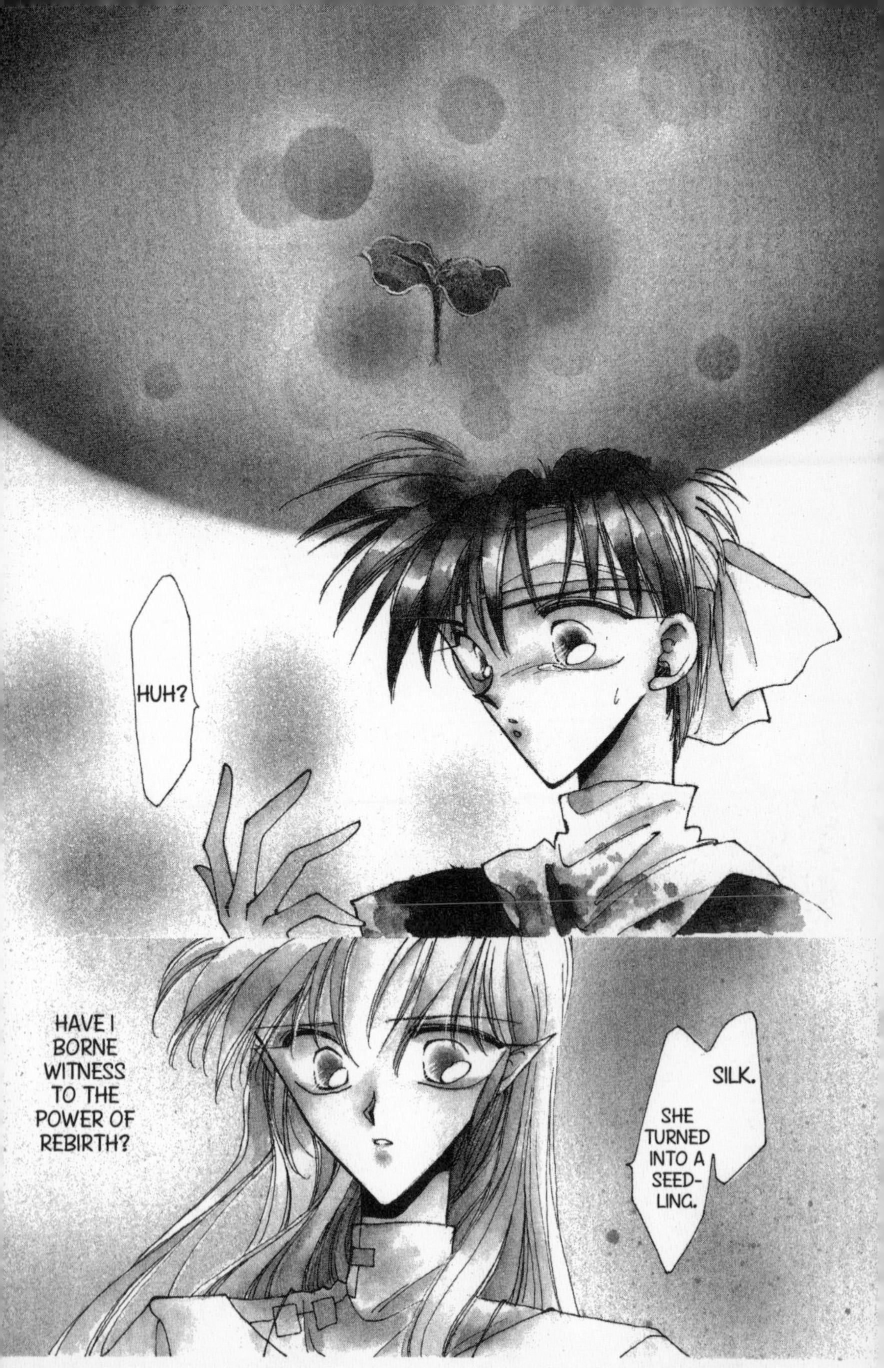
HUH?
SILK.
SHE TURNED INTO A SEED-LING.
HAVE I BORNE WITNESS TO THE POWER OF REBIRTH?

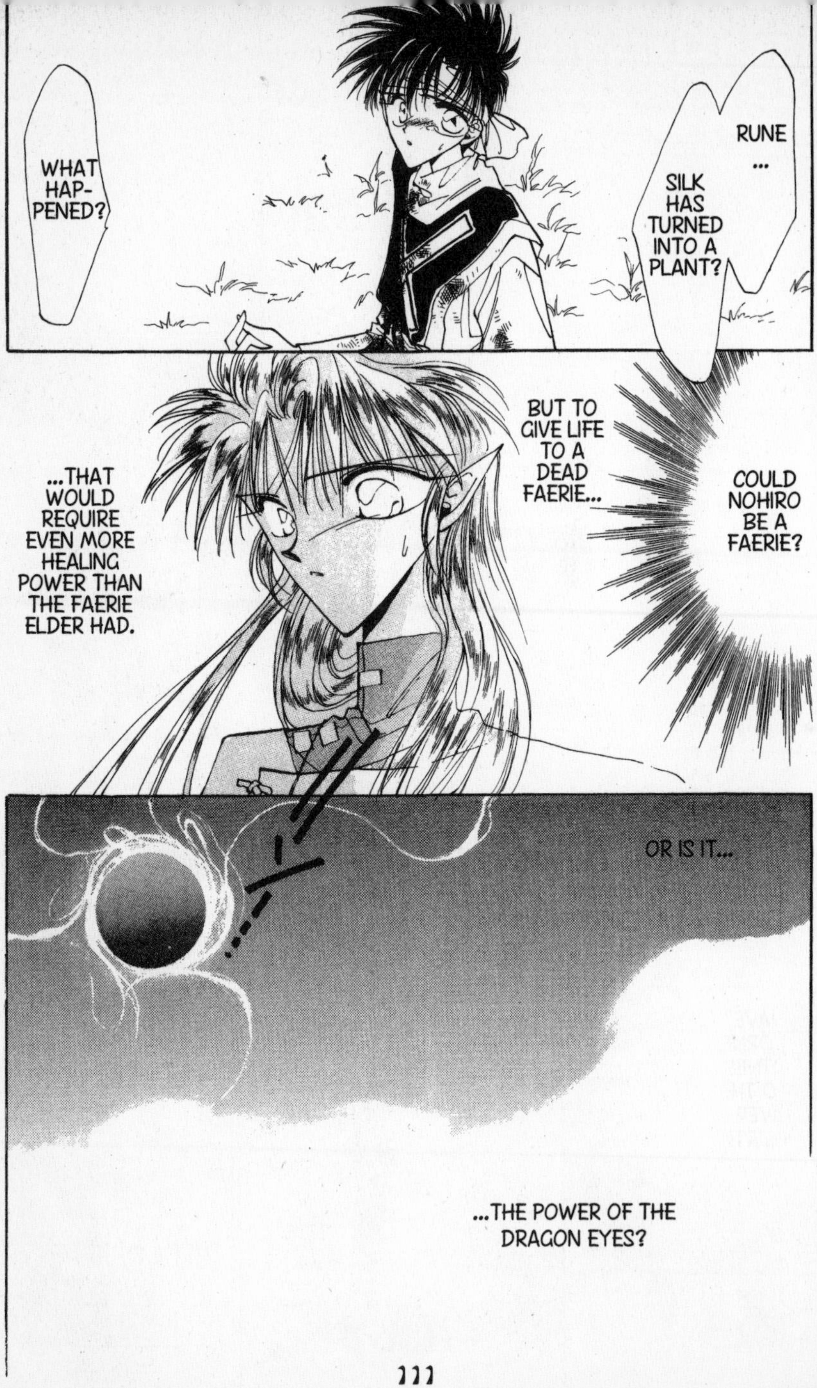
RUNE ... SILK HAS TURNED INTO A PLANT?
WHAT HAP-PENED?
COULD NOHIRO BE A FAERIE?
BUT TO GIVE LIFE TO A DEAD FAERIE...
...THAT WOULD REQUIRE EVEN MORE HEALING POWER THAN THE FAERIE ELDER HAD.
OR IS IT...
...THE POWER OF THE DRAGON EYES?

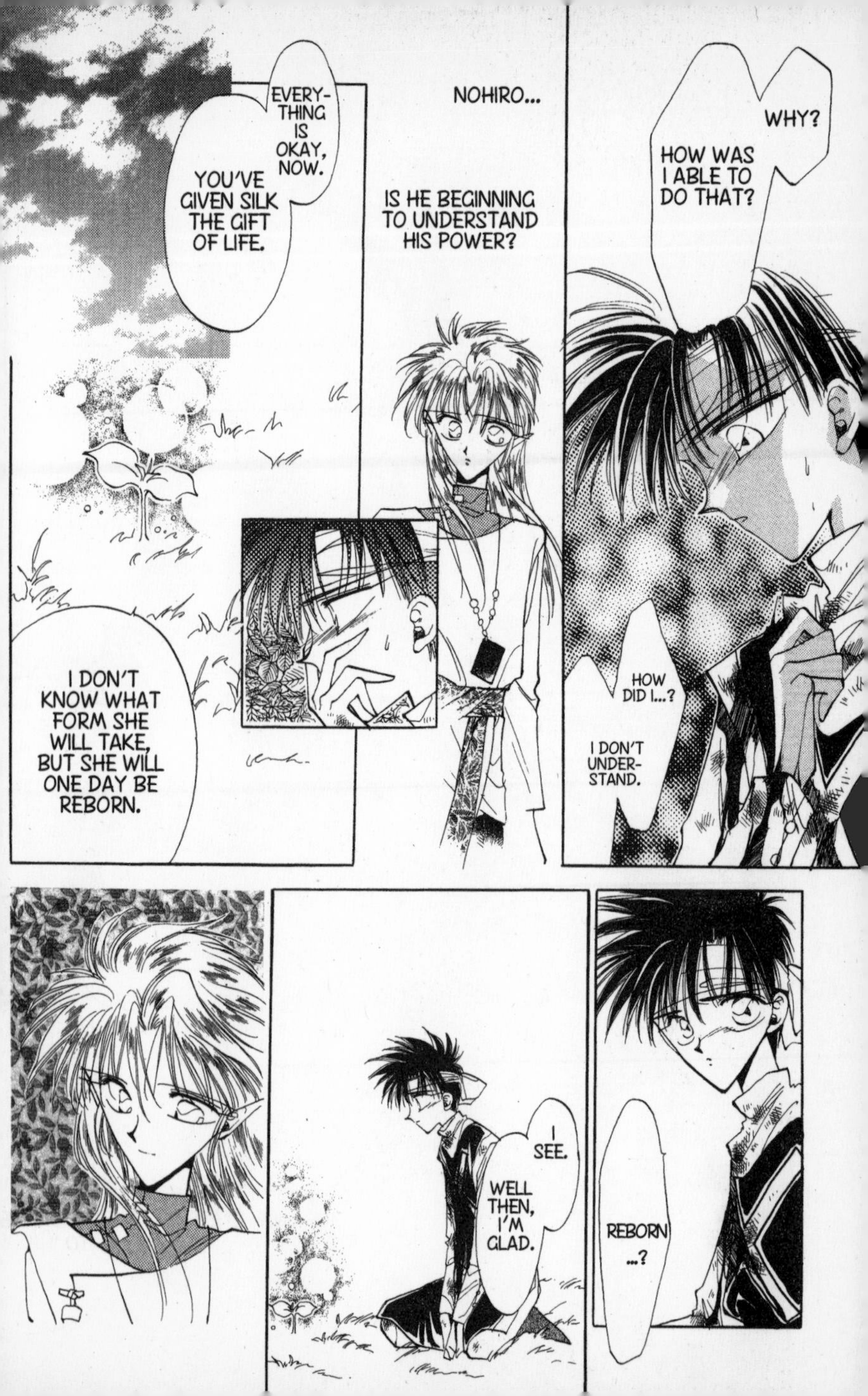
WHY?
HOW WAS I ABLE TO DO THAT?
HOW DID I...?
I DON'T UNDERSTAND.
NOHIRO...
IS HE BEGINNING TO UNDERSTAND HIS POWER?
EVERYTHING IS OKAY, NOW.
YOU'VE GIVEN SILK THE GIFT OF LIFE.
I DON'T KNOW WHAT FORM SHE WILL TAKE, BUT SHE WILL ONE DAY BE REBORN.
REBORN ...?
I SEE.
WELL THEN, I'M GLAD.

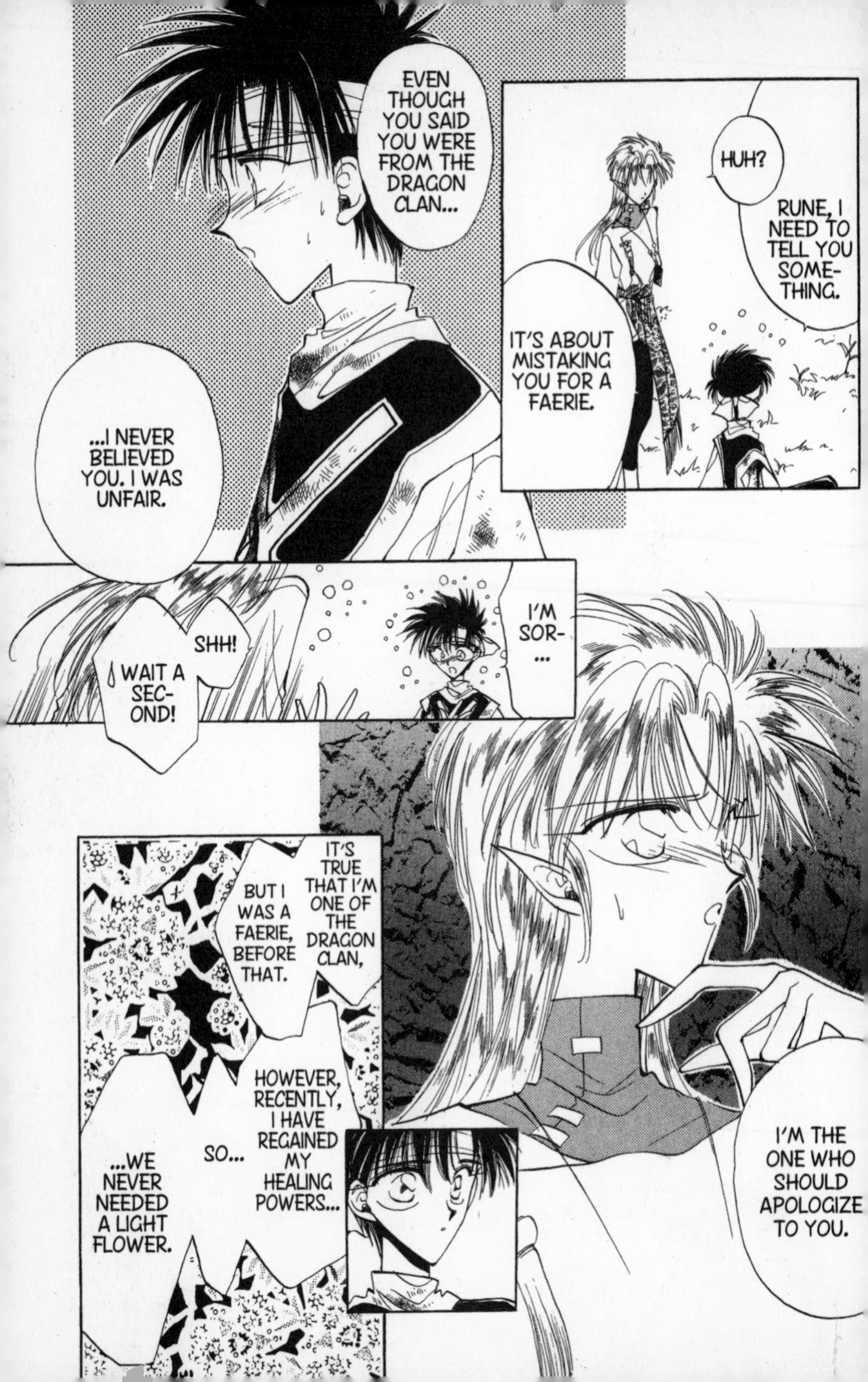
HUH?
RUNE, I NEED TO TELL YOU SOME-THING.
IT'S ABOUT MISTAKING YOU FOR A FAERIE.
EVEN THOUGH YOU SAID YOU WERE FROM THE DRAGON CLAN...
...I NEVER BELIEVED YOU. I WAS UNFAIR.
I'M SOR-...
SHH!
WAIT A SEC-OND!
I'M THE ONE WHO SHOULD APOLOGIZE TO YOU.
IT'S TRUE THAT I'M ONE OF THE DRAGON CLAN,
BUT I WAS A FAERIE, BEFORE THAT.
HOWEVER, RECENTLY, I HAVE REGAINED MY HEALING POWERS...
SO...
...WE NEVER NEEDED A LIGHT FLOWER.

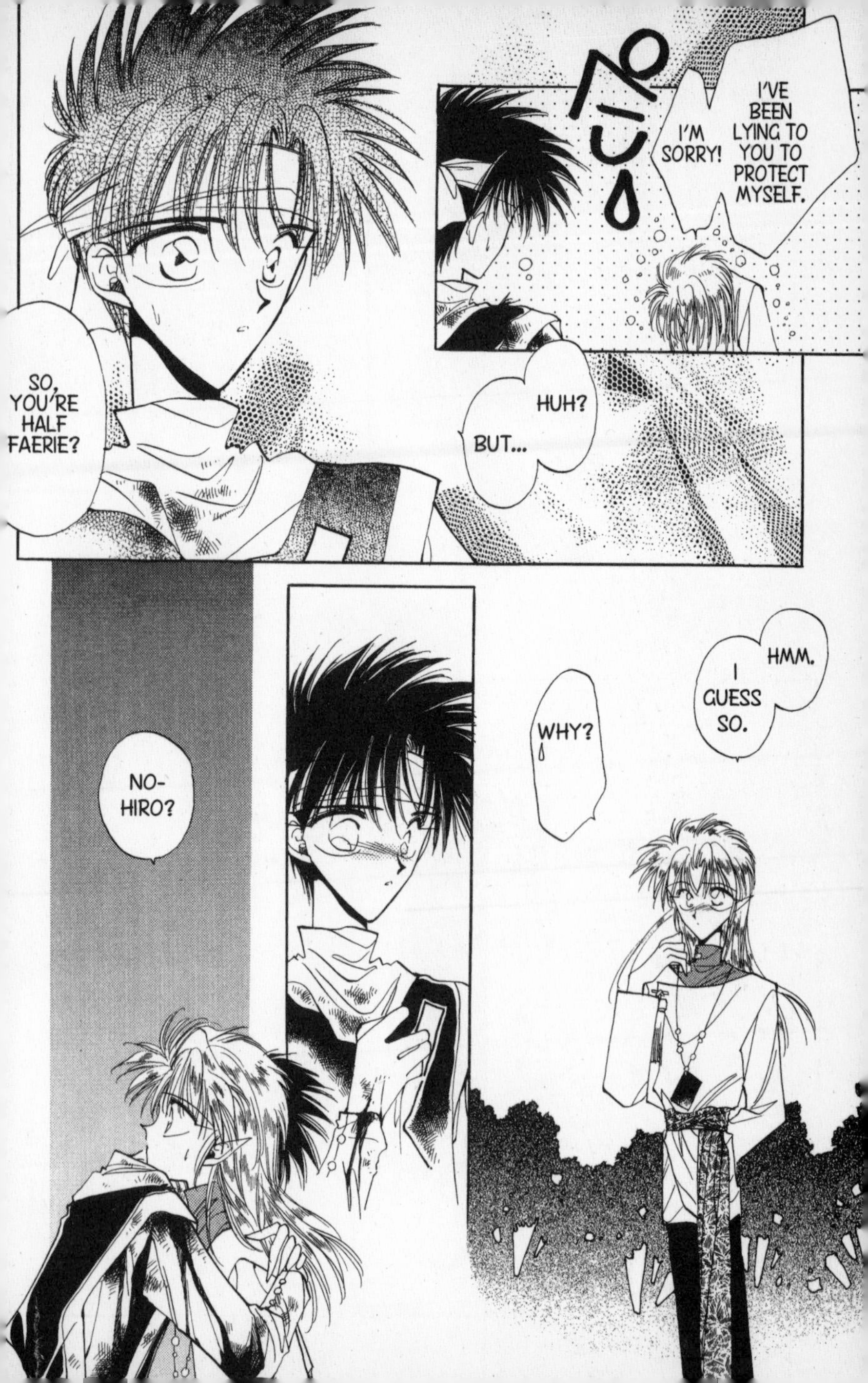
I'M SORRY! I'VE BEEN LYING TO YOU TO PROTECT MYSELF.
HUH? BUT...
SO, YOU'RE HALF FAERIE?
HMM. I GUESS SO.
WHY?
NO-HIRO?

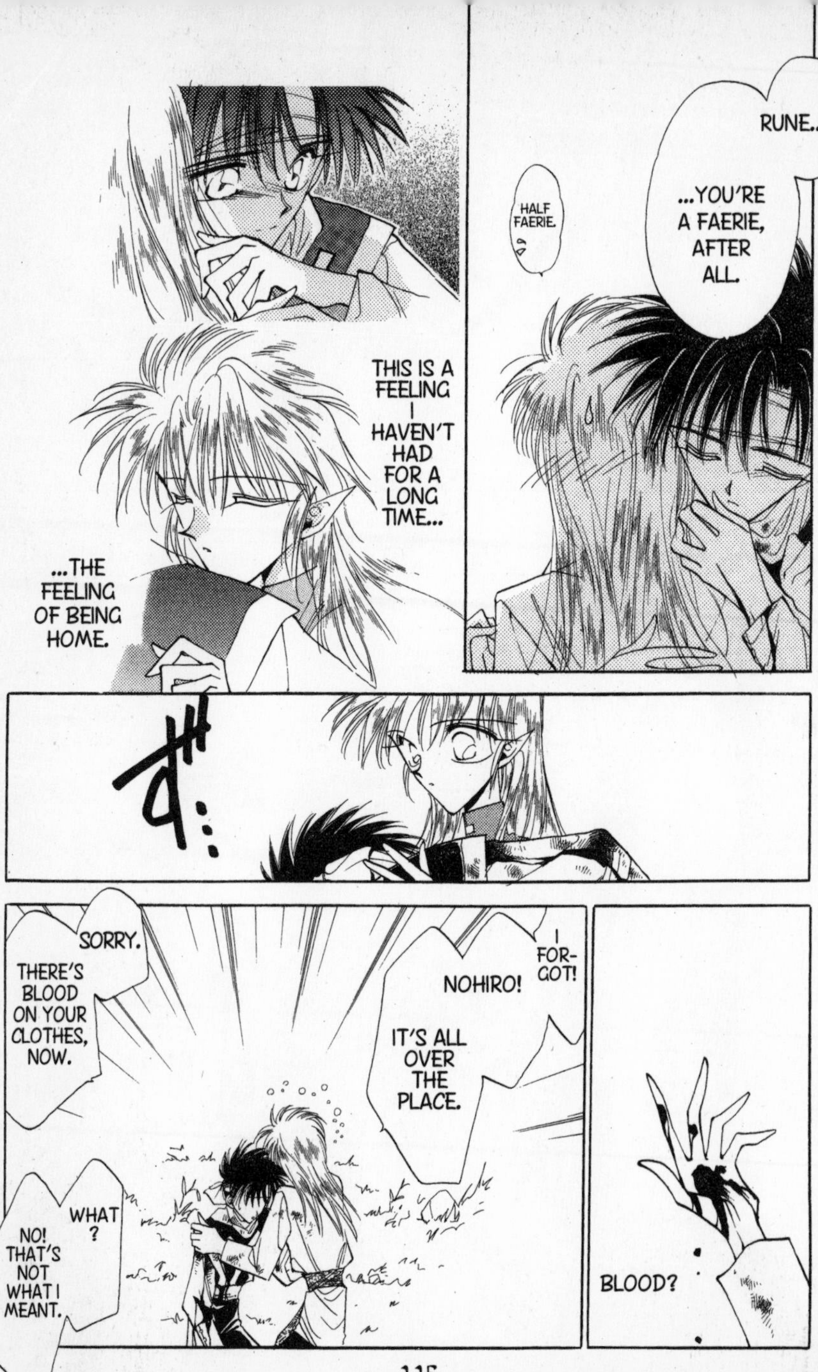
RUNE...
...YOU'RE A FAERIE, AFTER ALL.
HALF FAERIE.
THIS IS A FEELING I HAVEN'T HAD FOR A LONG TIME...
...THE FEELING OF BEING HOME.
ず...
BLOOD?
I FOR-GOT!
NOHIRO!
IT'S ALL OVER THE PLACE.
SORRY.
THERE'S BLOOD ON YOUR CLOTHES, NOW.
WHAT?
NO! THAT'S NOT WHAT I MEANT.

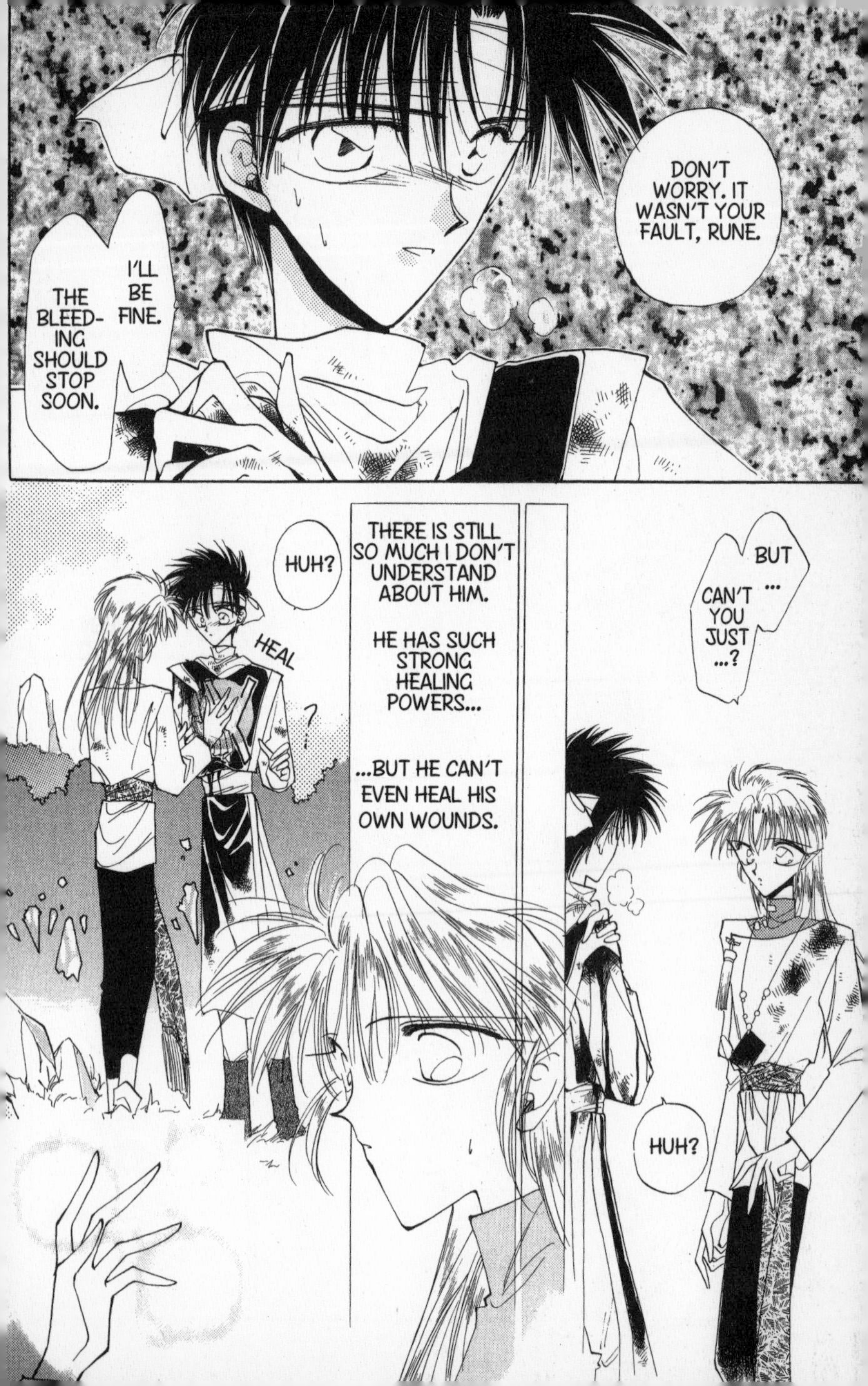
DON'T WORRY. IT WASN'T YOUR FAULT, RUNE.
I'LL BE FINE.
THE BLEED-ING SHOULD STOP SOON.
BUT ... CAN'T YOU JUST ...?
HUH?
THERE IS STILL SO MUCH I DON'T UNDERSTAND ABOUT HIM.
HE HAS SUCH STRONG HEALING POWERS...
...BUT HE CAN'T EVEN HEAL HIS OWN WOUNDS.
HUH?
HEAL
?

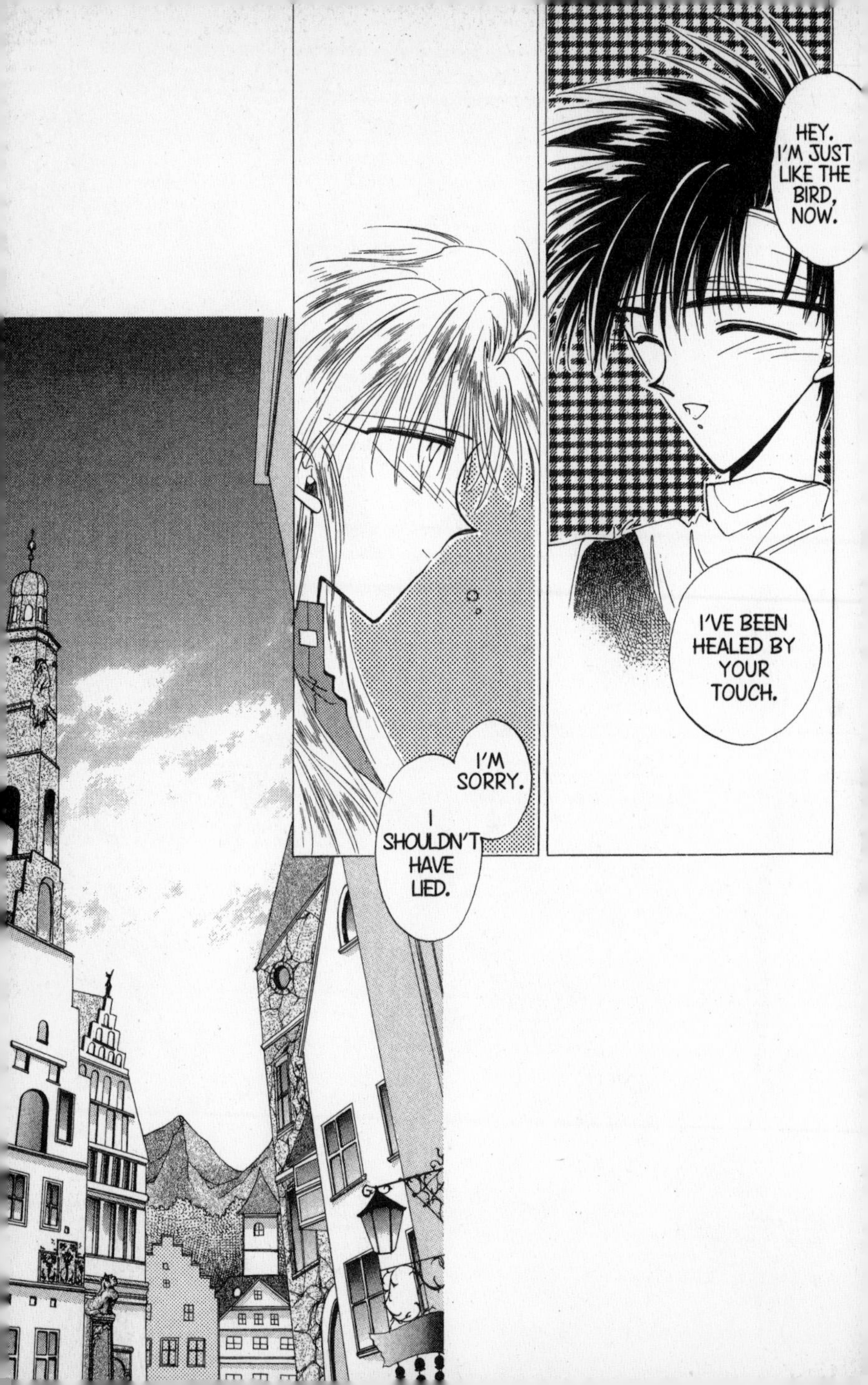
HEY. I'M JUST LIKE THE BIRD, NOW.
I'VE BEEN HEALED BY YOUR TOUCH.
I'M SORRY.
I SHOULDN'T HAVE LIED.

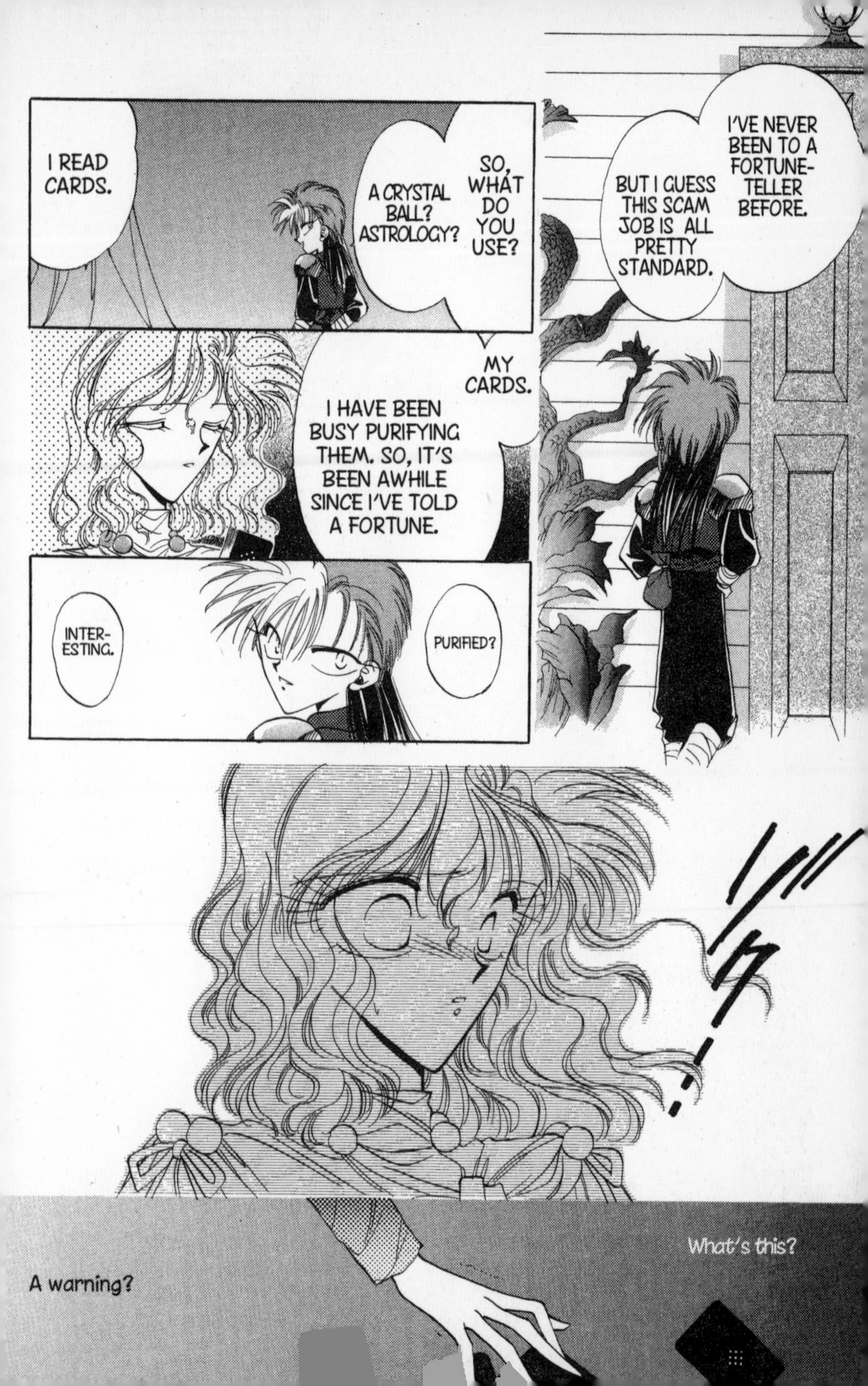
I'VE NEVER BEEN TO A FORTUNE-TELLER BEFORE.
BUT I GUESS THIS SCAM JOB IS ALL PRETTY STANDARD.
SO, WHAT DO YOU USE?
A CRYSTAL BALL? ASTROLOGY?
I READ CARDS.
MY CARDS.
I HAVE BEEN BUSY PURIFYING THEM. SO, IT'S BEEN AWHILE SINCE I'VE TOLD A FORTUNE.
PURIFIED?
INTER-ESTING.
What's this?
A warning?

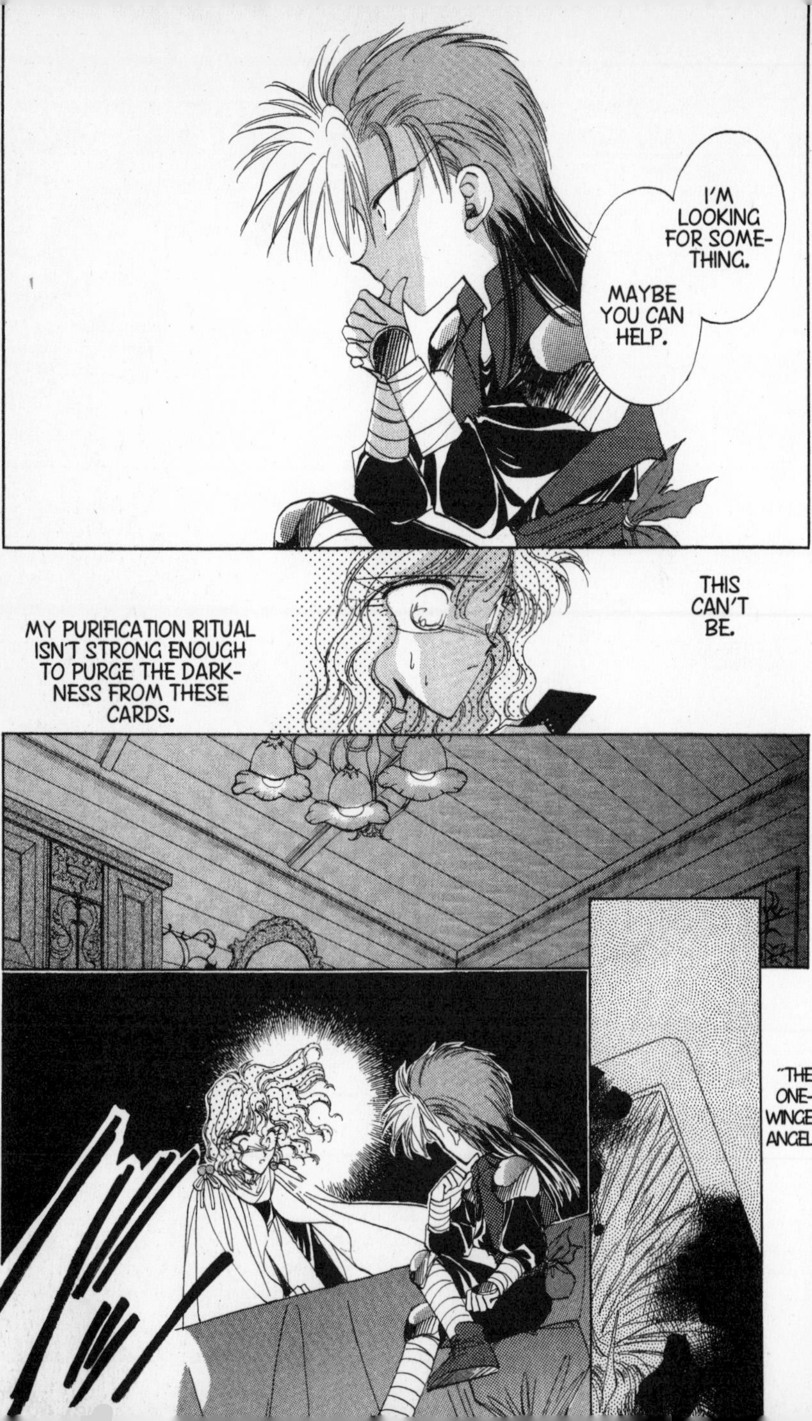
I'M LOOKING FOR SOME-THING.
MAYBE YOU CAN HELP.
THIS CAN'T BE.
MY PURIFICATION RITUAL ISN'T STRONG ENOUGH TO PURGE THE DARK-NESS FROM THESE CARDS.
"THE ONE-WINGED ANGEL!"

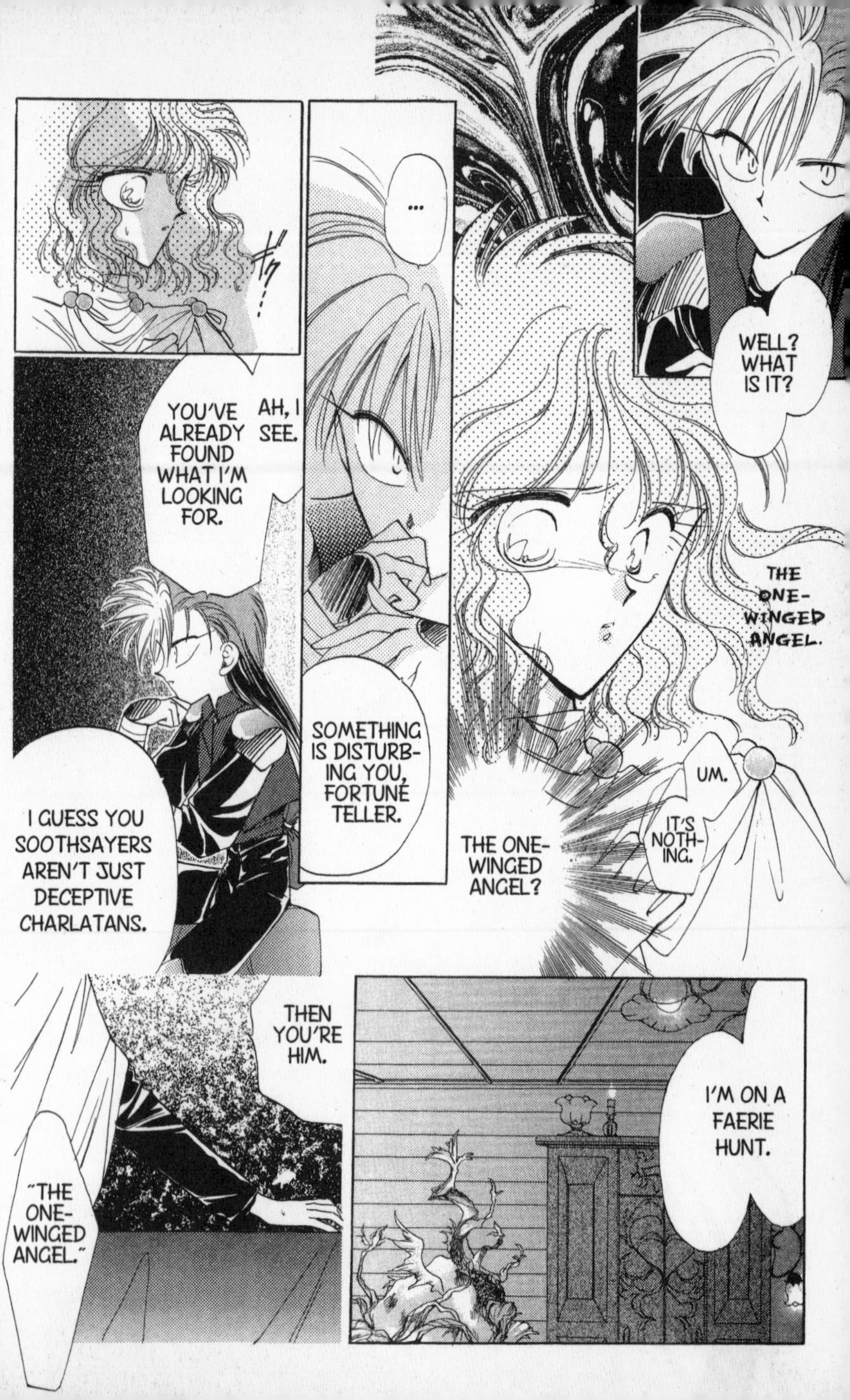
WELL? WHAT IS IT?
THE ONE-WINGED ANGEL.
UM.
IT'S NOTHING.
THE ONE-WINGED ANGEL?
...
SOMETHING IS DISTURBING YOU, FORTUNE TELLER.
AH, I SEE.
YOU'VE ALREADY FOUND WHAT I'M LOOKING FOR.
I GUESS YOU SOOTHSAYERS AREN'T JUST DECEPTIVE CHARLATANS.
I'M ON A FAERIE HUNT.
THEN YOU'RE HIM.
"THE ONE-WINGED ANGEL."

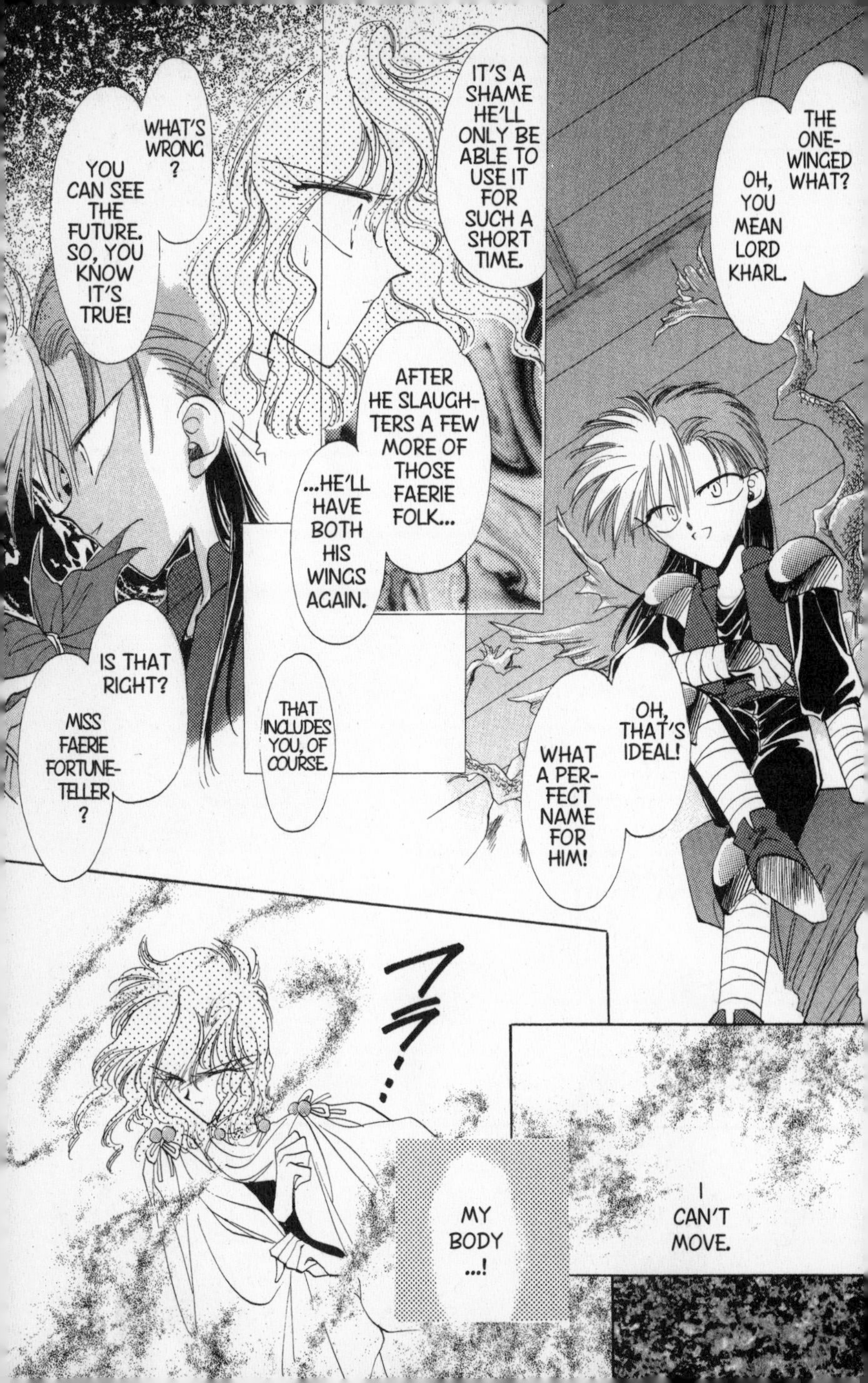
THE ONE-WINGED WHAT?
OH, YOU MEAN LORD KHARL.
OH, THAT'S IDEAL!
WHAT A PERFECT NAME FOR HIM!
IT'S A SHAME HE'LL ONLY BE ABLE TO USE IT FOR SUCH A SHORT TIME.
AFTER HE SLAUGHTERS A FEW MORE OF THOSE FAERIE FOLK...
...HE'LL HAVE BOTH HIS WINGS AGAIN.
THAT INCLUDES YOU, OF COURSE.
WHAT'S WRONG?
YOU CAN SEE THE FUTURE. SO, YOU KNOW IT'S TRUE!
IS THAT RIGHT?
MISS FAERIE FORTUNE-TELLER?
I CAN'T MOVE.
MY BODY ...!
フラ…

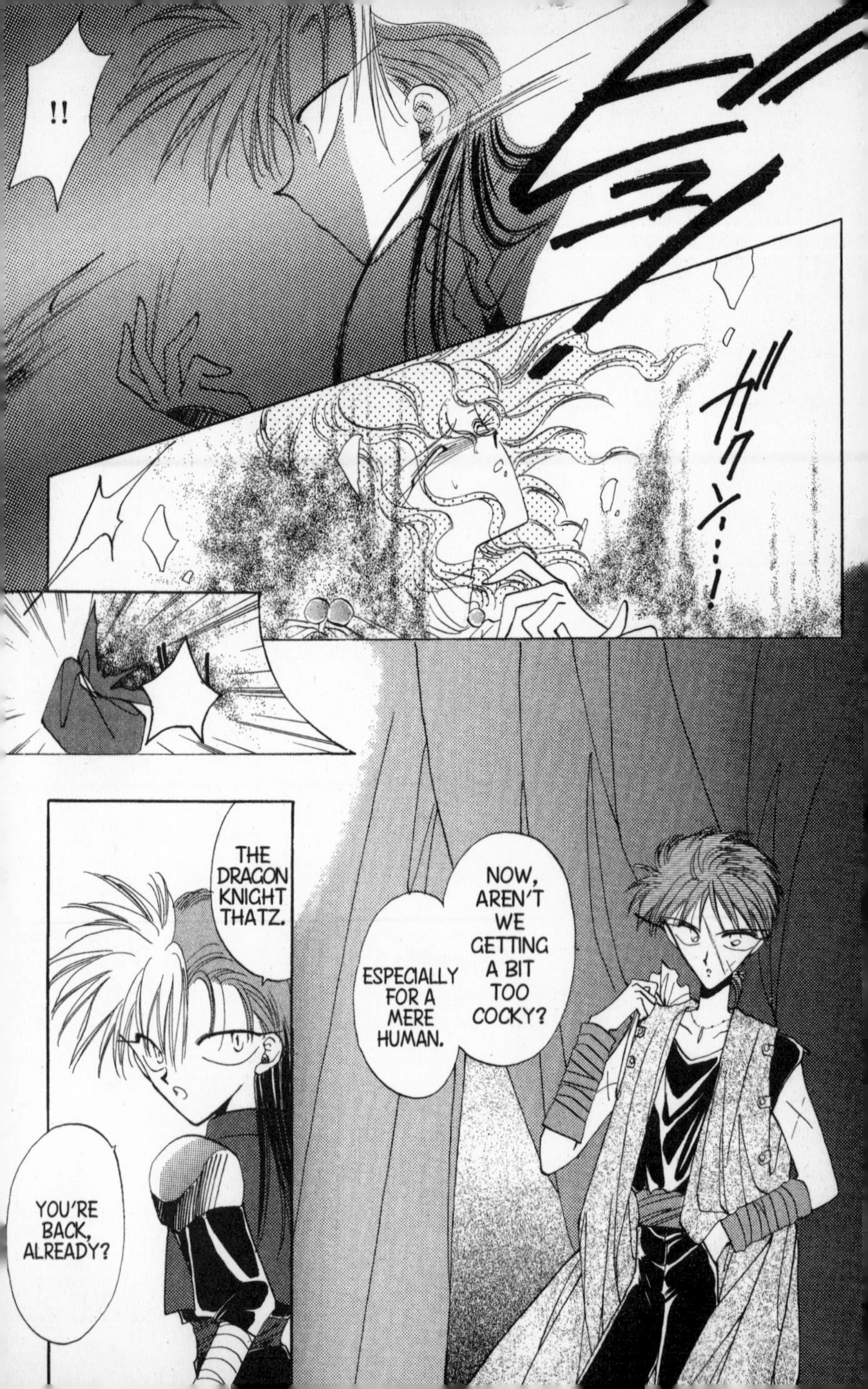
!!
ガクン…!
NOW, AREN'T WE GETTING A BIT TOO COCKY?
ESPECIALLY FOR A MERE HUMAN.
THE DRAGON KNIGHT THATZ.
YOU'RE BACK, ALREADY?

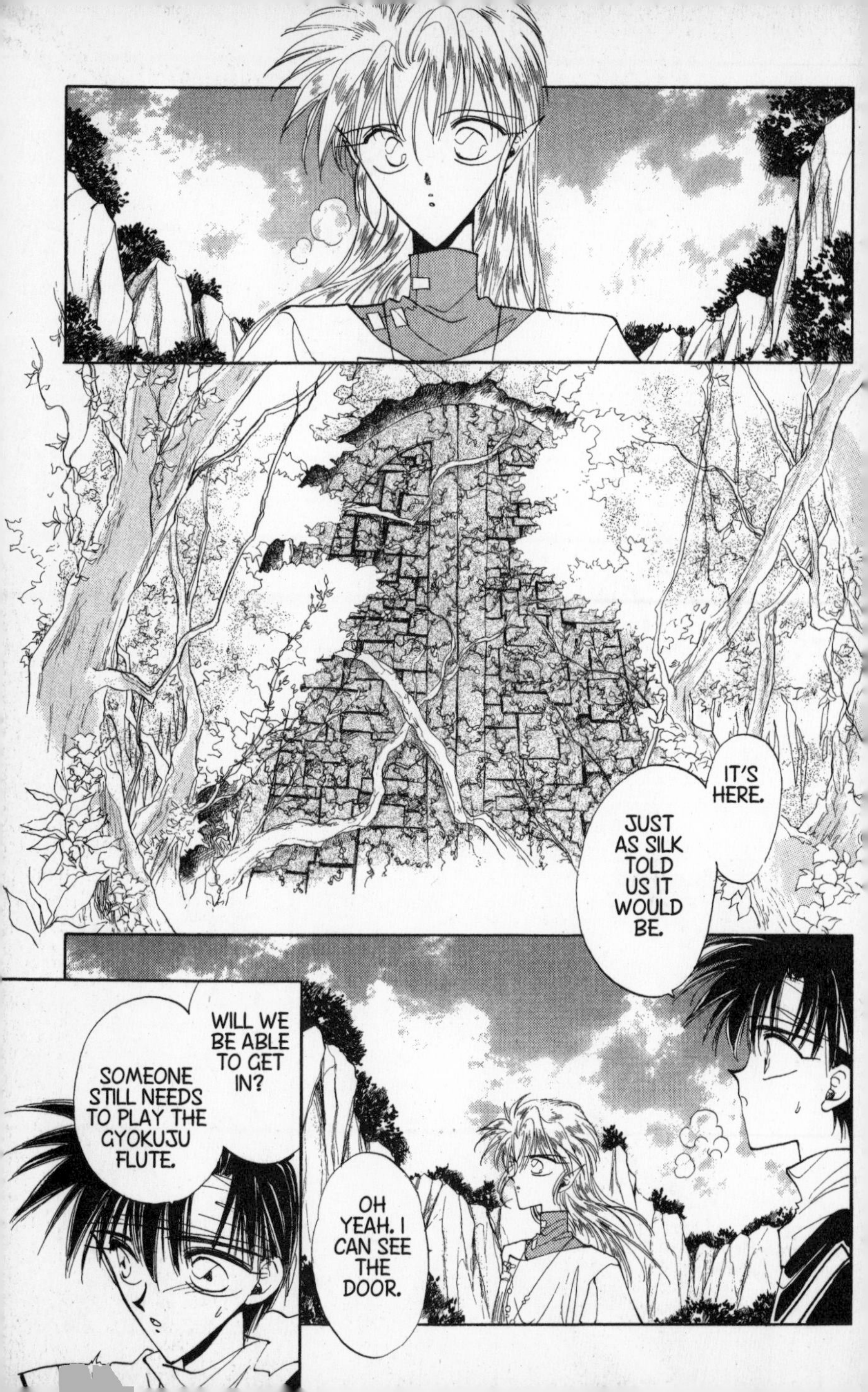
IT'S HERE.
JUST AS SILK TOLD US IT WOULD BE.
OH YEAH. I CAN SEE THE DOOR.
WILL WE BE ABLE TO GET IN?
SOMEONE STILL NEEDS TO PLAY THE GYOKUJU FLUTE.

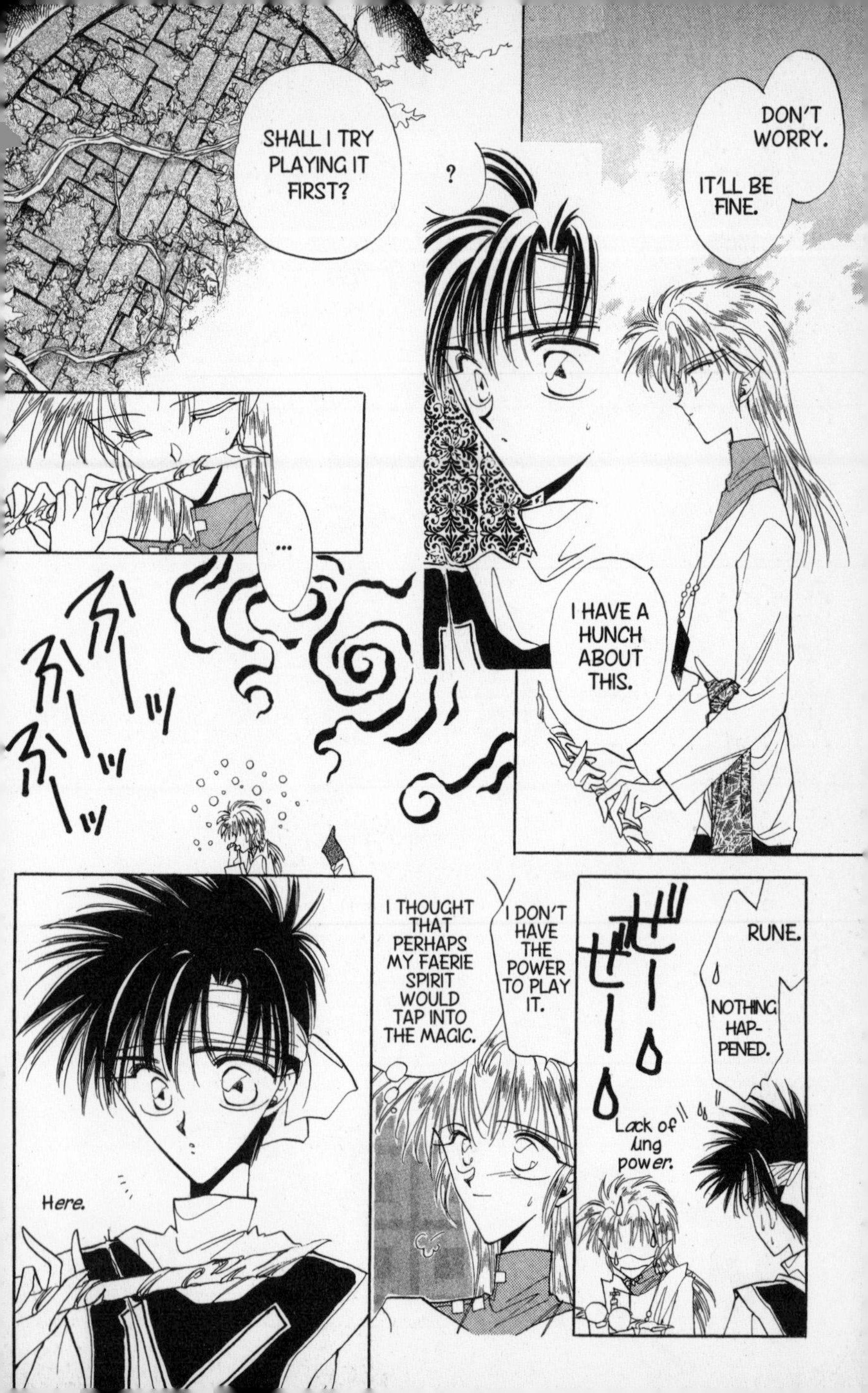
DON'T WORRY.
IT'LL BE FINE.
?
SHALL I TRY PLAYING IT FIRST?
I HAVE A HUNCH ABOUT THIS.
...
RUNE.
NOTHING HAP-PENED.
ゼーゼー
Lack of lung power.
I DON'T HAVE THE POWER TO PLAY IT.
I THOUGHT THAT PERHAPS MY FAERIE SPIRIT WOULD TAP INTO THE MAGIC.
Here.

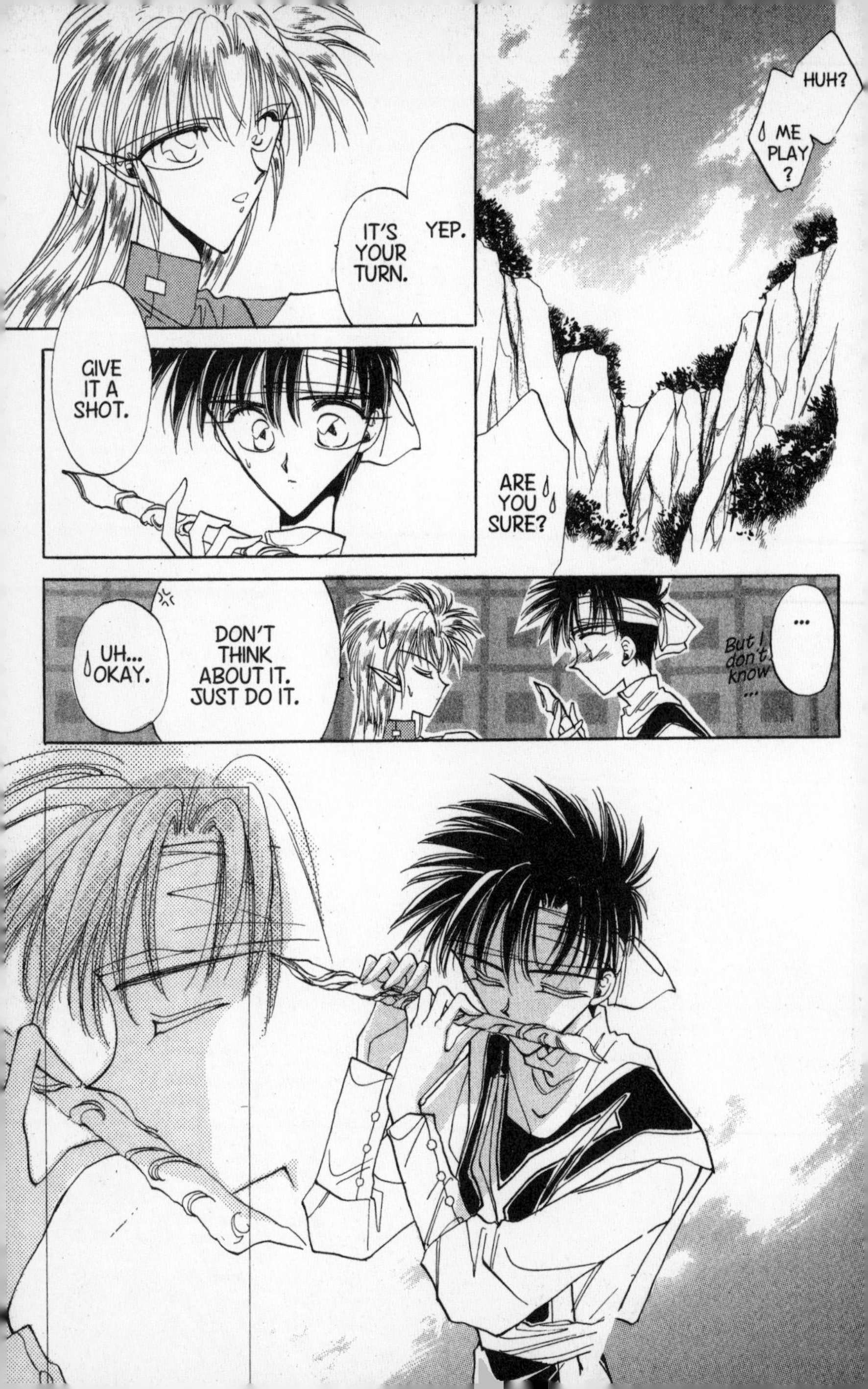
HUH?
ME PLAY?
YEP.
IT'S YOUR TURN.
ARE YOU SURE?
GIVE IT A SHOT.
...
But I don't know...
DON'T THINK ABOUT IT. JUST DO IT.
UH... OKAY.

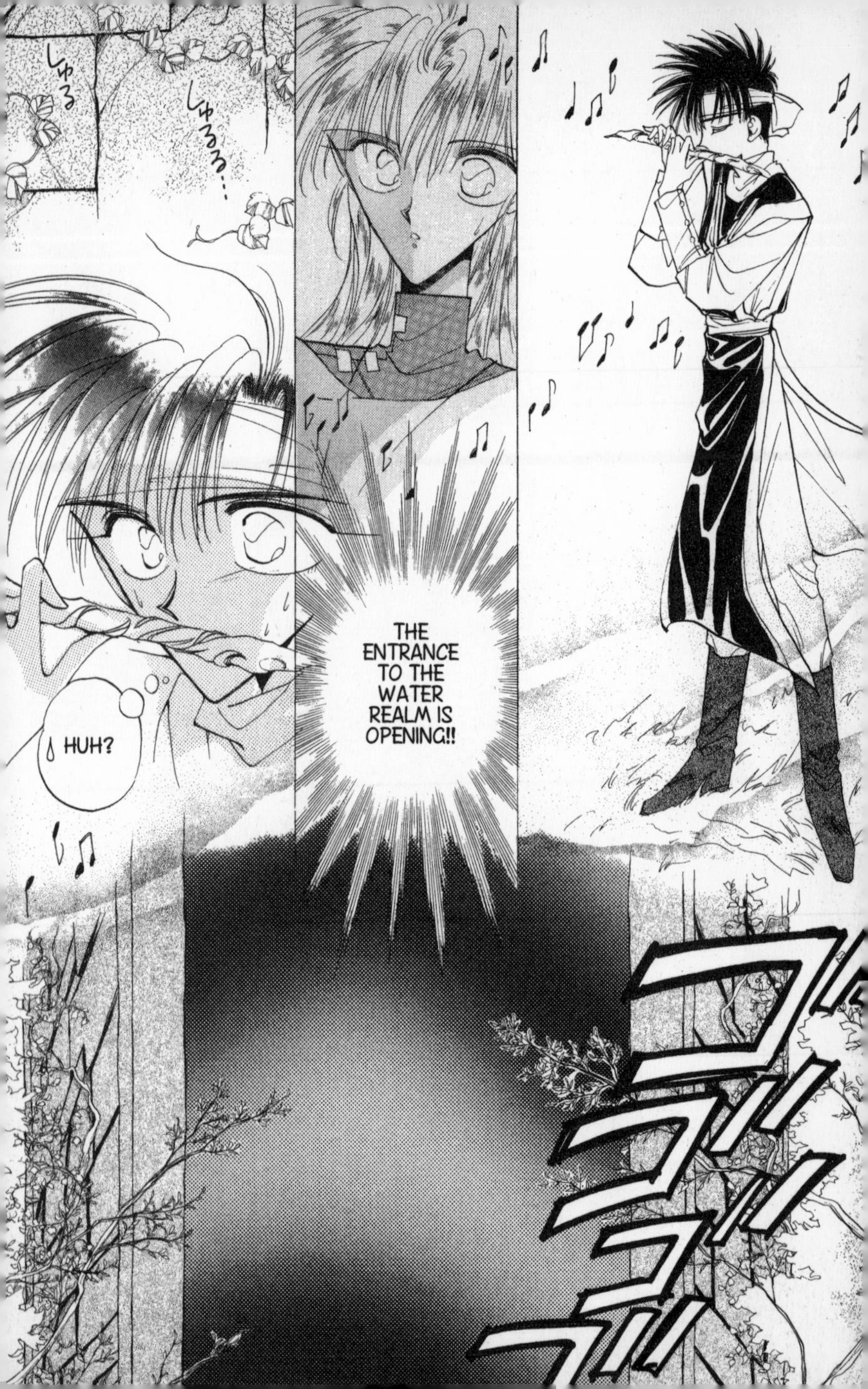
THE ENTRANCE TO THE WATER REALM IS OPENING!!
しゅる
しゅるる…
HUH?

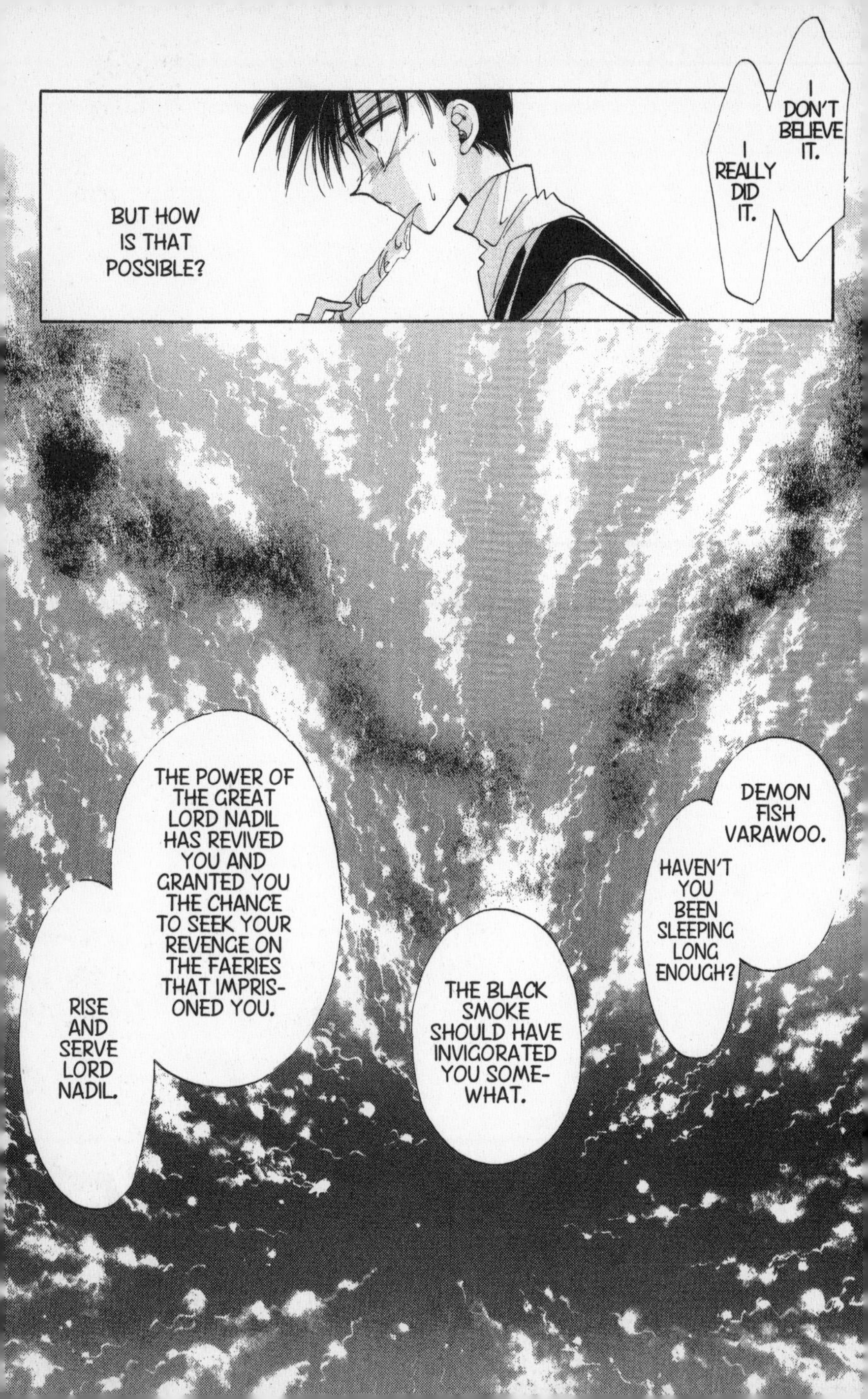
I DON'T BELIEVE IT.
I REALLY DID IT.
BUT HOW IS THAT POSSIBLE?
DEMON FISH VARAWOO.
HAVEN'T YOU BEEN SLEEPING LONG ENOUGH?
THE BLACK SMOKE SHOULD HAVE INVIGORATED YOU SOME-WHAT.
THE POWER OF THE GREAT LORD NADIL HAS REVIVED YOU AND GRANTED YOU THE CHANCE TO SEEK YOUR REVENGE ON THE FAERIES THAT IMPRIS-ONED YOU.
RISE AND SERVE LORD NADIL.

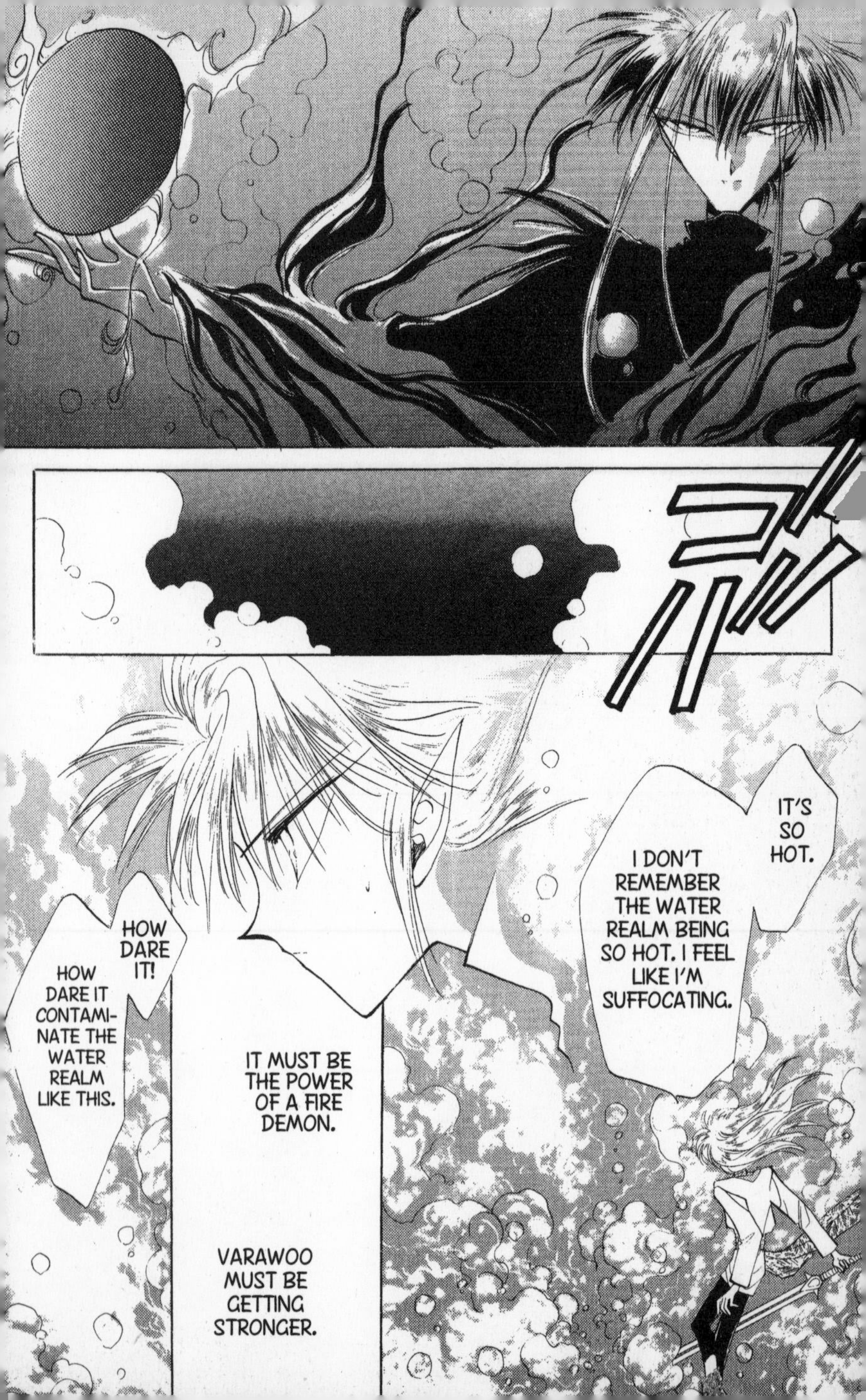
IT'S SO HOT.
I DON'T REMEMBER THE WATER REALM BEING SO HOT. I FEEL LIKE I'M SUFFOCATING.
IT MUST BE THE POWER OF A FIRE DEMON.
VARAWOO MUST BE GETTING STRONGER.
HOW DARE IT!
HOW DARE IT CONTAMINATE THE WATER REALM LIKE THIS.

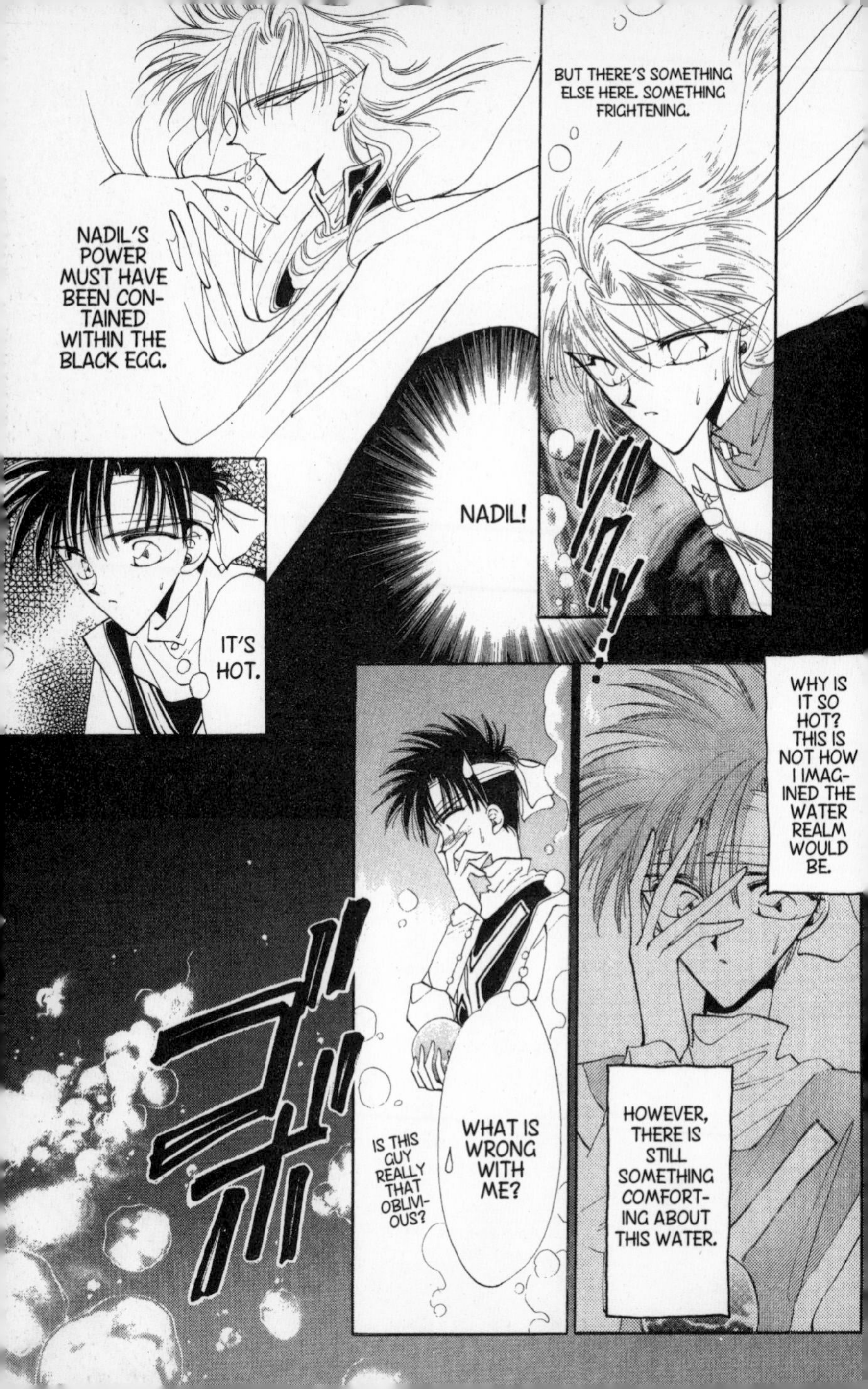
BUT THERE'S SOMETHING ELSE HERE. SOMETHING FRIGHTENING.
NADIL'S POWER MUST HAVE BEEN CONTAINED WITHIN THE BLACK EGG.
NADIL!
IT'S HOT.
WHY IS IT SO HOT? THIS IS NOT HOW I IMAGINED THE WATER REALM WOULD BE.
HOWEVER, THERE IS STILL SOMETHING COMFORTING ABOUT THIS WATER.
WHAT IS WRONG WITH ME?
IS THIS GUY REALLY THAT OBLIVIOUS?

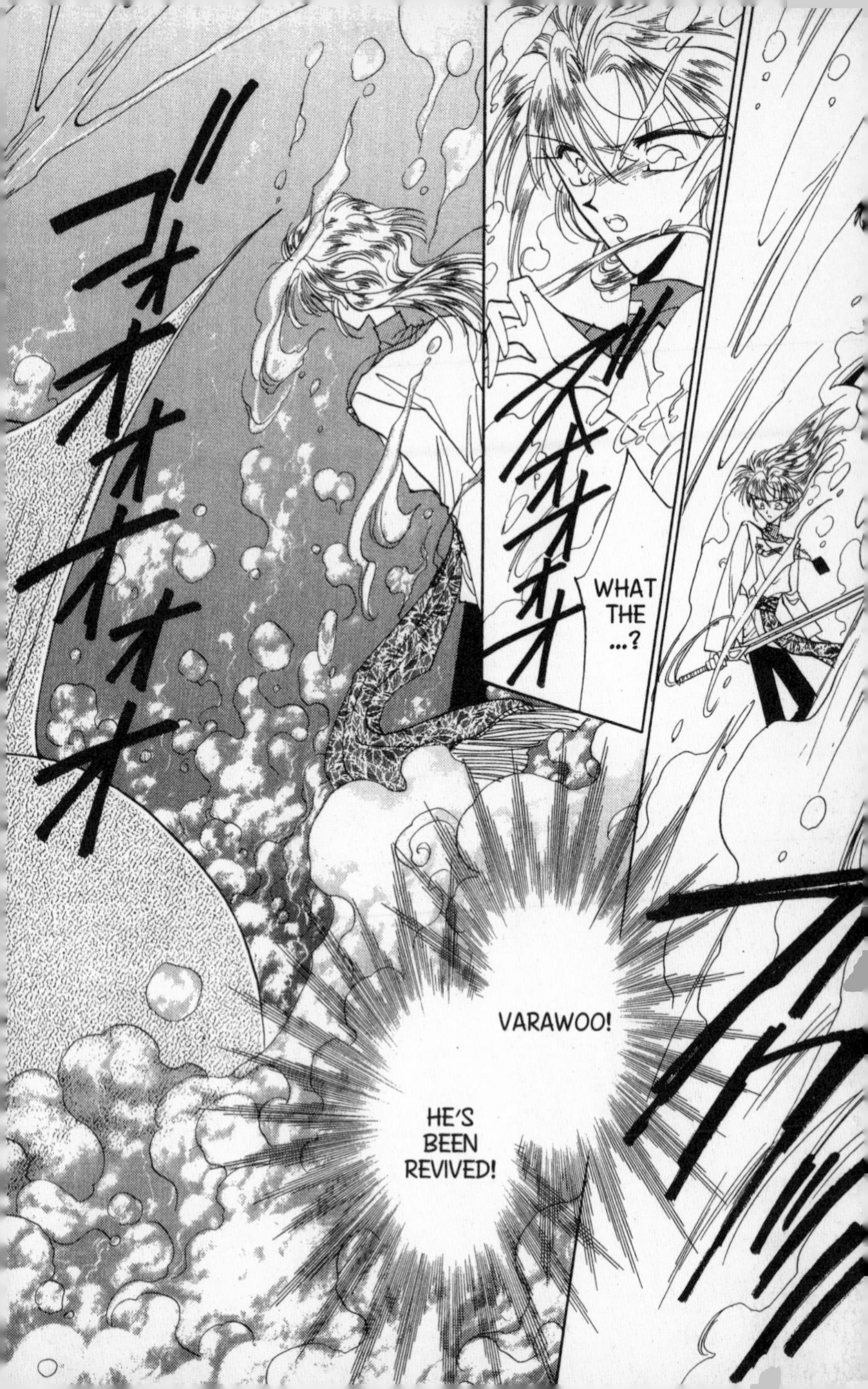
WHAT THE ...?
VARAWOO!
HE'S BEEN REVIVED!

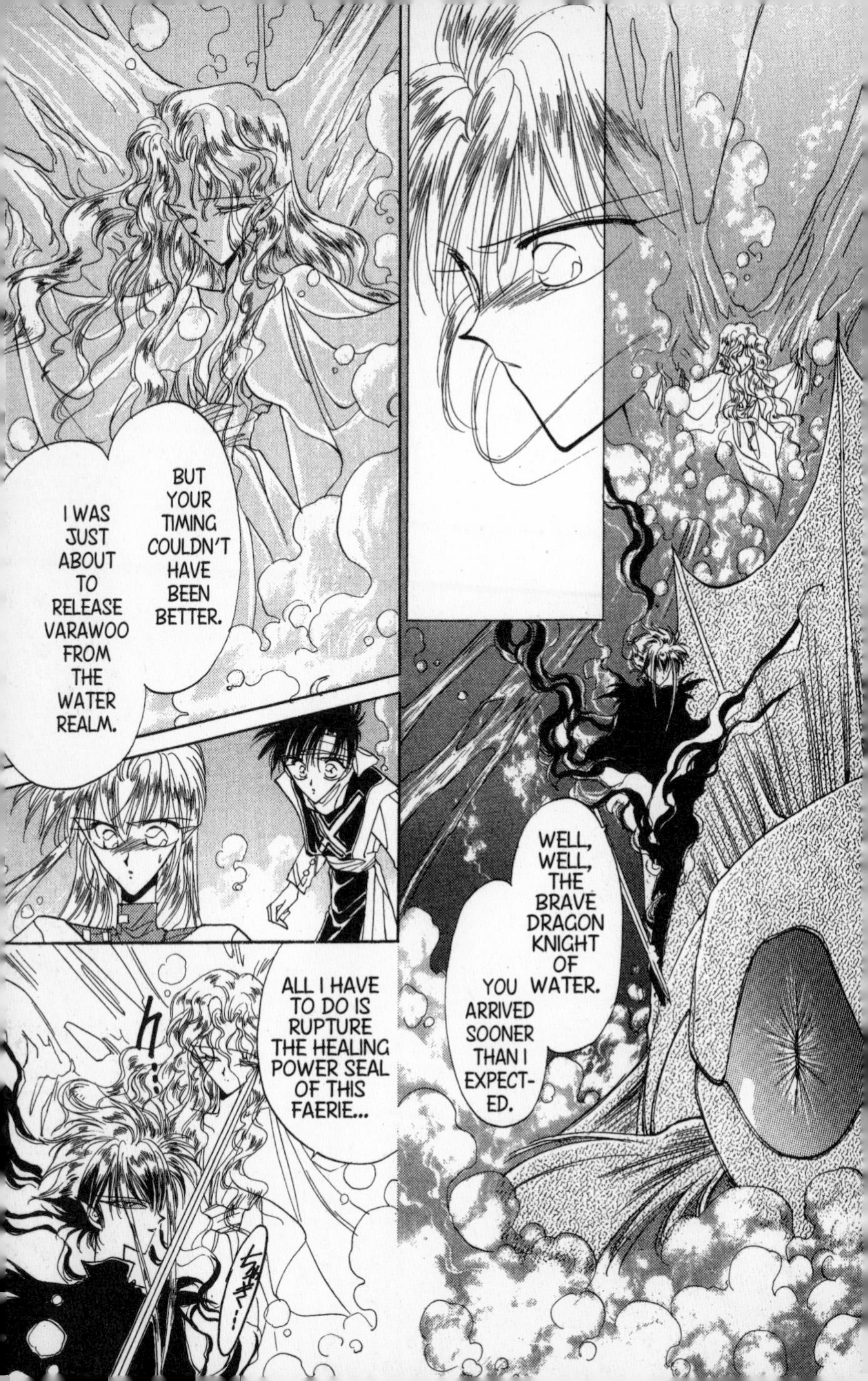
WELL, WELL, THE BRAVE DRAGON KNIGHT OF WATER.
YOU ARRIVED SOONER THAN I EXPECT-ED.
BUT YOUR TIMING COULDN'T HAVE BEEN BETTER.
I WAS JUST ABOUT TO RELEASE VARAWOO FROM THE WATER REALM.
ALL I HAVE TO DO IS RUPTURE THE HEALING POWER SEAL OF THIS FAERIE...

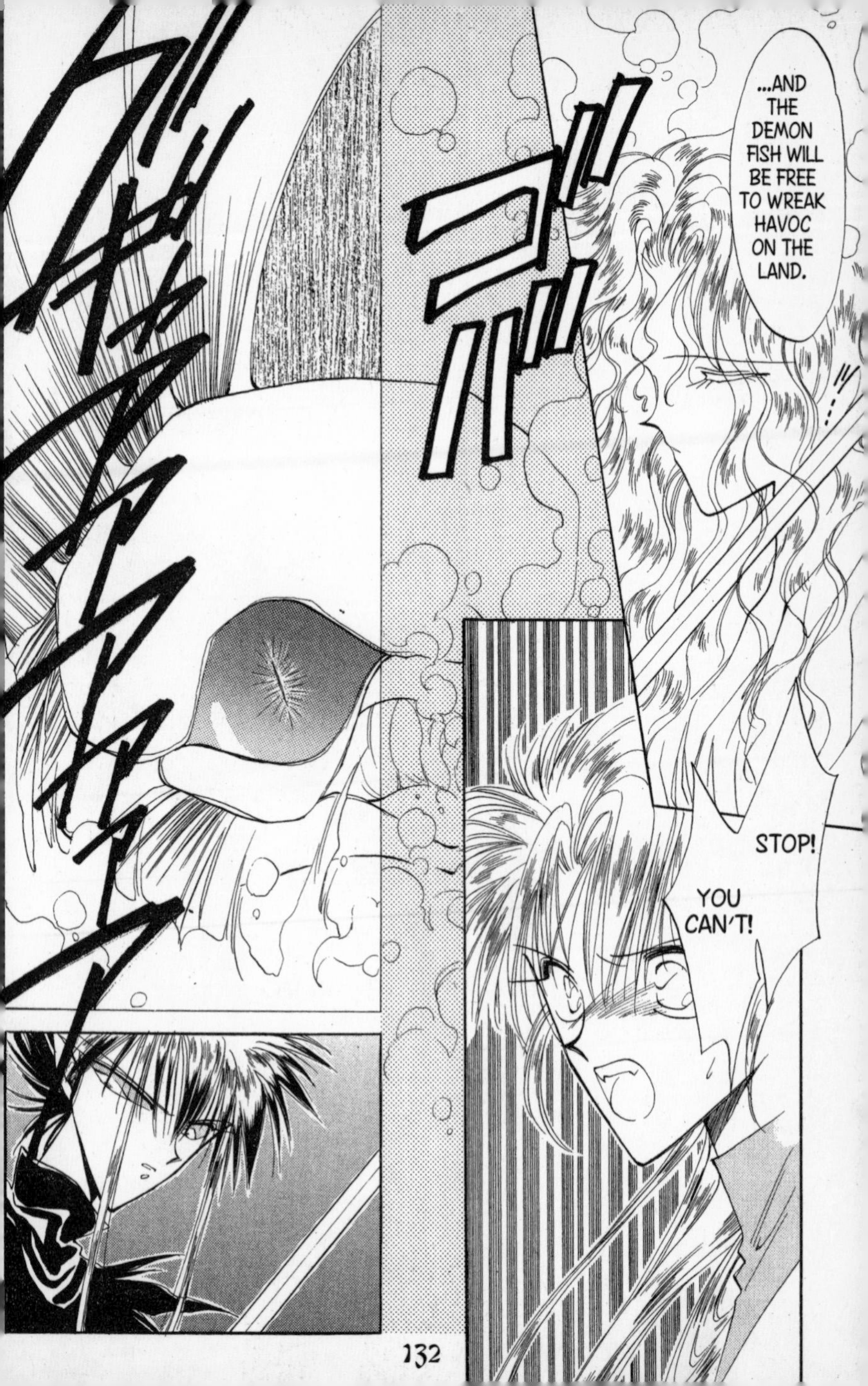
...AND THE DEMON FISH WILL BE FREE TO WREAK HAVOC ON THE LAND.
STOP!
YOU CAN'T!

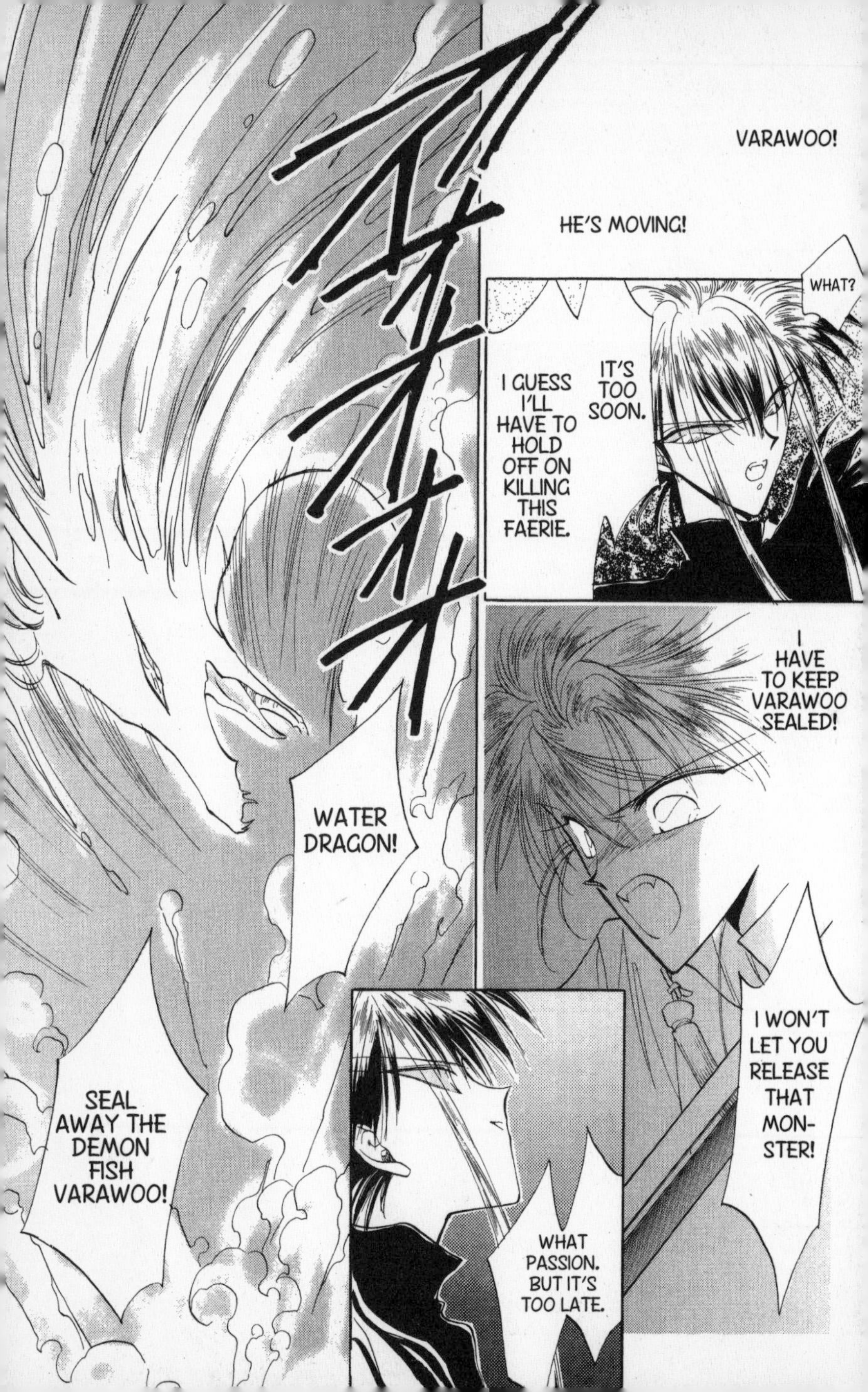
VARAWOO!
HE'S MOVING!
WHAT?
IT'S TOO SOON.
I GUESS I'LL HAVE TO HOLD OFF ON KILLING THIS FAERIE.
I HAVE TO KEEP VARAWOO SEALED!
I WON'T LET YOU RELEASE THAT MON-STER!
WHAT PASSION. BUT IT'S TOO LATE.
WATER DRAGON!
SEAL AWAY THE DEMON FISH VARAWOO!

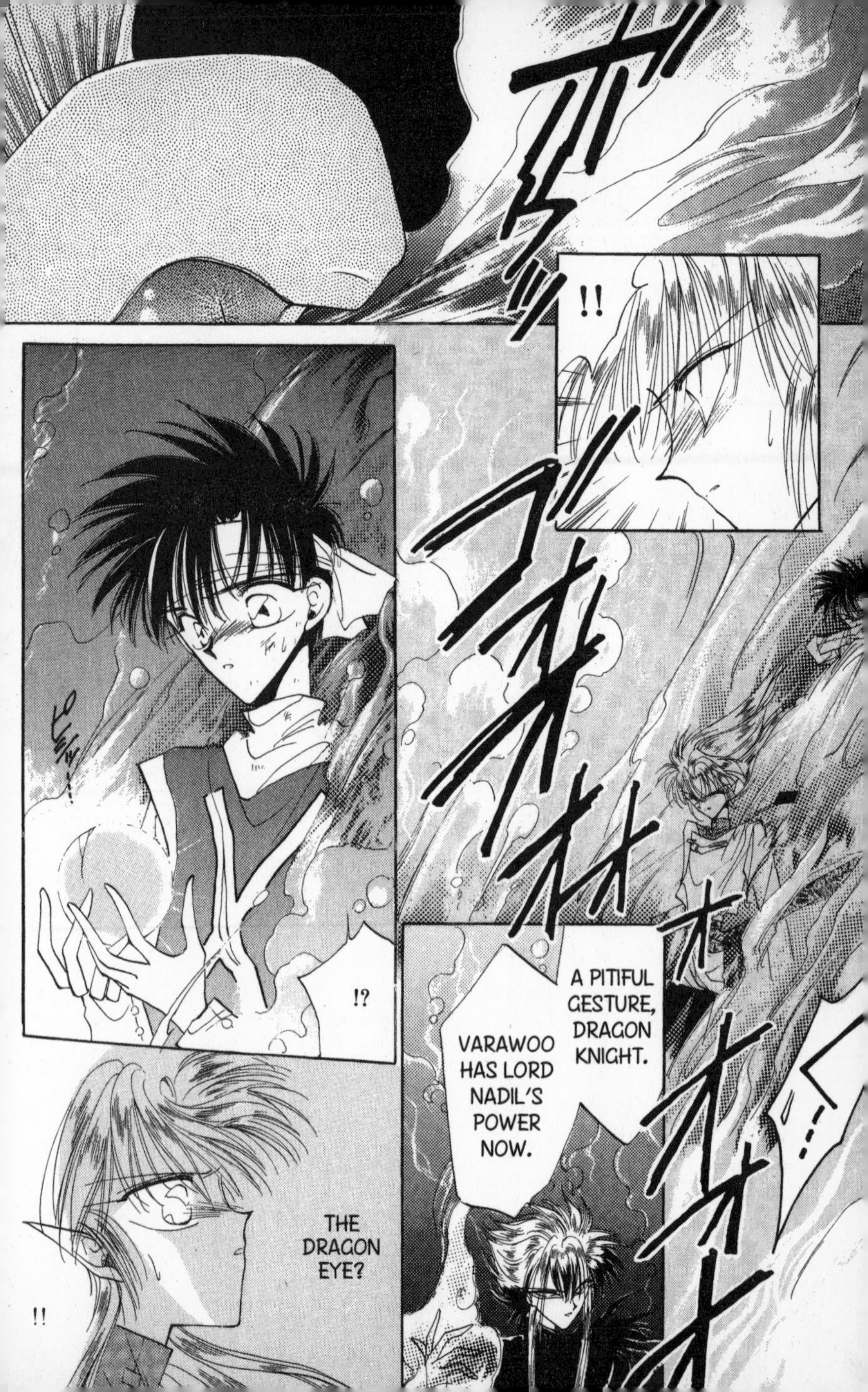
!!
A PITIFUL GESTURE, DRAGON KNIGHT.
VARAWOO HAS LORD NADIL'S POWER NOW.
!?
THE DRAGON EYE?
!!

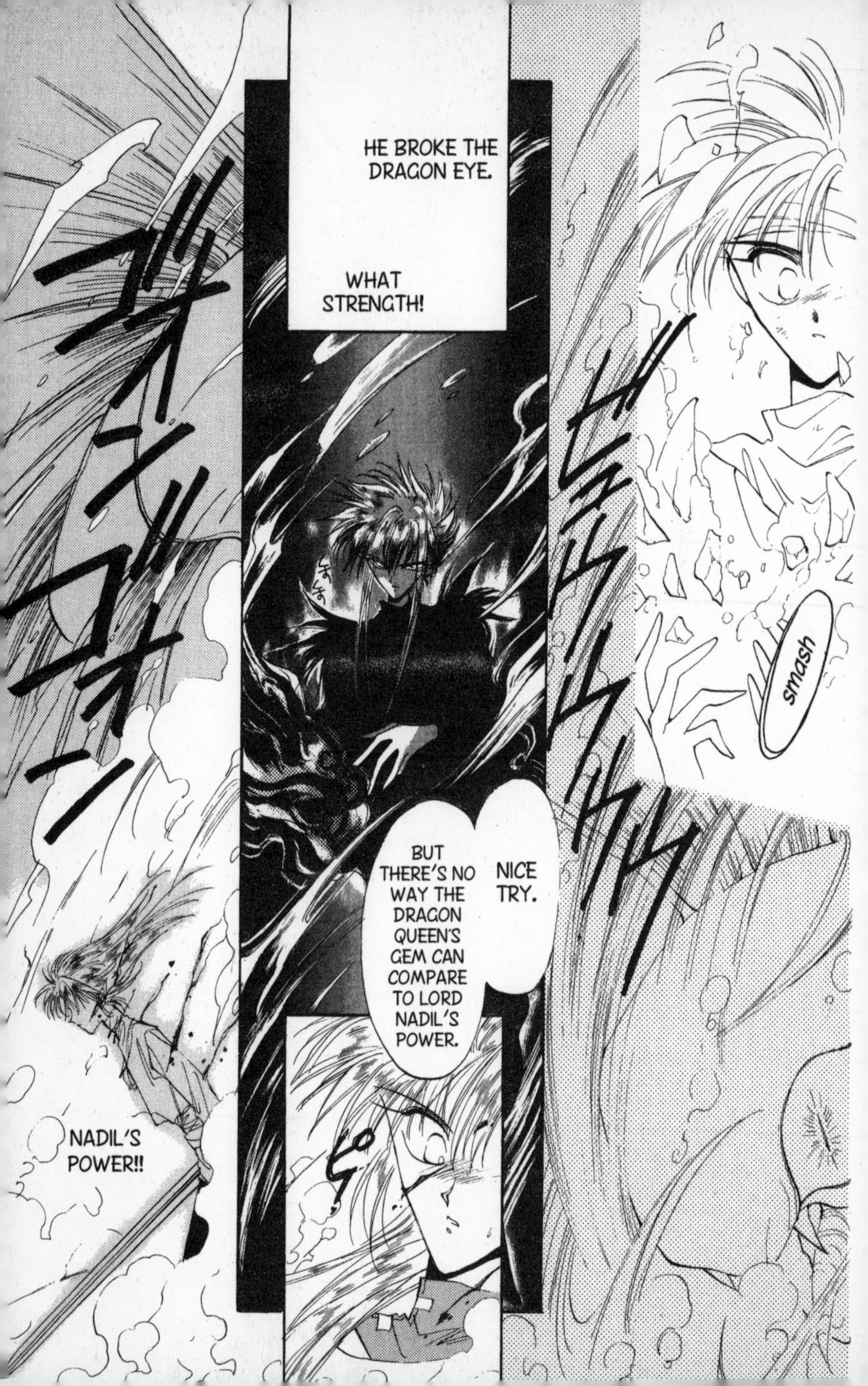
smash
HE BROKE THE DRAGON EYE.
WHAT STRENGTH!
NICE TRY.
BUT THERE'S NO WAY THE DRAGON QUEEN'S GEM CAN COMPARE TO LORD NADIL'S POWER.
NADIL'S POWER!!

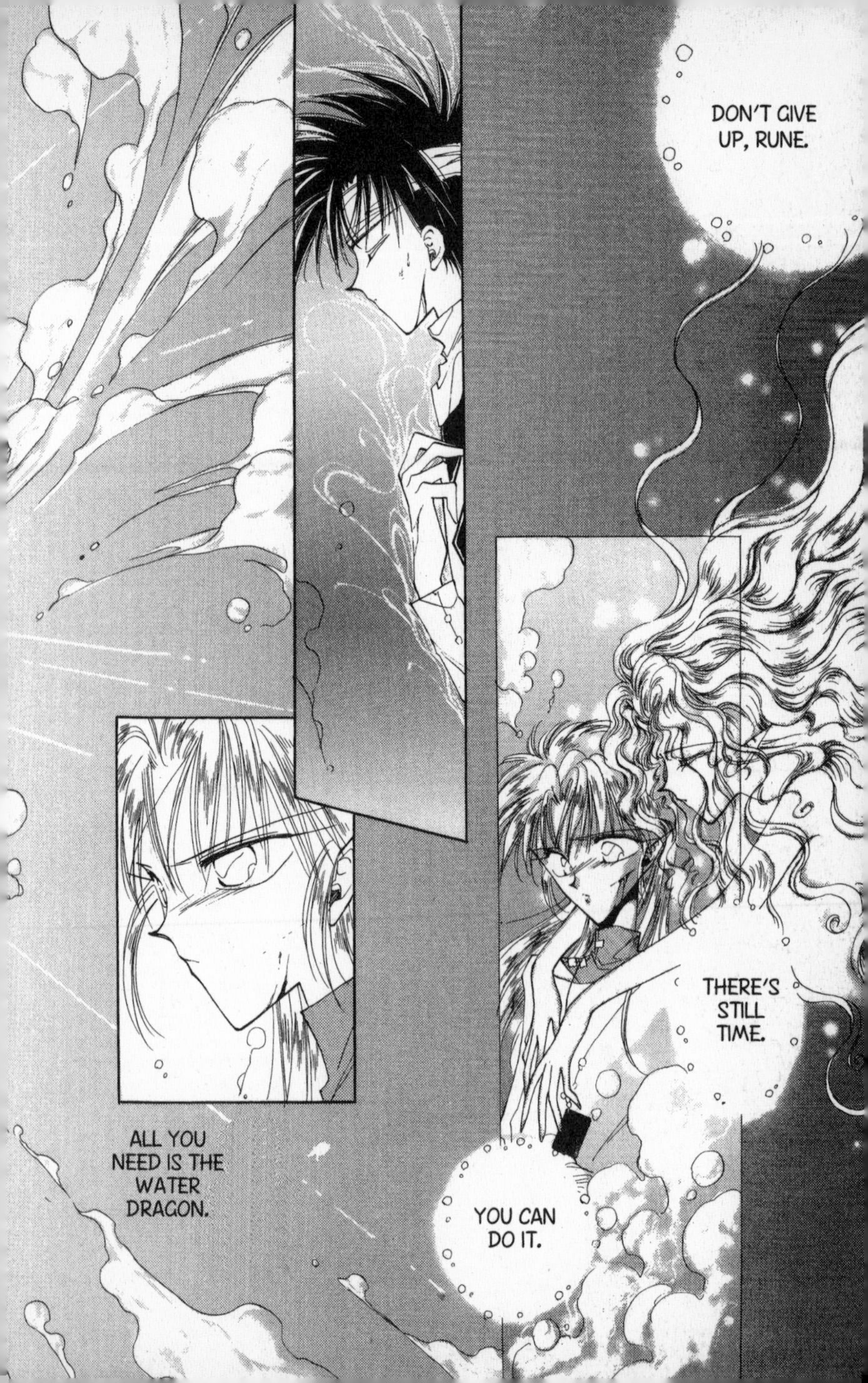
DON'T GIVE UP, RUNE.
THERE'S STILL TIME.
YOU CAN DO IT.
ALL YOU NEED IS THE WATER DRAGON.

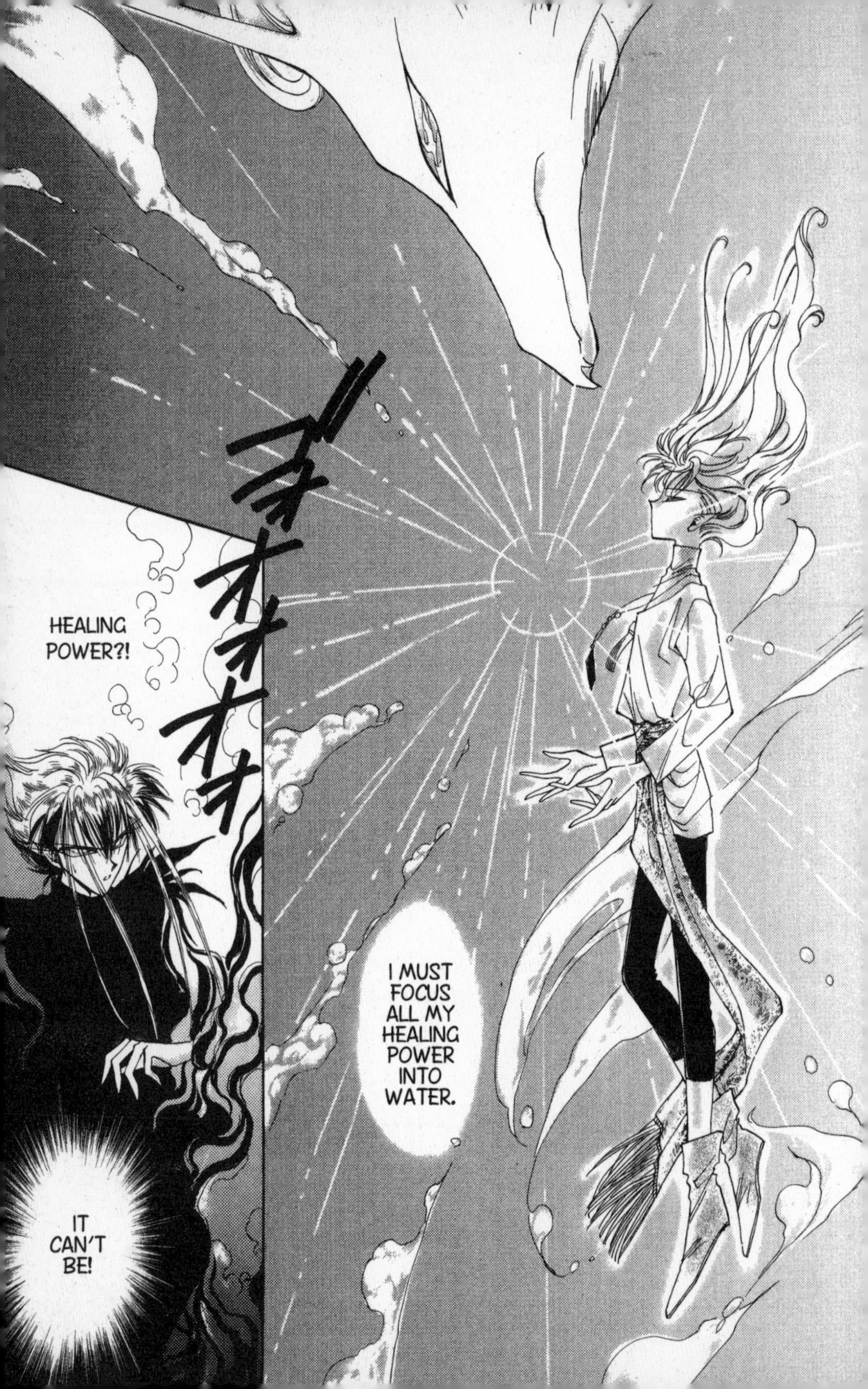
ゴオオオオ
I MUST FOCUS ALL MY HEALING POWER INTO WATER.
HEALING POWER?!
IT CAN'T BE!

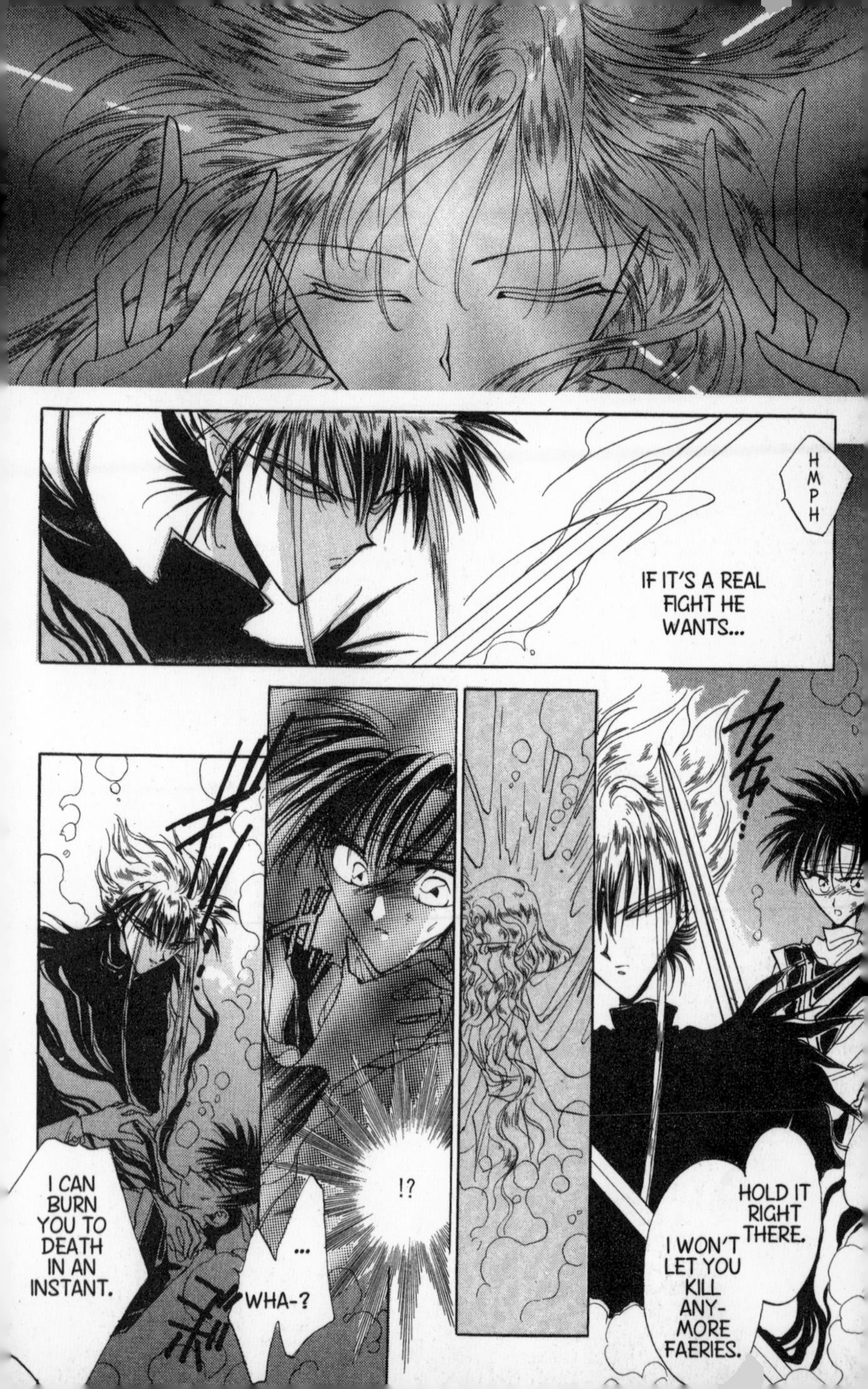
HMPH
IF IT'S A REAL FIGHT HE WANTS...
HOLD IT RIGHT THERE.
I WON'T LET YOU KILL ANY-MORE FAERIES.
!?
...
WHA-?
I CAN BURN YOU TO DEATH IN AN INSTANT.

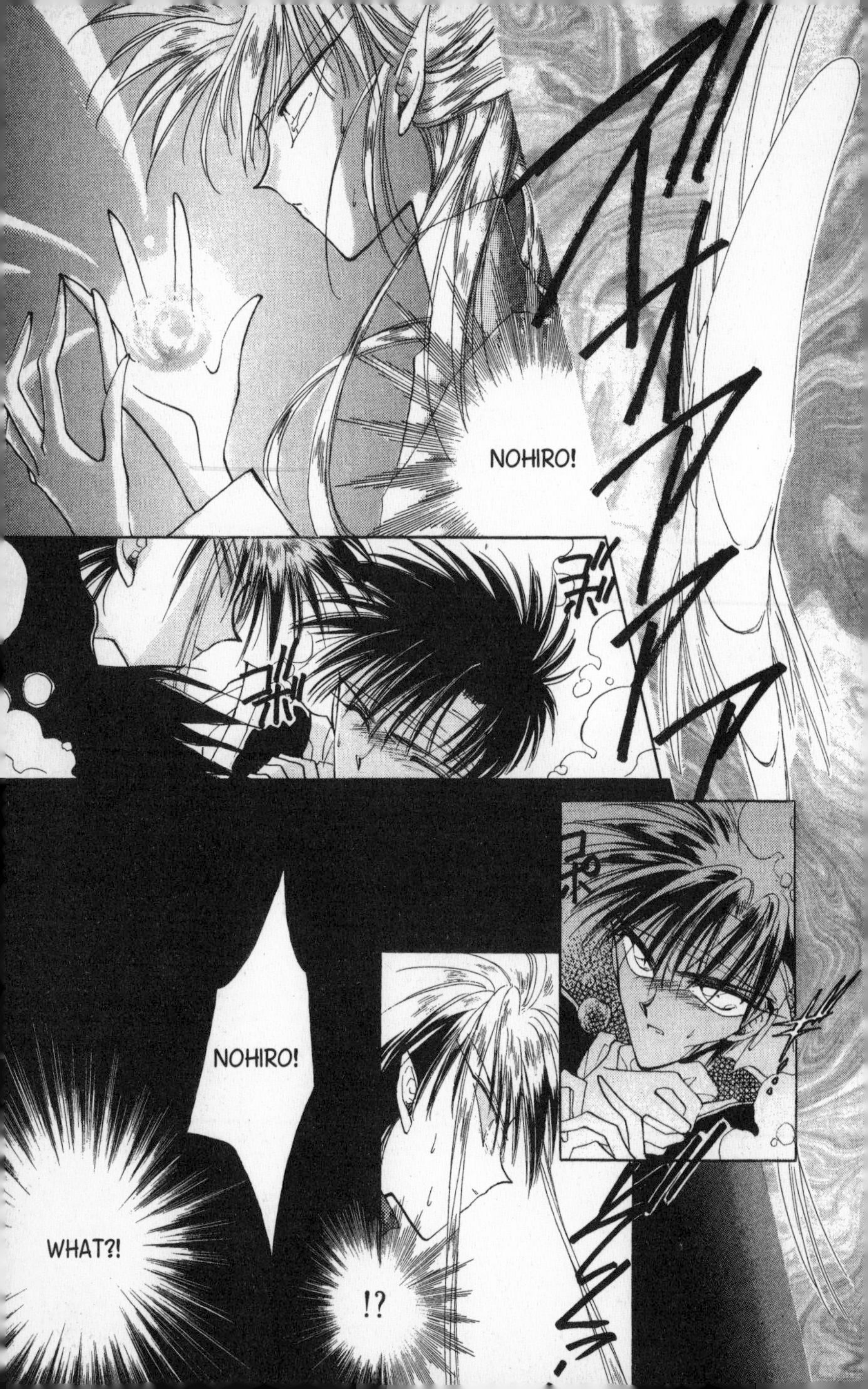
NOHIRO!
!?
NOHIRO!
WHAT?!

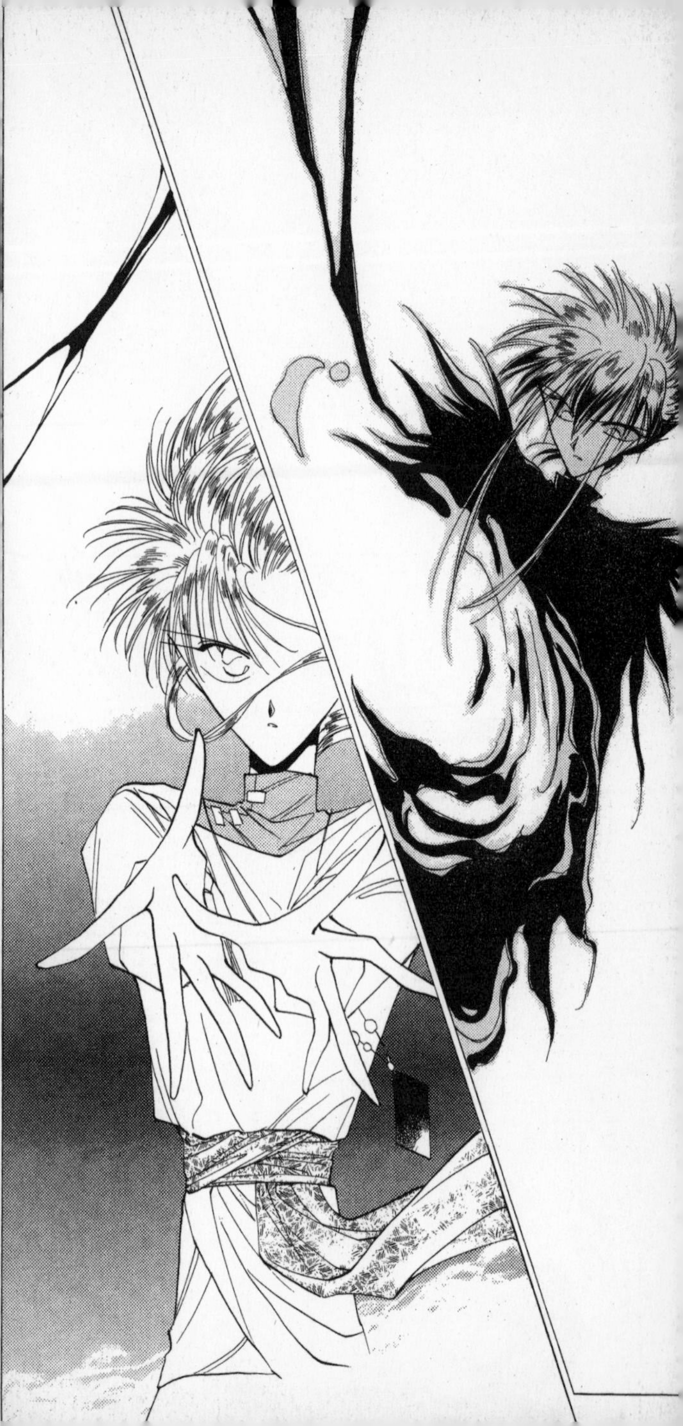

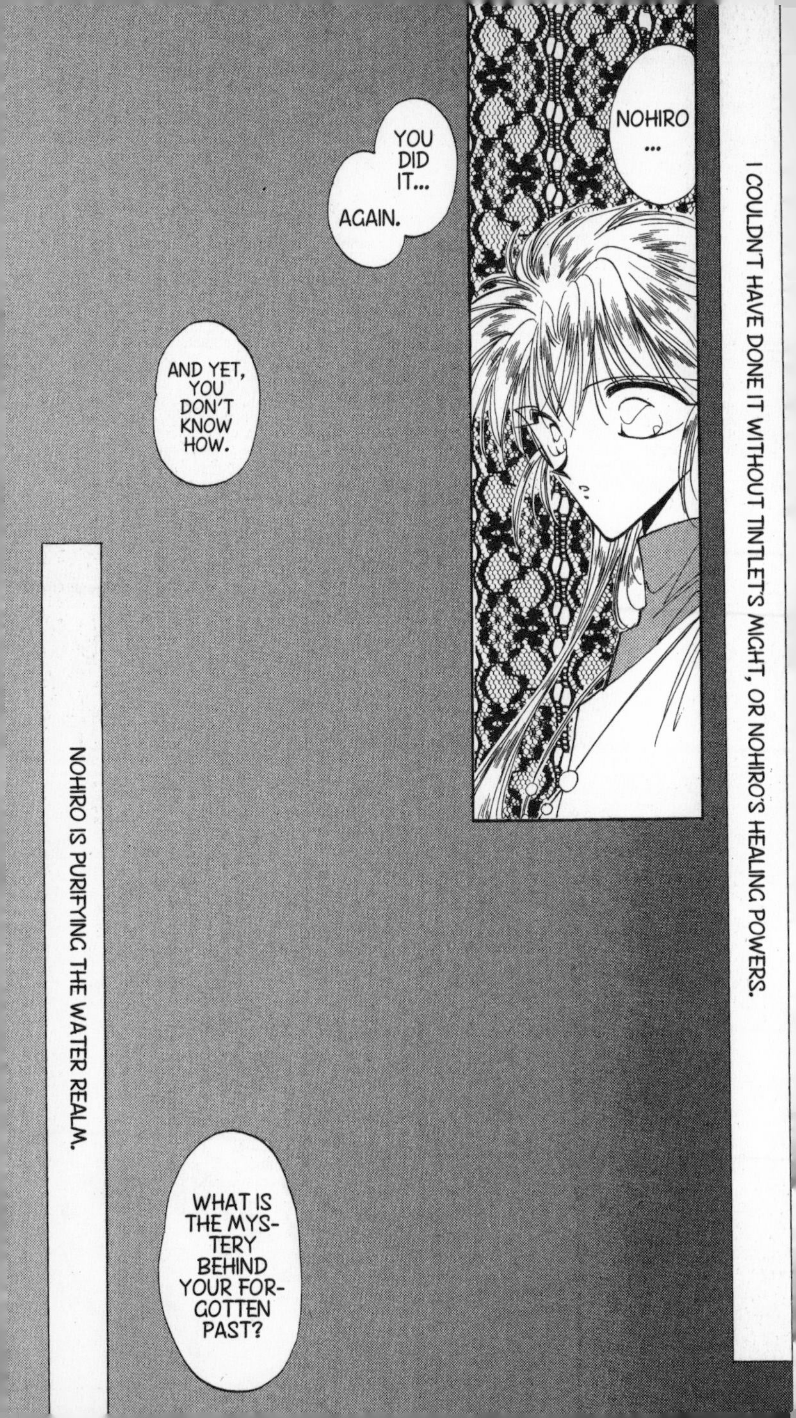
I COULDN'T HAVE DONE IT WITHOUT TINTLET'S MIGHT, OR NOHIRO'S HEALING POWERS.
NOHIRO ...
YOU DID IT... AGAIN.
AND YET, YOU DON'T KNOW HOW.
WHAT IS THE MYS-TERY BEHIND YOUR FOR-GOTTEN PAST?
NOHIRO IS PURIFYING THE WATER REALM.

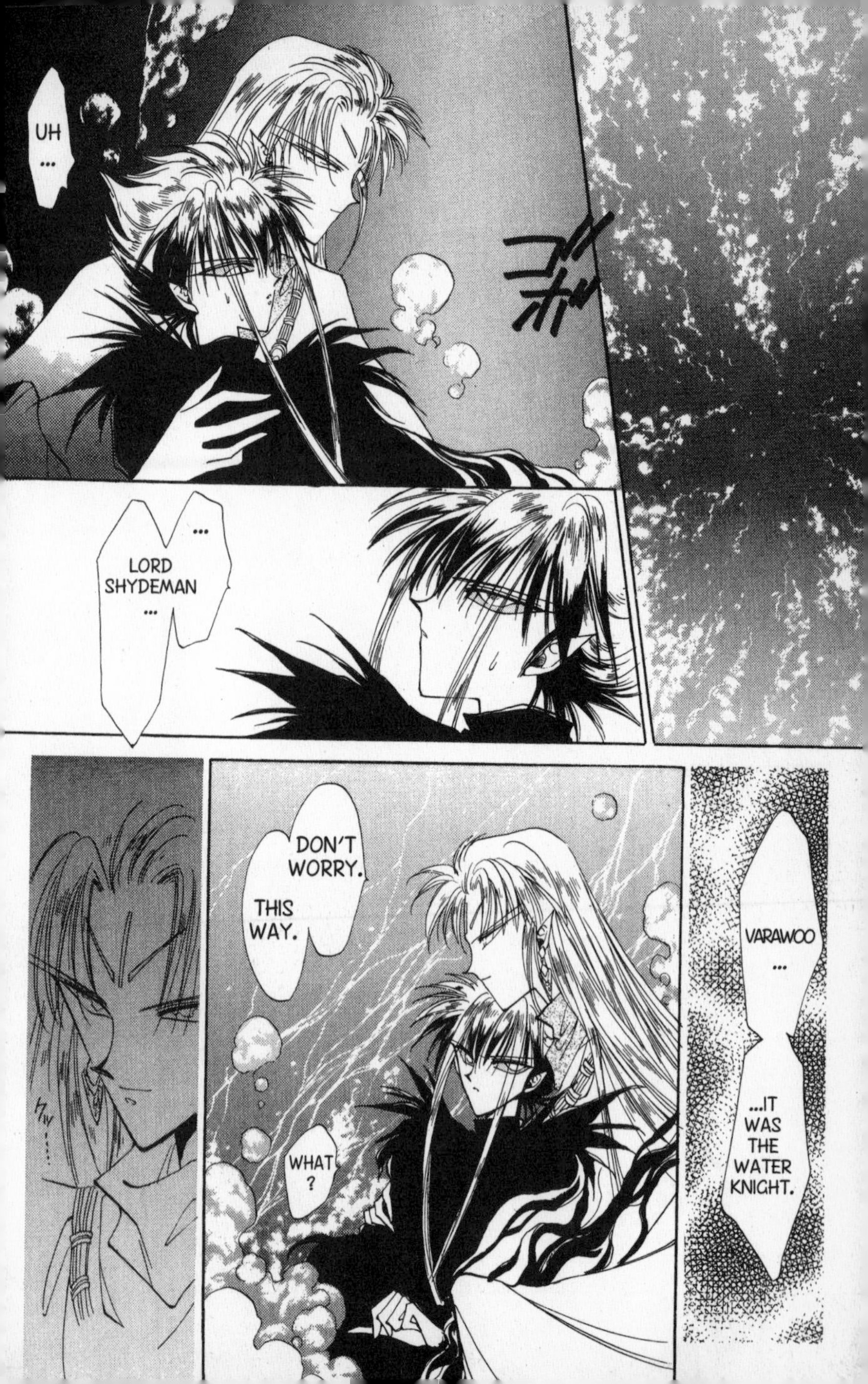
UH ...
... LORD SHYDEMAN ...
VARAWOO ...
...IT WAS THE WATER KNIGHT.
DON'T WORRY.
THIS WAY.
WHAT?

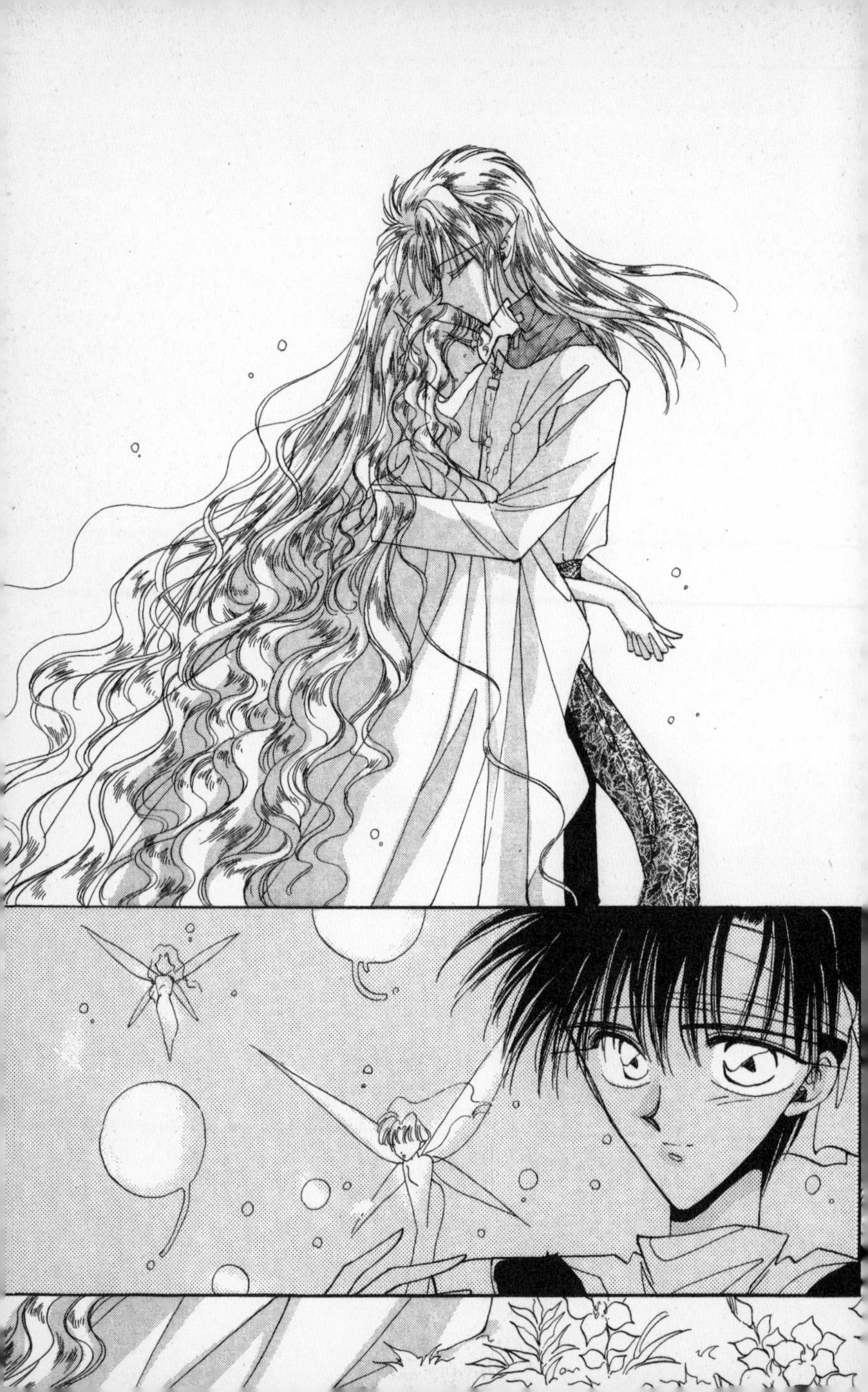

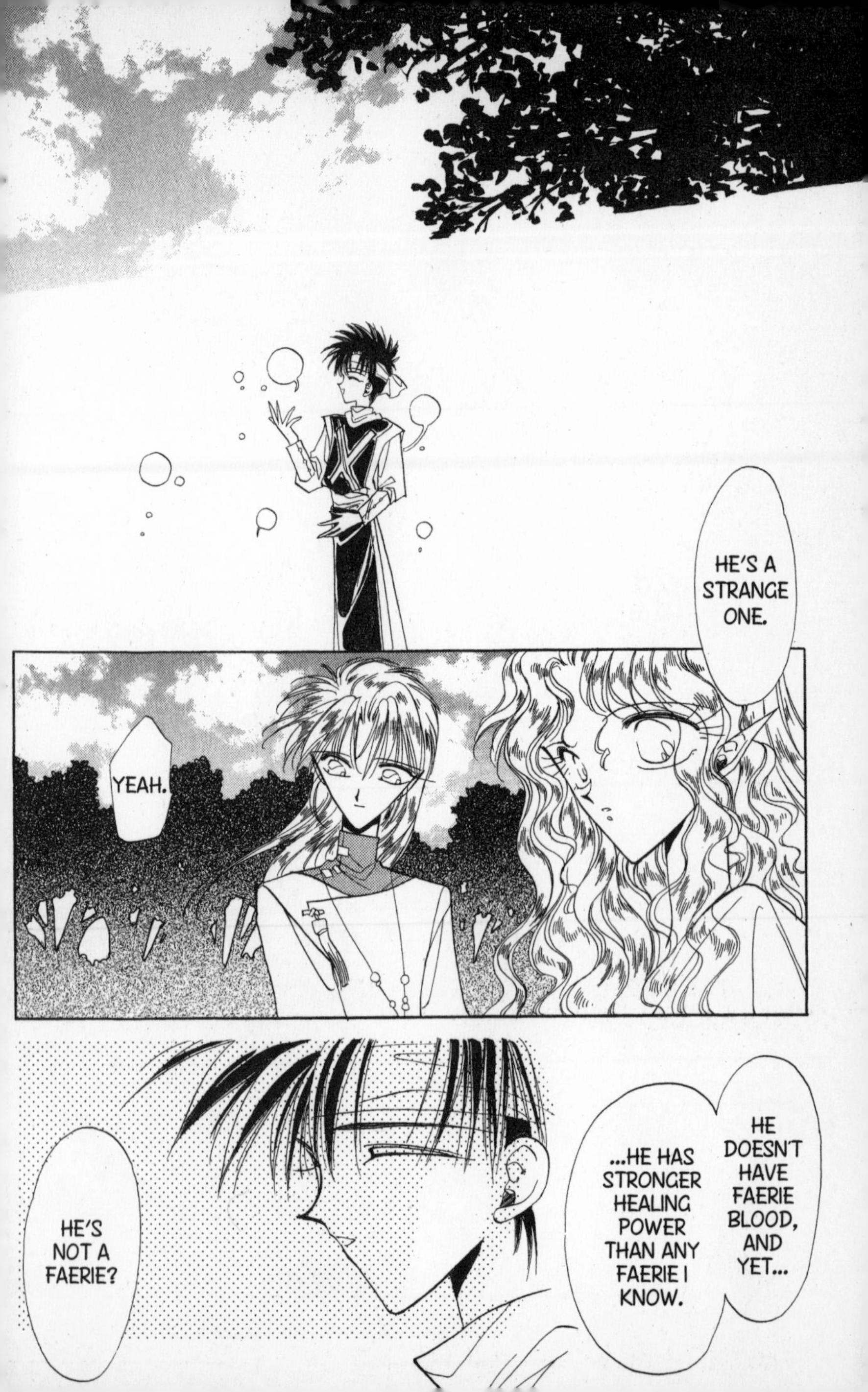
HE'S A STRANGE ONE.
YEAH.
HE DOESN'T HAVE FAERIE BLOOD, AND YET...
...HE HAS STRONGER HEALING POWER THAN ANY FAERIE I KNOW.
HE'S NOT A FAERIE?

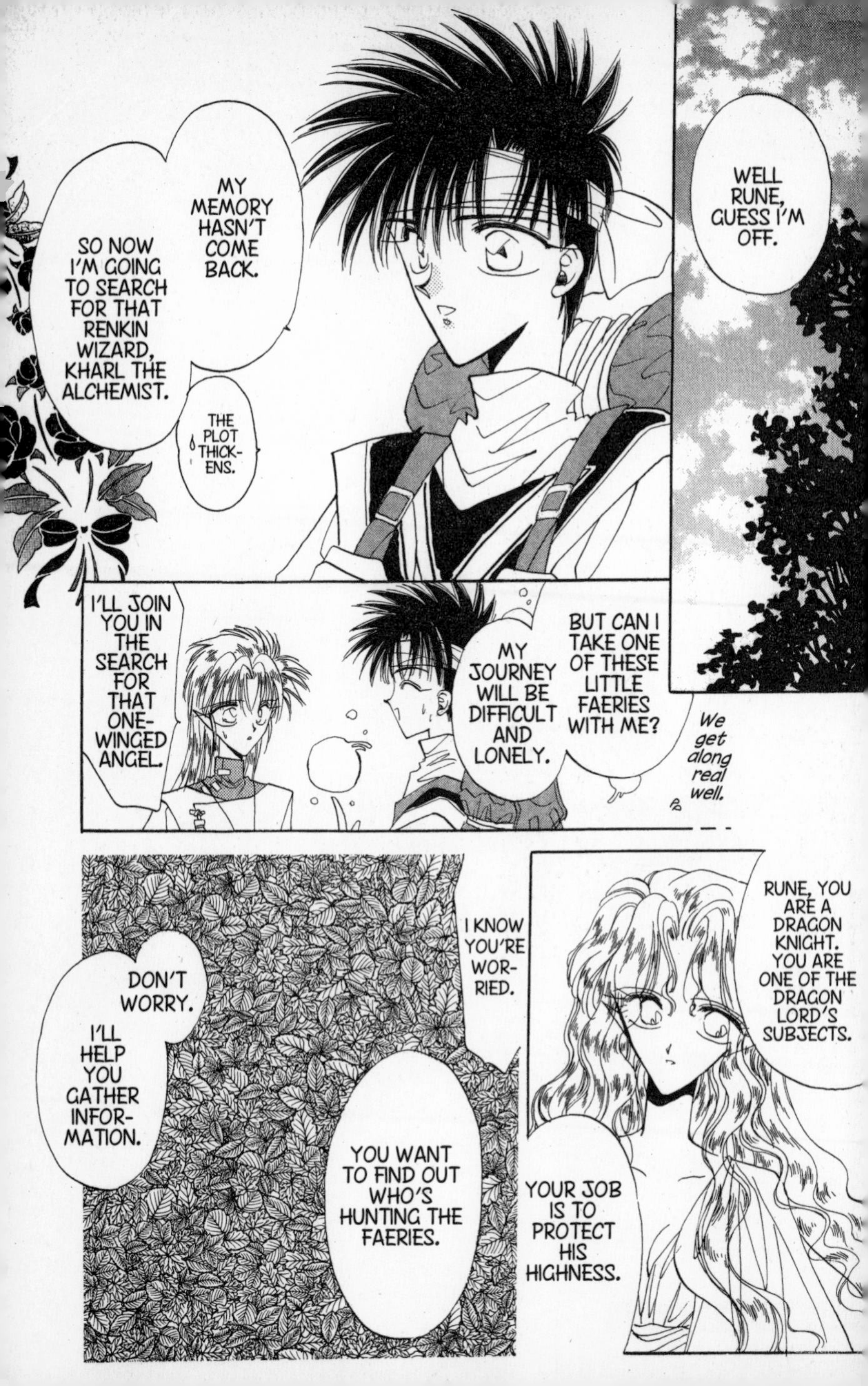
WELL RUNE, GUESS I'M OFF.
MY MEMORY HASN'T COME BACK.
SO NOW I'M GOING TO SEARCH FOR THAT RENKIN WIZARD, KHARL THE ALCHEMIST.
THE PLOT THICK-ENS.
BUT CAN I TAKE ONE OF THESE LITTLE FAERIES WITH ME?
MY JOURNEY WILL BE DIFFICULT AND LONELY.
We get along real well.
I'LL JOIN YOU IN THE SEARCH FOR THAT ONE-WINGED ANGEL.
RUNE, YOU ARE A DRAGON KNIGHT. YOU ARE ONE OF THE DRAGON LORD'S SUBJECTS.
I KNOW YOU'RE WOR-RIED.
YOUR JOB IS TO PROTECT HIS HIGHNESS.
YOU WANT TO FIND OUT WHO'S HUNTING THE FAERIES.
DON'T WORRY.
I'LL HELP YOU GATHER INFOR-MATION.

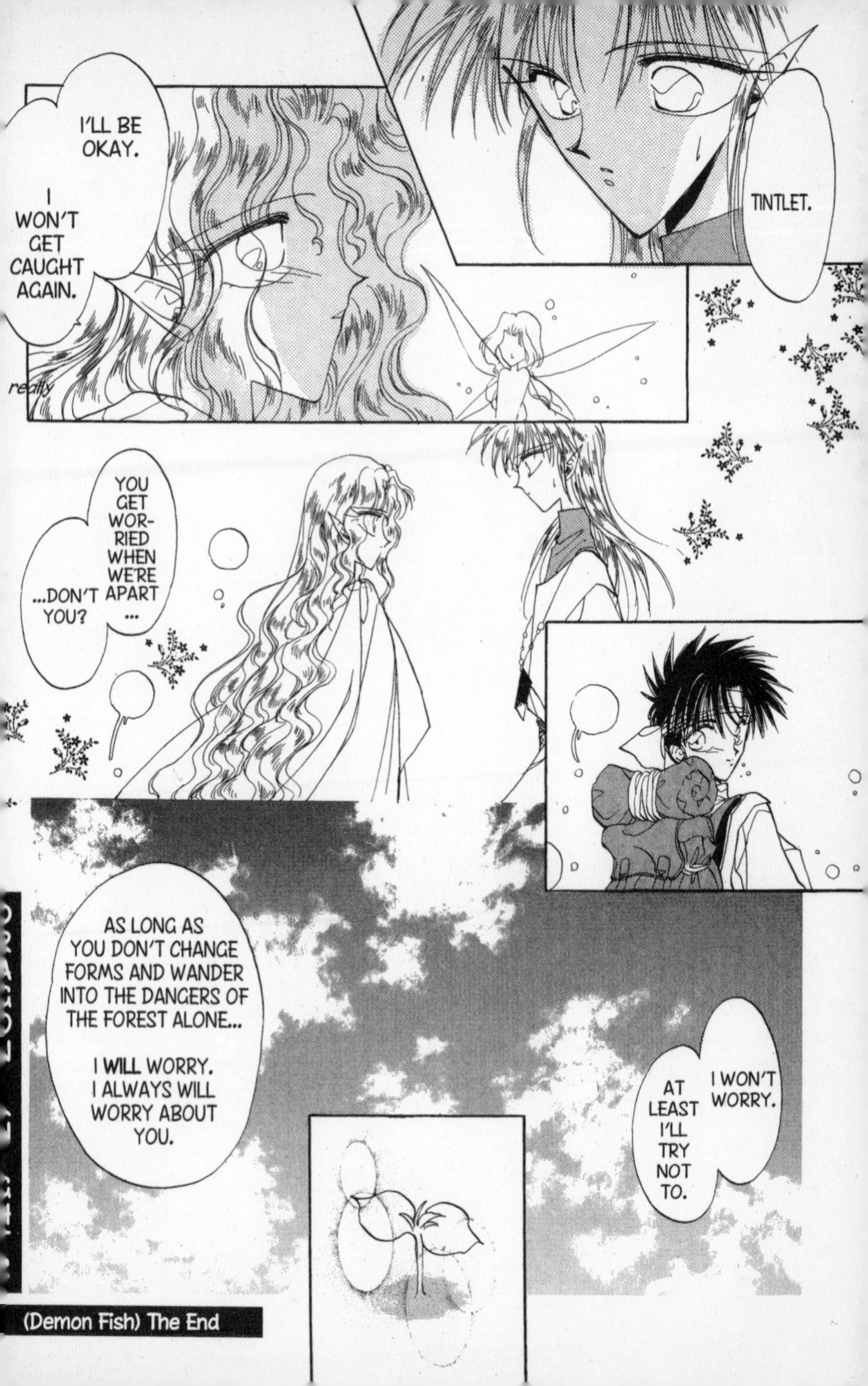
TINTLET.
I'LL BE OKAY.
I WON'T GET CAUGHT AGAIN.
really
YOU GET WOR-RIED WHEN WE'RE APART ...
...DON'T YOU?
I WON'T WORRY.
AT LEAST I'LL TRY NOT TO.
AS LONG AS YOU DON'T CHANGE FORMS AND WANDER INTO THE DANGERS OF THE FOREST ALONE...
I **WILL** WORRY. I ALWAYS WILL WORRY ABOUT YOU.

(Demon Fish) The End

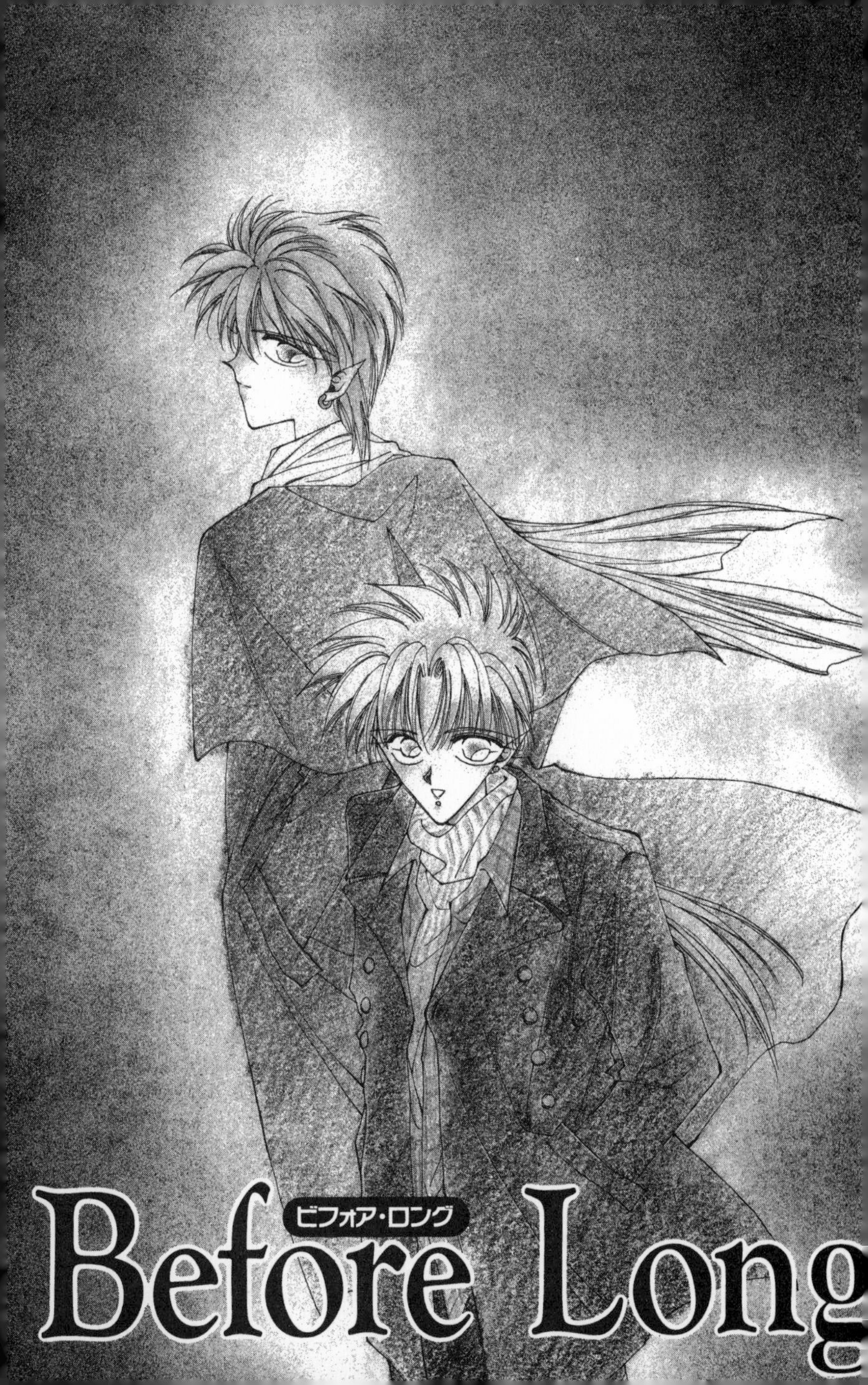
ビフォア・ロング
Before Long

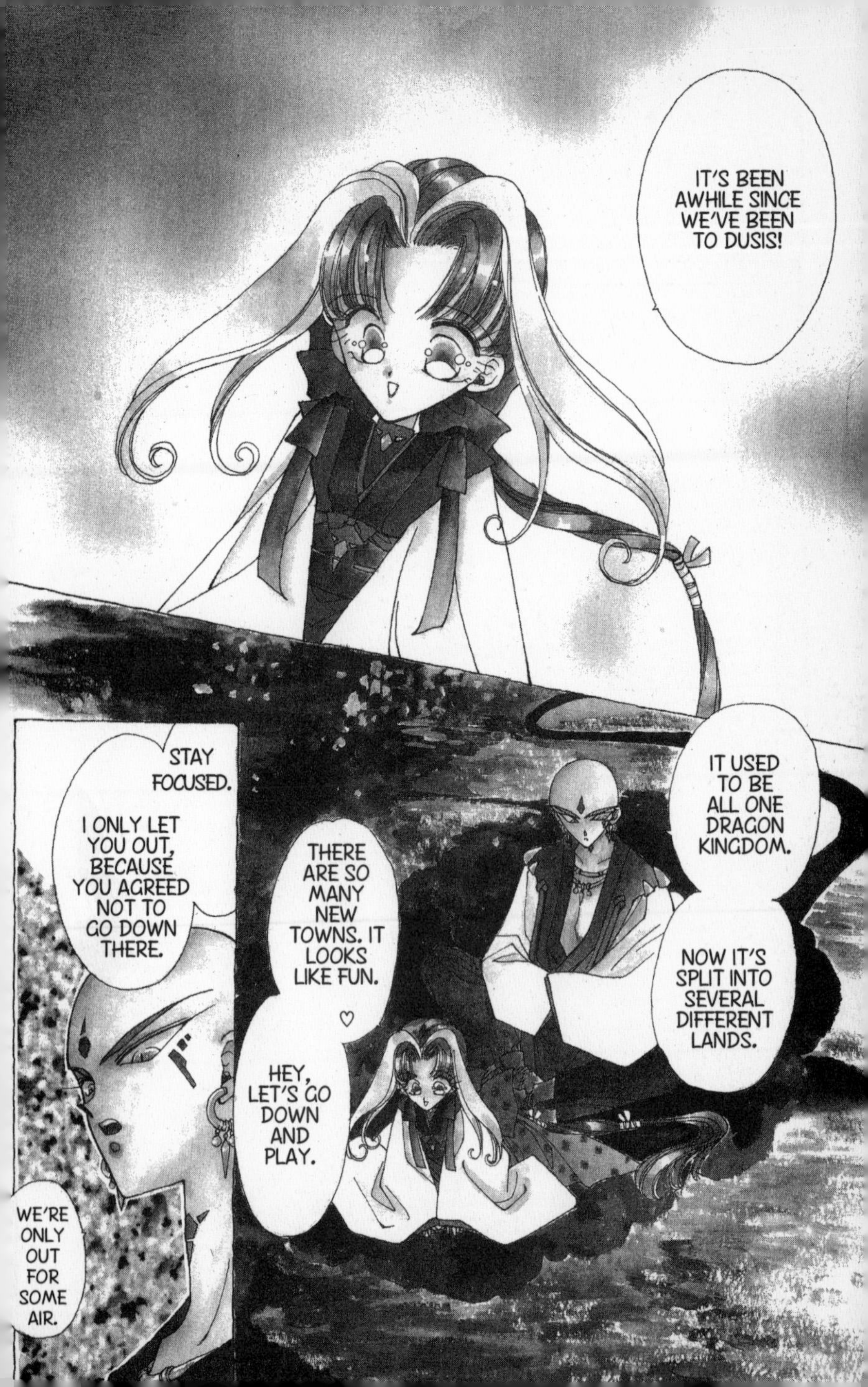
IT'S BEEN AWHILE SINCE WE'VE BEEN TO DUSIS!
IT USED TO BE ALL ONE DRAGON KINGDOM.
NOW IT'S SPLIT INTO SEVERAL DIFFERENT LANDS.
THERE ARE SO MANY NEW TOWNS. IT LOOKS LIKE FUN. ♡
HEY, LET'S GO DOWN AND PLAY.
STAY FOCUSED.
I ONLY LET YOU OUT, BECAUSE YOU AGREED NOT TO GO DOWN THERE.
WE'RE ONLY OUT FOR SOME AIR.

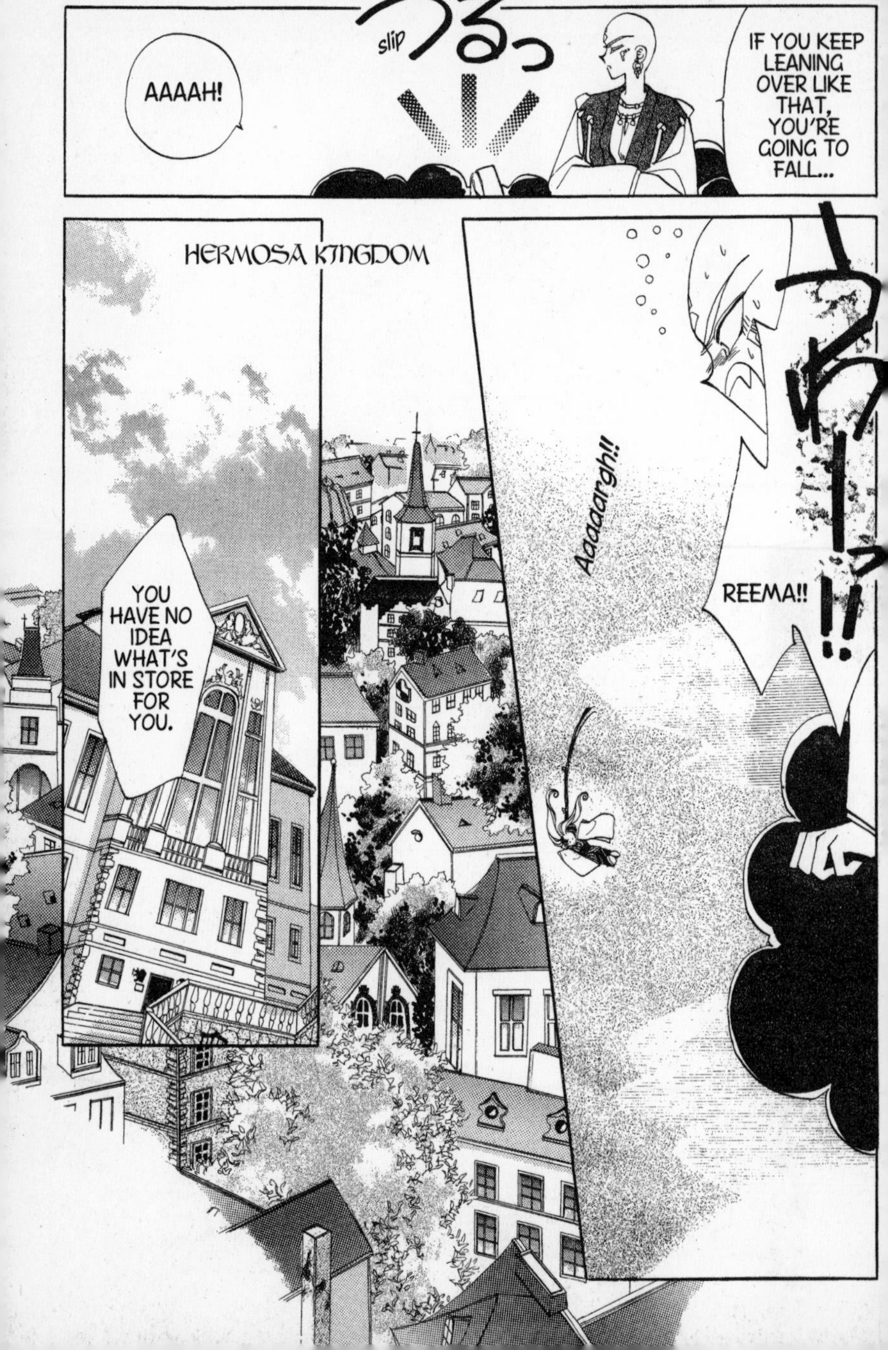
IF YOU KEEP LEANING OVER LIKE THAT, YOU'RE GOING TO FALL...
slip つるっ
AAAAH!
うわーっ!!
Aaaaargh!!
REEMA!!
HERMOSA KINGDOM
YOU HAVE NO IDEA WHAT'S IN STORE FOR YOU.

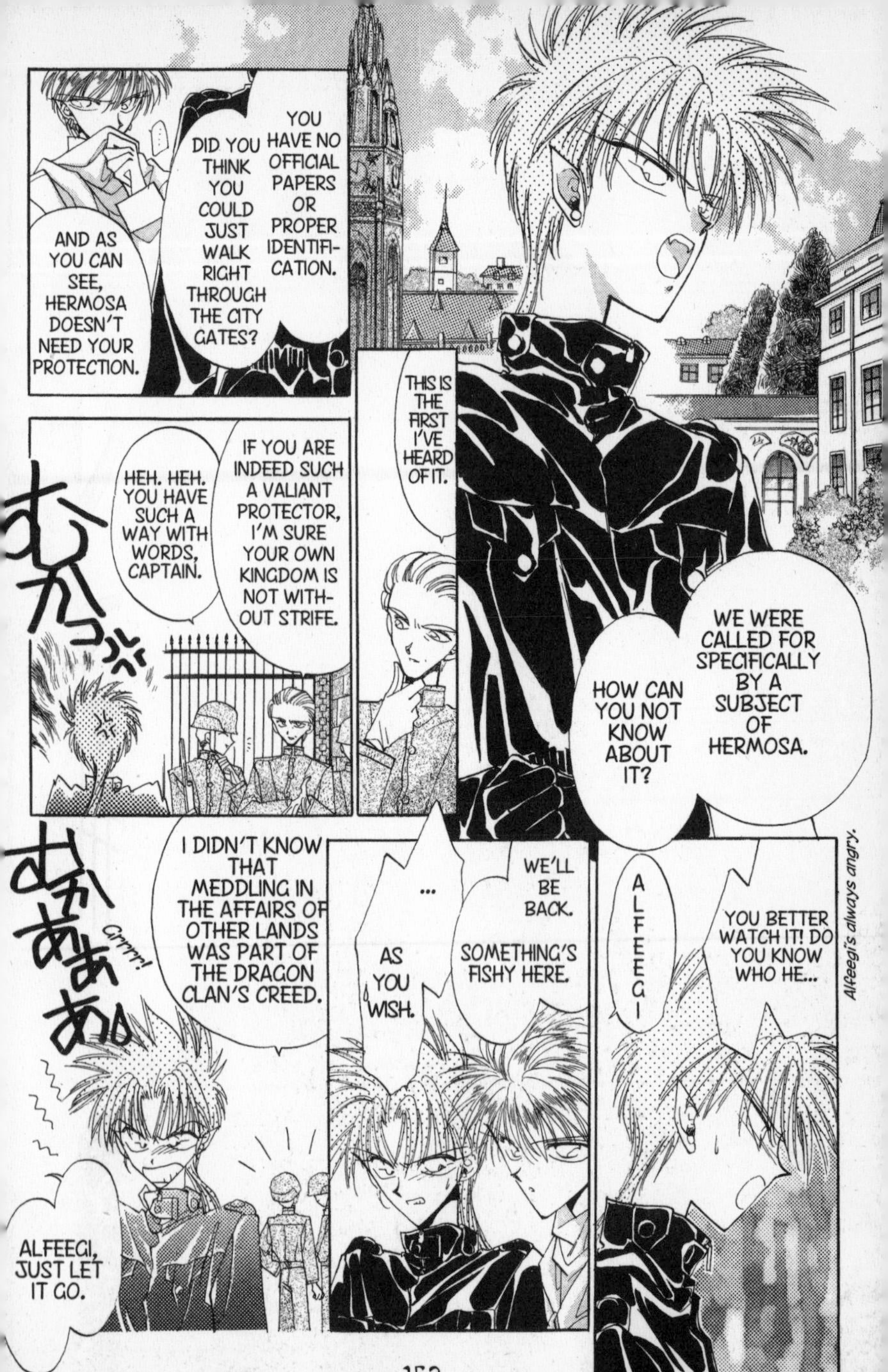
WE WERE CALLED FOR SPECIFICALLY BY A SUBJECT OF HERMOSA.
HOW CAN YOU NOT KNOW ABOUT IT?
THIS IS THE FIRST I'VE HEARD OF IT.
YOU HAVE NO OFFICIAL PAPERS OR PROPER IDENTIFICATION.
DID YOU THINK YOU COULD JUST WALK RIGHT THROUGH THE CITY GATES?
AND AS YOU CAN SEE, HERMOSA DOESN'T NEED YOUR PROTECTION.
IF YOU ARE INDEED SUCH A VALIANT PROTECTOR, I'M SURE YOUR OWN KINGDOM IS NOT WITHOUT STRIFE.
HEH. HEH. YOU HAVE SUCH A WAY WITH WORDS, CAPTAIN.
むかっ
Alfeegi's always angry.
YOU BETTER WATCH IT! DO YOU KNOW WHO HE...
ALFEEGI
WE'LL BE BACK.
SOMETHING'S FISHY HERE.
...
AS YOU WISH.
I DIDN'T KNOW THAT MEDDLING IN THE AFFAIRS OF OTHER LANDS WAS PART OF THE DRAGON CLAN'S CREED.
むかあああ。
Grrrr!
ALFEEGI, JUST LET IT GO.

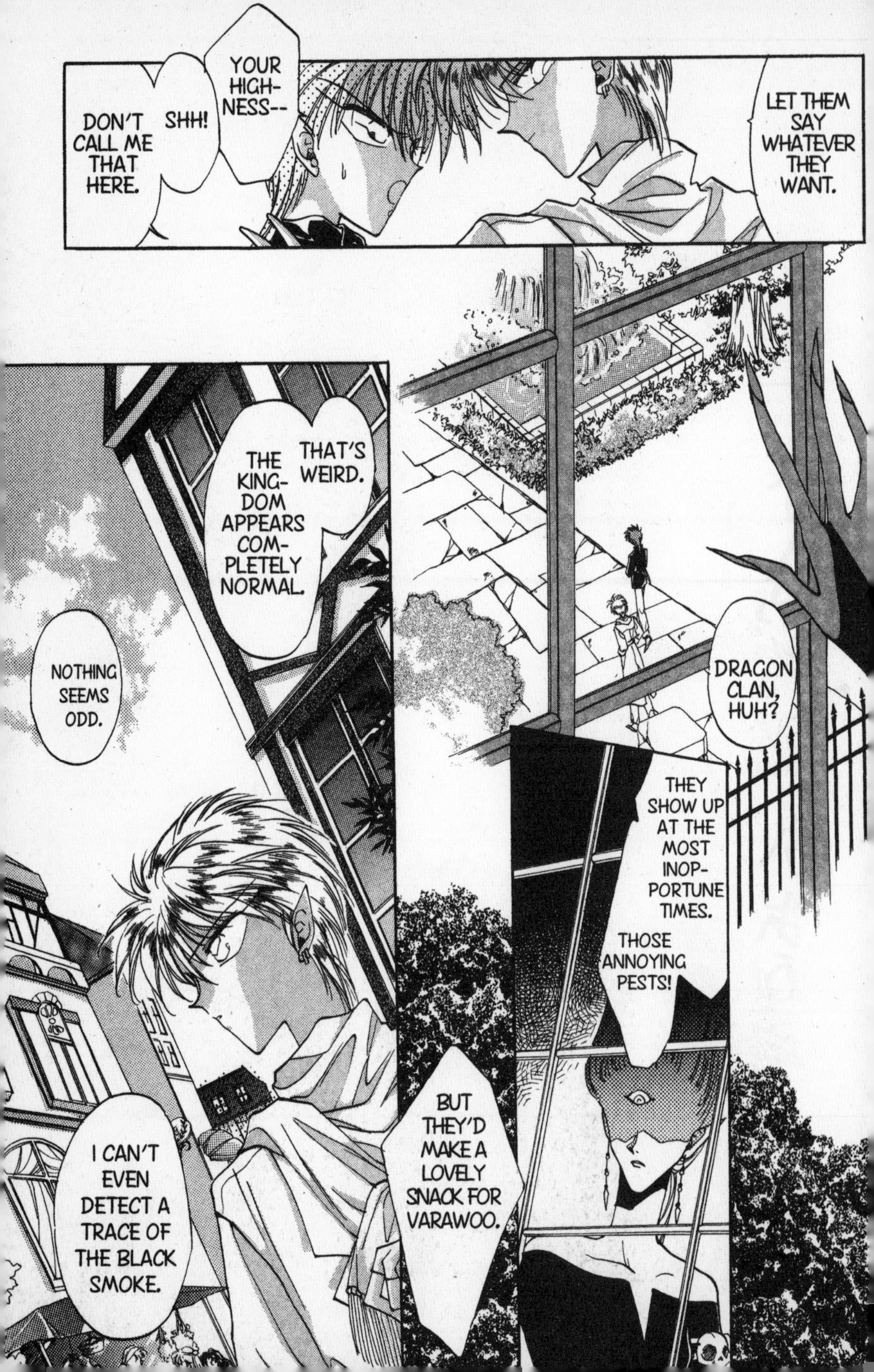
LET THEM SAY WHATEVER THEY WANT.
YOUR HIGH-NESS--
SHH!
DON'T CALL ME THAT HERE.
DRAGON CLAN, HUH?
THEY SHOW UP AT THE MOST INOP-PORTUNE TIMES.
THOSE ANNOYING PESTS!
BUT THEY'D MAKE A LOVELY SNACK FOR VARAWOO.
THAT'S WEIRD.
THE KING-DOM APPEARS COM-PLETELY NORMAL.
NOTHING SEEMS ODD.
I CAN'T EVEN DETECT A TRACE OF THE BLACK SMOKE.

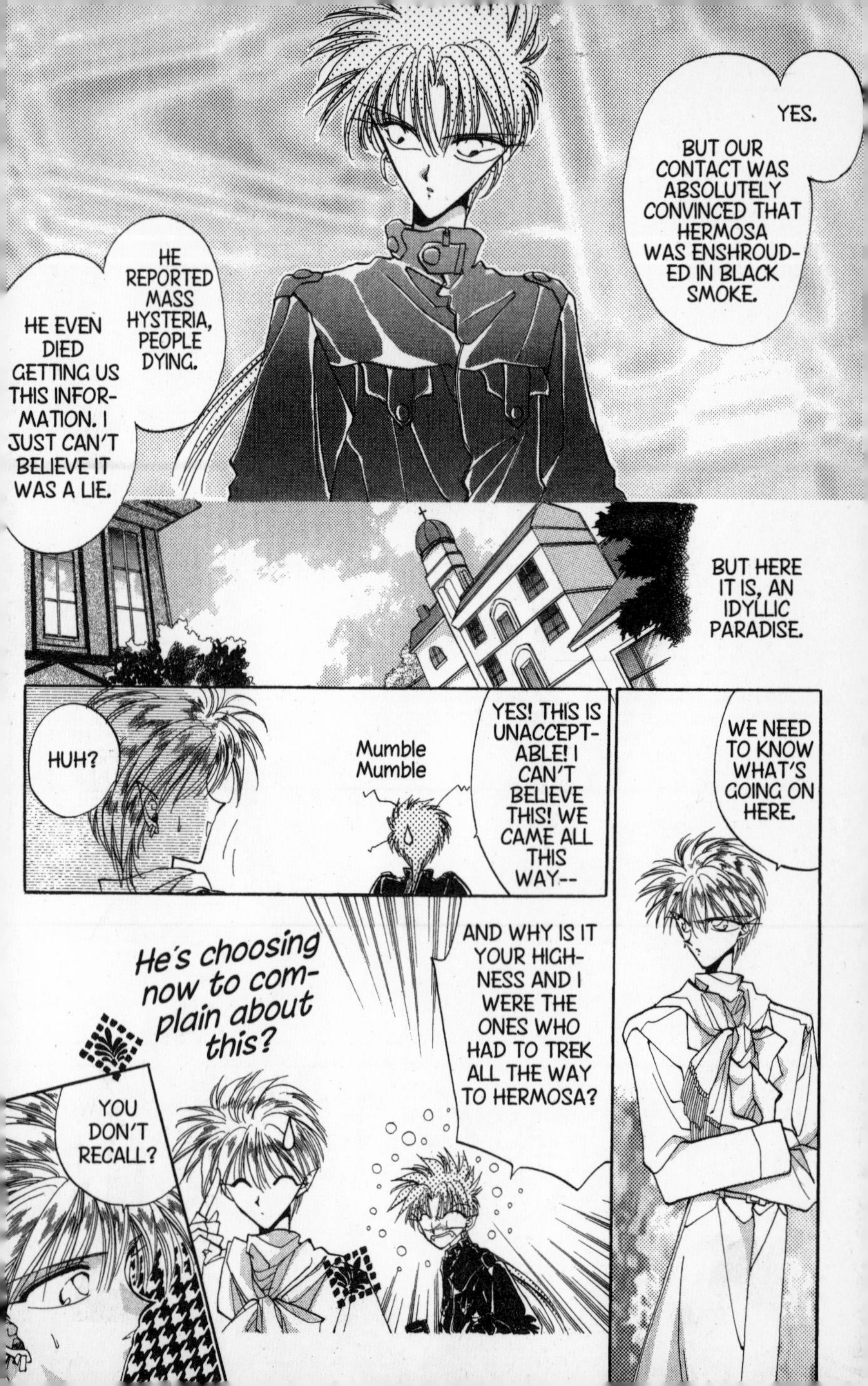
YES.
BUT OUR CONTACT WAS ABSOLUTELY CONVINCED THAT HERMOSA WAS ENSHROUDED-ED IN BLACK SMOKE.
HE REPORTED MASS HYSTERIA, PEOPLE DYING.
HE EVEN DIED GETTING US THIS INFOR-MATION. I JUST CAN'T BELIEVE IT WAS A LIE.
BUT HERE IT IS, AN IDYLLIC PARADISE.
WE NEED TO KNOW WHAT'S GOING ON HERE.
YES! THIS IS UNACCEPT-ABLE! I CAN'T BELIEVE THIS! WE CAME ALL THIS WAY--
Mumble Mumble
HUH?
AND WHY IS IT YOUR HIGH-NESS AND I WERE THE ONES WHO HAD TO TREK ALL THE WAY TO HERMOSA?
He's choosing now to com-plain about this?
YOU DON'T RECALL?

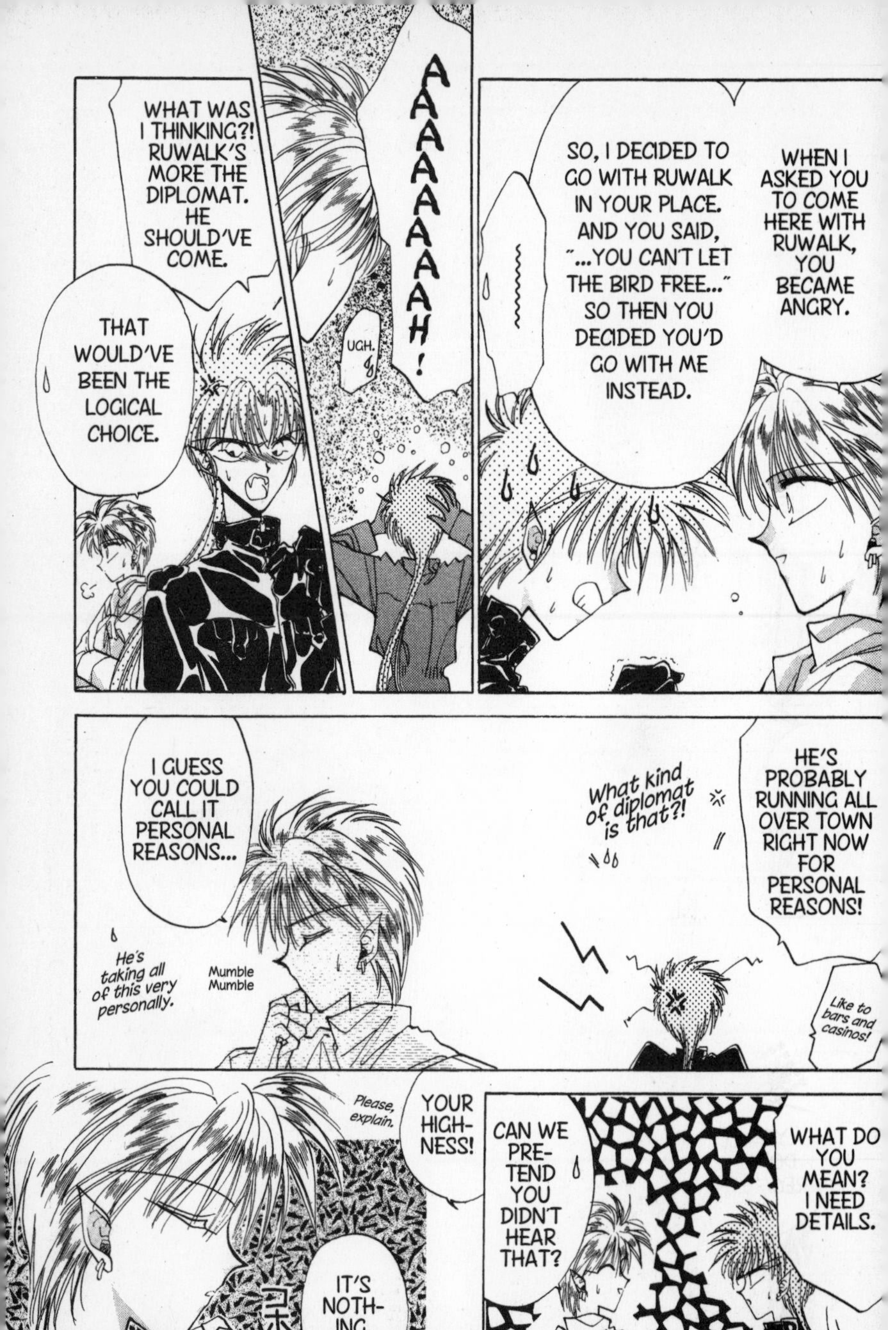
WHEN I ASKED YOU TO COME HERE WITH RUWALK, YOU BECAME ANGRY.
SO, I DECIDED TO GO WITH RUWALK IN YOUR PLACE. AND YOU SAID, "...YOU CAN'T LET THE BIRD FREE..." SO THEN YOU DECIDED YOU'D GO WITH ME INSTEAD.
AAAAAAAAH!
UGH.
WHAT WAS I THINKING?! RUWALK'S MORE THE DIPLOMAT. HE SHOULD'VE COME.
THAT WOULD'VE BEEN THE LOGICAL CHOICE.
HE'S PROBABLY RUNNING ALL OVER TOWN RIGHT NOW FOR PERSONAL REASONS!
Like to bars and casinos!
What kind of diplomat is that?!
I GUESS YOU COULD CALL IT PERSONAL REASONS...
Mumble Mumble
He's taking all of this very personally.
WHAT DO YOU MEAN? I NEED DETAILS.
CAN WE PRE-TEND YOU DIDN'T HEAR THAT?
YOUR HIGH-NESS!
Please, explain.
IT'S NOTH-ING.
コホ

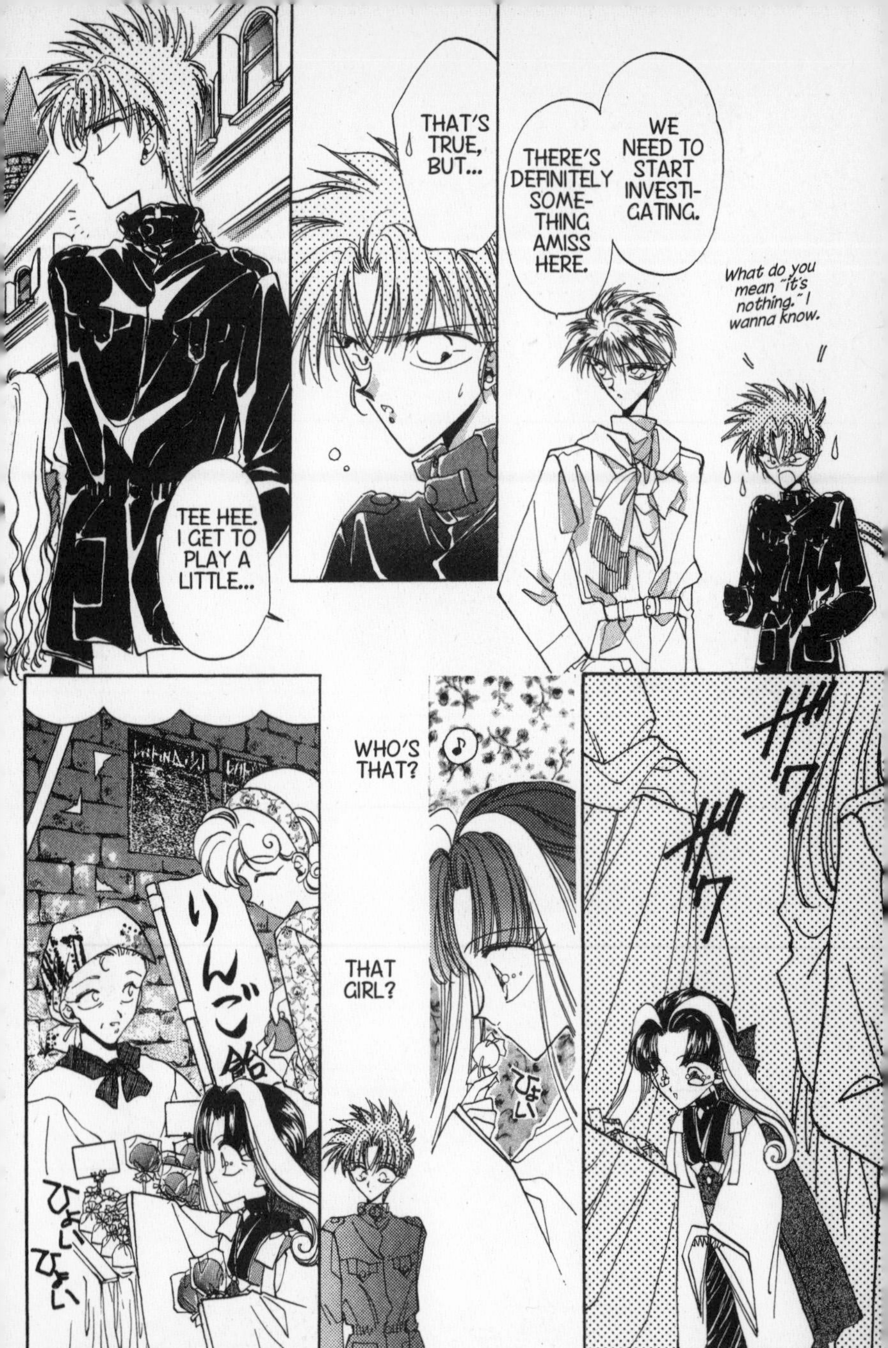

WE NEED TO START INVESTIGATING.
THERE'S DEFINITELY SOMETHING AMISS HERE.
What do you mean "it's nothing." I wanna know.
THAT'S TRUE, BUT...
TEE HEE. I GET TO PLAY A LITTLE...
ザワ
ザワ
WHO'S THAT?
THAT GIRL?
ひょい
りんご飴
ひょい ひょい

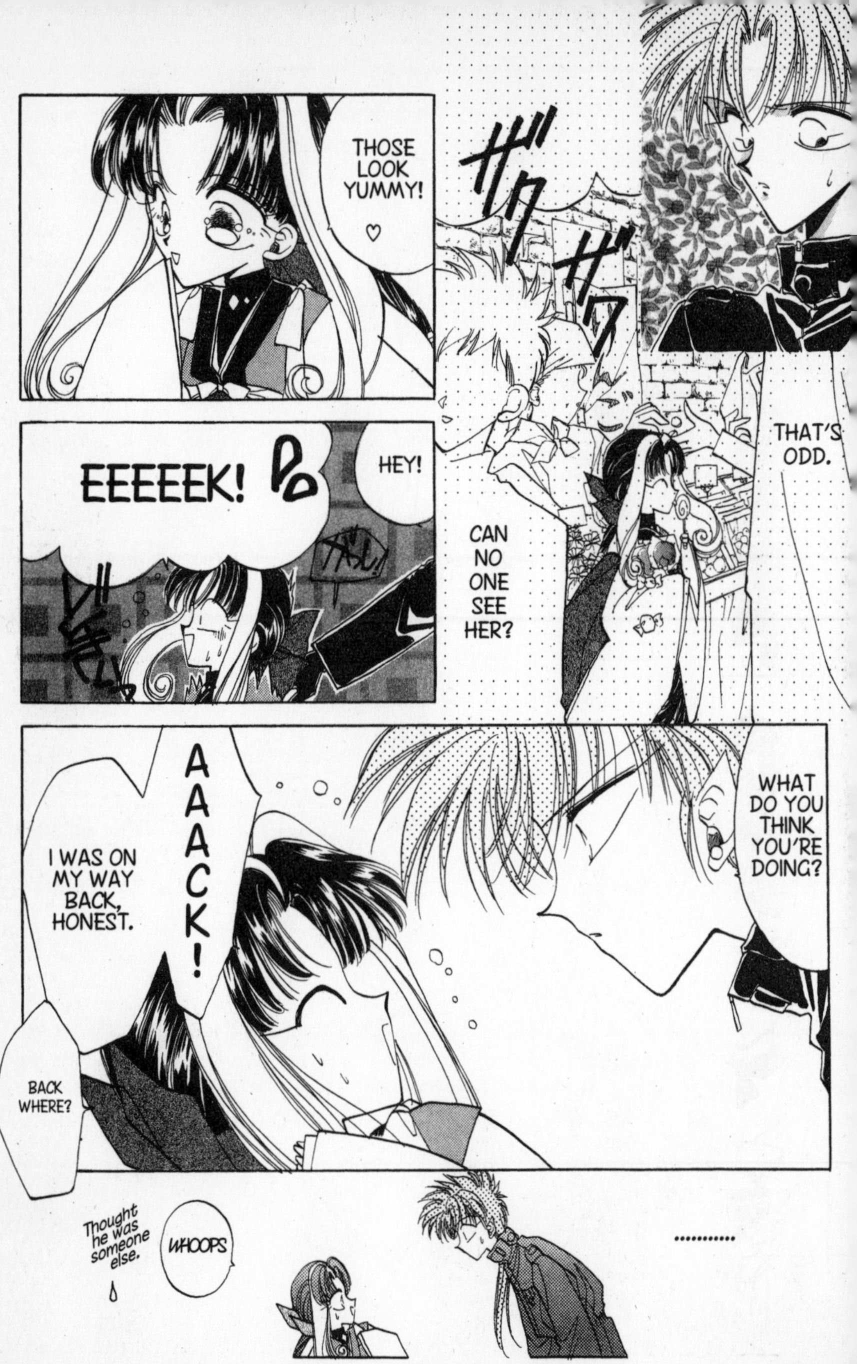
ザク ザク
THAT'S ODD.
CAN NO ONE SEE HER?
THOSE LOOK YUMMY! ♡
HEY!
EEEEEK!
WHAT DO YOU THINK YOU'RE DOING?
AAAACK!
I WAS ON MY WAY BACK, HONEST.
BACK WHERE?
....
WHOOPS
Thought he was someone else.

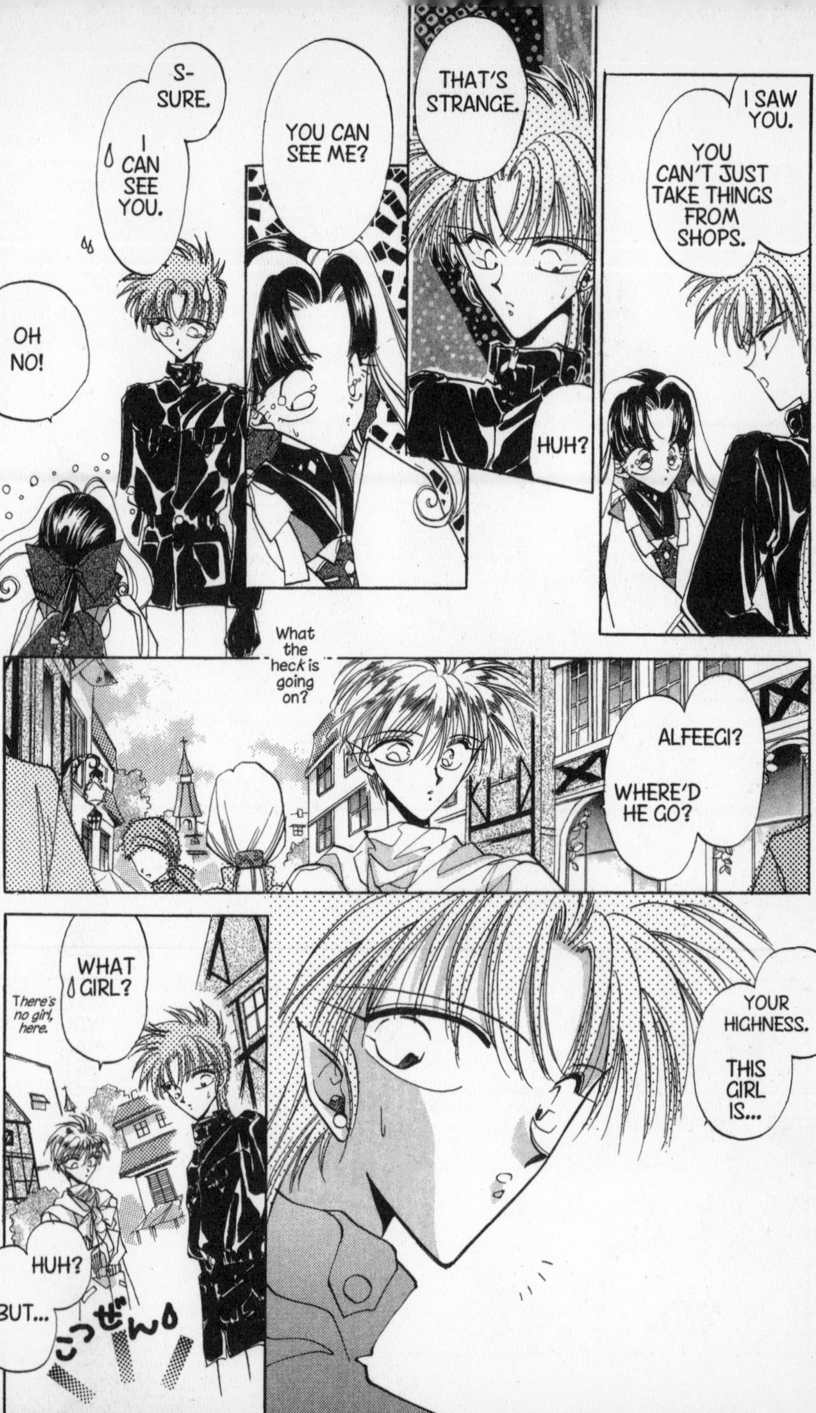
I SAW YOU.
YOU CAN'T JUST TAKE THINGS FROM SHOPS.
THAT'S STRANGE.
HUH?
YOU CAN SEE ME?
S-SURE.
I CAN SEE YOU.
OH NO!
What the heck is going on?
ALFEEGI?
WHERE'D HE GO?
YOUR HIGHNESS.
THIS GIRL IS...
WHAT GIRL?
There's no girl, here.
HUH?
BUT...
こっぜん

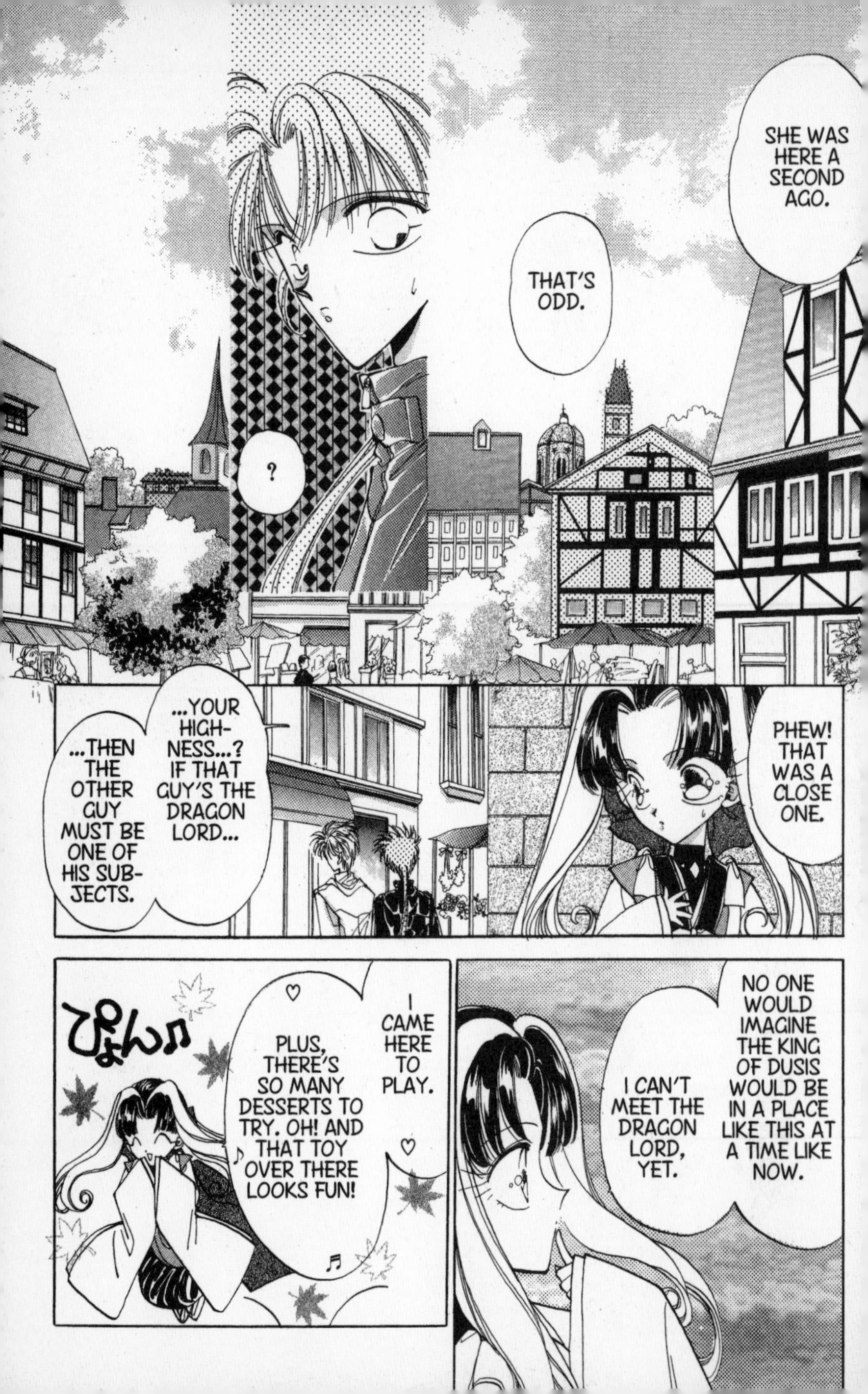
SHE WAS HERE A SECOND AGO.
THAT'S ODD.
?
PHEW! THAT WAS A CLOSE ONE.
...YOUR HIGHNESS...? IF THAT GUY'S THE DRAGON LORD...
...THEN THE OTHER GUY MUST BE ONE OF HIS SUB-JECTS.
NO ONE WOULD IMAGINE THE KING OF DUSIS WOULD BE IN A PLACE LIKE THIS AT A TIME LIKE NOW.
I CAN'T MEET THE DRAGON LORD, YET.
I CAME HERE TO PLAY.
PLUS, THERE'S SO MANY DESSERTS TO TRY. OH! AND THAT TOY OVER THERE LOOKS FUN!
ぴょん♫

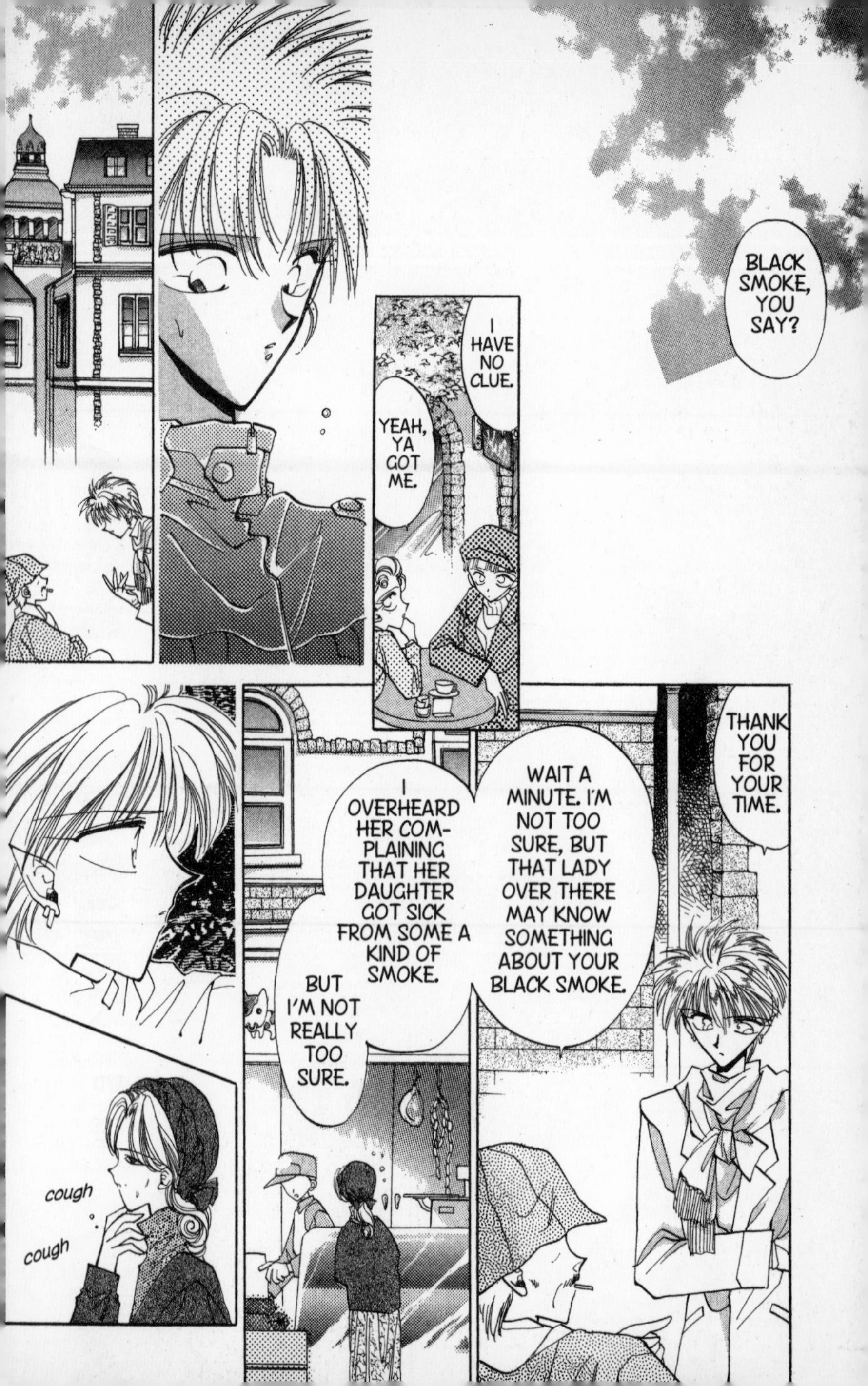
BLACK SMOKE, YOU SAY?
I HAVE NO CLUE.
YEAH, YA GOT ME.
THANK YOU FOR YOUR TIME.
WAIT A MINUTE. I'M NOT TOO SURE, BUT THAT LADY OVER THERE MAY KNOW SOMETHING ABOUT YOUR BLACK SMOKE.
I OVERHEARD HER COM-PLAINING THAT HER DAUGHTER GOT SICK FROM SOME A KIND OF SMOKE.
BUT I'M NOT REALLY TOO SURE.
cough
cough

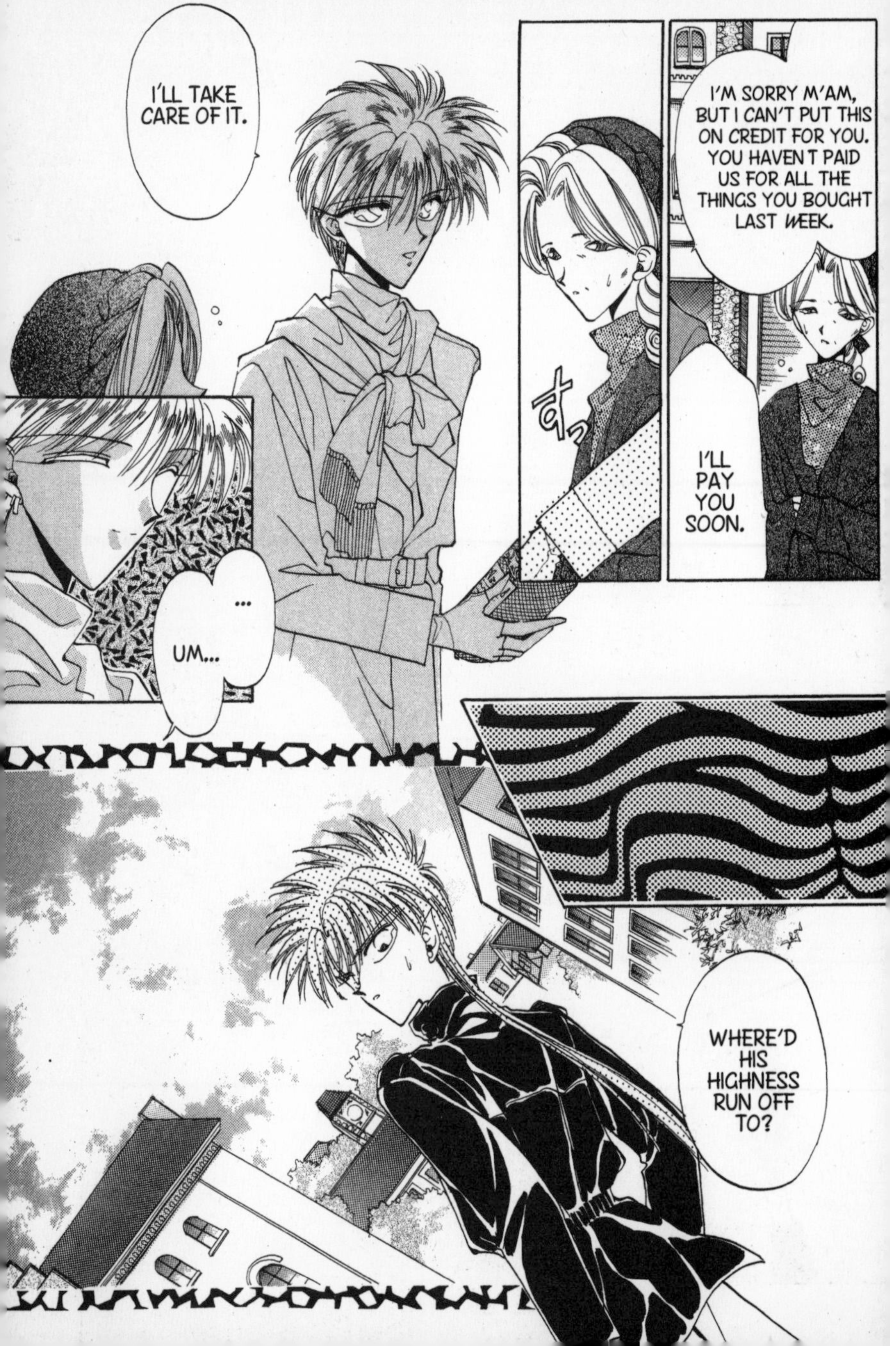
I'M SORRY M'AM, BUT I CAN'T PUT THIS ON CREDIT FOR YOU. YOU HAVEN'T PAID US FOR ALL THE THINGS YOU BOUGHT LAST WEEK.
I'LL PAY YOU SOON.
すっ
I'LL TAKE CARE OF IT.
...
UM...
WHERE'D HIS HIGHNESS RUN OFF TO?

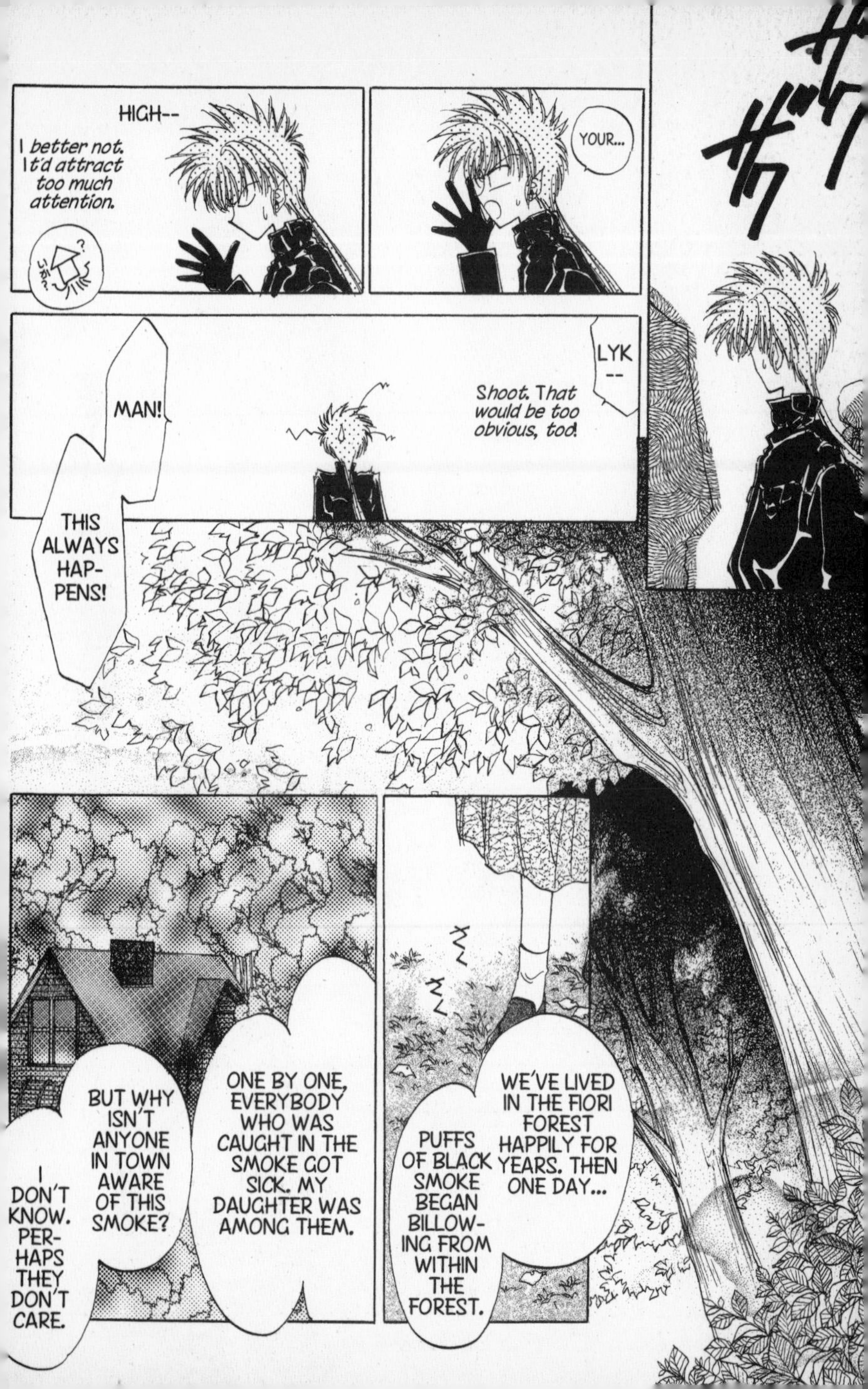
YOUR...
HIGH--
I better not. It'd attract too much attention.
LYK --
Shoot. That would be too obvious, too.
MAN!
THIS ALWAYS HAP-PENS!
WE'VE LIVED IN THE FIORI FOREST HAPPILY FOR YEARS. THEN ONE DAY...
PUFFS OF BLACK SMOKE BEGAN BILLOW-ING FROM WITHIN THE FOREST.
ONE BY ONE, EVERYBODY WHO WAS CAUGHT IN THE SMOKE GOT SICK. MY DAUGHTER WAS AMONG THEM.
BUT WHY ISN'T ANYONE IN TOWN AWARE OF THIS SMOKE?
I DON'T KNOW. PER-HAPS THEY DON'T CARE.

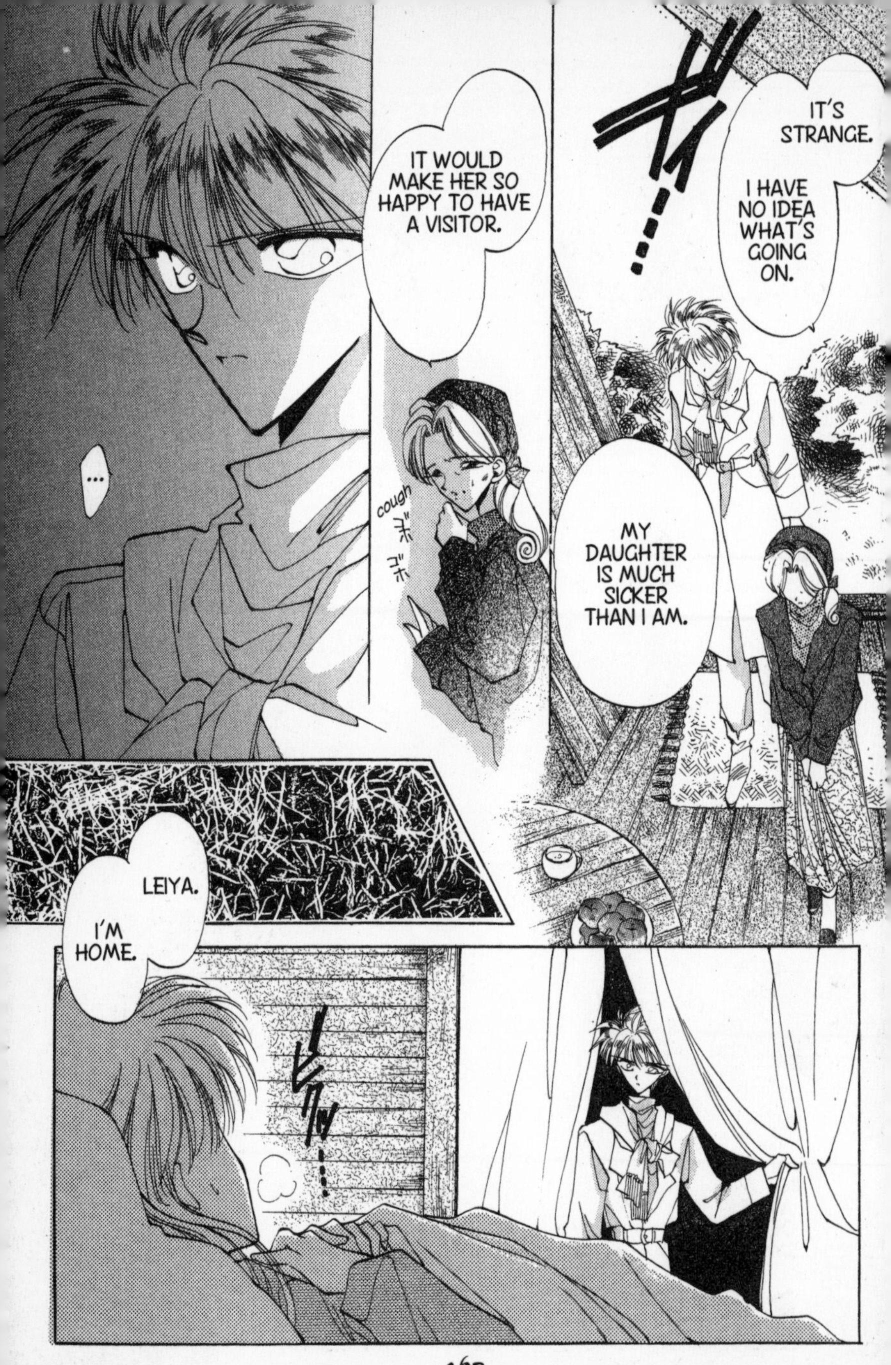
IT'S STRANGE.
I HAVE NO IDEA WHAT'S GOING ON.
MY DAUGHTER IS MUCH SICKER THAN I AM.
IT WOULD MAKE HER SO HAPPY TO HAVE A VISITOR.
cough
...
LEIYA.
I'M HOME.

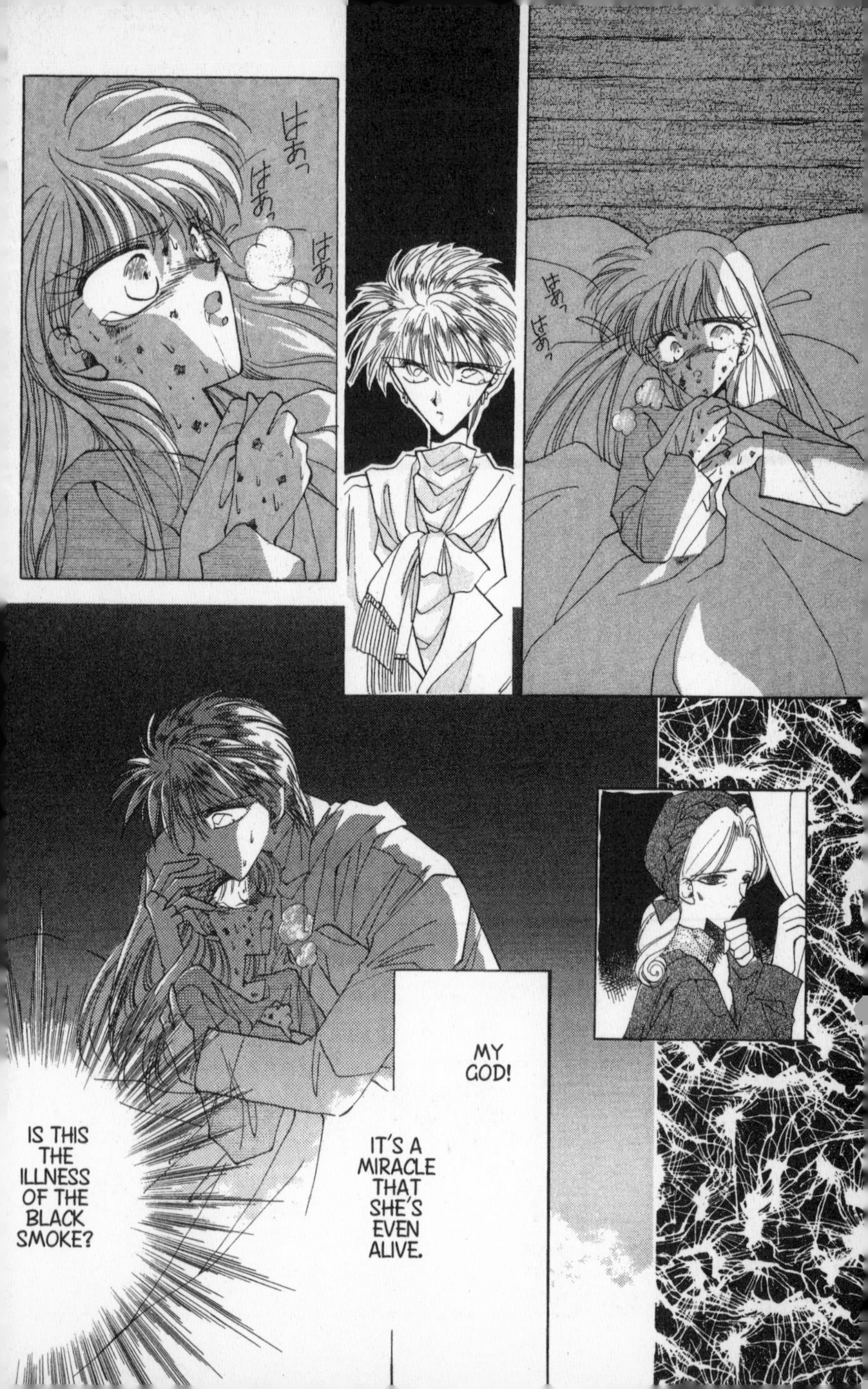
はあっ
はあっ
はあっ
はあっ
はあっ
MY GOD!
IT'S A MIRACLE THAT SHE'S EVEN ALIVE.
IS THIS THE ILLNESS OF THE BLACK SMOKE?

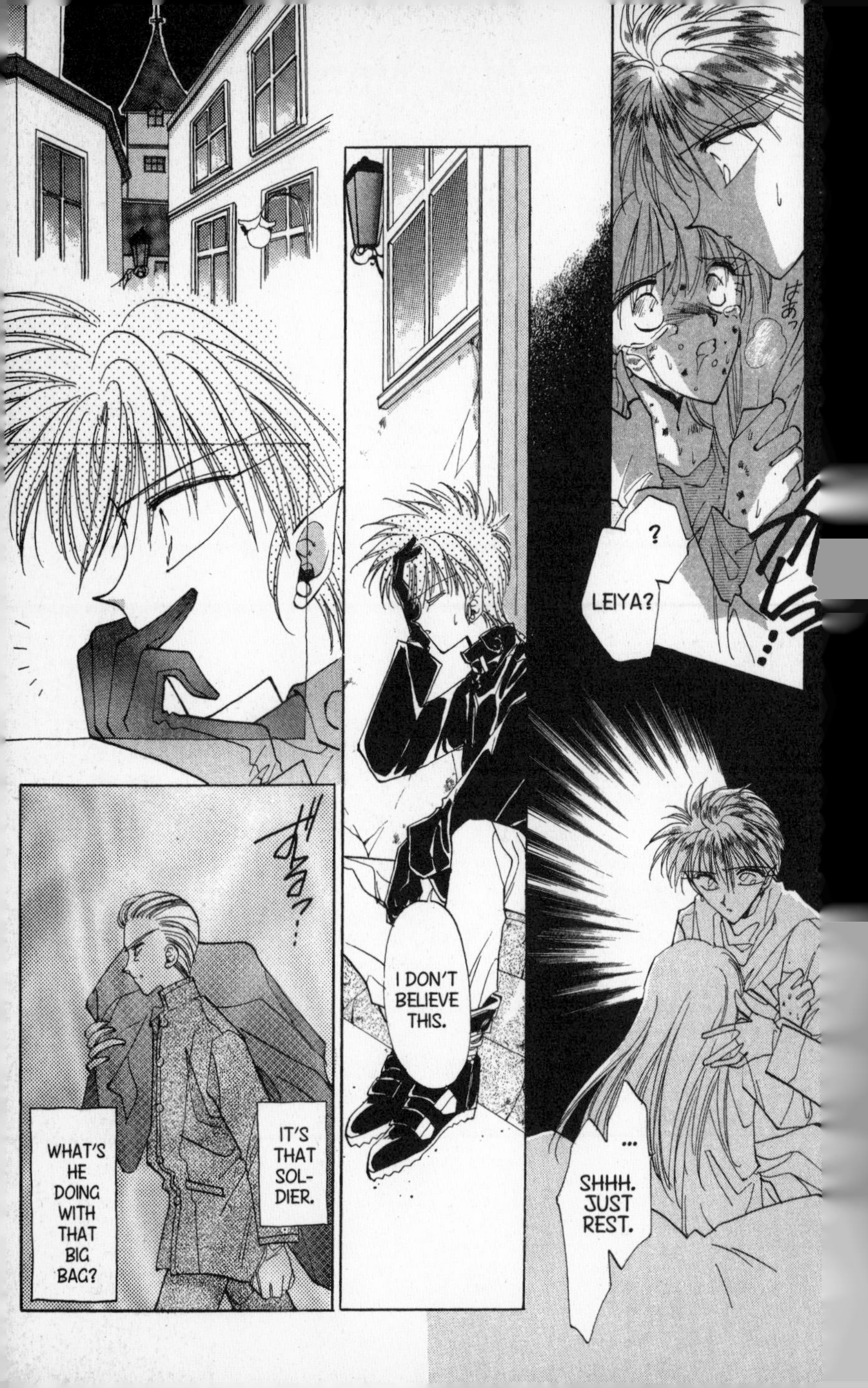
はあっ
?
LEIYA?
...
SHHH. JUST REST.
I DON'T BELIEVE THIS.
IT'S THAT SOL-DIER.
WHAT'S HE DOING WITH THAT BIG BAG?

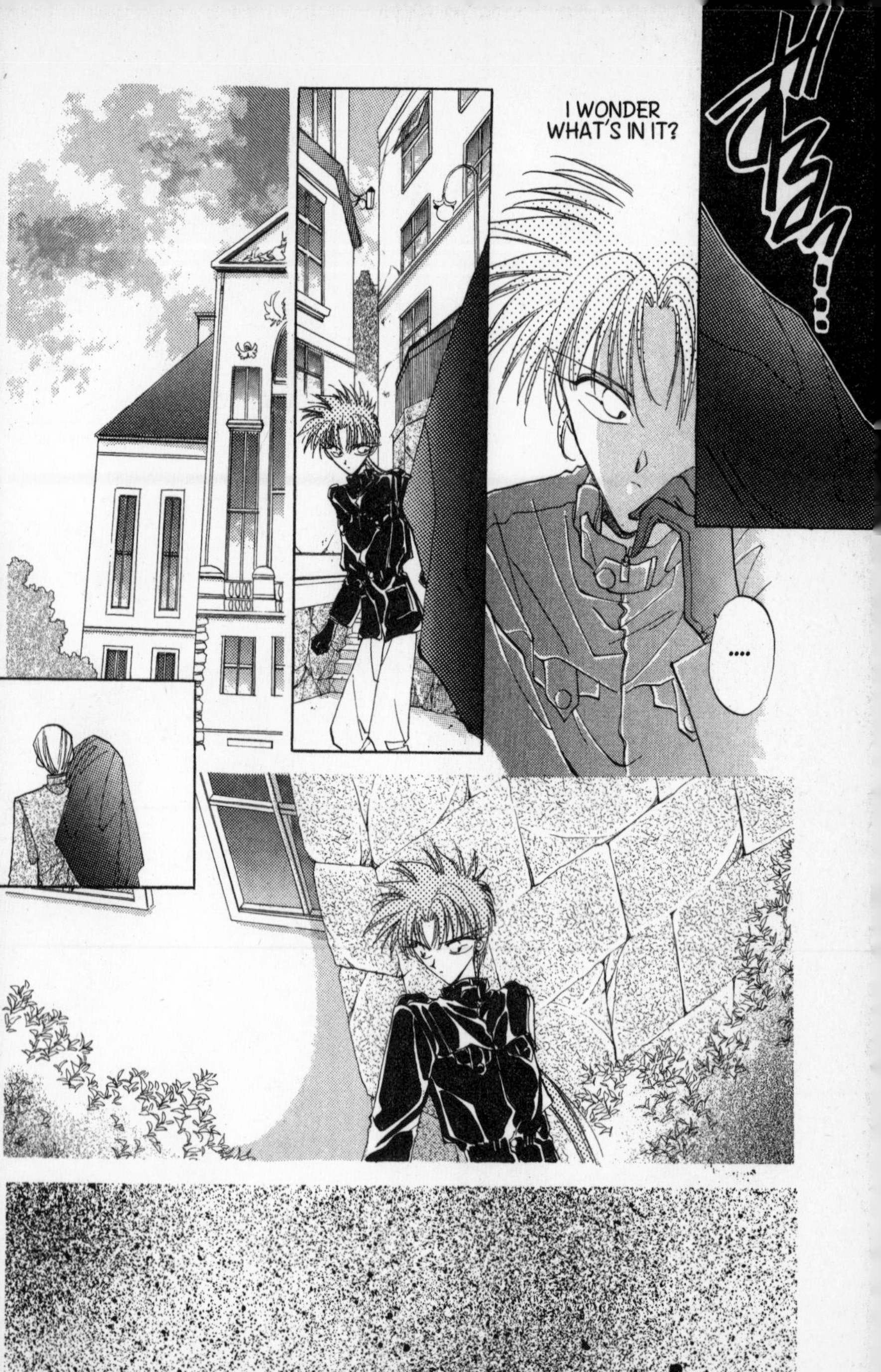
I WONDER WHAT'S IN IT?
....

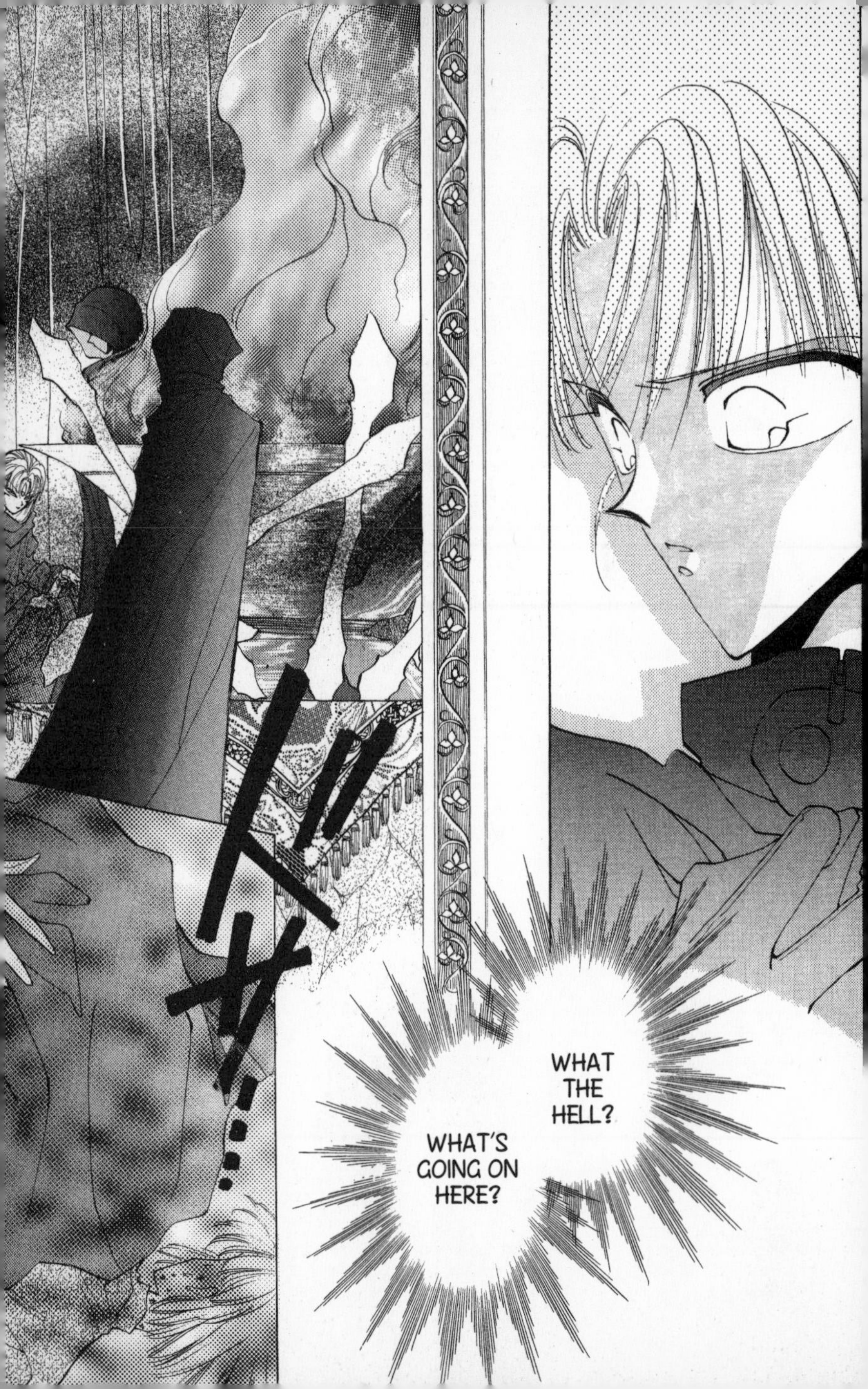
WHAT THE HELL?
WHAT'S GOING ON HERE?

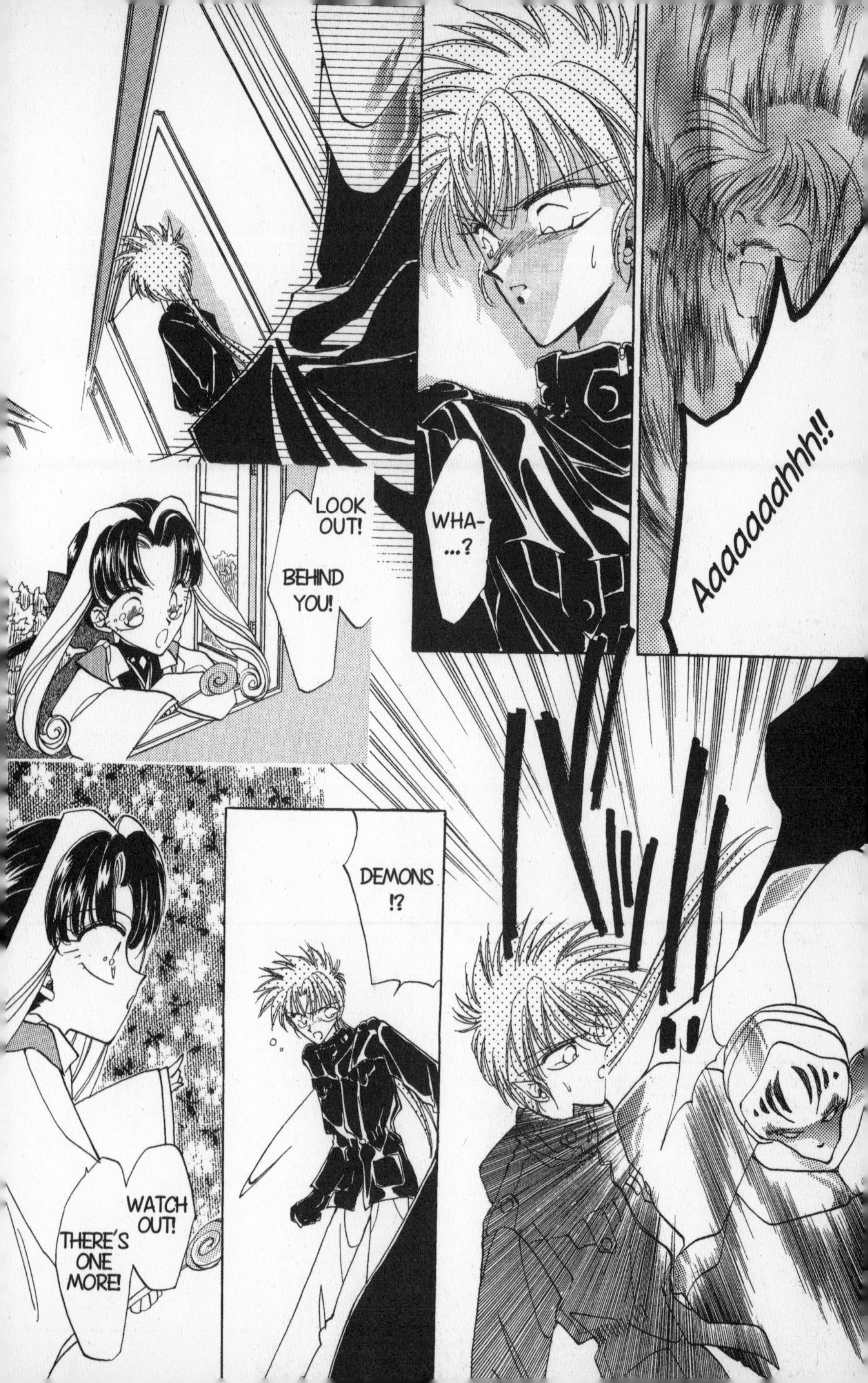
Aaaaaaahhh!!
WHA- ...?
LOOK OUT!
BEHIND YOU!
DEMONS !?
WATCH OUT!
THERE'S ONE MORE!

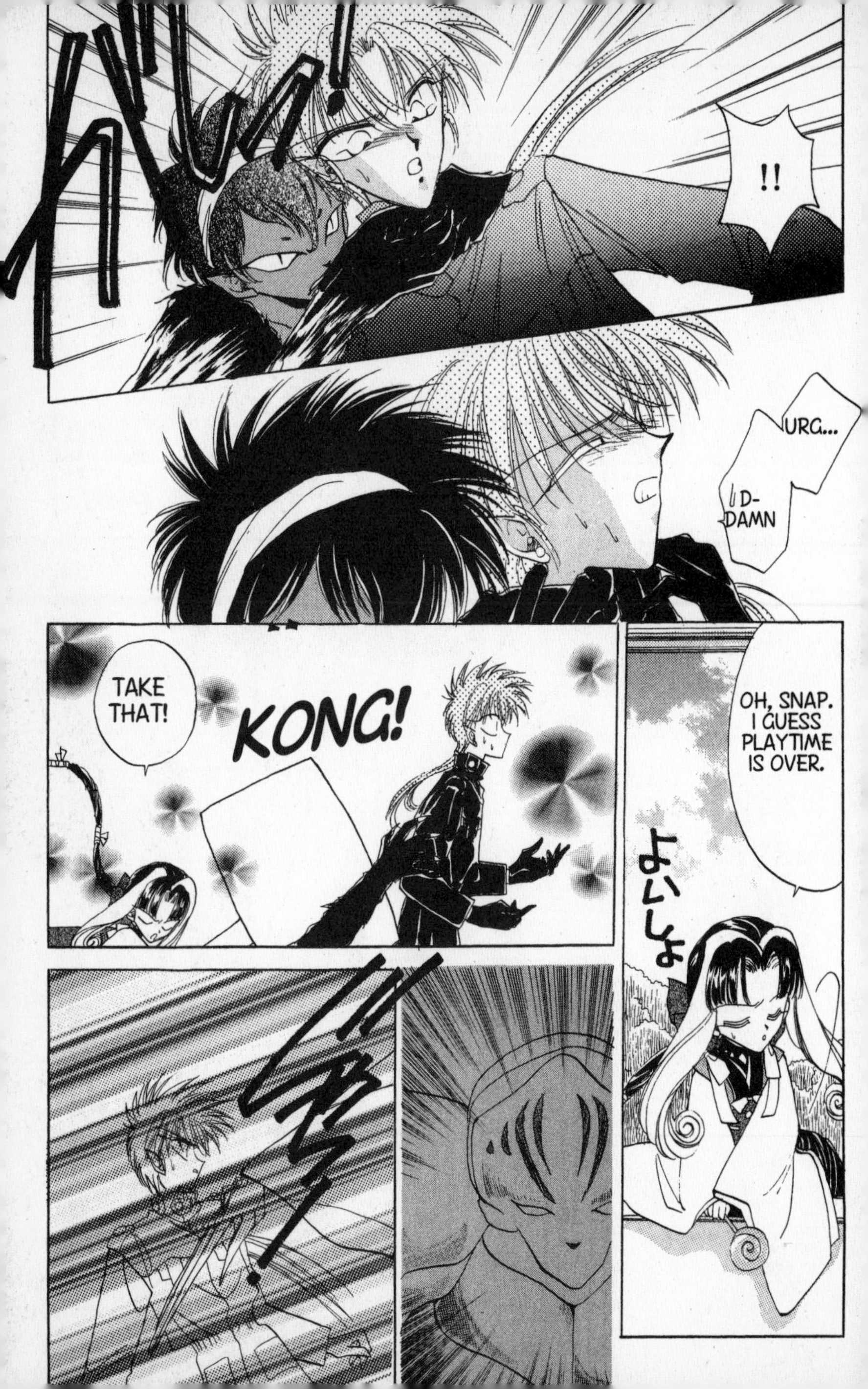
!!
URG...
D-DAMN
OH, SNAP. I GUESS PLAYTIME IS OVER.
よいしょ
TAKE THAT!
KONG!

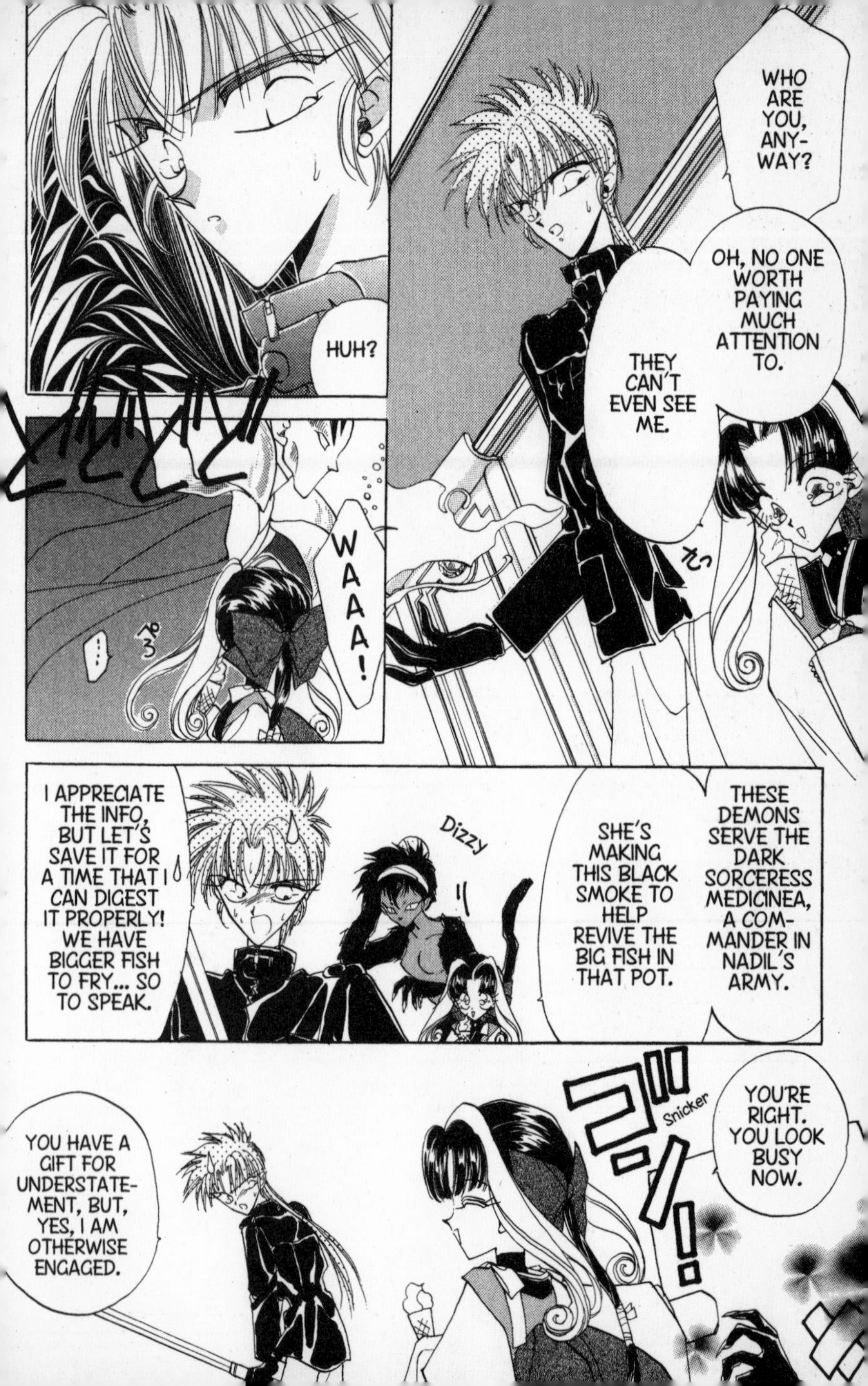
WHO ARE YOU, ANY-WAY?
OH, NO ONE WORTH PAYING MUCH ATTENTION TO.
THEY CAN'T EVEN SEE ME.
HUH?
WAAAA!
...
THESE DEMONS SERVE THE DARK SORCERESS MEDICINEA, A COM-MANDER IN NADIL'S ARMY.
SHE'S MAKING THIS BLACK SMOKE TO HELP REVIVE THE BIG FISH IN THAT POT.
Dizzy
I APPRECIATE THE INFO, BUT LET'S SAVE IT FOR A TIME THAT I CAN DIGEST IT PROPERLY! WE HAVE BIGGER FISH TO FRY... SO TO SPEAK.
YOU'RE RIGHT. YOU LOOK BUSY NOW.
Snicker
YOU HAVE A GIFT FOR UNDERSTATE-MENT, BUT, YES, I AM OTHERWISE ENGAGED.

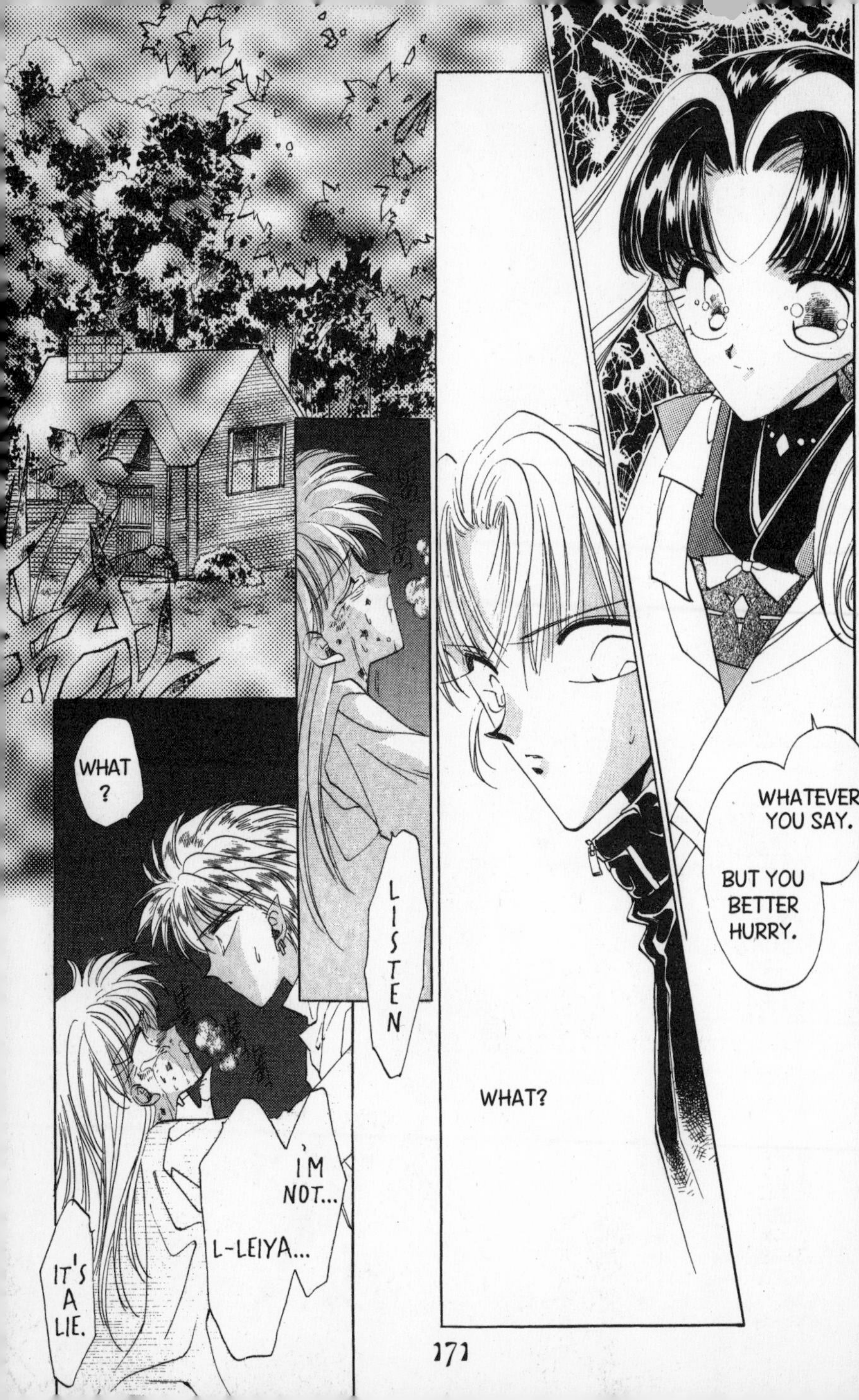
WHATEVER YOU SAY.
BUT YOU BETTER HURRY.
WHAT?
LISTEN
WHAT?
I'M NOT...
L-LEIYA...
IT'S A LIE.

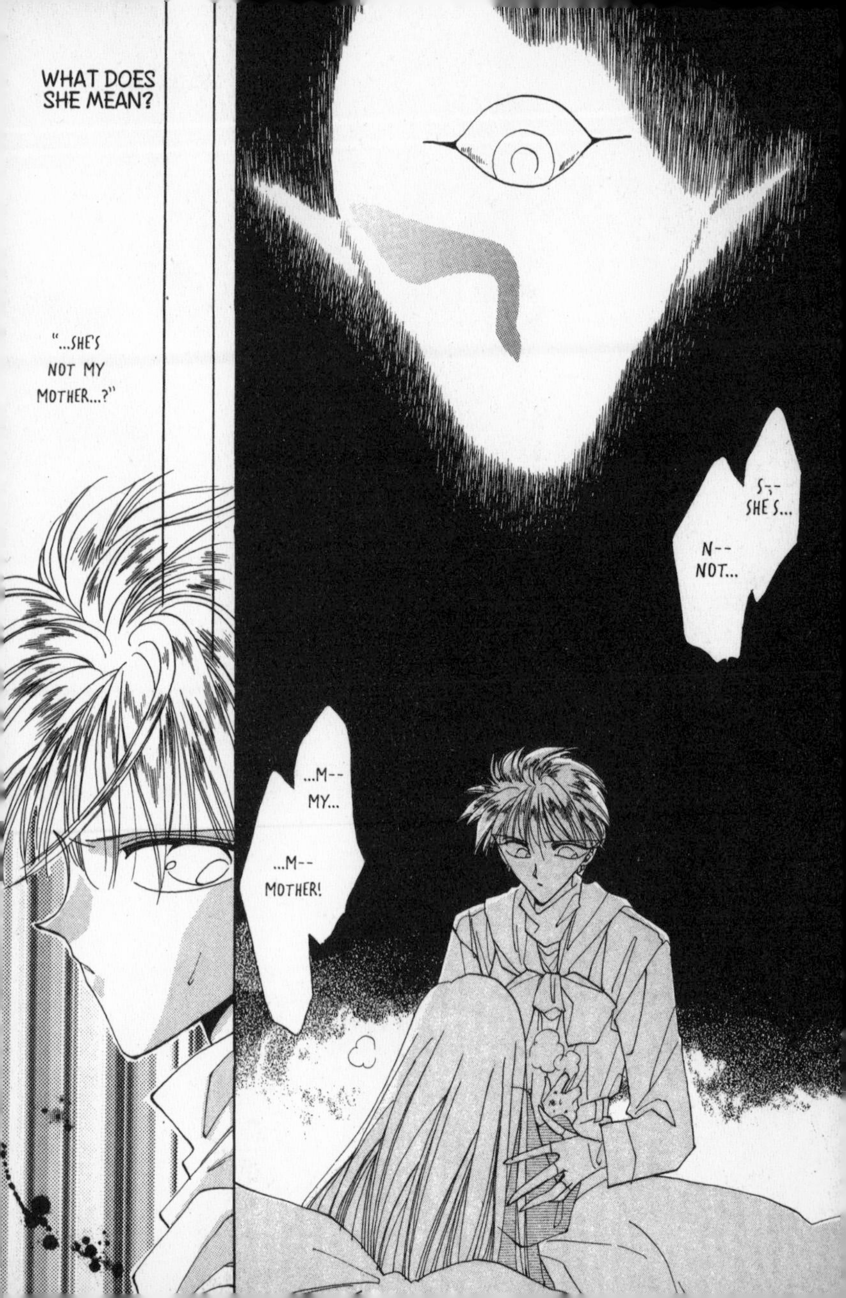
S--
SHE'S...
N--
NOT...
...M--
MY...
...M--
MOTHER!
WHAT DOES SHE MEAN?
"...SHE'S NOT MY MOTHER...?"

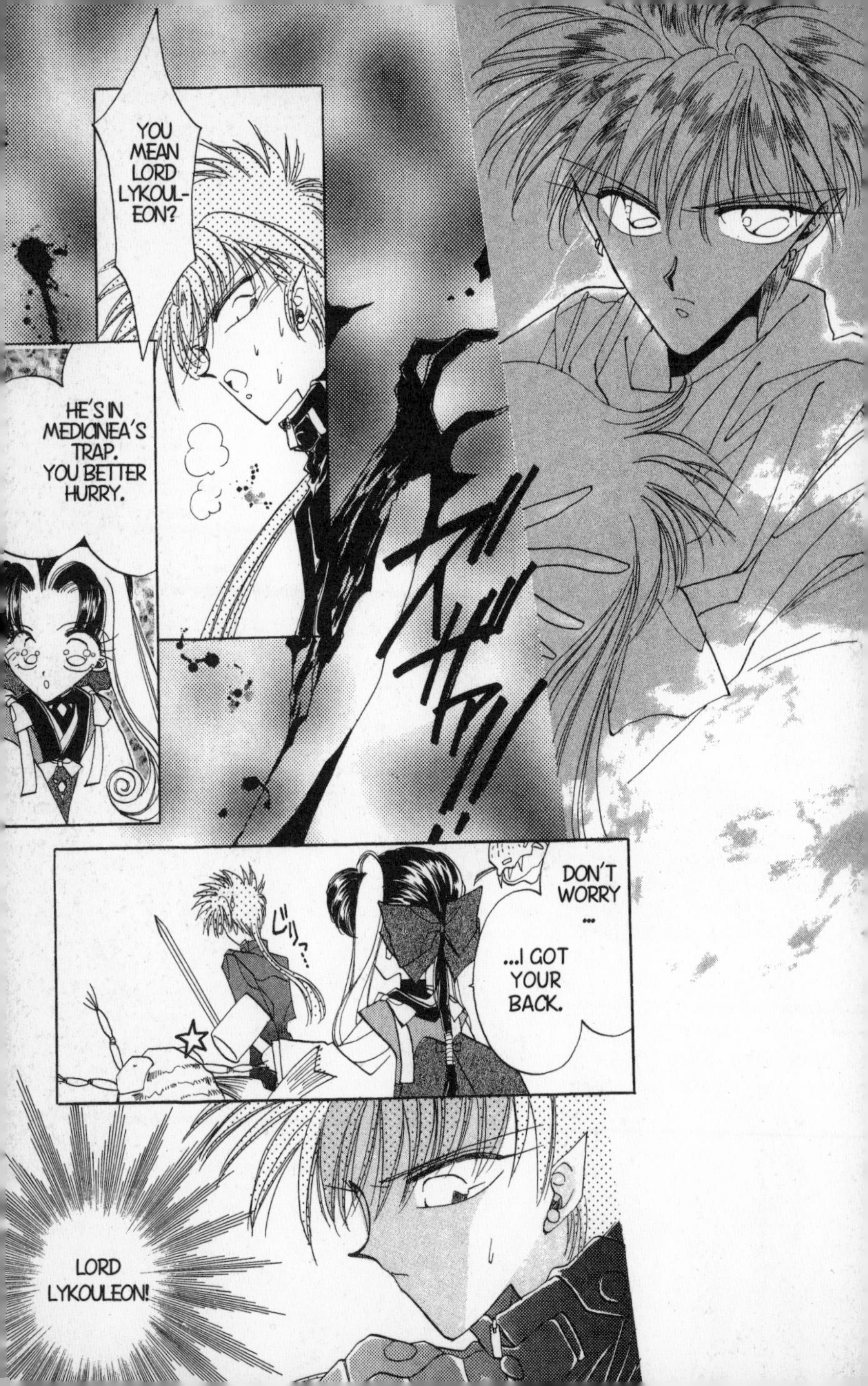
YOU MEAN LORD LYKOUL-EON?
HE'S IN MEDICINEA'S TRAP. YOU BETTER HURRY.
DON'T WORRY ...
...I GOT YOUR BACK.
LORD LYKOULEON!

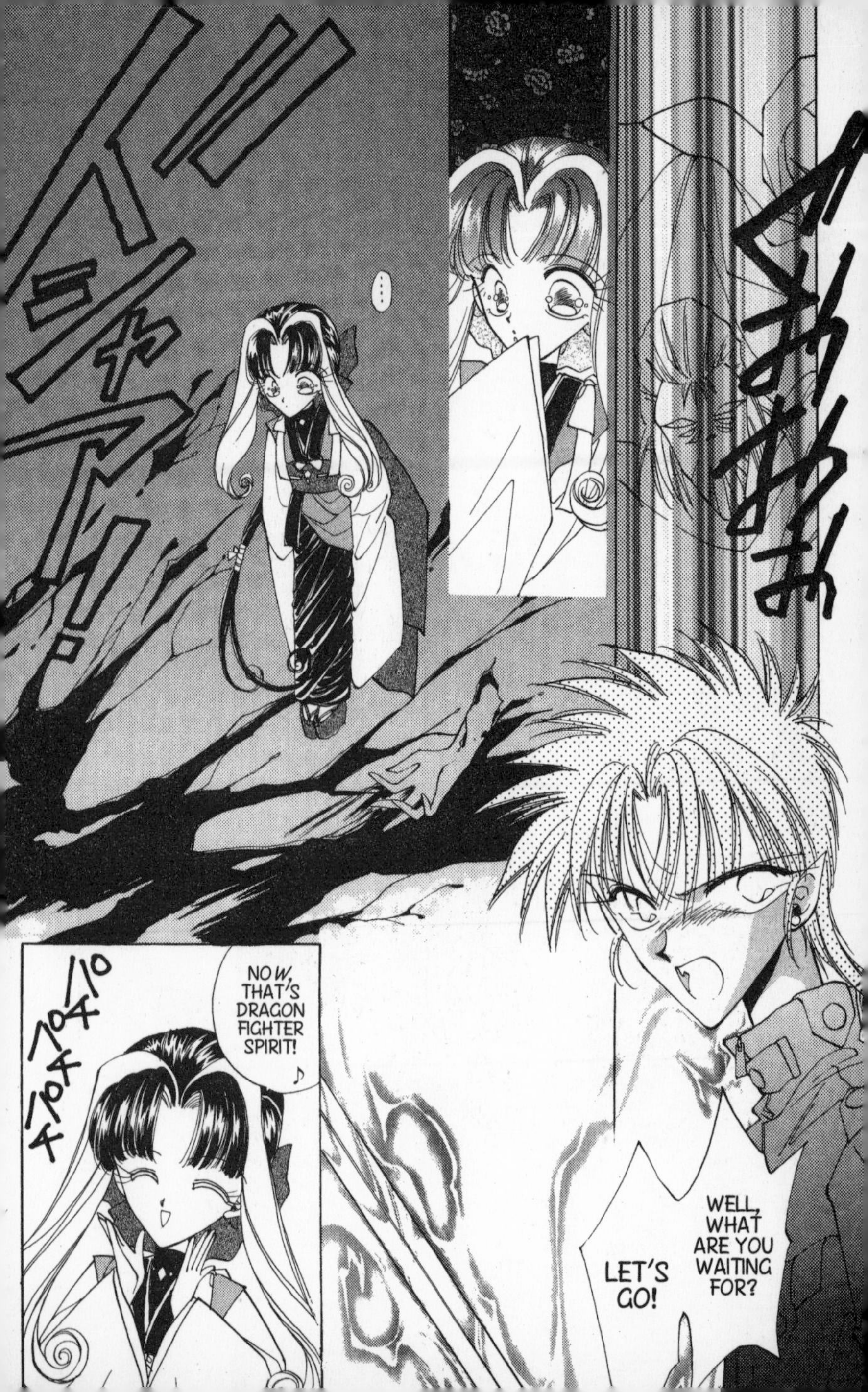
...
WELL, WHAT ARE YOU WAITING FOR?
LET'S GO!
NOW, THAT'S DRAGON FIGHTER SPIRIT! ♪

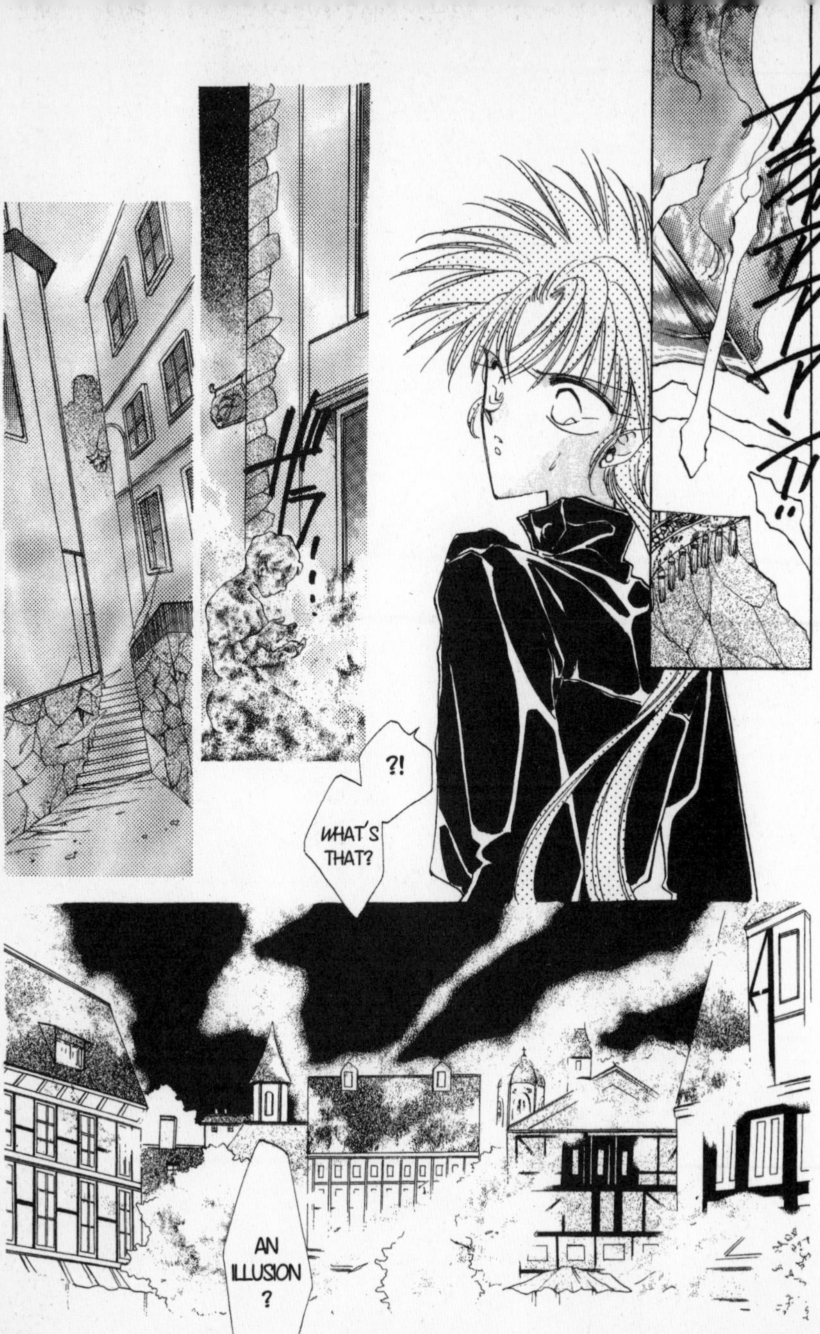
?!
WHAT'S THAT?
AN ILLUSION?

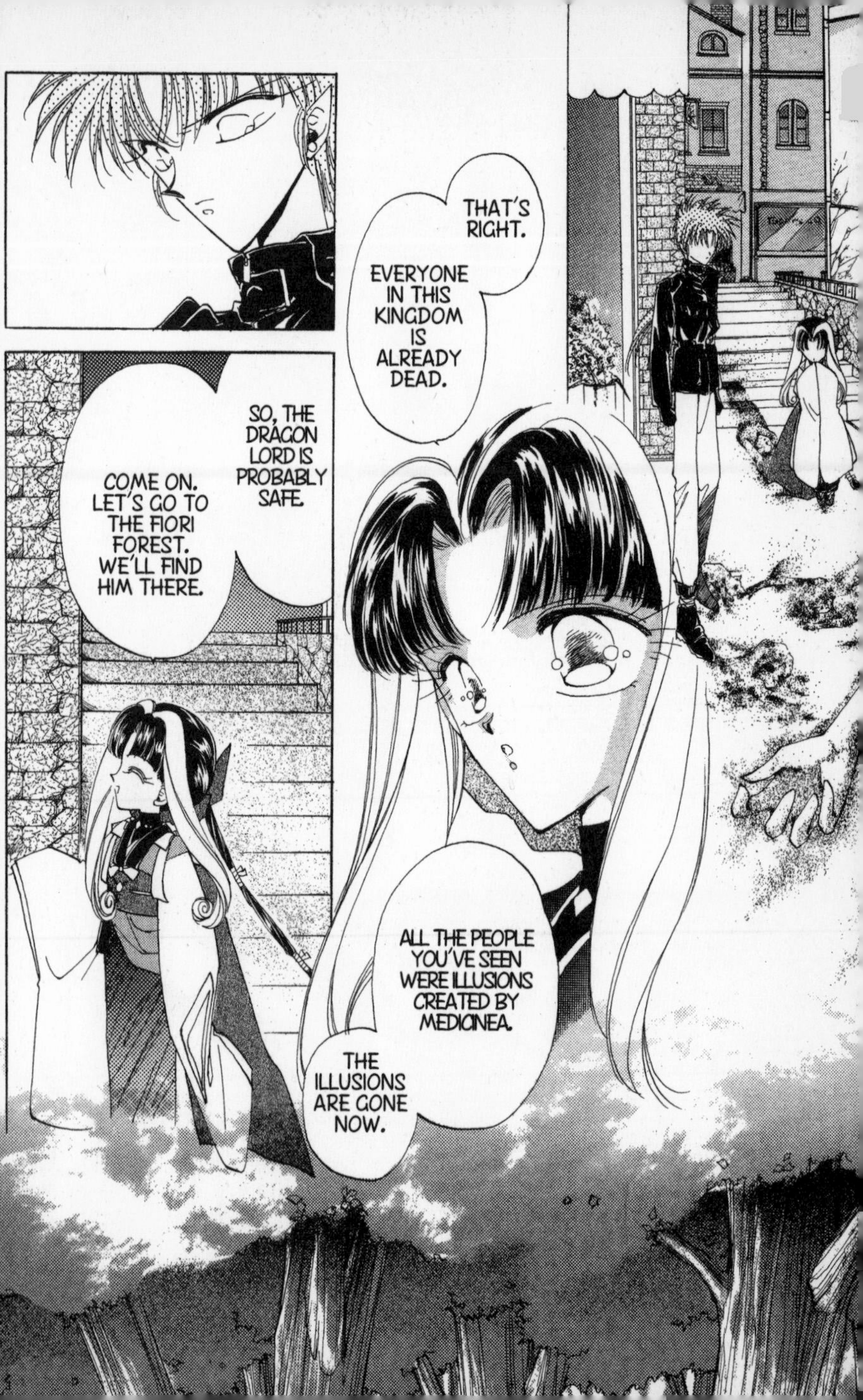
THAT'S RIGHT.
EVERYONE IN THIS KINGDOM IS ALREADY DEAD.
ALL THE PEOPLE YOU'VE SEEN WERE ILLUSIONS CREATED BY MEDICINEA.
THE ILLUSIONS ARE GONE NOW.
SO, THE DRAGON LORD IS PROBABLY SAFE.
COME ON. LET'S GO TO THE FIORI FOREST. WE'LL FIND HIM THERE.

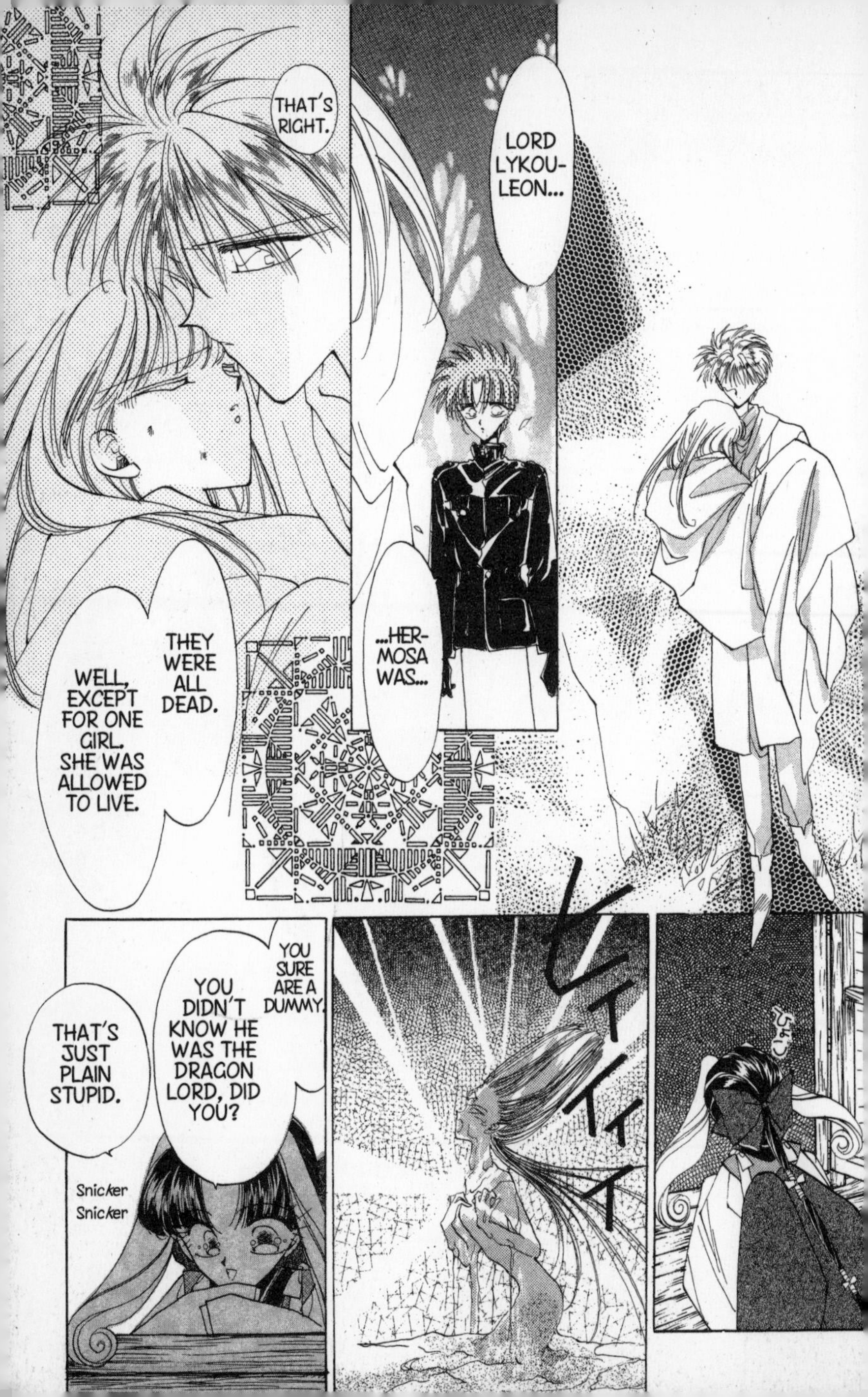
LORD LYKOU-LEON...
...HER-MOSA WAS...
THAT'S RIGHT.
THEY WERE ALL DEAD.
WELL, EXCEPT FOR ONE GIRL. SHE WAS ALLOWED TO LIVE.
YOU SURE ARE A DUMMY.
YOU DIDN'T KNOW HE WAS THE DRAGON LORD, DID YOU?
THAT'S JUST PLAIN STUPID.
Snicker
Snicker

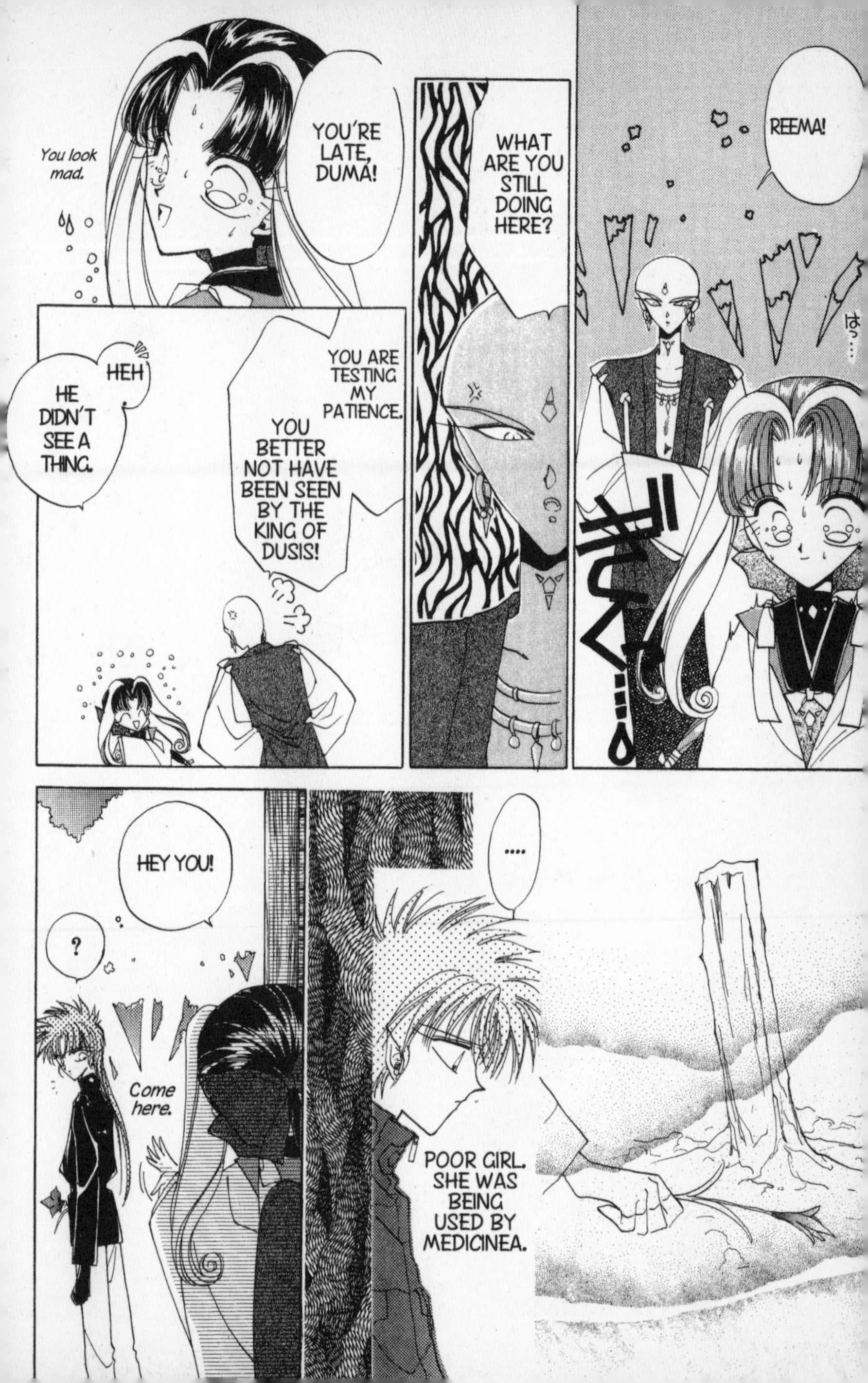
REEMA!
はっ…
WHAT ARE YOU STILL DOING HERE?
YOU'RE LATE, DUMA!
You look mad.
YOU ARE TESTING MY PATIENCE.
YOU BETTER NOT HAVE BEEN SEEN BY THE KING OF DUSIS!
HEH
HE DIDN'T SEE A THING.
....
POOR GIRL. SHE WAS BEING USED BY MEDICINEA.
HEY YOU!
?
Come here.

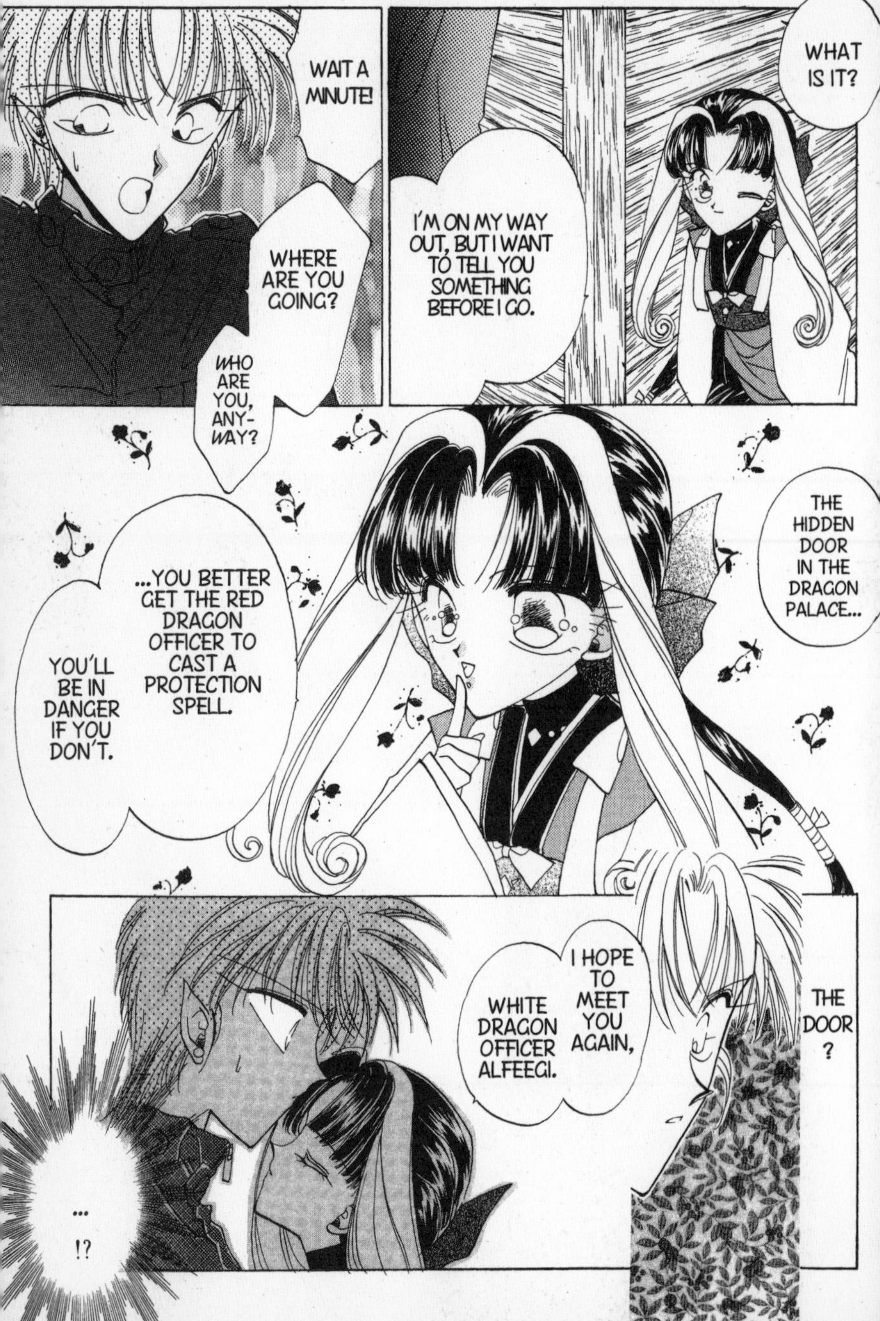
WHAT IS IT?
I'M ON MY WAY OUT, BUT I WANT TO TELL YOU SOMETHING BEFORE I GO.
WAIT A MINUTE!
WHERE ARE YOU GOING?
WHO ARE YOU, ANY-WAY?
THE HIDDEN DOOR IN THE DRAGON PALACE...
...YOU BETTER GET THE RED DRAGON OFFICER TO CAST A PROTECTION SPELL.
YOU'LL BE IN DANGER IF YOU DON'T.
THE DOOR?
I HOPE TO MEET YOU AGAIN,
WHITE DRAGON OFFICER ALFEEGI.
...!?

WHY DID YOU HAVE TO TELL HIM ABOUT THE DOOR?
What were you thinking?
IT DOESN'T MATTER.
TELLING THEM... WON'T CHANGE ANYTHING.
It doesn't matter?!
OH...
...QUIT YOUR WHINING.

The following special story is called "Dragon Knights: Dragon Corps"

It places the characters of Dragon Knights in an alternative setting. Please don't confuse it with the riveting tale you just read.

-The Author

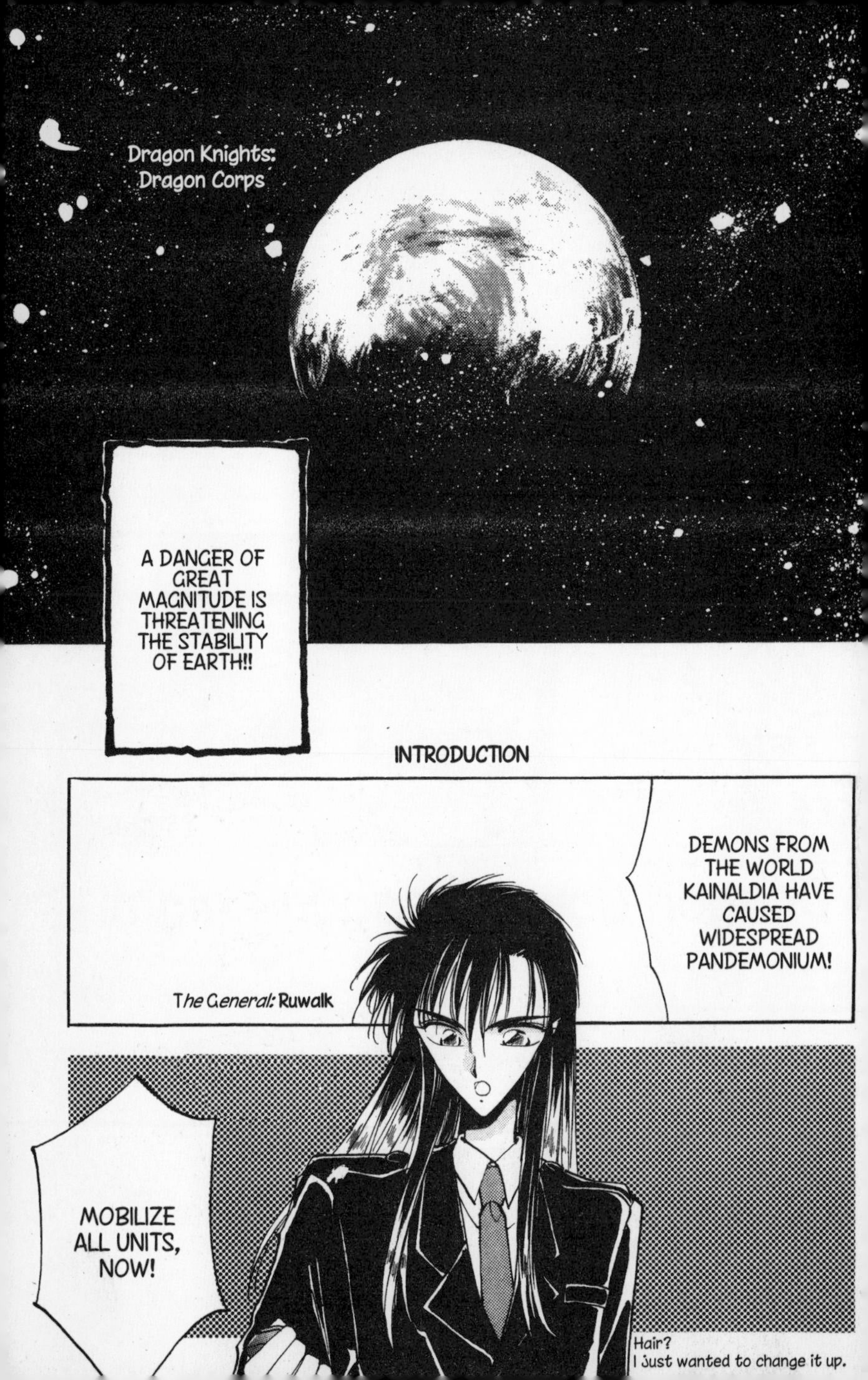
Dragon Knights: Dragon Corps
A DANGER OF GREAT MAGNITUDE IS THREATENING THE STABILITY OF EARTH!!
INTRODUCTION
DEMONS FROM THE WORLD KAINALDIA HAVE CAUSED WIDESPREAD PANDEMONIUM!
The General: Ruwalk
MOBILIZE ALL UNITS, NOW!
Hair? I just wanted to change it up.

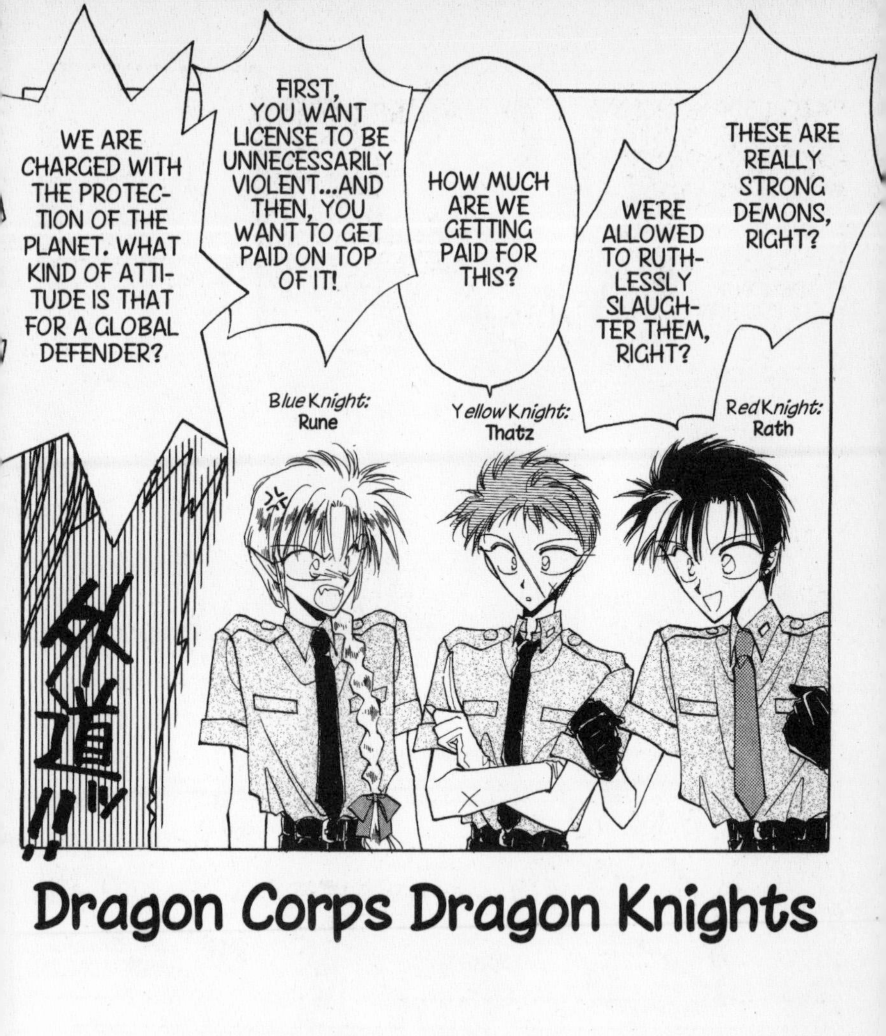
THESE ARE REALLY STRONG DEMONS, RIGHT?
WE'RE ALLOWED TO RUTH-LESSLY SLAUGH-TER THEM, RIGHT?
Red Knight: Rath
HOW MUCH ARE WE GETTING PAID FOR THIS?
Yellow Knight: Thatz
FIRST, YOU WANT LICENSE TO BE UNNECESSARILY VIOLENT...AND THEN, YOU WANT TO GET PAID ON TOP OF IT!
WE ARE CHARGED WITH THE PROTEC-TION OF THE PLANET. WHAT KIND OF ATTI-TUDE IS THAT FOR A GLOBAL DEFENDER?
Blue Knight: Rune
外道ッ!!

Dragon Corps Dragon Knights

ONCE AGAIN, THIS STORY IS COMPLETELY UNRELATED TO THE MAIN STORY OF "DRAGON KNIGHTS."

ACT. 1

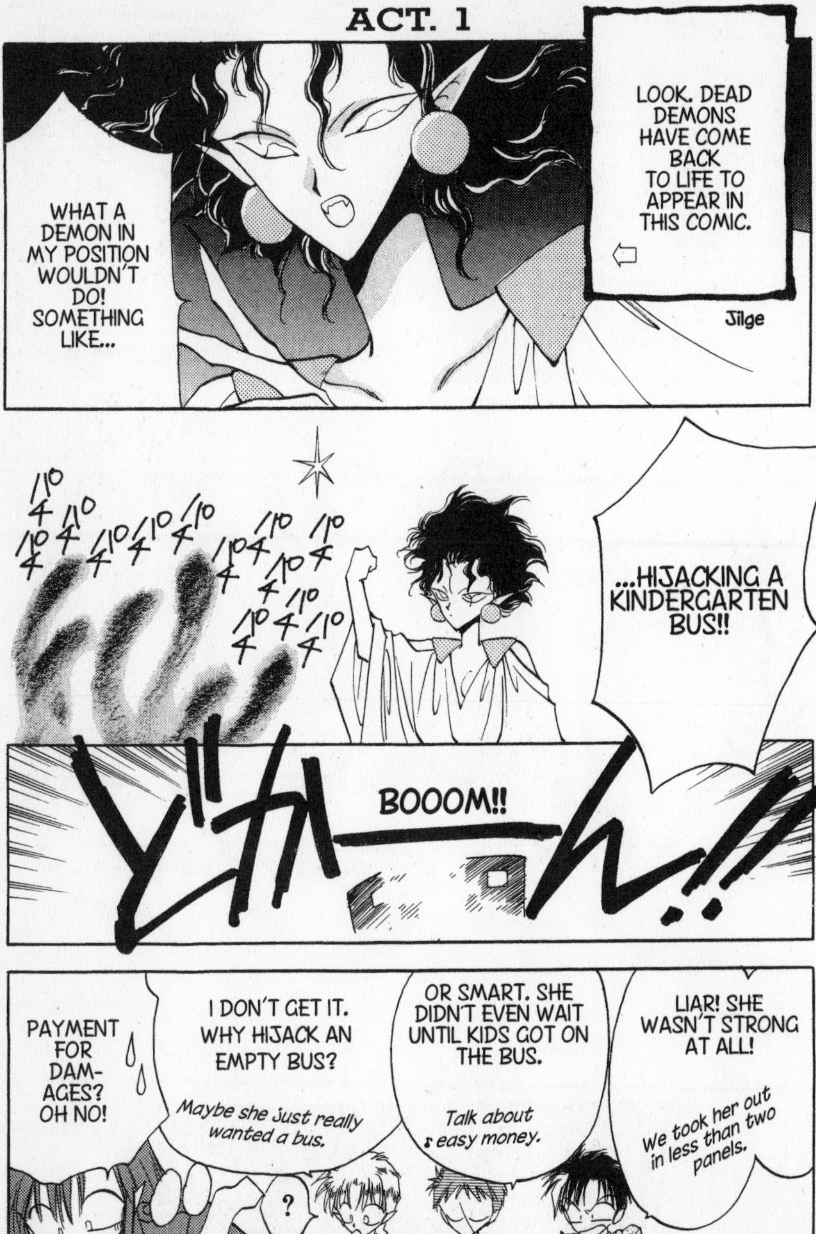
LOOK. DEAD DEMONS HAVE COME BACK TO LIFE TO APPEAR IN THIS COMIC.
Jilge
WHAT A DEMON IN MY POSITION WOULDN'T DO! SOMETHING LIKE...
...HIJACKING A KINDERGARTEN BUS!!
どかーん!!
BOOOM!!
LIAR! SHE WASN'T STRONG AT ALL!
We took her out in less than two panels.
OR SMART. SHE DIDN'T EVEN WAIT UNTIL KIDS GOT ON THE BUS.
Talk about easy money.
I DON'T GET IT. WHY HIJACK AN EMPTY BUS?
Maybe she just really wanted a bus.
?
PAYMENT FOR DAM-AGES? OH NO!

ACT. 2

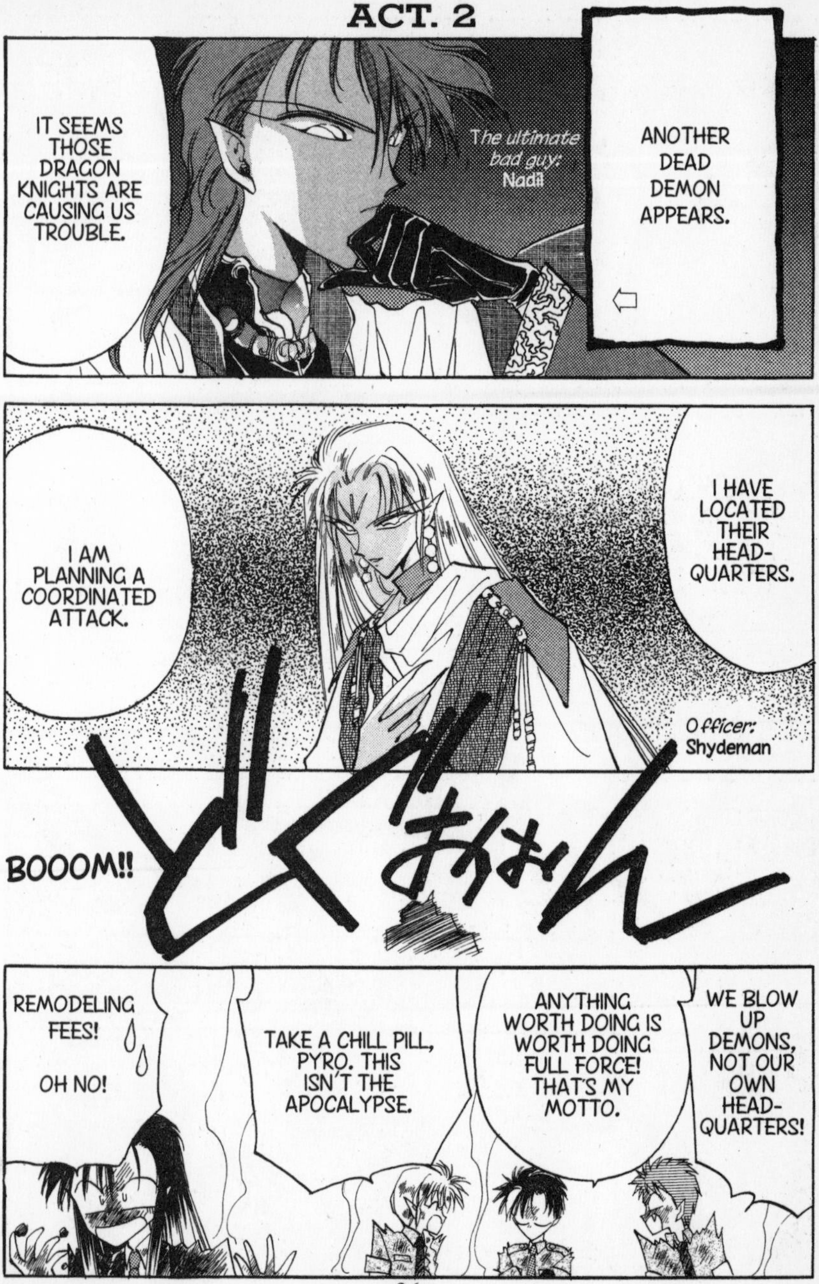

ANOTHER DEAD DEMON APPEARS.
The ultimate bad guy: Nadil
IT SEEMS THOSE DRAGON KNIGHTS ARE CAUSING US TROUBLE.
I HAVE LOCATED THEIR HEAD-QUARTERS.
Officer: Shydeman
I AM PLANNING A COORDINATED ATTACK.
BOOOM!!
WE BLOW UP DEMONS, NOT OUR OWN HEAD-QUARTERS!
ANYTHING WORTH DOING IS WORTH DOING FULL FORCE! THAT'S MY MOTTO.
TAKE A CHILL PILL, PYRO. THIS ISN'T THE APOCALYPSE.
REMODELING FEES!
OH NO!

ACT. 3

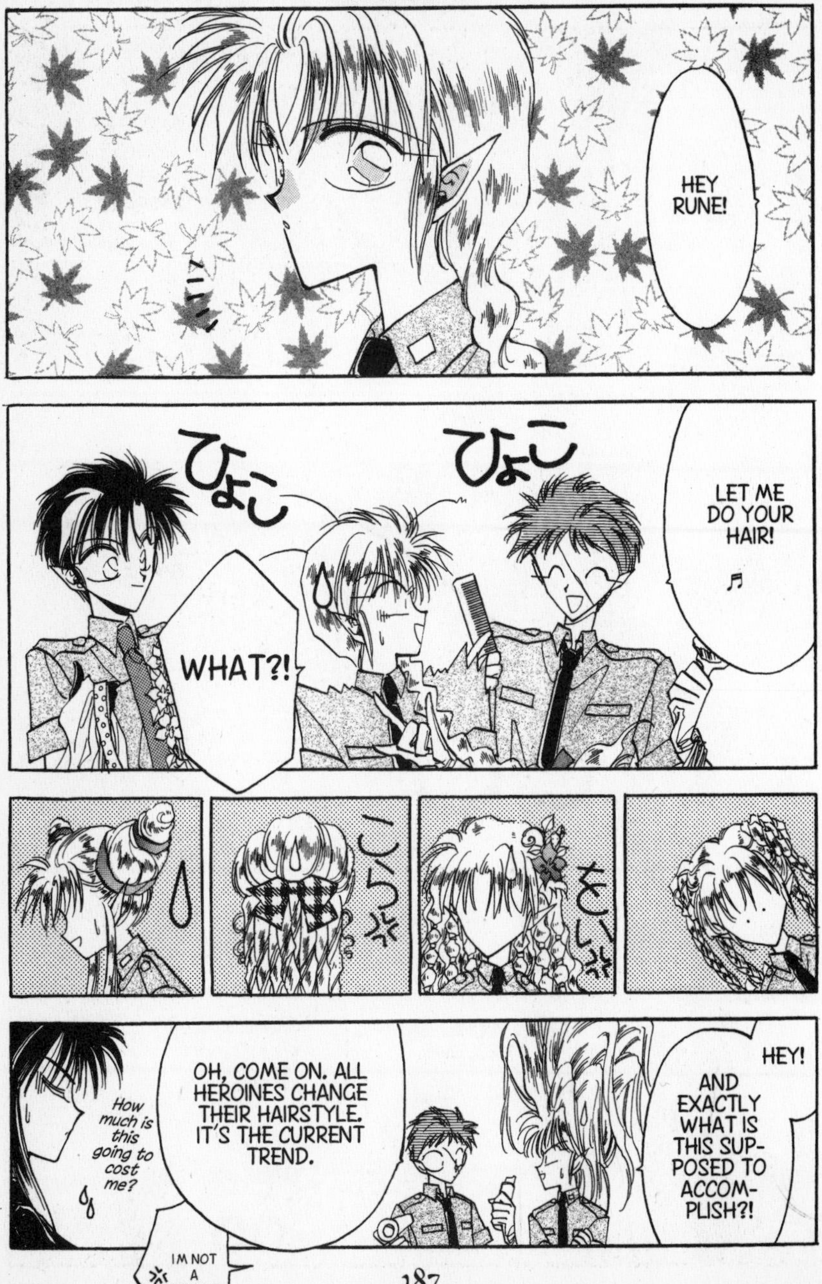
HEY RUNE!
LET ME DO YOUR HAIR! ♪
ひょこ
ひょこ
WHAT?!
をい
こら
HEY!
AND EXACTLY WHAT IS THIS SUPPOSED TO ACCOMPLISH?!
OH, COME ON. ALL HEROINES CHANGE THEIR HAIRSTYLE. IT'S THE CURRENT TREND.
How much is this going to cost me?
I'M NOT A HEROINE!

ACT. 4

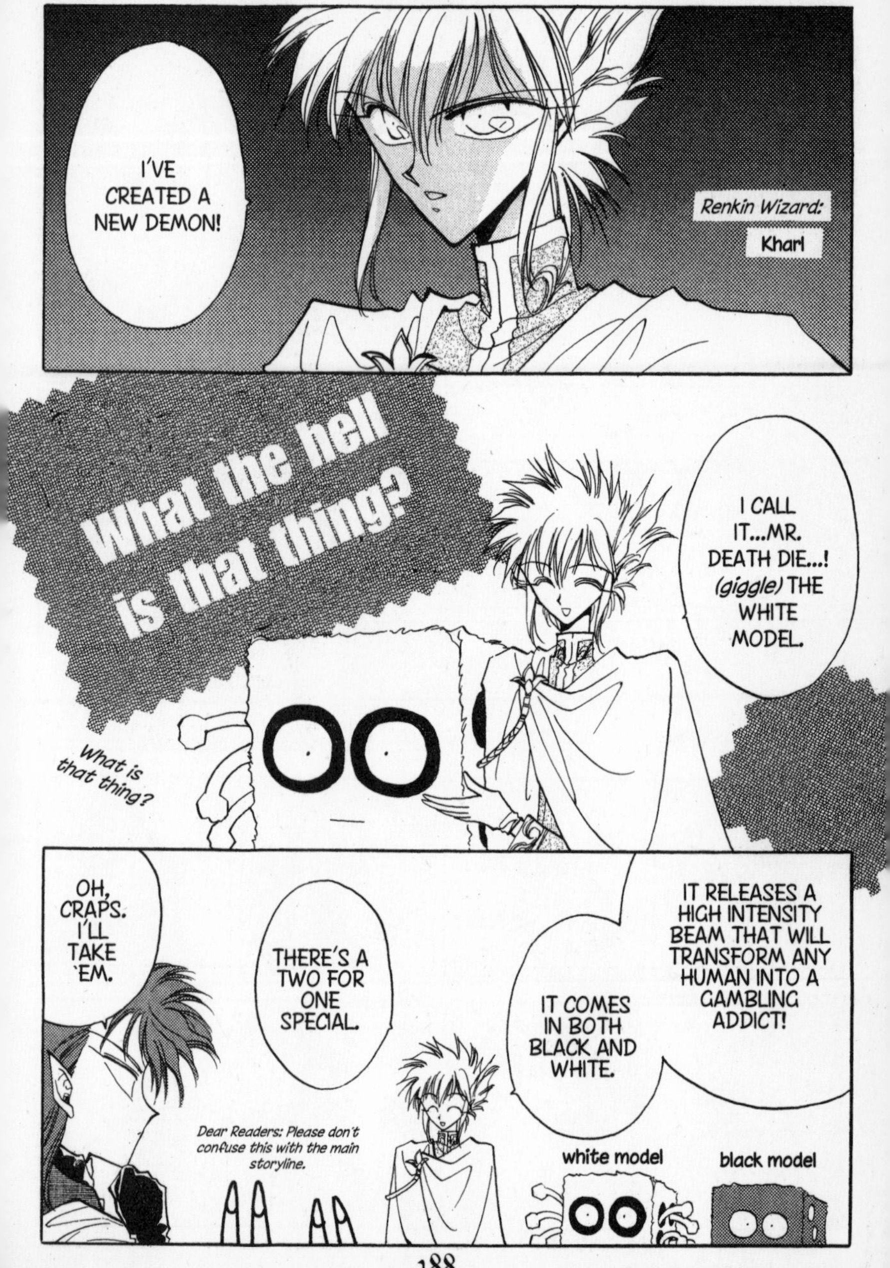

I'VE CREATED A NEW DEMON!
Renkin Wizard:
Kharl
I CALL IT...MR. DEATH DIE...! (giggle) THE WHITE MODEL.
What the hell is that thing?
What is that thing?
IT RELEASES A HIGH INTENSITY BEAM THAT WILL TRANSFORM ANY HUMAN INTO A GAMBLING ADDICT!
IT COMES IN BOTH BLACK AND WHITE.
THERE'S A TWO FOR ONE SPECIAL.
OH, CRAPS. I'LL TAKE 'EM.
black model
white model
Dear Readers: Please don't confuse this with the main storyline.

ACT. 5

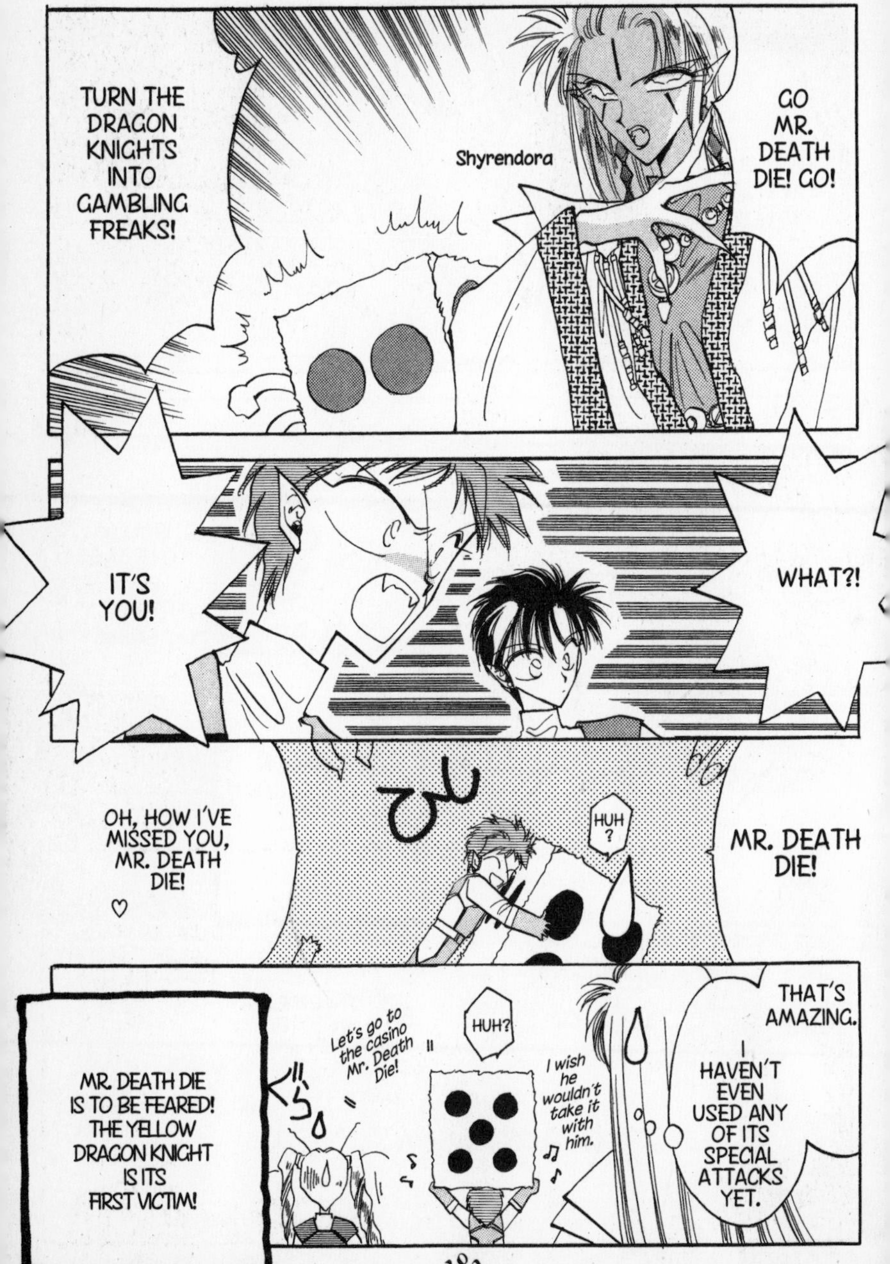

GO MR. DEATH DIE! GO!
Shyrendora
TURN THE DRAGON KNIGHTS INTO GAMBLING FREAKS!
WHAT?!
IT'S YOU!
MR. DEATH DIE!
HUH ?
OH, HOW I'VE MISSED YOU, MR. DEATH DIE! ♡
THAT'S AMAZING.
I HAVEN'T EVEN USED ANY OF ITS SPECIAL ATTACKS YET.
I wish he wouldn't take it with him.
HUH?
Let's go to the casino Mr. Death Die!
MR. DEATH DIE IS TO BE FEARED! THE YELLOW DRAGON KNIGHT IS ITS FIRST VICTIM!

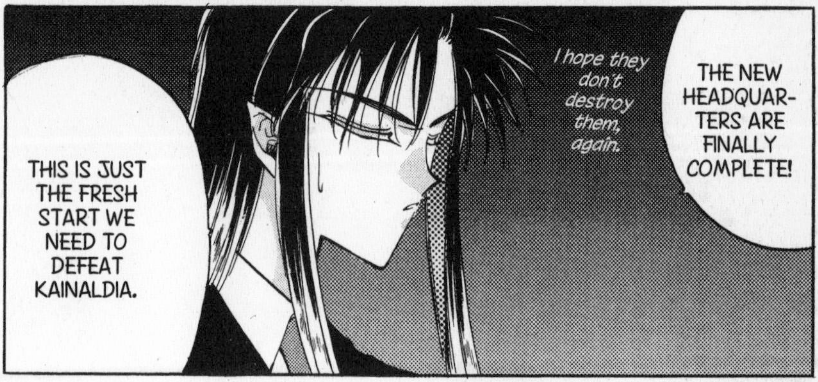
THE NEW HEADQUARTERS ARE FINALLY COMPLETE!
I hope they don't destroy them, again.
THIS IS JUST THE FRESH START WE NEED TO DEFEAT KAINALDIA.

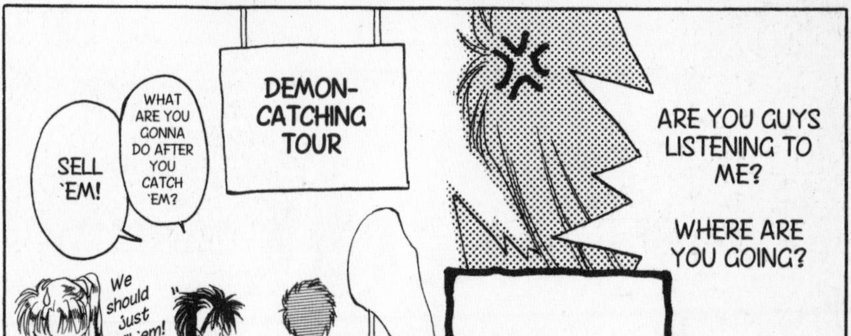
ARE YOU GUYS LISTENING TO ME?
WHERE ARE YOU GOING?
GO DRAGON KNIGHTS, GO!
DEMON-CATCHING TOUR
WHAT ARE YOU GONNA DO AFTER YOU CATCH 'EM?
SELL 'EM!
We should just kill 'em!

※ AND REMEMBER, DO NOT CONFUSE THIS WITH THE MAIN STORY.

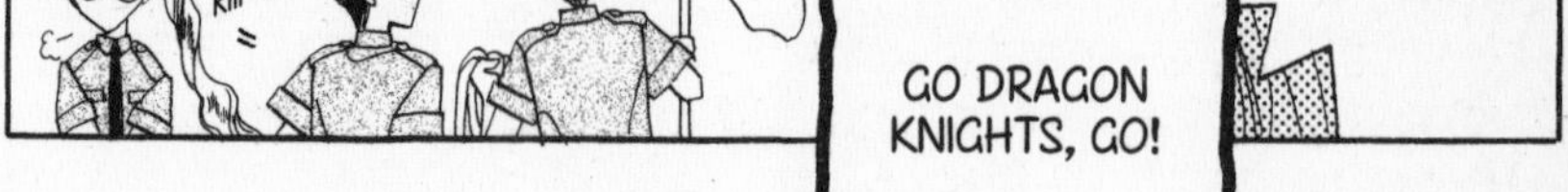
THIS IS MY NEWEST DEMON. IT'S CALLED KILLER SHRIMP. (laugh)
I CAN GIVE YOU A DISCOUNT.
SOLD.

★ MY LITTLE BROTHER DESIGNED MR. DEATH DIE AND KILLER SHRIMP. (OH, AND KHARL, TOO)

STOP!

This is the back of the book.
You wouldn't want to spoil a great ending!

This book is printed "manga-style," in the authentic Japanese right-to-left format. Since none of the artwork has been flipped or altered, readers get to experience the story just as the creator intended. You've been asking for it, so TOKYOPOP® delivered: authentic, hot-off-the-press, and far more fun!

DIRECTIONS

If this is your first time reading manga-style, here's a quick guide to help you understand how it works.

It's easy... just start in the top right panel and follow the numbers. Have fun, and look for more 100% authentic manga from TOKYOPOP®!

100% AUTHENTIC MANGA

Dragon Knights

Preview for Volume 7

The next installment of Dragon Knights returns us to Rath and Cesia's journey to Mt. Mfartha. Once again, Cesia falls victim to a strange spell, driving her and Rath to the Spring of Purification. However, she soon learns that one can be too pure if one indulges too long in the Spring of Purification. And it will take everything the two of them have to combat Nadil's Army, which has caught up with them and now threatens to lure them over to the Demon side. And Cesia also has to deal with a rather tangible and frighteningly deadly alter ego. So, she better get out of the water quick.

Mineko Ohkami

7